The Cutleaf Reader

Volume Three

EDITED BY

Keith Pilapil Lesmeister, Denton Loving,
Kelly March, and Walter Robinson

The Cutleaf Reader, Volume Three

Edited by Keith Pilapil Lesmeister, Denton Loving,
Kelly March, and Walter Robinson

Anthology

ISBN 978-1-958094-49-5

Book & Cover Design : EK Larken

✺

Cutleaf and *The Cutleaf Reader* are projects of EastOver Press.

✺

EastOver Press encourages the use of our publications in educational settings.
For questions about educational discounts, contact us at
www.EastOverPress.com or info@eastoverpress.com.

Published in the United States of America by

Rochester, Massachusetts
www.EastOverPress.com

The Cutleaf Reader

VOLUME THREE

www.CutleafJournal.com

Contents

Nonfiction

POETRY

Fiction

A Note from EastOver Press

Cutleaf and *The Cutleaf Reader* are both project of EastOver Press, a small independent press specializing in collection of short stories, nonfiction, and poetry.

Some of the authors in *The Cutleaf Reader* also have books published by EastOver Press, and we encourage you to take a look at those books on EastOverPress.com

Other writers featured in *The Cutleaf Reader* have had books published by other presses in 2023, and we encourage you to seek out their work as well. More information can be found in the Contributor biographies.

Recent and forthcoming books from EastOver Press *(Cutleaf contributor *):*

*George Singleton, *Asides – Occasional Essays on Dogs, Food, Restaurants, Bars, Hangovers, Jobs, Music, Family Trees, Robbery, Relationships, Being Brought Up Questionably, Et Cetera*
*Catherine Pritchard Childress, *Outside the Frame*
*Shayla Hawkins, *Exquisite by September*
*Joseph Bathanti, *The Act of Contrition*
*Tara Kelly, *No Last Words*
*Ralph Sneeden, *The Legible Element*
*Elijah Burell, *Skies of Blur*
*Ray Trotter, *And Dogs To Chase Them*
*Kari Gunter-Seymour, *Dirt Songs*
Andrea Rinard, *Murmurations*
George Choundas, *Until All You See Is Sky*
Richard LeBlond, *Homesisck for Nowhere*

Contributors to *Cutleaf* with recent and forthcoming books from other publishers:

Rannva Holm Mortensen, *Suntaste* (International Polar Institute; 2023), Matthew Landrum, trans.
BA Van Sise, *Invited to Life: Finding Hope after the Holocaust* (Schiffer Publishing, 2023)
Eileen Cunniffe, *Mischief and Metaphors* (Shanti Arts, 2023)
Jill McCorkle, *Old Crimes* (Algonquin, 2024)
William Woolfitt, *Ring of Earth* (Madville Publishing, 2023)
Brett Biebel, *Winder Dance Party* (Alternating Current Press, 2023)
Tara Stillions Whitehead, *They More Than Burned* (ELJ Editions, 2023)

Introduction

Welcome to the third volume of *The Cutleaf Reader,* a print anthology of work published in the online journal during 2023.

A print book brings something to reading that a screen cannot deliver. We publish the anthology because we know that some readers prefer paper, and because we believe in the power and persistence of the physical book. After all, *Cutleaf* is a project of EastOver Press, a small press that specializes in print collections of poetry and prose, and we take no small delight in bringing well-written and beautiful physical books into the world.

Cutleaf publishes work of all shapes and sizes. In this anthology you will read flash fiction and longer stories, hybrid essays and more traditional nonfiction formats, and poetry of many different styles and approaches. We hope *The Cutleaf Reader* is a snapshot of the best work in contemporary writing in English. We began the project with the ideal of engaging writers from around the world, and in this volume you will find work from writers in North America, Africa, Europe, and Asia. We also hope you find a variety of approaches to subject matter, form, and style.

We started *Cutleaf* three years ago, and we have relished the growth of the journal and the increasing interest in the work we publish. Each year we enjoy reading the work that writers send us, and we are pleased that the journal and the press are growing into a welcoming, vibrant community of writers and readers.

The four of us who edit *Cutleaf* are all writers ourselves. As writing is a (mostly) solitary activity, we have sought to build connections with the wider writing community through *Cutleaf* and the work of EastOver Press. We hope that as we now enter our fourth year, we can continue to "help uplift and support that community," as my fellow editor Keith Lesmeister put it in the introduction to the first volume of *The Cutleaf Reader.*

But most of all, we still want to have fun working with each other and with you, the readers and writers of *Cutleaf.* This project has been a joy for us during difficult times, and we are happy to share it with you.

Walter M. Robinson
Rochester, Massachusetts

NONFICTION

Chris Arthur

Snowglobe Coordinates

When I visit somewhere new, I like to find one of those publicly displayed maps of the area that has "You Are Here" clearly marked on it. An arrow, cross, or dot – often in red – indicates the spot where you're standing, looking at what's shown and trying to get your bearings. Sometimes they're so faded it's hard to make out the detail. Sometimes the scrawls and gouges of graffiti render them useless. But despite their vulnerability to aging, vandalism, and weather, and although their fixed perspectives may seem primitive compared to the navigational capabilities of mobile phones, I still find such "You Are Here" maps appealing. I like them partly for their obvious utility – they offer a rapid means of gaining a sense of orientation. But their main appeal, for me, lies in another direction entirely: I enjoy the sense of existential absurdity they engender.

"You Are Here" maps offer a reassuringly straightforward understanding of your whereabouts. They plot your position according to a few readily recognized points of reference. Once you've scanned your surroundings, noted key features, matched landscape to map-scape, understood the scale and symbols being used, a sense of knowing where you are is fostered. This provides sufficient confidence to set off and get successfully from a to b to c. If these maps had a voice their tone would be like a newsreader's – calm, unhurried, authoritative. Their assertion of "You Are Here" invites neither doubt nor questioning. To ask "Where?" in puzzlement or outraged disbelief would simply result in patient reiteration. Look at the arrow, X marks the spot, that dot shows where you're standing. Whatever sign is being used, it lets you see exactly where you are in relation to your surroundings.

In one sense, such maps are unproblematic. They place us in a way we can readily relate to. But their plotting of our location doesn't bear much weight of scrutiny. Beyond a superficial sense of direction, the coordinates they give are little more than flimsy fabrications thrown over the chasm of a larger truth.

I don't just mean that "You Are Here" maps are simplifications. Like any map, they're not attempts to replicate the area they show. Rather, they select and represent. A great deal is, quite deliberately, left out. If everything was included, we would end up with an unwieldy facsimile, not a map. The surreal impossibilities of such a thing – a map that reproduced a territory with flawless faithfulness, a point-by-point echo with everything mirrored in 1:1 scale – is nicely shown in Jorge Luis Borges' story, "Of the Exactitude of Science" (included in his collection *A Universal History of Infamy*). Maps are not copies of the world but readings of it that excerpt and emphasize, they show enough of somewhere to facilitate our grasp of it, without bamboozling us by including too much. In calling "You Are Here" maps fabrications, it's not cartography's necessary simplification that I have in mind. I'm thinking, rather, of the absence of any indication that there's a great deal more to the story than the tiny part of it they tell.

It's easy to be taken in, to confer upon such maps a degree of certainty they really don't possess. We assume the little fictions that they offer are straightforward facts, slip too readily into thinking that their version of our whereabouts is accurate, that we can accept where they place us as truthful snapshots of where we actually are. Yes, of course, they do provide some passing sense of orientation; they help us find our way around whatever area they're concerned with. But the pinpointing they offer is fractional, provisional, temporary at best. It gives no sense of the fundamental nature of our surroundings, or their scale, or where we fit into the astonishing picture they are part of.

*   *   *

When I'm musing about the nature of "You Are Here" maps, I often think of snowglobes. A snowglobe is a small transparent sphere of glass or plastic. Within its dome, some miniaturized scene is depicted – a village or a farmyard, a city street, a little rural landscape with hills and trees. Usually a few figures are included, sometimes animals as well. Model vehicles are often placed in urban scenes. Snowglobes are particularly popular at Christmas. Then, their cameos take on a seasonal theme – horse-drawn sledges, red-robed Santa Clauses, snowmen, reindeer, Christmas trees. The space enclosed within the snowglobe's dome is filled with clear liquid and scores of tiny white particles. When the globe is shaken, the particles are agitated and give the impression of a flurry of snowflakes. They make their slow descent through the watery atmosphere that holds them, briefly creating a miniature blizzard-effect. Soon they settle and the scene clears. It stays that way until the globe is shaken again.

Imagine a snowglobe where a fragment of a town has been modelled within the transparent enclosure – miniaturized streets and buildings, with a few vehicles and pedestrians appropriately positioned. There's a tiny figure standing in a carpark, looking at a "You Are Here" map that's displayed on a noticeboard. If you shake the globe the usual blizzard would momentarily appear. But instead of shaking, imagine this globe is a projectile that's been fired into the middle of the Atlantic Ocean. The little "You Are Here" map that's within shows the figure's location with a customary red arrow. It provides the necessary orientation to plot a route through the model town that's built inside the glassy encasement. The position of anything within this sphere is shown on the map relative to the other features that the globe contains. But there is no mention anywhere – still less any mapping – of the miles of sea in which this snowglobe is bobbing. The depths and distances of the environing Atlantic are ignored. No hint is given of its powerful waves and currents. The few millilitres of liquid within the globe define the boundaries of its cartography. Its

"You Are Here" map gives no indication of the megatons of water separated from its world by only a thin, transparent membrane.

Just as the imaginary map within this castaway snowglobe ignores what's all around it, so the real "You Are Here" maps we consult are similarly blinkered. In fact the coordinates they give are even more curtailed than those within a snowglobe drifting in the ocean. At least the sea, even at its deepest, is something we can fathom; there is the certainty of seabed somewhere beneath us. And, however far from them we might be, there are vessels, islands, coastlines – all known phenomena – that offer the triangulation of familiarity. There are also fish and whales and seaweed we can name. But the snowglobe of our Earth is floating in an expanse that makes the Atlantic seem like a dewdrop, and within the enormous ambit of what surrounds our planet there is little we can confidently label.

* * *

The Solar System gives a kind of stay of execution against being overwhelmed by immensities we can't map, it preserves for a while longer the sense that "You Are Here" is an intelligible concept, that we can weave a comforting cocoon of coordinates around ourselves. Looking at the Solar System may pull the rug away from locally measured estimates of our whereabouts, but it still provides a sense of what we mean by "here." In pointing to the sun, "Solar" brings with it a sense of light and warmth, the familiar feel of summer days. "System" suggests something ordered and purposeful, a pace of proceeding we can reliably predict and chart. Our family of planets orbiting the sun moves in patterns we can grasp. We can take soundings of Earth's size and position relative to its nearest neighbours. We know we're on the third planet from the Sun, 93 million miles from the fiery star that sustains us. Our planet is the fifth largest in the System. As names we recognize, "Sun," "Earth," "Moon," "Mercury," "Venus,"

"Mars," "Jupiter," "Saturn," "Uranus," and "Neptune" bestow a sense of being in familiar conceptual territory. Seeing them written on the page kindles a homely feeling of belonging and may even provide a bulwark against what lies beyond them. But such reassuring resonances soon fade when we consider the wider picture.

The Solar System is just one small group of planets located in a galaxy called the Milky Way, a disc-shaped assemblage of numerous stars. It would take some 120,000 years for light to travel across the expanse they cover. And the Milky Way is just one among a multitude of galaxies. One estimate suggests there are at least 200 billion of them. They range in size from dwarf galaxies, consisting of just (just!) a few hundred million stars, to giants that contain one hundred trillion. There are more stars than there are grains of sand on all Earth's beaches, more than every speck of dust we've ever seen.

Cosmologists organize galaxies into groups, clusters, and superclusters. Our Milky Way is part of a collection of galaxies in the so-called Local Group. One of these, the Andromeda Galaxy (2.5 million light years from us) is twice the size and four times the mass of the Milky Way. The Local Group in turn belongs to the Virgo cluster (65 million light years from us). Virgo contains at least a hundred galaxies. But this cluster, gigantic though it is, is dwarfed by the almost inconceivable immensity of a supercluster of galaxies that's aptly named Laniakea (Hawaiian for "immeasurable heavens"). Laniakea consists of more than 100,000 galaxies.

The size of the universe – home to this plethora of galaxies – is not known. The possibility that it is infinite cannot be ruled out. It has been expanding since it came into being and is expanding still, which means that though it would now take light 500 million years to cross the expanse of Laniakea, it will take even longer in the future (and would have taken less time in the past). The universe is not a static entity. The flux of expansion ripples through it. It is not thought to have a centre or an edge. If it was possible to go in any direction fast enough and for long enough, eventually you'd reach the edge of the observable universe. Beyond that lie unobservable realms. They are so far away that no light from them has reached Earth or any of its telescopes. Who knows what such realms may contain? And if you travelled for aeons, on a journey lasting so long it would witness the birth and death of all the stars, it may be – if the cosmologists are right – that you would return precisely to the point you set out from. I like the way that supposition sends a shiver of locational vertigo through our looking at any simple "You Are Here" map. It gives a very different sense of the possibilities implicit in our present position. "Here" becomes a kind of portal into the mystery of time and space.

It's hard to grasp these stupendous astral distances and dimensions in any kind of meaningful way. They slip through the fingers of what seems credible even though the evidence for them is incontrovertible. They're not easy to hold in mind as features of existence, characteristics of the reality in which our lives unfold from day to day. Despite the massiveness of galaxies, they seem strangely insubstantial, almost spectral, haunting the edges of belief rather than occupying its centre. Though they are there, now, defining this – as every – moment, these Laniakean vistas lack the impress of immediate sensation. They exist beyond any direct confirmation from sight, or sound, or touch, or taste, or smell. I take Laniakea on trust from those whose calculations and observations have revealed it. I know it's there; I know we're part of it. And yet…

* * *

In their six-volume *The History of Cartography* (1987), J.B. Harley and David Woodward define maps as:

Graphic representations that facilitate a spatial understanding of things, concepts, conditions, processes, or events in the human world.

Some indication of the variety this definition can encompass is shown in Stephen Hall's "I, Mercator," a brilliant essay that first appeared in the Spring 1994 issue of *Orion* magazine. Hall writes:

> There are maps to anywhere: chromosomes, galaxies, the brain, the cell, the spaces between atoms, cracks in the double helix. The edge of time.

With each of these maps, it would be possible to introduce a "You Are Here" indicator. But the coordinates it gives take on a quality of mirage as soon as we glance at what they connect to and recognize where such connections lead us.

Master cartographer Tim Robinson's explorations provide a rare depth of topographical and cultural insight into the ground he studies. In *Stones of Aran: Pilgrimage* (1986) – in a passage that surely applies to any map – he talks about the way in which his careful walking and map-making bring him into contact not just with the obvious ground beneath his feet on Ireland's Aran Islands, but with nothing less than "the network of being." It is a network dense with multiple nodes of interconnection. Robinson suggests that it consists of "tangle within tangle within tangle, indefinitely." Faced with such an intricate series of interrelationships – every feature, place, time, event leading always to others – perhaps all we can do is "tease out a thread or two here and there," as Robinson does with such engaging elegance. The tapestry as a whole remains beyond our grasp. As Stephen Hall puts it:

> The most important thing a map shows, if we pause to look at it long enough, if we travel upon it widely enough, if we think about it hard enough, is all the things we still do not know.

The same sentiment surely lies behind the famous line

in Herman Melville's *Moby Dick*, when Ishmael says of his friend Queequeg's island home, Kokovoko: "It is not down in any map; true places never are." The true place of where we really are, beyond the snowglobe coordinates of our quotidian cartographies, is similarly resistant to being pinpointed.

It's not just a case of disorientation being ignited as our scale of inclusion increases, with distances soon reaching stupendous expanses when we think of stars and galaxies in their scattered billions. Something similar happens if, instead of looking outwards (Earth, Solar System, Milky Way and beyond) we look inwards. Apply microscopes instead of telescopes and you'll soon discover there's uncharted space inside us. Think of our multi-millions of cells, think of the atoms that make them, the electrons orbiting the nuclei, the tiny planetary systems of atomic particles that arc their transits through these inner emptinesses. Sequestered within interiorities we rarely consider are nanospheres laden with the potential to corrode the coordinates we use to plot our everyday positions. These nanospheres are as caustic to the certainties of straightforward "You Are Here" maps as are the exteriorities of Laniakean perspectives.

* * *

My own snowglobe coordinates are easily enough laid out. Like everyone, I was born at a particular time in a particular place. In my case in Belfast on a cold February morning. There had been snow the night before. The roads were icy. The perils of driving to the hospital became an often-told family story. There was a skid when my father almost lost control. When we passed that spot in years to come, it was always pointed out. I've often wondered what different patterns my life might have taken if the car had left the road. For the time between then and now, I could sum up in a paragraph or two the main factors that have given me my underlying sense of "You Are Here," that foundation-feeling of present consciousness that pulses out its guiding beacon of identity and location throughout a life. I don't mean by this any self-conscious effort at map-making, but simply the soundings of people, places, times and seasons by reference to which the contour lines on our personal sense of whereabouts are drawn. Wherever we happen to be, and whoever happens to accompany us, provides a background continuum of reference, creates touchstones that offer a sense of everyday orientation. For me, a handful of people and places – my personal polestars – have been welcome constants.

What I find hard to bring into focus is the relationship between my straightforward sense of who and where I am and the wider picture that I know it's part of. How does the spot on that County Antrim road where, as we headed towards my birthing, my father almost skidded, relate to the enormousness of Laniakea? Can I bring into any meaningful alignment the baby born on that February morning in Belfast with a bloodline that reaches back, through innumerable forbears, not just to recognizable ancestors we can name but to the crucible of creatures that emerged when life's presence first sparked into existence on this third planet from the Sun? Can my present point in time-space, sitting at a computer in an attic room typing the words of this sentence, look anything other than ridiculous – minuscule, ephemeral, insignificant – when it's put beside the immensities of time that stretch out on either side of it?

In one sense, "You are Here" is a simple matter. It's determined by the immediate coordinates – geographical, social, psychological – that define our place and person at any given moment. But there is so much more looming beyond such simple pictures. Even the sketchiest knowledge of it creates such a magnification that ordinary coordinates risk being crushed in the massive atmospheres of cognitive pressure that result. Sometimes I picture myself standing in front of some straightforward "You Are Here" map in a town I'm visiting for the first time, but instead of it offering the ready reckoning I want, its snowglobe enclosure of manageable proximities cracks and I'm left floundering in Atlantic expanses.

* * *

In *You Are Here* (2004), her fascinating compilation of what she calls "personal geographies and other maps of the imagination," Katharine Harmon suggests that the urge to map, "like our opposable thumbs, is part of what makes us human." Not every outcome of this urge is expressed through drawing; there are thought-maps and word-maps. Our sense of where we are comes from a range of sources, not all of them obviously cartographical. But whatever form the maps that we rely on take, it's clear a need for orientation runs clamant in our veins. We are salted with a thirst to know where and who we are, where we've come from, where we're going between (beyond?) the obvious markers of or birth and death. I don't think that thirst can be more than momentarily slaked by the kind of straightforward coordinates "You Are Here" maps give.

Harmon's book presents a richly diverse collection. Not just maps of the world drawn according to expected conventions, but maps that make use of imagination, humour, fiction, that explore ideas, dreams, and emotions as well as well as landscapes, maps that offer pictures of our interior worlds as well as of the external landscape. Among the examples she includes are: a map that shows the incidence of Halloween lanterns in an American suburb; a map of air routes over Britain by day and by night; a map of Srinagar embroidered in fine wool on cloth; Edwin Morgan's visual poem "Chaffinch Map of Scotland"; Seymour Chwast's "A Map of Lovemaking," with the anatomy of a couple in coitus depicted as a contour map. There's a sixteenth century Tibetan map of the body's interconnecting blood vessels; prehistoric hunting maps incised on rock; maps of gene expression in the body of a fruit fly. Behind all of these maps is the urge to understand our surroundings. Driving all of them is the thirst for insight into the nature of the things around us, for soundings that will reveal, piece by piece, the coordinates of our whereabouts.

* * *

I like "You are Here" maps because they stimulate my sense of what I've called "existential absurdity." By contrasting their everyday positional parameters with measurements that utterly dwarf them, I can savour a rush of vertigo at the vast disparity in scale. Beside the distances I travel in an average day, the "immeasurable heavens" of Laniakea, seem somehow surreal. But there's another reason I like "You Are Here" maps. They appeal to me because they constitute such an obvious transition between reality and representation. The ones I like best include a representation of themselves – a little laminated noticeboard displaying the map is drawn on the map itself. This makes such maps feel like thresholds where you can almost witness the world metamorphosing into the symbols we use to try to catch and manipulate its elements. A "You Are Here" map pictured on a "You Are Here" map means that thing symbolized and symbol are for a moment co-existent, able to touch hands, exchange breaths, beckon us to walk between them as a kind of transubstantiation happens. Mapping, like writing, lets us translate the surge of sensation and information our existence brings, allows us to channel the raw impress of things upon us into tokens we can trade in the commerce of our cognitive transactions. This symbolic currency enables us to purchase some trace at least of sense – even if our little economies of scale are left bankrupt by amounts that overwhelm all the refinements and confinements of language.

Perhaps on some distant planet, in some distant time, there will be displayed a massive "You Are Here" map of such stupendous size and sophistication that everywhere can be marked, where the tokens of representation will somehow be underlain by a gold standard which means that they can be exchanged for the true coordinates of where whoever stands before them really is. It's hard to judge whether looking at such a map would do more to terrify or enlighten us.

* * *

I realize, naturally, that "You Are Here" maps are drawn for routine, limited purposes – to help us get from the carpark to the bank, or find the track that leads to a mountain viewpoint; they're not designed to plot our whereabouts beyond that. It would be unreasonable to expect them to show our position in the universe. They're not interested in galaxies or superclusters, but rather how we can best walk or drive between nearby locations. I don't doubt the usefulness of that. But, for me, such maps, as well as fulfilling their quotidian function, almost never fail to spark a sense of bizarre limitation in terms of where they say we are. Talk about not noticing the elephant in the room! You'd never guess from their little markers that in fact we're on the surface of a spinning planet, formed some 4,500 million years ago, that it's orbiting a giant burning star, part of a family of planets in a Solar System, located in a galaxy that's one of countless others threaded through the immensity of a 13.8-billion-year-old universe. No, you are here, in the carpark, 500 yards from the bank. It's maybe just a few minutes' walk in that direction to the leisure centre – but how long did it really take me to get to this spot? That question prompts the lineage of *Homo sapiens* into mind, the long bloodline of which we're a part. Behind any "You Are Here" lurks a journey that has extended over aeons.

I sometimes think of all the different "You Are Here" maps that must exist, how each person has a sense of where they are; our personal orientations of self and place. The maps we carry invisibly within us will be drawn according to the particular life-situations in which we find ourselves. There will, of course, be many similarities – because of the common ground of our essential biology – but considerable variation too. I sometimes think about my grandmother's sense of where she was, how she would have understood the "You Are Here" arrow that pointed at her life. I doubt if she thought much outside the territory of her strong sense of local and familial placement. Beyond the immediate coordinates that did so much to define her – living, widowed, with three daughters on a farm eight miles from Belfast – did she have much sense of her whereabouts? The unsophisticated theology that informed her faith might have given her a few Biblical pointers. But I think it's unlikely she thought of being on a planet spinning in space, one tiny particle in a universe of stupendous span and age. Even if she'd had time for star-gazing and daydreaming, astronomical knowledge at the time she lived was rudimentary compared to how it now is.

So long as we can get from one place to another in terms of navigating our everyday needs, does it matter what we think about where we are? How much, if at all, do our different senses of whereabouts influence the lives we lead? If you could lay them side by side, I suspect there would be significant differences between my grandmother's "You Are Here" map and mine. No doubt mine will seem as primitive to those a century hence as hers strikes me today. But is there any reason to believe that my coordinates serve me any better than hers served the life she led? I'm reminded of the passage in Sir Arthur Conan Doyle's *A Study in Scarlet* when Dr Watson discovers that Sherlock Holmes "Was ignorant of the Copernican Theory and of the composition of the Solar System." Challenged about his ignorance of what Watson sees as fundamental knowledge, the great detective's riposte is: "What the deuce is it to me? You say that we go round the sun. If we went round the moon it would not make a pennyworth of difference to me or to my work."

* * *

In *The Wild Places* (2007) Robert Macfarlane writes:

> Maps organize information about a landscape in a profoundly influential way. They carry out a triage of its aspects, selecting and ranking those aspects in

> an order of importance, and so they create forceful biases in the ways a landscape is perceived and treated.

I think Macfarlane is correct about maps creating "forceful biases" in terms of the ways we read the world. He warns that we have fallen under the spell of roadmaps. By ignoring many features of the natural world, they exert "distortive pressure" on the imagination. The land is seen "only as a context for motorized transport" – an outlook that promotes "the elimination of wonder."

Laniakean perspectives are a long way removed from any concern about our stewardship of the particular habitats we occupy on Planet Earth. They are seemingly remote from the many immediate threats that preoccupy environmentalists. But perhaps the usefulness of cultivating existential vertigo lies precisely in its boosting of wonder, in the way it can recalibrate a sense of just how wild the places are that we inhabit, however much we treat them as domesticated. Stand back from our routine "You Are Here" maps – whether they're of a city-centre or a nature reserve – and think about where we really are beyond the snowglobe coordinates they give. Yes, that may cause feelings of angst and cosmic lostness, of complete individual insignificance, but it seems likely also to ignite a blazing sense of untamed wonderment.

Greg Bottoms

Getting Dressed, 1981

My clothing, how I appear to others, matters marginally. Then one day when I am almost eleven, in 1981, a new awareness flares, like a flint spark. I become part of a new grid of social meaning. I am seen by the world of the school, the world at large. Call it the end of comfort.

I turn over in bed, thinking (without precise words, cogent contextualizing thought patterns, descriptive verbal ability): *How can I control how they see me?* Or maybe: *How can I make it so they adore me…or like me…or at least accept me?*

Light filters beneath the white, plastic blinds of my bedroom. Our suburban house is new and smells sharp and chemically, like fresh paint and the synthetic green carpet on which I've already spilled dark soda. The walls are white and bare. This is because what you put on bedroom walls is important, defining. I'm learning this by visiting with friends, seeing their bedroom walls decorated with posters of basketball stars, handsome quarterbacks, rock bands, even centerfolds in one case. I don't want to portray myself through sports stars. It is the rock stars I want to showcase. But who? Elton John—cool outfits—and I'm gay. U2 and I'm a self-serious moper. Judas Priest and I play records backwards for subliminal satanic messages and probably abuse animals. Who speaks a part of the story I want to tell about myself to the world? What *is* that story?

And every morning this strange, new problem. A mysterious tightness in the crotch, swelling, a pressure. Should I be embarrassed? Is there something wrong? (Nowadays I'd have a smart phone and more illicit, if largely incorrect, knowledge about my body and other bodies and what bodies can do to other bodies according to essentially crowdsourced fetishes from millions of male minds. But this is 1981, the personal computer is a novel idea, Reagan is the newly elected president, the "moral majority" is actually a phrase I've heard at our Methodist church, and the minds of middle-class children in the western world have not yet been co-opted and colonized by technology. Anxiety rates and eating disorders and suicides among kids my age at this time are a small fraction of a fraction of a fraction of what they will become when I am a parent and writing this and the world some days feels like it's on fire and there is no turning off a visual culture of capitalist surveillance and consumerism and toxic ideologies with their scintillating, enthralling, and addictive prodding of desire and shame, fear and loathing.)

I stand up quickly in only white Fruit-of-the-Loom underwear, which my mother buys every six months or so in four packs from K-Mart and places, freshly washed, in the top drawer of the walnut-colored dresser. At a certain point—she must conclude—the careless skid marks of boyhood won't wash out.

I walk to the door, open it a crack, and look into the short hallway. Empty and quiet.

I share a bathroom with my older and younger brothers, who each have their own room in this new house, identical to mine in size and dimension, on different sides of the hall. My older brother, fifteen, is already experiencing concerning symptoms—brief dissociation, forgetfulness, mild aural hallucinations, unprovoked mood swings—of early-onset paranoid schizophrenia, which no one will understand or diagnose for a couple of years (psychiatrist at places like Harvard are still blaming schizophrenia on concepts like the "cold mother" in the early eighties). This brother will later refuse treatment and become homeless and later still try to burn this house down with everyone in my family inside except me, away at college at the time. This brother will also go to prison for twenty years, then get out and kill himself within a year, at age forty-eight, while in a psychiatric facility. My younger brother, so dear to me as a six-year-old in 1981, a great thudding love in my life, will later struggle with his own, if less dramatic, problems, as I suppose I will, too, the three of us—American boys and then men of a certain time and place and kind—heading toward what sociologists will later refer to as potential "deaths of despair." But those are other stories in other books. Right now, wearing my crisp, new, skid-mark-free Fruit-of-the-Loom briefs from the local K-Mart, I simply want to make sure the bathroom is open so I can get ready for school before my brothers stumble, wild-haired and also wearing white Fruit-of-the-Looms, out of their rooms to demand I hurry up through the locked door.

The bathroom is small, maybe six feet by eight feet and part of the ceiling slopes down with the roof line of the house. I stand in front of one of the two sinks, both rimmed with dried toothpaste, and stare into the large, water-spotted mirror. This obsessive looking never occurred to me only months ago. Now it is as if I've become two people: the one acting and the one observing and critiquing the acting.

I wash my face with bar soap from the plastic dish. The bottom of the bar is soft and wet and slippery, and I often have to pick off a snaking black pubic hair or two from my older brother's fast-developing body. After the face wash and rinse, I wet my medium-length, sandy-blond hair and spend minutes trying to create a straight part in the middle of my head. I comb the hair down from the part and then back; it flops forward. Try again; same result. I put my older brother's Old Spice deodorant—the scent like a Christmas tree dipped in my grandmother's Kentucky bourbon—on my bald armpits, smell the white stick, then run it up and down my chest and stomach, like someone sloppily painting the bare wall of some other new house in our half-built neighborhood.

I obsess. I perseverate. I have recently seen snippets of the film *Saturday Night Fever* on cable TV, on posters, mentioned in magazines in convenience stores as an important reference, a touchstone, some shorthand in mass culture—positive or negative, historical or ironic or mocking—even though it is four years old and many of the older boys I know were not long ago into the "disco sucks" phenomenon (kids gathering in crowds to destroy makeshift disco balls; rail against the movement as gay; proclaim the superior, macho aesthetic of heavy metal). My parents won't let me watch the movie, now available on one of the new movie channels—I see the brown cable box with black buttons on top, a thick cord mysteriously snaked into the wall—but I covet, replay mental images from, and "get" (an important verb: *Do you get it? Can you get it? Get this? Got it, man, got it*) its central story and message about manhood. Sex is key, the essential quest. Style is essential, too, something to get right because it is part of the sex, which is not just an act—an act I do not understand—but a larger ritual, a way of presenting oneself in the world. Hard work, understanding and performing this ritual, but it needs to seem easy, natural, simply the way the man exists. I am, in a way, in love with the images of John Travolta I have seen, or at least enthralled by them. They possess a power, a beauty, though I am not sure that is the right word, the word I'm looking for. (Later, in grad school, say, I might use a word like "signification" or "mystification," something semiotic or Marxist, pretentious.) Anyway, a powerful force or aura or ambience starts out *there*, in the world, in music and fashion and magazines and TV and movies and representations of gestures and walks and expressions and speech patterns, and then it moves in *here*, to this mirror that holds aloft my smooth, soft, round face, my now-musky smelling and sticky ribcage and chest and nipples and armpits.

Recently, my mother bought me a yellow polyester shirt with an extra-wide collar and realistic images of large blue and purple tropical fish printed all over it. A disco shirt. A clearance sale shirt from a decade now gone, tightly packed like a wet page in an old book against other unwanted clothes on a circular rack in the back of a store. She thought I'd love it, and I do. It reminds me of John Travolta as Tony Manero in *Saturday Night Fever*. I am also a fan of the dance shows *American Bandstand* and *Soul Train*, which I watch with my mother on Saturday mornings sometimes and even dance to, unless my father and a little breeze of shame enters the TV room. This shirt would be at home in those dance studios during tapings, might even draw the attention of a camera, its light like an all-seeing eye assessing me, exalting me.

I walk back to my bedroom, into its bare look of new construction and the Elmer's-glue smell of latex paint. I lock the door (my family's old house didn't have locks on inside doors, or two bathrooms, or *two sinks* in one bathroom, an almost absurd opulence). I open the top dresser drawer and remove the carefully folded tropical fish shirt, rough fingertip skin catching on the shiny chemical compound of the material. I fluff the bed sheets and flatten them. I unfold the shirt carefully and then arrange it on the bed in the shape of an invisible man midway through a jumping jack.

Now the pants. But what pants? Should I match the glory of this shirt or go more subdued on the bottoms to accent the top? Or is contrast the way to go?

I place a pair of jeans below the shirt. They are dark blue, stiff. They barely change shape with a person in them, bend like a thing with hinges. I stand back and look at the arrangement on the bed. Maybe. Remove the jeans and replace them with a burgundy pair of slightly bellbottomed corduroys, luxuriously soft, hand-me-downs from my brother, maybe a size too small for me this school year, but flashy, telegenic, something that both compliments and contrasts with the shirt.

I can hear my brothers now (still alive, still healthy, I haven't a clue of the sorrows that await us)—one locked in the bathroom, one outside the bathroom door pleading to get in to pee. Let them argue. I am concentrating, coming to a decision. Pulling on the burgundy corduroys, yanking and shimmying to get them up my thickening thighs, straining to button them, I try to ignore the uncomfortable fit and focus more on the color pallet, the way they will accent the clearance-sale shirt. I turn to face the mirror. Flesh bulges above my waistband. The material strains and stretches around the hips. I am a little chubby, no doubt, which won't do, not at all, certainly not for a fine TV-room dancer, but that can't be fixed this morning.

I carefully pick up the shirt, the bright magisterial polyester, like some regal garment from South Asia, button it up and stare into the mirror above the dresser. Broad freckly face, dark blue eyes, hair parted in the middle and uncooperative even when, in the recent past, I have secretly tried my mother's Sunday-school, industrial-strength hairspray. The yellow shirt with its blue and purple fish, two buttons undone. Pants squeezing but the color palette feeling right, fashion-photographic. Stylish. *Sensuous*, I might say, if I knew that word.

Forget, for now, the mortification that happens later at school, or how the school day becomes a collection of agonizingly slow seconds once I realize, running into some eighth-grade boys just after the first bell, the monumental mistake of these clothing choices, the fashion *faux pas*, the way they cast me on the wrong side of a mysterious something. *Disco dick*, I will be called. *What baby did you steal those pants from? Nice little red sausages, those thighs of yours? I can see your cellulite! Fish? Purple fish? Are they sucking each other's asses or French kissing or both? Was this a dare? Did your mom dress you? Did your brother see you leave the house like this?*

But this hasn't happened yet. In the mirror, in this moment, I am a super-sexy celebrity, a pop star, Tony Manero, dressed for the marveling of the masses. I'll skip breakfast to make sure these colorful corduroys don't get any tighter and split. Should I go with three open buttons instead of two? Perfume up with more deodorant? Plaster on more of mom's hairspray? I wish I had a gold chain, maybe with a cross on it like one of those cool and hairy-chested New York Catholics in *Saturday Night Fever*. A blessing that the future is only knowable once it transforms into the past. I look forward to the day ahead.

Evan Brooke

Like a Dazzle

We called it the Dick Book, but it wasn't actually a book. It was a magazine—*Teen Beat*, Kirk Cameron on the cover—with several polaroids of a naked man tucked in between pages. We found it—more than once—while walking home from school, planted in the middle of a sidewalk or just off the sidewalk. But really, the Dick Book found us.

We were ninth graders, thrilled and relieved to be out of middle school, but confused by the fresh set of edicts required by a new school. Sports became a refuge, a place where the rules were very clear: what we wore, where we stood, what we said, when we came and went. On the off season, we often walked into town after school to buy junk food or makeup at the pharmacy and then we'd continue on to the home with the best snacks or the fewest possible disturbances.

Elizabeth grabbed it, thinking she had scored a free copy of *Teen Beat.* The polaroids slipped out as soon as she picked it up.

"What—is—that?" Meghan yelled, never quite aware of her own volume. She was high energy all the time.

"It's a dick," Elizabeth whispered, her rowdy curls tamed only by the sunglasses on top of her head. Taking the lead as she usually did, Elizabeth grasped one of the photos by the corner and held it up as if it were nuclear waste. Our heads tilted as we examined the picture sideways.

"No, it's a lot of dicks," Jenny observed, her eyes darting between the fallen polaroids. Jenny was the problem-solver of the group, and often accessorized with a key-filled carabiner clipped onto a belt loop of her jeans. We wondered how anyone could know so many doors.

"Like different dicks?" I asked, barely audible. I preferred not to be heard or seen. Anything that might attract attention—like my freckles—was cause for misery.

"Same dick, different positions," Christine said with authority.

She had an older sister; she knew things.

We were young and immature enough that to use the word penis was absolutely out of the question, as it was far too accurate a word — *pee-nis* sounded like what it was, like you "pee out of this." We were old enough to know what a dick was; there were dicks all around us—our older brothers, occasionally our fathers, Señor Porter, Assistant Coach Tom.

~

Though unproven, some zoologists have theorized that zebras have stripes to confuse predators because it's harder to identify individual zebras when they are in a group. A group of zebras is called a dazzle, which would be a fine name for a group of teenage girls who prefer to travel in groups, who feel like they might only dazzle when they are together. Our stripes—those things that made us feel like we stood out—blended when we were together. Our awkwardness became consensus. We were brace-faced and gap-toothed; we were flat-chested wishing for more chest and big-breasted wishing for less breast; we were lining our eyes with Go-You Green and glossing our lips with Boom-Boom Berry; we were pretending to know every song The Pixies ever wrote while we sang every word to "Unskinny Bop" by the band known as Poison.

Fellow girls were supposed to be our biggest threat. We had been warned: they are cutthroat and backstabbing, which sounded dangerous. We certainly didn't want to stab or cut anyone, but we stayed on high alert, especially when we weren't in the dazzle. Being alone was terrifying back then not just because we became conspicuous, but also because we were forced to become more conscious of our singular selves, more vulnerable.

Lions prey on zebras: they are known to stalk their prey during the day, hiding behind vegetation, sometimes giving themselves away by peeking. They go for the kill at night. If attacked, zebras will first try to outrun a lion and if that doesn't work their legs can kick hard enough to break jaws or sometimes knock out the predator. For the most part, zebras are completely fucked when preyed on.

Fortunately, we found the Dick Book during the day. It disgusted us and enthralled us, it may have even flattered us. At fifteen, we had all seen a penis, but not all of us had seen a dick. The photos did not reveal the man's face, but offered plenty of angles of his lower half. "Does he think he's hot?" we asked, genuinely curious. "Does anyone think this is hot?" The exhibitionism astounded us, that anyone could feel that confident about their nakedness, especially since our own bodies were still so mysterious. It certainly did not sell us on being heterosexual—or sexual at all—it was gross, perverted, and yet somehow not imminently threatening. It created the tiniest of fissures, room enough for an unnamed and unspoken message to seep in and warn us that the world wasn't safe, not even here in our small, leafy New Jersey town. When a pebble hits the windshield, it sometimes leaves a small crack, a crack that might only obscure a distant traffic light, but over time that crack has the potential to spread into rivulets and then shatter the entire thing. Danger had crept into our quiet suburb and was following us behind the pachysandra. We acknowledged only that the Dick Book had an author, but he remained anonymous and it scared us for a minute, but we kept walking home and ate our Funyons along the way. We didn't think too much about the drafting of that book, the distribution of it, or the probability that the author was waiting around to sign copies.

~

A group of ducks is called a flock or more obscurely known as a brace. Originally, the term brace meant a pair of ducks, but evolved to include a group. The term "sitting duck" originated with hunters who found the animals easy targets, especially when they were just chilling in the water minding their own business. Ducks have few ways of defending themselves—rounded beaks, dull nails, and the domesticated ones (i.e. those that live in the suburbs) can't fly. The only thing we knew about defense in high school was how to protect your teammate. We could be vicious to our opponents—verbally and physically—but off the field we presumed we had nothing to fear. We didn't need to brace ourselves for anything.

Male ducks will flirt with females, attempt to capture attention by stretching their necks or splashing their heads into the water like some of the headbangers we knew. Most birds don't have penises, but male ducks apparently have dicks and use them violently. According to *National Geographic*, the mating season is traumatic for females: "There are even socially organized groups of males pursuing females to force copulation. This is really physically harmful for the female ducks. They are stressed out. They fly away, dive, and do everything they can to avoid it. Sometimes they even drown because ducks often copulate in the water." Biologists call this "forced copulation" while our health teachers called it rape.

~

We got reckless as we ventured further into high school—took the train into New York to buy booze, had parties when our parents left us alone, drank stolen grain alcohol, took the car out for license-less joyrides, at least one of us had unprotected sex, another a try-on eating disorder, the other a full-blown eating disorder—but the ending was always clear. All would eventually end, if not well, then okay. You get pregnant, the end is an abortion. You get really drunk, the end is throwing up a lot, feeling like shit for a day and you might even get caught, but it's not like you would die. You get nabbed by the cops at a party, your parents bail you out. You stop eating for a while, you start up again as long as your mom has stopped saying you look fat in your spring formal dress. You find the Dick Book, you lose it and walk home.

~

A murmuration is a flock of starlings that fly synchronously. They swirl in one enormous mass, a dark cloud, a moving constellation. There is strength in their numbers, sometimes hundreds, sometimes thousands. A 2013 analysis by a group of scientists suggests this aerial phenomenon shows the "birds' ability to manage uncertainty while also maintaining consensus." The swarm is beautiful and alarming, a reaction one might feel towards a swarm of teen girls. We were no swarm, but like the starlings, we were loyal to our formation. Rarely less than three or more than five, we stuck together, pushing our desks closer, clustering at the lunch table, walking like a moving dam on the sidewalk, piling in the back of our mothers' station wagons. We were afraid of our singular identities, of our vulnerabilities as individuals. There was no *I* in team, our coaches always told us. So we avoided the *I* for as long as we could.

Falcons and hawks are natural predators to starlings, but humans are the primary threat. In the U.S. starlings are invasive and considered to be a major pain in the ass. They are everywhere, which means so is their poop. They deprive other birds of food sources, they damage crops, and can transmit disease. They have caused airplane crashes. Advice on how to control or kill them abounds on the internet—trap, electric shock, poison, or shoot are common suggestions—so it sort of makes sense why they would stick together. We were misunderstood, otherwise more people would have seen our value, our uniqueness. As a group, we certainly felt more protected, but we also felt like we could be beautiful.

~

A year after we found the Dick Book, we were drinking wine coolers at Christine's house and hightailed it as soon as we saw her mom's headlights in the driveway. We made our way down the road and landed at the park. Memorial Field was the hub of recreational life in town. It's where the Fourth of July fireworks went off, soccer games were played, the annual fair happened. It had tennis courts and basketball courts, two playgrounds, one with a seesaw that made you feel like you were getting shot out of a cannon. The field was encircled by a pebbled track, none of it lit up at night to prevent kids like us from loitering. We were huddled on the sidewalk that bordered the field to discuss our next destination when a white van pulled up. Given the curtains on the back windows, we thought it could possibly be a friendly van. But it was dark and the van had pulled over and we paused in between the grass and the track wondering what this van was doing. Soon, four masked bodies jumped out of the van and ran towards us. We split into different directions, booking it into the darkness of the open field as the bodies ran after us. Our formation had been broken, the murmuration had splintered. In an instant, our "we" became "me."

I remember thinking how this couldn't possibly be happening, that really I was back at the house being lectured to by Christine's mom. But reality struck when I was grabbed from behind, and lifted up in a straitjacket hug. I screamed and twisted wildly, eventually maneuvering in such a way that I bit into the scalp of this person, which made him let go. It wasn't intentional, but I probably said it was in an effort to prove I wasn't as defenseless as a duck. I don't remember how long this went on, but it felt interminable and terrifying, and ended once each of us managed to unmask them. They were a mix of 10th, 11th, and 12th grade boys. We were friends with at least one of them, friendly with the rest. They thought it would be funny.

"Total dicks," we said, and then eventually, after the terror wore off, we acted like it was funny too because we were tough and we weren't going to let them think otherwise. For a few moments, the end felt certain, we'd be assaulted or killed. But that danger was an illusion and offered proof to us that we were always going to be fine. All would eventually end well. In many ways, getting older is that process of realizing that we weren't always going to be fine, that there will be moments when you can't deny your vulnerability.

~

We did reach Meghan's house safely, and left the Dick Book for someone else to find. It found us one more time after that in a different location, but by then it wasn't as interesting any more. How unoriginal, we may have thought. Pathetic even. We can only speculate now how our lackluster response may have been received by the author, if he was watching, as we still suspect he was. That was the point. He knew teenage girls would not find his polaroid porn arousing—but he knew he had power over us, that his anonymity may have been cowardly, but it gave him the perch he needed to watch us, exploit us, prey on us. The van incident widened the fissure the Dick Book created. Those masked boys used their anonymity too—until we took it away from them. They terrorized us not just by physically threatening us, but also by showing us we could be hunted and harmed by people we knew.

The van incident wasn't just a cruel prank, it was also a warning: there were men out there who felt entitled to our bodies. Some men engaged in bizarre mating rituals; some men showed off their penises like lions do with their manes; some men forced copulation. We felt less invincible, but more convinced of the strength in our number. As we got older, we would learn that our bodies could betray us too—that danger could arrive in the form of a tiny fucked-up cell, causing depression, infertility, cancer.

Over the years, our formation resumed: straight-lined as bridesmaids, bent-elbowed as bar patrons, flocked as aunties, kneeled as mourners. When we are in the group, we manage the uncertainty of getting married, of having babies, of getting sick, of death, more bravely, like the starlings. Now middle-aged, at last, we are comfortable with who we are, insist on the frequent use of *I* since we abdicated it for so long, but settle into the solace and safety of *we* because we choose to.

~

The International Union for Conservation of Nature (IUCN) maintains a database of threatened species that evaluates the vulnerability of animals and plants globally. Each species is given a rating to assess their "extinction risk status," ranging from "least concern" to "extinct" with other markers in between. The zebra is considered "near threatened," one notch away from "vulnerable." Humans are to blame: farming, hunting, warring, climate-destroying. Surely, the zebras are not as oblivious to threats as we were—they can at least sense a predator hiding in the bushes. And yet we survived, close call after close call. That denial of our own vulnerability is what kept us close, what convinced us we could run into a dark field without consequence. The opposite is true now—our expressed vulnerabilities are what hold us together.

We come together again in that leafy New Jersey town, pewed like crows, sitting six excruciating feet apart, mourning the last of our fathers. We blend in black, but each of our stripes still stands out. There is Elizabeth, her perfect posture, sunglasses still serving as a headband; and Meghan, still unable to whisper, her impeccably neat short hair feigning reserve underneath; Christine streams in from Vermont, still so chic in her laid-backness; my freckles have shifted into larger constellations; I am still disheveled, inside and out. And then there is Jenny, who sits even farther away, up front, her deep red locks a little less fiery on this day because she can't solve the biggest problem. Her father had called her Red.

Outside the church, we huddle, defying the danger of a global virus, the danger of known and unknown predators, and we hold each other—so briefly safe in each other's arms.

Sarah Butkovic

Castles, Books, and Submarines

SOMEWHERE ON THE SOUTH SIDE OF CHICAGO May 12th, 1925. Dorothy "Dotsy" Elich was born under the sign of the bull and year of the Ox on the Chinese calendar. If that astrological mumbo-jumbo counts for anything, I attribute it to making my aunt the most stubborn and fiercest woman I know.

SWEET, STICKY DISNEYLAND

"When I turned 20 I told myself I needed to get out of the house. So instead of my sister, who was too fragile to step out the door without a man to guide her, I sucked it up and packed my bags. No risk, no reward. And as soon as I left the tirade of my parents, I went to the only logical place I could think of. Hot sun, smiling faces, cute caricatures running around... They called it the happiest place on Earth for a reason, right?"

Dotsy moved into a worn-down studio apartment about five blocks away from Disneyland California and commuted to work on foot. With the park in the middle of a staff expansion, Dotsy was given the title of "management team member" without even reviewing her (admittedly spare) resume. She thought landing a job so easily, and at the largest tourist venue in America, was just the Disney magic rubbing off on her. She was wrong. The job was a hellish loop: she took inventory of the merchandise flooding the warehouses every day, then dished out Mickey ears and castle T-shirts until her arms wore out. Day after day for a year and a half. Dotsy had scorned her friends for being stuck in a hamster wheel of maternal monotony-- cooking and cleaning and kissing their kiddos goodnight-- but now she was stuck in the same way they were. Every Monday through Friday, Dotsy plodded through the unforgiving sun watching children prance around with scuffed-up shoes and dried ice cream plastered on their faces like sticky birthmarks.

She began to pity herself and despised maintaining a happy-go-lucky facade for kids who barely noticed her.

"I realized that I needed to get out and make a difference in the world. I felt stagnant after a while, slipping further and further into a job and farther away from a career. Disneyland taught me that those words have different meanings--job and career--and God help the poor souls who think they're the same."

THE ONLY MIRROR SHE OWNED

Dotsy joined the Marines in 1948 law just as they began to accept women. She remembers how it felt slipping on her uniform for the first time, the crisp, unforgiving fabric hiding her feminine curves to give off the illusion of a straight-cut figure. It made Dotsy feel like those plastic toy soldiers her older brother played with when they were kids: stout, stoic, and able to withstand a nasty tumble down the basement stairs.

"Too many times, being a woman stopped me from doing what I wanted. I stood in my bathroom gawking at myself like I was Narcissus, and in fact, I would've put him to shame. That uniform was my escape--a way to be powerful and serve a purpose."

While every other doll-eyed woman was blissfully frying ham and eggs for her breadwinning husband and gaggle of cherry-lipped children, Dotsy was preparing for something bigger.

"I'd rather go to Hell and back than become a housewife. Every poor woman trapped in that fantasy was starring in their very own Groundhog Day. I had friends whose schedules I memorized because they did the exact same things at the exact same time every single day of the week. Not saying what they were doing wasn't important--raising the next generation is a noble task, indeed--but I wanted something more for myself: a life of my own."

A DUSTY LIBRARY THAT HELD MORE THAN A DREAM

According to Dotsy, being a lesbian in the civilian world in the 1950's was just as dangerous as in the Marines; there was widespread homophobia in an era where many women gathered dust like trinkets on shelves. Dotsy was no trinket and she planned to gather no dust.

"It was like owning a speakeasy, except the secret room downstairs was your heart you only let people with the password into. That's why I moved to California-- to open my own speakeasy and stop pretending I ran a run-of-the-mill business without any hidden doors. I couldn't get away with being gay at home. My parents were smart and more judgmental than that lady on CBS…You like how poetic that was?"

The lady my aunt was referring to, as I later found out, was Judge Judy.

"I had been unsure of my sexuality for a while—I always caught myself drooling over Audrey Hepburn instead of the Ken Dolls co-starring in her films. But the day I met Maggi Kennedy in the library was the day I knew women were the only ones allowed in my speakeasy."

Dotsy doesn't remember the name of the library, but she does recall the hexagon path leading up to the entrance and how hard she tried to avoid the tip of her kitten-heels falling into the cracks between the bricks. She remembers the way the dust particles, stirred up by the *whoosh* of the double doors swinging open, would float around the room like dandelion fuzzies. And most importantly, she remembers the glum face of the front desk clerk that was squashed under dainty hands and a name tag that simply read "Mag."

"Maggi looked bored to tears the first time I went in there. And if I'm being honest, which you know I always am, she looked just as bored each time after that. Except when I came in. She had this sort of adorable pout-- almost as if there was a vendetta between herself and the wall clock across from her. She would angrily stare it down to intimidate the hands into ticking faster than they should so her grueling shift would end. It never worked, of course, but that didn't stop the girl from trying."

Their first conversation occurred when Dotsy checked out two books about Belize and international tourism. After Maggi inquired if Dotsy planned on traveling while ringing her up, the small talk that followed quickly evolved into a lengthy conversation about foreign culture. Maggi, who had never been out of the country before, wrote short fantasy novels about the exoticism of overseas adventures in her free time. Dotsy, enamored by this, promised to indulge her with the details of her trip and perhaps photos upon returning. Catching Maggi up on the highlights of her which was something that became a regular occurrence.

Infatuated by Maggi's radiant smile and intellectual edge, simply pining after her from afar was something Dotsy no longer had the patience for. On a hazy day in September and donned in her Sunday best, Dotsy strutted down that gilded brick pathway with fervor and finally asked Maggi out for coffee.

EGGSHELL LEATHER SEATS

"The kiss happened after a drive-in movie. I was so nervous I can't remember what was playing to this day. Neither of us had revealed ourselves at that point--we were both riding on the bold assumption that the other was gay. Thank God we were right because after I drove her home in my father's old Ford I stole a quick kiss on the cheek when it was safe in the dark, and then she stole one back on the lips, and damn me if I was gonna let her have the last one so I kissed her back a second time."

FRANCE, 1991

Maggi and Dotsy traveled. And traveled. And went home to make sure their apartment hadn't burned down in their absence and then traveled some more.

They saw almost every region in the world in less than twenty years; no foreign language or culture was too daunting as long as the two of them faced the unknown together. My aunt-- and I don't mean this as a hyperbole-- is probably one of the most worldly and astute people in America. I remember hearing horror stories about some of her misadventures when I was younger, like when she traveled to China during the 1960's and lived off processed cheese balls for three days because the first restaurant she visited served her fried pigeon, or when she lost Maggi in France and only knew how to say *revoir!* and *oui oui!*

Maggi, whose parents emigrated from Paris, spoke the language fluently and was deigned to be more of a translator than a partner to Dotsy while they were in Marseille. She ordered all of Dotsy's meals (sometimes "inadvertently" asking for the wrong one if she was feeling particularly thorny) and constantly explained dialogue between the characters on the sitcoms that played on their hotel room TV.

'Maggi up and left in the middle of an evening stroll. I remember bending down to fetch my runaway wallet which had landed on the cobblestone street, and when I stood back up to make a joke about my clumsiness Maggi was nowhere in sight. I wandered the square for the longest twenty minutes of my life before I finally found the bastard picking flowers from a private garden closed off for the night. I wanted so badly to be mad at her but all I could do was stand there and laugh. Moments like those are so small but the ones I look back on most fondly."

SHERMAN OAKS, CALIFORNIA

And now, after a whirlwind of 96 years, Dotsy resides in a small yet chic bungalow on the quaint side of town. Her traveling is mostly limited to grocery store trips and coffee shop runs, but her frail bones and sagging skin (which, she notes, is a sign that the devil is trying to drag her down to hell) hasn't taken the zeal out of her spirit. In fact, her mind is still acute enough to point out the sentence fragments and dangling participles in the writing that I send her; she's probably going to have a field day marking this up when she reads it. Reading is a hobby she initially loathed but begrudgingly came to love since the written word was Maggi's lifeblood as a writer. After Maggi's death in 2017, my aunt has made exercising her brain her top priority in order to preserve the encyclopedia of memories they've made together.

'Maggi's been gone for four years and I miss her more than ever. But I've got her here with me every time I wake up and every time I go to sleep. Her book collection still takes up half the shelves in the house and her stories are kept in the desk I do all my brooding on."

She pauses to flip a page of something. Possibly a photo

album.

"People nowadays seem to be obsessed with minimalism and throwing away everything they own until they've got nothing left. But I say a big fuck you to that. Pardon my francois. Because when you're dead and gone, your imprint on the world goes with it. Memories are only good when you've got a working brain to keep them in. Maggi survives in my head for now. But when I'm dead she will still be alive through the things she owned and the things she touched and the things she loved and I think someone like her, and hell, maybe even someone like me, deserve to keep on living."

Kathryn Chiariello

On Impermanence

I shared an elevator with a child, once at a hotel in San Antonio. He was a baby almost, a brown-eyed, round-cheeked chunk of a fellow, perhaps ten months old. While his father struggled with several suitcases and his mother balanced him and a shoulder bag and her heavy purse, he stared out the elevator's open doors, looking toward everything that happened, everything that existed in the wide hotel lobby. The counter where a line of people waited, the waxy plants and bright paintings, the huge urns of coffee, the concierge who talked on the phone behind the desk.

"Six, please," the father said to me, as the mother wiped her hand across the child's forehead to shift his damp hair away from his eyes. The doors closed. The child's gaze followed them intently, his un-furrowed brow trying a furrow. His wet, dark eyes shone, and his mouth puckered into an "o."

"Look," his father said, pointing out the glass back of the elevator toward the tall atrium and the walled, greenish river beyond it. "Look at us go up."

The atrium view didn't interest the child, especially not after the lighted panel next to the elevator door dinged for floor two, then three, then four. We stopped. The door slid open. This was a hall far different from the lobby we'd left. A narrow iron table and mirror stood next to a close wall. Two hotel guests waited with magazines and flip flops and sunglasses that announced to all of us, save the child, that their destination was the rooftop pool. Every muscle in the child's body contracted, as if in fear or confusion or anger or frustration. The father made a joke. The child wailed.

Jean Piaget hypothesized that children develop an understanding of object permanence when they are around eight months old. After, perhaps, they've already ridden in an elevator. If you show a four-month-old a ball and put the ball under an opaque box, she will seem surprised when you lift the box and reveal the ball. By a year, most babies will be surprised if a clever researcher has played a trick to secretly remove the ball—a trapdoor under the box, for example—and the ball is not there.

Contemporary developmental psychologists believe children gain the understanding of object permanence over a spectrum of experiences and through a longer period than Piaget supposed. Acquiring it starts sooner and takes longer to completely master. We need a range of experiences to understand what in the world—what of the world—is here to stay and what will go, what is shaped by our perceptions and emotions and what by matter. (A complication, the wave-particle duality, means unreconcilable ambiguity is at the heart of physical reality.) No wonder we can't master it overnight. The child entered the elevator and watched the doors close on the world. We stopped. The doors opened. The world had changed. The game was one of wish fulfillment and unknown terror, both. I might wail, too.

Attaining a sense of object permanence leads to a paradox. Once we understand that the world exists and remains outside ourselves, we can begin to imagine interacting with our environment as an exercise of desire. We can stash a red foam ball or a Hershey's Kiss in the corner behind the embroidered couch at grandma's house and there it will be when we come back for it later. At the same time, we begin to recognize that the world's reality separate from our experience of it is the very thing that renders it outside our control. Grandma, after all, is a diligent housekeeper.

Most of us live much of our lives as incrementalists. We shape ourselves and our experience of the real by daily habit—the goodnight kiss when we are small, the place we hide during a family fight. We grow up. We brush our teeth. Go to bed. Wake up. Decide what to do when we have a day off. We reach for a creased hand at a matinee. Clear the dishes. One year follows another, so much faster. *I can't believe how fast time goes these days*, we say to ourselves, or, if we are lucky, to old friends who remember our faces when they were young.

Sometimes, rarely, but often and irregularly enough that we are almost conditioned by random reinforcement to expect it, the world changes all at once. A son's aneurism explodes. A bomb does. Elections are suspended. A condom breaks. The cure works. A tree crushes the roof. The promotion comes through, or the move to Hawaii. A double pirouette feels suddenly automatic. The femur breaks. You wake up blind. You wake up alone. You wake up with the winning lottery ticket, Covid-19, the tune in your head that will earn your first gold record, finally the words to tell your spouse you are leaving, or that you love him, or that you love him and yet you are leaving. Your son will survive. No, you will survive your son. As you walk across the thin, synthetic carpet laid over the thick, hard ground of winter, the box is still, and empty of anything of your son that mattered. It will be the same tomorrow—forever different.

Two floors further up, I left the elevator. Even from down the hall, I could hear the child's cries. I tapped my key card and opened the door to my empty room, a rectangle, a prism. I could imagine him in his mother's arms where she tried to comfort him, his dark hair matted around his ears, the damp skin of his forearm as he dragged it across his face, the tight arch of his back as he struggled—and failed without words—to ask, to understand, how can it be that the world is first one way and then it is another. I had nothing to tell him. Some things stay. Some things go. It takes our whole lives to know which will be which.

Maybe, if he had the language or wanted my solace, or if I had the time or the words, I could have said that the world shapes us, and then we shape the world. Maybe I could have said, "Everything was transformed when you were born," or,

"You are no more than a grain of sand." Maybe I could have tried to explain that confusion and fear and loss are everyday occurrences in his life not because he is so young, but because he simply is; not because he doesn't understand the nature of things, but because in some sense, he already does. I didn't though. Of course, I didn't. I couldn't explain to him about the ball. Not yet. Not about the ball. Not about the box.

Eileen Cunniffe

The Last Picture Show

When the opportunity presented itself, I didn't hesitate to take Winnie to see "Belfast." I'd already seen it once, and I knew she would love it. I also knew she wouldn't mind me selecting the movie we'd see; she'd always been deferential when we were making plans, no matter how hard I tried to extract her preferences: "You decide," she'd say. "Wherever you want to eat is fine." "What's a good time for you?" (It must be noted this trait applied only to unimportant decisions; Winnie never hesitated to express an honest opinion—or ask a probing question—when it mattered.) This time, however, I didn't ask; I just knew I had to take her.

One of the reasons we became friends so easily, even though I was fresh out of college and Winnie was nearly 40, was our Irishness, and our big, rollicking Irish-American families. Winnie's parents, like my grandparents, were born in Ireland. From Winnie, a redhead with a melodic laugh, I'd learned to call Irish fiddling "deedle-dee" music. From me, she'd learned to expect Irish soda bread for St. Patrick's Day and Christmas. We'd consumed barrels of tea in each other's company over the years, and when we gave each other gifts, they were as likely as not to have some connection to tea, and/or to Ireland. Sometimes we joked about the sappy sentimentality of the Irish; other times we got sentimental together over practically nothing.

I knew Winnie so well that even before we got to the movie, I was anticipating how she'd react to certain characters and scenes. I knew she would love Jude Hill, the young actor who plays 8-year-old Buddy in 1969 Belfast. I knew she'd want to talk afterwards about the boy's wise and funny grandfather, played by Ciarán Hands; and then about the bottomless marvelousness of Judi Dench, who plays the boy's granny. Then once the lights went down, even in the dark, I knew Winnie would be swaying along to the Van Morrison soundtrack, like me. (Later, over an imagined thermos of tea in my car, because, you know, Covid, Winnie and I would agree that while Morrison's music remained irresistible, his support for anti-vaxxers was inexcusable.)

As the movie unspooled, I could sense the familiar, exaggerated roll of Winnie's bright blue eyes every time religion was used to stir up trouble; and I could feel her solemn approval every time a counterpoint was offered. I knew she would think the actor who played Buddy's father was handsome. I knew she'd remind me later that she'd worn miniskirts like Buddy's mother way back then, and what were they ever thinking? But the moment in the film she liked best—as I had known she would—was when the tipsy aunt belts out "Danny Boy" at the end of a family gathering in front of Buddy's house, in plain view of the neighbors. I felt Winnie elbow me in the ribs pretty hard during that scene.

*

When Winnie and her husband Paul suddenly moved to Florida seven years ago, he kindly wrote to tell me what had happened. She was settling into a memory care unit, while he had an apartment nearby in the same senior community. Almost overnight, in her early 70s, Winnie had gone from a physically active, mentally sharp, engaged retiree who doted on her college-aged grandkids and volunteered for several community organizations to an often-agitated Alzheimer's patient whose memories had mostly been erased. For a few years, I learned, there had been some early signs of dementia—mood shifts and other atypical behavior; certainly not anything I had noticed, although by then Winnie and I only saw each other once or twice a year, and stayed in touch mostly through email. But something had snapped, and she'd needed specialized care, quickly. Her sister in Florida had found a place where Winnie and Paul could both move in, right away.

In the intervening years Paul sent a few updates, including a picture of Winnie blowing out candles on her 75th birthday cake. Her hair was pure white by then, not a hint of that gorgeous auburn remained. But her smile was the same. I still thought of Winnie often, because she'd been such a presence in my life. It haunted me that I'd not had a chance to say good-bye to the friend I'd known, although I was a little bit relieved that I'd only known her "before," and never seen her "after." Sometimes I had news I wanted to share with her; sometimes she was the person I most wanted to gripe with about the news-news. In November 2016, I dared to hope Winnie never had to know the outcome of the presidential election; although I knew that if she did, she'd be every bit as outraged "after" as she would have been "before."

Then last September, I got another email message from Paul, after a long interval. "Winnie has died," it began. Peacefully, thank goodness, at the age of 81. He told me there would be a funeral mass in Delaware the day before Thanksgiving, and I assured him I would be there. Online, I found an obituary that noted "her zest for life" had made her the longest-tenured resident in the history of the memory care unit where she'd lived her last chapter. Zest, oh my, yes. Winnie was one of the zestiest people I will ever know.

At the church, I was welcomed as a member of the family, introduced as Winnie's dear friend, my name familiar to her nearest kin, even some I'd never met. Her kids were happy, but surprised, to see me, because they hadn't known how to reach me; I explained that their 91-year-old father still had my email address. It made my heart happy to see Winnie and Paul's three beautiful, grown-up grandchildren, whose early years I'd enjoyed witnessing through photographs and occasional encounters. Their son Tim confirmed for me that Winnie had, unfortunately, understood the outcome of the 2016 election, although perhaps not the 2020 result. Damn. He didn't mind the question, but he did remind that me that I'd best not mention that topic to one of his aunts. I told him I knew to tread carefully there.

The reception after the mass was held in a rustic room

built into a hillside overlooking Ashland Nature Center, one of Winnie's favorite places. Several people in that room had walked around Ashland with Winnie, some of them many, many times. Often a dog or two was involved. A wall of windows was lit up by the midday sun, filtered through November's bare tree branches. Winnie's ashes sat in an unadorned white marble box, next to a vase of flowers, on a small table by the door. She would have liked that—being tucked into a corner where she could watch this gathering unfold.

By way of introduction, as I moved around the room and met nieces and nephews, grandkids and in-laws, I'd told them Winnie and I had worked together for close to 25 years, in two different organizations—first at a children's hospital, and later (basically across the street) at a pharmaceutical company. I explained we'd stayed in touch long after we'd both moved on from that second place, back in 2005, although we didn't see each other quite so often after that. I told them it had occurred to me recently that I'd probably had more lunches with Winnie than with any other person in my life. When we worked together, we weren't always in the same department, or even in the same building; but we often sought each other's company at lunchtime. We shared a cast of workplace characters that stretched all the way back to my first job out of college. Most of those characters are all mine now—no one but Winnie would remember them, or at least not in the way we had remembered them together over the decades.

Winnie's daughter, Erin, offered a beautiful eulogy at the reception. She celebrated the fact that her free-spirited mother had at last been released from the illness that had stolen some (but not all) of the joy from her closing years. Erin then invited others to share their memories. And that's when the real fun began. Because it was impossible to remember Winnie without laughing out loud at her mischievous ways, her irrepressible spirit, her wicked sense of humor. Some of the stories that made me happiest took place in Florida—"after"—when Winnie's essence shone through her illness. She seemed to have understood that whatever had been taken from her had also endowed her with extra cover for being "naughty" on a regular basis.

When the stories began, I'd only planned to listen and smile along with the family. I thought—maybe we all did—that Paul, along with Winnie's sisters and two sons, might add a few words to what Erin had said, and then everyone would quietly slip off to finish Thanksgiving preparations. But one story led to another, and suddenly the room was filled with laughter, warmth, and Winnie. The memories were bumping into each other left and right. People were competing for the next chance to speak. Winnie was right there with us—as a sister, a wife, a mother, an aunt, a cousin, a godmother, a grandmother. I realized I was the only person out of the three dozen or so in that room who was not related to Winnie by blood or by marriage. I was the only one there who had known her strictly as a friend and a co-worker. She was someone who'd always made friends easily, someone people confided in, and trusted. I'd met some of her same-age friends years ago, women who'd been young suburban moms together in the 1970s. The two I could recall had long since moved to other states. The ones we used to work with—including Winnie's "lunch ladies," because she and I didn't always eat together—maybe hadn't known why she'd disappeared from Delaware years ago, and could easily have missed her obituary in the local paper back in September.

So I waited for an opening, and I took my turn. I started by explaining that I'd met Winnie nearly 40 years ago, and so when it came to her extended family, "I know stuff," I said. Big laughs, especially from Winnie's two surviving sisters. I told them Winnie had known stuff, too—about me, and my extended family. I also told them I grew up in the same kind of family as theirs, that my Dad's sisters all went to the same Catholic girls' high school in West Philadelphia as Winnie and her four sisters. I mentioned all the movies, all the plays, all the lunches, all the cups of tea. I told them Winnie was a great person to work with, always generous with ideas and willing to roll up her sleeves to get things done. I told them I'd learned a great deal from her, about work, about life, about family. I could have spent an hour reflecting on all the ways the world of work had changed—and yet stayed the same—over the decades we'd known each other; and especially for women, of Winnie's generation and of mine.

Then I mentioned that something Erin said made me remember that Winnie had long been one of my best book buddies. Beginning in the early 1980s, whenever I found a book I loved, I couldn't wait to share it with Winnie. She did the same with me. Once we'd both finished a book, we'd have to get together for a debrief. I told her family that Winnie and I gave each other dozens of books over the years. Winnie's sister Ronnie chimed in: "I can vouch for that. Because one year you gave her a book with a lovely inscription for her birthday, and later she wrapped it up and gave it to me. I still have it!" Two more people popped up with similar regifting anecdotes, and that led to more laughter, more memories, more stories. Winnie never seemed to care about possessions. I can't recall one single time when she said, "I wish I had a …" She preferred to keep things circulating, rather than holding onto them. She flat-out loved letting go of objects. I recalled that Winnie was philosophically opposed to locking doors—to houses or to cars. "Help yourself," was the implied message, "maybe you need it more than I do." Until the book stories started at the reception, I'd forgotten that decades ago, Winnie had given me her mother-in-law's ancient (original?) copy of "Joy of Cooking," because I had just moved into my first apartment, and she had a thing that maybe I could use.

My favorite family memory came from Winnie's youngest sister, Patsy. Parts of the story were familiar. I remember Winnie telling me that their oldest (and bossiest, sorry, but I do know stuff) sister, Maryellen (may she rest in peace), would sometimes insist that all five sisters converge at their beloved mother's grave. Then, arms linked, she would lead them in a rousing (or not so) rendition of a maudlin old Irish emigrant song, "A Mother's Love's a Blessing," exactly the type of sentimental pap that provoked Winnie's patented eyeroll. (By the time I was 10, I knew the words to this and countless other Irish songs by heart. Every gathering at my paternal grandparents' home included an Irish sing-along.) The last line of the chorus is: "…For you'll never miss a mother's love 'til she's buried beneath the clay." As Patsy told the story, every time Maryellen instigated this ritual, she would belt out the words while the other four sisters would sway along and softly sing something like: "hmmm hmmm hmmm hmmm hmmm…" Every time, Maryellen would yell at them for mumbling; and every time, Winnie would insist they didn't know the words. And Maryellen would say, "Yes you do." "No we don't." "Yes you do." Months later, they'd repeat the whole show again, four grown women trying not to make a scene in a cemetery, one aiming to do precisely that. Until the one time Winnie came prepared, with five copies of the printed lyrics, so at last they could satisfy Maryellen. Which they did not do, because when she started belting out *her* version of the lyrics, while the rest of them confidently sang the words from the printed pages, it became clear Maryellen had never known the actual words to the song. Classic Winnie.

I've never had so much fun at a funeral. I wasn't watching the time, but the stories went on for well over an hour, probably closer to two. I didn't want to leave, because I knew this really was the end of the long good-bye I'd been saying ever since Paul had told me about their move to Florida. I said my farewells to the grandkids, to Paul Sr., and Tim. Paul nearly did me in when he said, "This is probably the last time I'll see you." I'd barely recovered from what he'd said earlier: "You were the first person I sent a message to after Winnie died."

I could see Erin standing near the door, and saying goodbye to her would be the hardest. More than anyone there, she understood what Winnie and I had meant to each other as friends, and as independent-minded women navigating a world that was not optimally designed for us. I remembered a conversation with Winnie—maybe our last one, while we ate ice cream under a tree in July—where she mentioned Erin had a milestone birthday on the horizon. "I must be getting old, I said. Erin was just a kid when I first met you." Winnie had responded, "*You* were just a kid when I first met *you*. You're not much older than Erin." True. But Erin was still in high school, and I was already a working girl. A very young working girl, but still.

As I started to say good-bye, Erin asked if I wanted to join a few family members who were going to scatter some of Winnie's ashes at the top of a hill at Ashland, her favorite lookout for hawks. I hesitated, even as Paul Jr. approached with a short stack of small cardboard boxes containing ashes that had been withheld from the white marble box, which would be interred two days later. "Or," Erin offered, "you could just take one of the boxes and scatter the ashes somewhere else." I knew in a flash that Winnie would have wanted me to carry a trace of her home with me. And so I took a little white box with a blue label from the crematory affixed to the top, confirming the legitimacy of its contents. I most certainly had not expected to leave this gathering with a party favor, especially not one with such deep sentimental value. I felt honored to be given this gift. I assured Erin I'd think of someplace special to scatter the ashes. But then it hit me: I didn't have to scatter them right away. I could still have one last little adventure with Winnie. Something we could enjoy together, and then talk about after it ended. On the spot I announced to Erin and Paul Jr., and a couple of their cousins, "I'm going to take her to see one last movie." "Belfast"? Erin asked, because I'd already recommended she see it. "Belfast," I agreed. "I just know she's going to love it."

*

I drove back to Pennsylvania with the little cardboard box safely lodged in the passenger seat behind my purse. At home, I gently placed it on my coffee table. It took me days to get up the nerve to remove the rubber band and look inside. This was as close as I'd ever been to anyone's cremated remains. Under the lid I saw a tiny plastic bag that held just a few teaspoons of Winnie. Teaspoons. That was it. I hadn't wavered in my intention to see "Belfast" with Winnie. But I'd been fretting over the logistics. Should I buy one ticket or two? Should I keep the little box out of sight at the bottom of my purse, or should I place it on the seat beside me?

I have a collection of teapots and teacups, more than one of which came from Winnie. I selected an elegant porcelain teapot—designed for brewing just one cupful—which I bought in Ireland more than 20 years ago. I lifted the tiny lid, and tucked those few teaspoons of Winnie (still in their plastic bag) into this most perfect vessel for a most unusual outing.

This being a special occasion, I took a day off from work in early December and bought a ticket for a matinee screening of "Belfast" at my favorite arthouse theater. The wee porcelain teapot slipped easily into my purse. When I got to my reserved seat in the sparsely populated theater, I nestled it into a cupholder. Throughout the movie, my left hand gravitated toward that teapot, gently cupping its lid, while being careful not to jiggle it. Winnie would have found it hilarious if I'd inadvertently scattered her ashes on the floor of the theater; I, however, would have been mortified, even though it's the kind of place where they would have understood, even celebrated, her presence there in that way.

As I've reported, Winnie loved the movie, like I knew she would. I kid you not when I say I could feel her poking my ribs when that tipsy aunt sang "Danny Boy." I imagined Winnie throwing her head back and laughing heartily at the clichéd scene, and the sentimental song, which always strikes a chord for those of us with Irish roots. In my father's family, it was the grand finale for any sing-along: voices had to be warmed up before the high notes could even be attempted.

After the movie, I took my little teapot full of Winnie back home. I incorporated it, along with the movie ticket, into the Christmas decorations on my dining room table. I decided to keep her with me a bit longer because…why not? A few days after Christmas, I finally released my few teaspoons of Winnie back into the universe. I'm not sure I should say where, although I did Google "scattering ashes in Pennsylvania" first. Let's just say I have every reason to believe the sprawling lilac bush beneath my kitchen window, and a few other garden favorites, will be zestier than ever this spring. If you happen to wander by, you might catch me humming "Danny Boy" into the lilac blossoms, or you might pause to listen to the toe-tapping deedle-dee music floating out through an open window.

Bill Cushing

Drinking with St. Nick

"Look at that, an empty table," Richie said to me as we walked in, pointing me towards a far corner of the raised dining room that adjoined the bar.

"Great," I told him. "Go ahead and grab it while I get a pitcher."

Ordering our beer and an appetizer to justify taking the space in the dining area, I also sprang for a couple of shots of whiskey to make some boilermakers.

That seemed a good way to toast in Christmas morning. December 24, 1971: I was home on leave from the Navy and Richie and I decided early in the evening to visit Patrick's Pub, the local pub in Little Neck, the place where my dad bought me my first legal beer only a year before and the place I would spend many nights and early evenings over the decade to come. You usually needed a reservation to get in to Patrick's on a holiday night, but since it was only a bit after 10 at night when we left his place and midnight mass hadn't begun yet, we took a chance on getting a table. With money in our wallets and hope in our hearts, Richie and I drove over and found that our luck held out.

I opted to go in uniform that night. I still ran into veterans at Patrick's, and being in uniform proved a good way to sometimes score free drinks while there, swapping stories. The older guys had the better and livelier ones; I hadn't been in long enough to gather my own.

*

Not long after midnight, we—along with everyone else in the back room—heard a booming, boisterous "Ho! Ho! Ho! Merr-r-ry Christmas, everyone!"

There, in the side door that led to the parking area, Santa stood in all his glory. The outfit and beard were perfect, but his basso voice was the real attention-getter. Santa wended his way to the first table, sat down between two couples, and started singing "Jingle Bells." Everyone in the place joined in while Santa sat there conducting the chorus with a mug of beer he'd grabbed off the table.

The tune over and all applauding, St. Nick now moved to another table and started in on "Oh, Christmas Tree," refilling his empty mug from that pitcher of beer. At times, St. Nick forgot some of the words but filled those gaps by loudly belting out "Da-Dadada-Da-Dadada" followed by "Da-Dadadada-Dada!"

That carol done, he stood and moved to the next table. Once there, he started in with "Silent Night." Of course, now everyone quieted down to reverently sing when I noticed that Santa was refilling his mug from their pitcher.

I nudged my friend and pointed.

"Santa's getting tanked on everyone else's beer. I think I wore the wrong outfit tonight."

*

As the night went on, we noticed he never hit any table that didn't have both an obvious couple and a fairly full pitcher within reach. Santa spent time with a different group, leading them in song while siphoning—at times spilling—the contents of their pitcher into his own glass.

Later the crowd thinned out, leaving behind the last few stragglers, including Richie and myself, and one snoring Santa. The bartender came over to wake him. "Come on, Santa. Time to get back to the North Pole and the wife." He removed the hat and wraparound beard, then stood back.

"Anyone know this fellow?"

None of us still there recognized the guy now collapsed against the side of a dining room bench. The bartender eventually called a cab after checking his wallet for a name and address. With daybreak approaching, the rest of us left, and I trudged home to face the daunting task of trying to wrap presents under the influence.

I still don't know how Santa does it.

Gary Fincke

In the Heart

During the first summer of the pandemic, Japan reopened its amusement parks, roller coasters, once again, climbing to precipices meant to prompt mass shrieking. Aware of how that response encouraged the spread of the virus, the government declared, "Please, scream in your heart." Immediately, on social media, that phrase trended as if silent screaming was rare.

The Internet bloomed with short films of cars and buses traveling narrow, uneven roads carved into cliff sides thousands of feet above certain death. When I imagined the screams of the passengers if the bus tipped over the edge, the sounds were comic book shrieks meant to be heard only in the minds and hearts of readers, ones always written in a series of vowels of varying lengths depending on the distance of the fall.

Years ago, I screamed in my heart in a friend's jeep as he inched us along a road better described as a ledge overlooking, without guardrails, a fall of several hundred feet. "You're not the worst," he said, referencing my terror. "Someone once curled up on the floor." My internal shriek was nothing like a comic book wail. In my imagination, I remained mute all the way to the base of that cliff.

For sure, when I examine Edvard Munch's famous eponymous painting, that wide open mouth always suggests unendurable horror because I believe it makes no sound.

Likewise, it's not surprising that one of the most recognizable images in silent films is the scream of the nurse watching the baby carriage tumble down tiers of steps while soldiers slaughter Odessa's population in Sergei Eisenstein's *The Battleship Potemkin.* That extended scene concludes with a close-up, the nurse's pince-nez shattered, her face contorted by unvoiced terror.

Some of the figures in Francis Bacon's "Screaming Popes"

paintings replace the head of Pope Innocent X as painted by Velazquez with the agonized face of Eisenstein's wounded nurse. Bacon, when asked, remarked that during the silent era, the image in films had tremendous force, "sometimes very powerful, very beautiful."

Very powerful, in movies with soundtracks, is Janet Leigh's open-mouthed horror as she is stabbed in the shower during Alfred Hitchcock's *Psycho*. Hitchcock added shrieking violins to heighten Leigh's scream, but his first intention was to use no soundtrack at all for the scene.

A memorable tag line in movie advertising is "In space, no one can hear you scream." Yes, but even the closing confrontation between Ripley and the monster is nearly entirely silent. Her repressed screams, the ones in her heart as she tries to outwit the Alien, are ones the audience "hears".

Home from my freshman year in college, I rode with a high school classmate, seat belts ignored, radio cranked. The road we lived on was so familiar either one of us could have been speeding, but he was at the wheel when a car backed across both lanes from a garage. He braked hard, the car four-wheel-drifting toward a row of junipers as I gripped the door handle and braced until his father's car spun and stopped so close to the other that I could see the shape of that driver's inaudible scream.

Within months, a girl I knew was catapulted through a car's windshield when it crashed. Decades later, I used that girl's death to fuel a short story's conclusion. "What happened to your friend is not your story's truth," an editor cautioned, asking for a revision that avoided that literal recreation. So, I saved her, though ambiguously, the choices she made perhaps maiming or killing her on another reckless evening. I left her being sped through expectancy, that thrilling car still unscathed, her body nervous, but excited. Still unharmed. Screaming only in her heart.

The most terrifying minute of my life happened in the library of the college where I was teaching. My son was three.

The librarian, because she thought he was both adorable and well-behaved, gave him a lemon sourball that, a short while later, became stuck in his throat. He turned absolutely silent. No gasps. No coughs. I didn't say a word. Pre-Heimlich and panicked, I pounded on his back. When nothing changed, I turned him upside down and pounded until, somehow, the candy dropped to the carpet.

My son was so young that he has had only my storytelling to let him know what happened. How I screamed in my heart. Though, in his case, there's no way of knowing, how he must have, too.

Lauren Harkawik

House on Wheels

It's when it touches the guardrail that I realize it's someone's home. It doesn't even scrape. Just a little bop to the corner of the front of it. And I think, *that's someone's house* — and they're going to live in it and they're never going to know that somewhere between towns, the person towing their house misjudged. And then I drive behind someone's home for another twenty miles.

A light fog dances over the road. Later today, everyone will declare winter over, spring sprung. In light of the occasion, we are all — all of us, every Vermonter — wearing the new dress we just bought, the one with short sleeves and airy fabric. The people who'll live in the house won't know this: the weather, the dress, or that somewhere between the school and the next town, the house travels alongside a brook teeming with melted snow barreling itself toward a bigger place.

They won't know the bumps we heave over as we curve through the mountains. Or how the potholes left behind from the months of ice give my tire a sickening thud when I forget to swerve around them. They won't know that whoever is driving their house is getting more daring the longer this ride goes on, crossing the double yellow lines, or that at the bend near the cutout in the rocky wall, an 18 wheeler sounds its horn because the unruly house gets too close.

The horn sounds like a foghorn; reminds me of the ocean, and then I wonder where this house is going. Whether the air will be salty once it's a home, or whether it'll be enveloped in fog on a March morning, on the day when winter is over, when all of them, every person who lives there, will wear the new dress they got, the one with the short sleeves and the airy fabric, because spring has sprung.

Craig Holt

Drinking the Ocean: Notes on Travel and Drowning

Right up until the point when I drowned, it was a pretty good day. I held the tiller of an empty nineteen-foot Zodiac, drifting just outside the surf zone of the Tuamotus atoll of Pukarua, a picturesque ring island of coconut palms, frangipani, and torch ginger with a maximum elevation of six feet above sea level and a population of just ninety-five souls. All around me, blade-winged black and white shearwaters skimmed the wave troughs while onshore my elderly passengers wandered around the village of Marautagaroa gawping at the residents and poking their heads, uninvited, into people's homes. Behind me, farther out to sea, our ninety-passenger "expedition ship," the MV Discovery, held anchor. My rare moment of peace was almost over, though. Already, a few of our passengers were making their way to the crumbling concrete jetty and stepping gingerly back into one of the other Zodiacs to take a seat on the edge of the boat's black pontoons, all facing each other with their backs to the ocean.

Seas were heavy, but the warm air carried a tiare blossom and coconut oil scent that bamboozled everyone into thinking they were having an adventure even though, really, they were bobbing around in the South Pacific on a small, well-appointed cruise ship. In fairness, the trips were educational thanks to a staff of naturalists, anthropologists and ornithologists who regaled everyone with daily lectures about the places they visited. We also kept passengers active, with plenty of hiking, snorkeling, and birding walks along the white sand atoll shores and jungle clad mountains of the younger islands. But adventure? No. Regardless of what the brochures promised, it's hard to call it an adventure when you spend most of your time on a luxurious ship, sipping cocktails at an admirably stocked bar and eating decadent meals.

I was the only one having an adventure that day, and it wasn't my intention.

I'm sure our passengers knew they weren't participating in an intrepid exploration, but they seemed happy to spend an unholy amount of money for the privilege of listening to lectures, going on long walks in the bug-whirring heat, and being shuttled around in rubber boats. What I couldn't quite figure out was what motivated me to quit my first day job at a specialty coffee roasting company and leave my wife behind to take another gig as an Expedition Leader, the one responsible for passenger safety and for convincing them the trip was worth the thousands of dollars they'd spent. I was twenty-nine at the time, and most of my friends had already settled into careers, started making real money. They had savings accounts and medical insurance, while I had a beat-up passport and a wealth of stories about suffering food poisoning. They saw the people they loved every day, and I was bobbing around in the Pacific Ocean for a month with a bunch of retirees, five-thousand miles from my wife. They knew how to be content while I kept jumping on planes and heading off to find… what? Excitement? Perspective? Fulfillment? Some weak approximation of adventure that would convince me I was an interesting person? Sometimes I told people I traveled because something was going to kill me, and it might as well be something cool. The truth was, I had no idea why I kept skipping out on real life to wander the planet. But whatever drew me away, it was powerful enough to make me hop on a plane again and say goodbye to my wife for six weeks.

*

Our route took us from Easter Island to Papeete via Pitcairn, the Gambiers, Tuamotus and Marquesas, with a stop in Bora Bora. The route was new to me, but I had a lot of experience with the work. The captain ran the ship, but I ran the trip, determining the itinerary and activities, managing the lecture staff, and leading hikes and snorkeling outings. I was also a stand-in naturalist/anthropologist/historian and a regular

Zodiac driver. Obviously, an amazing job, but not without its stresses.

I was the focal point of blame for the passengers, the German officers, the Filipino crew, and our international team of well-respected (but fussy) ornithologists, anthropologists, and marine biologists. Satisfying all those factions at once was impossible, so a significant portion of the population of that one-hundred-and-sixty-five-person community was always ticked off at me. Passengers always wanted to spend more time hiking, birding, and snorkeling, but the ship's Bremen-based officers were focused on keeping to the schedule. The crew were more flexible than the officers, but they tended to push back against my habit of scheduling extra activities: spontaneous mid-ocean stops in the Sea of Cortez to snorkel with manta rays, sunrise landings (4:00 am) at the king penguin colony on South Georgia Island. My little extras for the passengers were a huge pain in the ass for the crew, and they resented me accordingly.

The primary source of my anxiety as an Expedition Leader, though, was the significant risk of passenger injury or death. Taking passengers on hikes across the Antarctic ice or having them climb out of Zodiacs in heavy surf in the Faroe Islands was risky for even young and healthy people, and our normal mix of passengers ranged in age from the early sixties to the mid-nineties. With that demographic in those situations there was bound to be the occasional tragedy. I had seen more than my share.

I'd experienced a passenger death on each of my first three trips as expedition leader-- Congestive heart failure at the Mayan ruins of Tikal; heart attack while snorkeling at Half Moon Cay in Belize; fatal stroke while anchored off Little Corn Island, Nicaragua-- so the risks were painfully real to me. During my first three-year stint as an expedition leader, I'd dealt with so many passenger deaths that the company I worked for asked me to write a manual on how to clear a cadaver through customs in a foreign port. But understanding the logistics of death at sea did nothing to ease the shock of watching someone die, or – worse – seeing the grief their life partners suffered at that loss. As a twenty-two-year-old, I spent three days in Belize City helping a recently widowed passenger navigate the grim bureaucracy of death after losing her husband of sixty years. She was remarkably brave about it, but it is terrible to bear witness to that much grief. And it wasn't her heartbreak that had me crying in my room at night, it was her courage; it was the realization that someday that kind of strength would be required of me or my wife.

Naturally, avoiding passenger deaths became something of an obsession for me, so my job mostly consisted of making them feel like they were having an adventure while making damn sure they avoided anything even remotely hazardous. Sure, I'd let them snorkel with manta rays, but by God they would wear life jackets while doing it.

*

It hadn't been a good trip up to that point. The ship was five days late picking us up from Easter Island which meant we'd miss several stops on the itinerary. Then, a storm hit the first night underway and stayed with us. By the time we got to the Tuamotus we'd banged through a week of heavy seas and had nearly flipped a Zodiac as we tried to bring passengers into the speck of a harbor on Pitcairn Island, where the descendants of the Bounty mutineers still live.

The captain and I were at risk of our own mutiny by the time we finally caught something of a break in the weather at the tiny atoll of Pukarua. The place is a ring island with a sizable lagoon in its center, a huge basin that breathes the ocean in and out with the tides, pushing the bulk of the tidal flow through a manmade channel the Polynesian government blasted out of the reef. The channel allows smaller boats safe passage into the lagoon, but when the tide runs out any waves pushing into the southwest side of the island get doubled up by the lagoon's outflow. This makes entering or leaving the harbor at that time… well… kind of an adventure.

But I, enjoying my rare moment of solitude in my Zodiac, wasn't aware of that danger to our passengers. I drifted happily, idling with my face tipped to the sun as I watched the sea birds slip over the waves. I was dressed in my usual uniform: stinky old sandals, salt bleached cargo shorts, and a water-activated life vest--less bulky than a standard life vests, worn around the neck and held down by black straps around the back and between the legs. If you went in the drink, it inflated and brought you back to the surface, or that was the idea. I told myself that this was what I'd come for; a chance to feel competent and in charge, a break from the small miseries of team meetings and Excel spreadsheets, some time to think about why I was so restless at home. In that calm moment, I was relieved to have the passengers off the ship and doing what they were supposed to do—getting sunburned, ogling the birds (and the people) of Pukarua through their binoculars, feeling oh so very far from home. Since the passengers had finally enjoyed a bit of shore time, I looked forward to a pleasant evening free of their angry questions about missed stops and threats of lawsuits related to the truncated itinerary.

So, imagine my disappointment when a zodiac full of passengers rounded the pier, hit one of those huge waves and went airborne, launching a passenger named Heidi backwards into the breakers.

Heidi, a round and smiling retiree from Stuttgart, was, understandably, not prepared for her dismount into the crashing waves. Hence, her goggle-eyed look of horror as she exited the boat, and the energy she brought to choking, screaming, and flailing when her life ring inflated and brought her, at last, back to the surface.

Heidi's situation was, technically speaking, Very Bad. The seas were maybe six feet, but because the tide was running out from the lagoon to double up the surf she floundered in breakers as high as ten or twelve feet. The boat from which she had so unceremoniously disembarked couldn't help her because the fully loaded Zodiacs tended to wallow, and another wave like the monster that sent them airborne in the first place would almost certainly flip them, littering the beaches of Pukarua with critically injured senior citizens. The driver, a seasoned Filipino deckhand named Benjie, wisely chose to get out of the surf zone and head back toward the ship, frantically radioing for help the whole way.

Rather than watch Heidi get rag-dolled onto the coral by the implacable sea, I twisted the throttle and rushed in to play the hero.

*

The first part goes great. I roar across the stormy ocean, salt spray in my face, my poofy hair swept back. Sure, the trip has been a disaster so far, but by gum I'm saving a life! In my mind, hero music.

By the time I get to Heidi, though, I'm riding up the wave backs at crazy angles, the world lost behind walls of black water as I drop into the troughs, and I think *This shit is dangerous.* The hero music stops, drowned out by the growling motor, Heidi's yelps as she rises to the wave tops, the boom and crash of big waves annihilating themselves on the reef.

I crest a steep wave and come down nearly on top of Heidi, throw the Evinrude into reverse and gun it briefly so I stop with the bow inches from her. I enjoy a moment of idiotic pride in my Zodiac skills as I flick the engine to neutral and rush to where Heidi, pale and wide eyed, already has a death grip on the ropes.

"I fell out of the boat!" she shouts over the wave roar.

"Yep." I lean over the pontoon, head down and hips high, to grab her by the armpits and pull her to safety.

She says, "Oof!" but she doesn't come out of the water.

Her shoulders slide up, the life ring smooshing her cheeks, but I can't lift her. It's like she's chained to the sea floor. I'm genuinely shocked to discover I can't lift a hundred-and-fifty-pound person out of the ocean while bent over with my ass in the air and my feet scrabbling for purchase on the slippery deck. Looking back, I realize my leverage was all wrong. But in the moment, because I'm an idiot, I blame Heidi.

"You gotta let go!" I holler, tapping one of her white-knuckled hands.

"I was so scared!" she says, as if she's already safe.

"Let go!" I haul at her armpits again, my hero narrative still demanding I lift her into the boat and whisk her to safety. This *Little Man Versus Gravity* micro drama lasts just a few seconds. But by the time I realize Heidi can hang onto the ropes while I drag her away from the breakers, we've drifted nearly onto the reef, into the heart of the surf break. I sprint back to the motor and kick it into reverse.

"Where are you going?!" Heidi says.

I twist the throttle, glance over my shoulder and shout, "Hang on!"

"You said let go!" she says, keeping her grip on the ropes.

I turn to face the waves. We're backing into a twelve-foot wall of water.

Have you ever stood in a little rubber boat staring up at a twelve-foot breaker? I can tell you it is very humbling. From a distance a wave like that looks cool; the graphite sea rising up in a wall of shimmering blue; steep, then vertical, then trembling, seemingly still, before curling over to thunder on the reef and rush up the sand with a hushing sigh. From a distance, big waves inspire poetry, garish paintings, the invention of boogie boards. But when you are sliding backwards toward one in a dinghy, dragging a waterlogged pensioner behind you, a twelve-foot breaker looks like nothing but a serious problem.

Realizing how badly I've screwed up I make my only half-decent decision of that day. I gun the motor so we climb the wave face at a good clip. Just before my prop cuts through the back of the crest, I jam the tiller hard to starboard. The boat pirouettes, the bow swings out over the top of the wave and centrifugal force whips Heidi out to sea; not far, but far enough. I'm pretty sure she's out of immediate danger.

Me, on the other hand, not so much.

The wave goes nearly vertical, shoving the Zodiac backward

onto the reef. I cling to the outboard to keep from going over the stern. I'm pretty sure it'll flip and I'll get smeared across the coral with the boat on top of me. But the bow drops over the back of the breaker, tossing the boat farther up the reef.

The Zodiac is upright and facing out to sea. The motor still works. The prop is in the water and, importantly, I'm not dead. Heidi is nowhere in sight, which I hope is a good sign. Things are looking up! I hop to my feet, twist throttle and head for safety.

The second wave knocks me on my ass again, filling the boat with water.

I repeat this Sisyphean slapstick several times, but with the Zodiac taking on water and the seas so high, I can't make any progress before the big waves push my bow into the air and dump me back on the coral. I'm in deep shit, but I'm still not panicked. I still can't imagine a scenario in which I don't come out of this unscathed. I get back on my feet for maybe the seventh time, and gun the motor.

That's when a real monster of a wave sucks all the water off the reef. My boat grinds to a stop on the exposed coral, nose angled down. The prop whirls in the air, the motor screams on my behalf. I brace myself, waiting for the sea to do its thing.

It plucks me up, tips the boat vertical and slams it stern-first on the reef. I fall, crack my lower back on the transom, and flip backward into the water.

I sink through wave roar and the motor's scream. The propeller whirls just over my head, so close the prop wash tugs at my hair. By rights it should've pureed my brain, trapped as I am between a boat and a hard place. But luck is (kind of) on my side. I've gone overboard at a cleft in the overhanging reef, slipping into deeper water as the Zodiac washes into the lagoon.

Hooray!

Pop! My life ring inflates.

Another wave drives me shoreward just as I gain buoyancy, slamming me into the underside of the reef and trapping my arms and legs. The light-deprived coral here is long dead, but still jagged enough to tear my skin. Now, I'm pinned underwater, snagged on the coral, and highly buoyant.

I try to thrash free, but the water presses me deeper into the gap. If you've ever tried to fight back against the ocean, you'll understand when I say that it is a profoundly demoralizing experience. Until this moment, I've had an intellectual understanding of humility. It isn't a strength of mine, but I can, you know, use the word in a sentence. Now, mashed against a reef, six feet underwater and held in place by billions of tons of ocean, I experience a cellular-level humbling. I realize I'm going to die.

Hard to say how long I'm under water, twitching and bleeding, but it's long enough to see swirling lights behind my squinched-shut eyes. *Holy shit, is that The Light?* I open my eyes on burning darkness and take my first gulp of the ocean. Weirdly, I'm not scared. Swear to God, I'm mostly annoyed. I think, *I'm dying. This is so stupid.*

I wonder what the hell inspired me to step out of my perfectly good life back home just to go on some corn dog "adventure" with a bunch of seniors. I wanted an escape from boredom, and instead I've punched my ticket for the sweet hereafter. Huffing ocean water, I can't remember what I thought was wrong with a quiet life lived on a small scale. Isn't it enough to be safe and loved? For me, apparently not. And because of that, I'm sucking salt spume under the sea. And I feel, in my dying moment, like a jackass.

Another huge wave rips me out of my little death chamber, takes me to the surface and hammers me onto the coral. I'm going to live!

Maybe.

I can't dive through the waves with an inflated life ring on, so I'm caught in a brutal spin cycle for a while, waves lifting me high and pounding me on the reef. I hit, drag and roll, hacking up water whenever I surface. Finally, once my arms and legs are sliced and gouged, I've broken my thumb and gotten a concussion, the sea rolls me into the lagoon so it can get on with the business of being a relentless force, the cradle of life, etcetera.

On my hands and knees in a foot of water, I puke and cough, then get painfully to my feet. I'm bleeding heavily from punctures and tears all over my arms and legs. I've bitten through my tongue.

On the plus side, I don't see any German ladies washed up in the shallows. Hopefully, Heidi's back at the ship enjoying a glass of wine.

Three young guys from town splash toward me, shouting. When they reach me, they whistle and shake their heads at all the blood, ask me if I'm alright.

I give them a broken thumbs up. Then I vomit.

They laugh and slap me on the back.

I say, "The woman who fell in. Is she alright?"

A handsome teenager wearing a Bart Simpson muscle shirt points to the ship, which floats calmly a hundred yards out. "They took her back. She seemed okay."

My knees ache with relief. I lean over with my working hand on one knee, swallowing past a lump in my throat.

When I look up again the local guys are farther into the lagoon, muscling my battered Zodiac back toward the pier. The prop is mangled and the port side pontoon is half deflated, the hard bottom scrapes the living coral with a peevish grumbling sound.

Thanks to my concussion - plus a heady mix of relief, pain, shock, and shame - I'm pretty muddled. But I know now what to do after narrowly avoiding death; I limp over to the Zodiac, trailing blood and shaking all over, and use my good hand to help push the boat toward the jetty. I can at least help clean up the mess I've made.

But the question I asked myself under the reef resurfaces. *Why did I even come here?*

*

I left the expedition ships for good after my South Seas

adventure to work in the coffee industry, thinking I was mostly done with the traveling life. But I kept going. And ever since my little fuckup in the South Pacific, the question of why I keep wandering has dogged me. During my particularly exciting times abroad—confronted by Congolese rebels at a roadblock outside Goma; going blind in one eye in northern Thailand; enduring the worst food poisoning of my life in an empty hotel in Houthi-controlled Sana'a—I keep wondering, *Why do I do this to myself? Why do* any *of us do this?*

Travel is not, after all, a de facto good. It is expensive, inconvenient, and – the way many of us do it – sometimes dangerous. Also, there are elements of travel and tourism that look a little grubby if closely examined. But for all these negative implications, I'm not ready to dismiss the urge to ramble across the planet as an entirely corrupt behavior.

For many, the urge to travel is fundamental. A dream and a goal in its own right. Possibly, it goes as deep as our DNA-level curiosity about the world, our origin as foragers and persistence hunters. At some level, travel could be an unconscious attempt to replicate the wandering that was so vital to our early survival. Whatever the case, whatever the problematic implications and downsides of it, human beings keep leaving the safety and comfort of home to explore their world.

We all have our reasons for striking out into the great elsewhere. For some, the physical distance from our obligations gives us license to relax. Others go in for the *What happens in Vegas stays in Vegas* approach, the indulgence of appetites. Gaggles of missionaries fly to Africa and Central America all kitted out in matching tee shirts and quick-dry pants with zip-off legs, because apparently all the disadvantaged folks in America have already been helped. Still others travel because they want to know culture as a living, breathing thing, and learn through experience.

For me, it's a bit of all these things - aside from the missionary urge. Traveling, I'm untethered from my obligations and free to be whatever version of myself the place and people draw from me. My Colombia self is a laidback guy who laughs a lot, drinks aguardiente on horseback, and goes dancing. Friends back home, for whom my irritability and impatience are sources of endless amusement, would think Colombia Craig is an imposter who is wearing my face. My wife, who lives with my dumb jokes and horrible singing, refuses to believe that my Japan self is quiet and serious. At home, I'm not a hugger and I'm twitchy about my personal space. But my Uganda self is warm and open. When friends in Kapchorwa and Mbale embrace him and hold his hand the whole time they talk, he does not freak out. Not even a little bit. Clearly, all of those other Craigs are part of me. (So why do they only show up when I'm at least three time zones from home?) And I still love learning about the places I visit. Every trip is an excuse to by books about a new culture, history, and natural environment.

But none of this quite explains why I continue to absent myself from home even though I've missed my wife and family every day of every trip I've taken. Why, after months and months of cumulative jet lag, several guns pointed in my face by angry men, countless cases of the fiery hopping shits, numerous visits to foreign emergency rooms and one near-drowning, I keep going back for more. Maybe I'm afraid that without my travel stories I'll cease being interesting to other people. Or to myself. Who knows, maybe I'm just restless and easily bored. Whatever the case, I'm no longer comfortable unless I'm out of my comfort zone. I can't explain why, at the time of this writing, I'm booked on an unguided trip across Northwestern Scotland on a miniature motorcycle that looks more like a circus prop than a mode of transportation. It's a stupid thing to do. I can't wait to go.

My urge to travel is like trying to drink the ocean; you can't take it all in, but once you try that first sip you might as well have another. My urge to wander hit when I read *20,000 Leagues Under the Sea* as an eight-year-old, and I've been thirsty for adventure ever since. I still don't know why I'm addicted to travel, but I know the answer is out there somewhere. To find it, I'll have to keep going.

Armaan Kapur

Olympus of Nothing

It's too early on the ferry, but here I am, buying champagne for breakfast. The attendant at the bar rolls his eyes, or maybe he's secretly delighted – it doesn't matter. When he turns around and retrieves the bottles, the pint-sized miniatures suggest a small and accomplishable happiness. In a short spell, consummate happiness will be mine to ingest.

When I return to the counter a few minutes later, you clear your throat. You aren't eating or drinking anything, so your presence confuses me.

'Two more bottles, please,' I request the bartender.

Behind my ears, the Cyclades lap and languish like green curtains. Mountains and promontories rise and wither, like unearthed artefacts. The gust of wind is a dominant hand in my hair, my shirt, my seven AM buttons are quite undone, and you, to me, are just another coin in the chaos, a drop in the Grecian spring of my youth. Who are you anyway, staring at me like that?

'Are you celebrating?' you ask, in an ambivalent tone. Your eyes flash to the recesses of the ferry, where my friends are, listening to music, laughing, breezing.

At your question, I go cold.

Whenever I travel internationally, my natural reaction is to stiffen when addressed by any stranger, outside consumer transactions or visits to bars. An interlude too unanticipated, I fear, will be followed by a predictable remark, a slur, or some unbidden, rampantly unnecessary challenge from the curious party, as regards my proficiency to function on foreign land. '*You* drink alcohol? *You* eat meat? *You* drive cars, not elephants?' Inside these small denigrations, what irks most is not knowing whom to pin my distaste onto: do I go after the questioning party, for not exhibiting a precise yet encyclopaedic knowledge of other cultures? Or do I turn inward for the reprimand, reflect on my own deficient outlook, that places American and British output as the global foci of aesthetics and sensibility? If asked, could I name *one* South Asian superstar, some prolific writer emerged from Tagore's school, as my literary influence? I couldn't. Instead, each time I stare in the mirror, my first thought is, 'You like a classic style.' Quietly disposed, not easily excited. Combed hair, splash of eau de toilette behind the ears. 1950s, Madison Avenue. Bespoke tailoring and Queen's English, spot of whisky for breakfast. A bad time for all involved (especially my sort).

I glance sideways and reply with facticity. 'Yeah, we're celebrating.'

Your careful gaze measures my stoicism, while the bartender hands me the bill. The transaction is over, the script maxed out, but I persist in place a minute longer. With furtive looks, I determine you aren't a local. You possess all the makings, of course: tan complexion, comfy cotton outfit, sun-tousled strands of blonde, and a laissez-faire spirit to match. But your eyes are grey, blue, very icy, from somewhere niche and indifferent. As I grasp the champagne and turn around, the bell of reason clangs in my skull to ask, 'Who's being presumptuous, now?'

After my third stint, the astonished bartender decries, 'The champagne is over!'

By then, you've moved away from your post. You stand by the metallic railing on the side of the deck, admiring the oceanic view with your back turned to everything. For the fourth and final round (beers only), I time myself perfectly so the two of us coincide again.

'Where are you from, exactly?' I ask, tipsy, audacious. 'I can't place your accent.'

We converse fleetingly, in vacation shorthand. The ferry docks in Paros an hour later. Arriving at the resort, my friends slump to their cottages with weary shoulders, but the butterflies are soaring, still. Everyone decides to meet after a nap, but I can't lay myself down; I'm too wired. Stepping out, I encounter a pair from my group sitting under an umbrella, next to the pool. 'Too early for gin—?' we philosophise, for the sake of discussion.

The young bartender who serves us—Milos—is working on his English, and he cracks a lot of jokes. Amply he's aware of his own charm, which ironically renders him a bit charmless in the end. We all become friends, nonetheless. I enquire if there are any hiking spots nearby, and he nods yes, but adds that the weather is brutal and it would be dangerous to venture out by myself. 'I've no intention of going by myself,' I nearly admit, but refrain at the last minute.

At night, I declare myself the designated driver, refusing to indulge and risk the potential hangover. Expectedly, as the evening proceeds, hastened pride about my club soda status turns into metaphysical distress about 'missing out on fun,' so I drown one shot of Jägermeister, then another. Am I fine? everyone asks, as we trundle down the paved flagstones of Naoussa Village – the quaint and yellow quarters of the weekday club scene. Music, blues or electronic or Latin, thumps out like different tempers, red pill, blue pill, jarring alternate to the family-oriented cafes, dessert parlours, and glassy pizzerias that huddle soberly alongside. There are shops too, open till late, selling bangles and dream catchers, kaftans and straw hats. Blush-cheeked teenagers hang from artisan balconies overhead, everyone the same shade of hopeful, not the least bit desperate. Even so, the scene appears too immaculate to be representational in any real sense; everywhere we look, it's tourists galore, who are visibly dissimilar to us, yet they act entirely the same.

At one red-clad venue, our gang charges in and is met by an equally boisterous set of owners, who encourage us by playing a Bollywood song on the sound set. Another round of Jäger then, to applaud this meeting of the minds. When the third crowd-pleasing number hits, I break out of the bar, telling everyone I need to make an urgent call. The outside air, now clear of the early dinner crowd, spins in sea-kissed circles. My enervation drips away like sweat, as I stagger past alleys and take out my phone. The black screen resembles an inert stone with some magical propensity, and scarcely deliberating the opportunity cost, I leave you a message.

Calmer then, I amble forward and arrive at two benches that overlook a quiet span of water. Dinghies lop and blink in front, and in the distance, an expanse of dunes lies suffused in grades of darkness. At one perch, a group of young men lounge and chat in Italian, sharing joints and cigarettes. They appear plucked from the same nest: of muscular build, military style haircuts, piercings, loose black t-shirts, and tight pants. The inflection of their intimacy confuses me. Not friends. Lovers? The image of one of them—the handsomest in my opinion and particularly dark featured—plays over my eyes, and I conjure us both, entangled under a remote arch somewhere, smoking and kissing. The music and signs of life long forgotten, the only concern our intimacy, the shape of our delight. But I revoke the sentiment harshly, like another paltry shot of liquor, when one of my friends catches my shoulder from behind.

Returning to the bar, I announce to everyone, 'I'm going for a hike tomorrow, very early. Would anyone care to join?'

Before sunrise finds me, your car arrives. I slink into the passenger seat, and am introduced to your Siberian husky, Sasha. 'Isn't it unpleasant for her?' I consider, gauging the muted draught outside, and scorching temperatures to follow. 'I brought her from Alsace,' you explain. 'There was no alternative.' But the insinuation frazzles you somewhat; you roll up the windows pointedly, and turn on the air conditioning, full blast. We travel in chilled silence, arriving at the foot of my memories: the diffused mountain expanse from last evening.

'Lefkes,' you describe, as we exit the car towards a prism of whitewashed cottages, shrouded in twilight blue. A narrow and winding map leads us sauntering uphill, to the breast of a walking trail, where we halt before a detached chapel and single, grandiose olive tree. A strong gust overtakes us, and I'm swept by a sudden, strange fear for my life. 'I'm terrified of snakes,' I abruptly confess. Your unspeaking silhouette doesn't placate my fears, only your head shakes, as if to say, 'It's too late now.'

Making the ascent—somewhat rocky, rewardingly pastoral—the two of us cross professions, palates, the countries we've both travelled to. You love sushi, yet you're a marine biologist. You haven't gone to India, but *Oh*, the stories you've heard. You ask if I'll ever visit France. 'I've been twice, actually. But only to Paris, and nothing spectacular happened. I didn't let the city unfold naturally, I was too cautious.' I signal the shape of a trench coat over my chest, perhaps a straitjacket, and you nod knowingly; a glint of kinship sparks briefly, between us.

Some fig trees and terraced hills later, at the cusp of a curved trail, we stop and overlook a verdant valley, where I forget what worry tasted like, though my glands are tear-jerked, overworked. Down the poignant view, dawn breaks across the Aegean Sea, where craters of land metamorphose and alternate, to designate the clearest blue of my entire life. To hold your hand (or anyone's) would emphasise the specialness of the moment, but I refuse to make the first move, to embarrass the goodwill I've accrued during our last hour of small talk.

You guide me through the trees, into a secluded copse, where we kiss. In your chaffed lips, all of morning's grit becomes known to me, creates an intimacy beautiful and rancid in equal measure. While Sasha rests, we make a carpet of our strewn clothes and repose in the bristling shade of overhanging leaves. I embrace your body with unbridled sentiment, wrapping my arms and legs tightly around your frame. It's untenable, my straitjacket and passionate sentimentality, but I am exacting to my cause. The remainder of my life is and remains a blanket intoxicated dullness, so I crave a flash of clear lucidity, where I can reveal myself, and in turn, be acknowledged skin to cell – completely. From the craters of your eyes, I sense you don't hate how hungrily I joined myself to you, but you are surprised anyway, taken aback, taken. Afterwards, we don't kiss, but you weave your fingers between my own, and there follows silence, a conciliation of spirit, an agreement of mutual space.

'What were you thinking?' you query, when we return to the car in the late afternoon. The view outside the window changes; by the time I reply, the spiritual vista behind us has long vanished.

'I was just living in the present,' I answer. 'I wasn't thinking about the next time, or if I'd ever speak to you again.'

'Why, won't you miss me?'

Your manner is sly, and your hand moves towards mine, but by now my other self has returned, restoring with it the apathy of our mutual origin, an inhumanity I've so well-adopted, like a third mask, over the second, over the first. To suffocate passion is imperative. Foisted between a heteronormative social order, and the desolation of casual dating life, there are but a few taut seconds where I can tear into existence and adore myself, so please, let respite lie still, and don't dissect the enjoyment out of me.

At the resort, my friends are only now rising for lunch, and I join them directly, opting not to shower first. Over cloches of fruit and sausages, one of them sniffs and signals at my muddied outfit. 'I didn't think you liked to trek,' she says. 'I can't see you getting your hands dirty, for whatever reason.'

I smile self-effacingly, and bring a slice of melon to my lips. The nectar is sweet and juicy, but still I prefer that rare fruit, that grows only in the desert. Taking a seat next to my friend, I nod sincerely and profess – 'Now that you mention it, I can't think of getting my hands dirty, either.'

And the matter is always forgotten, before it ever begins.

Rimma Kranet

Stakanchik

There's a new man behind the checkout counter at the "Royal Bazar". He has a large tattoo covering his shaved head and tapering off down the back of his neck. I am not sure what it depicts. He's half turned away from me, so I cannot make out the features of his face.

I place the jar of twenty-four percent fat sour cream on the counter. The only kind mother uses in her Borscht.

"Three fifty" he says.

His tone is stern, non-negotiable.

I can see his muscular forearms up to where the black fabric of his t -shirt stretches unnaturally across their circumference. That's as far as I dare lift my eyes while fishing for the correct change.

"Thank you." I mumble.

"*Pojalusta.*" he says, handing me the receipt. His fingers are also tattooed. He must be a "new Russian", those who disdain any form of restraint.

I turn to look for my mother.

There is no better place to feel the duplicity of my life than on these trips to West Hollywood, where the intersection of Santa Monica Boulevard and Fairfax abruptly delineates a three-block neighborhood of Soviet era grocers and English as a second language.

A month ago, this place was run by a woman who sat behind the register on a cracked, brown leatherette swivel chair, facing the front door. She followed you with her gaze, sizing you up, assuming you were there to inspect or pillage rather than buy a loaf of rye bread and a package of buckwheat.

The guy with the tattoos is a new attraction. His body is stiff, like the steel pots and pans, towers of colorful mugs and starched linen tablecloths.

It still smells of fresh deli meats and smoked fish sweating into the aquarium-like display. Along with a variety of cheeses: *borjomi, tvorog, kefir,* there are small glass jars of red and black caviar, the only allure for a bargain seeking American. Grey, sagging cardboard boxes limp from bearing the weight of their contents are stacked against the far wall, while others are haphazardly tucked into corners. Inside are items that come and go without lingering long enough to merit a designated space of their own. There is a sense of having dropped in on someone who is in the process of vacating the premises.

My mother walks up and down the aisles, letting her fingers flutter gently above the merchandise. Her mind is trigger happy, hungry for anything that brings on a memory.

Fine dust covers the once glistening lacquer *Palekh* boxes with intricate scenes of national folklore: fairytale lives, heroic acts of bravery and idyllic scenes of love. We once had a suitcase filled with similar souvenirs. We redeemed them for money and food.

"Look at these plates, this tea set, they're from the factory in Leningrad. They used to be so expensive.... I wonder how they were able to get these... they must be leftovers...."

She turns a small cobalt blue and gold dessert plate over in her hands, searching for the familiar *Lomonosov Imperial Porcelain Factory* seal which would confirm that she is right. Being right is her form of self-validation. Instead, "Made in China" takes up the space of the *St.Petersburg,1744* trademark.

"I have this entire service, the real thing, it's packed away under the stairs. Remind me and I will show it to you when we get home."

"Why don't you ever use it?" I ask, undermining the importance of possession.

Abundance breeds security. This is the immigrant mentality.

You need to have a lot of something to prove that you have enough.

"Oh, I have plenty of dishes. I'm saving it for you."

"Saving...you" is what I hear.

My mother has been trying to save me ever since I was six, when Professor Amosov discovered that I had a heart murmur.

I want to tell her it's not her fault, that I forgive her for keeping a noose around my neck like a wool scarf in winter. Her overprotectiveness pushing me away, her helplessness drawing me in.

"Ask that man in the front if they carry that ice cream that I love so much, you know *"stakanchik"*, the one, the one with vanilla..." mother asks.

I know what she wants, and they don't have it. They don't produce it anymore, not even in Russia. But she doesn't understand and you can't make her. She has the stubbornness of eighty-seven years working against me.

She wants to find her way back to her "before life", where the sweet taste of vanilla stifles any recollection of me being called a "Dirty Jew" on the playground.

They throw rocks at me and I run.

My smooth dark hair cut razor sharp at the chin, lips chapped, eyes foggy and moist.

I run.

After I hit the asphalt, mother holds a rag to my head as the blood tickles down the outside of her arm, into a trembling puddle beside me. Empty clotheslines cut across the sky.

I want to go home, but if I don't ask about the ice cream, there will be a scene. I return to the man.

"Sorry to bother you; my mother…she wants to know if you carry that ice cream in the wafer cone with vanilla filling?"

It is a crown. A thorny crown inked into his perfectly shaped skull.

"*Stakanchik*. Yeah, I don't have that. They stopped making

it because it cost too much to use real whipping cream. That's what made it taste so good, the whipping cream, but the factories don't do that nowadays. It's too expensive."

I am surprised at this bit of trivia and his Moscow accent. Although my Russian is perfect, anyone who hears me speak can tell by the way I shape my "ch" sound, how it casually slides into a "sh," that I am from the Ukraine. My annunciation is not etched with the sophistication of the Muscovites, who are known for their literary Russian.

"Okay. Thank you anyway." I smile, waiting for him to say something back. He stares.

"You here with your mother, that's nice. You gotta have respect for the elderly, for everything they've been through. It's not easy for them."

I wonder where his mother is.

"It looks painful." I squint and gesture timidly at his tattoo.

"Jesus died for our pain. Now we owe him."

He starts to laugh, showcasing his gold canines. The knuckles on his left hand are engraved in Cyrillic with the word *Sudba.* Destiny.

"They don't have your ice cream. Can we go home now?" I call out impatiently.

She is coming, her gait leisurely as she moves through the familiar disarray, hips swaying unevenly from a late onset of arthritis. She has found something else to buy, something she is gripping tightly with both hands, afraid that it will fall, slip clumsily on to the floor and break. It is a cluster of glass eyes with large blue pupils strung together on to a twisted chord. They are reminiscent of fisheyes that stare into nothingness. Glossy, smooth, compliant.

Triumphant she approaches the counter, her thin white hair pulled loosely off her face, her mischievous smile soaked through with red lipstick.

"To ward off the evil eye, *chto bi tebia ne zglazili"* she says. "To bring you luck."

Her giddiness has survived the transformation into old age. It seeps through the discomfort of her body, the deceptive nature of her mind. She is a schoolgirl with long skinny braids and hand sewn dresses, square shoulders and raspberry lips standing in a field of wheat on Ukrainian soil.

Ghosted

1. Ghosts

Things moved.

My husband would set a wine glass on the mantle only to find it later on a side table. Doors opened themselves, and periodically books just up and went somewhere. H blamed it on me initially and, fair enough, I've been known to put things away with too much enthusiasm. His theory fell apart when my work took me out of town for weeks at a time, and it was just H and our dog in the house.

The dog would sit still as a statue for long stretches in the kitchen doorway, laser focused on the hall beyond, looking *at* something or someone, tracking them as they stirred.

I was not there, and things kept moving.

Captain John Pollard died a few days before Christmas,1864 in Petersburg, Virginia. Since battles still raged right down the road, burials were suspended at Blandford Cemetery. So, into the backyard he went, swallowed at last by his beloved Virginia.

The Siege of Petersburg ground the city down to its knees, depriving it of food and supplies, of its sons, and of peace. After nine months and sixty thousand dead, the Confederates withdrew from Petersburg, limped west to the Appomattox Courthouse to surrender, and that was that. Depending on who you asked, if they were Black or White, Petersburg was where the Civil War was won or lost. It is no surprise there are ghosts there. It's the south, rising again.

In the early 2000s, we owned the house on Adams Street where Captain Pollard lived and died. We learned of the captain's demise from his great, great grandson. Surely, this Pollard had a first name, but everyone called him Judge. He first voiced the idea that the place might be haunted.

"Y'all ever feel like there's ghosts in the house?" Judge

Pollard asked one day while talking with H. Like this was a normal thing to say over sweet tea.

We moved from Chicago to Petersburg settling into a Greek Revival with so much history it had its own name: the Syme-Pollard House. The imposing slate blue home, built in 1842, had dozens of soaring windows with black shutters to either side and a massive porch spanning the front from which to appreciate the park beyond. Out back were box turtles, pecan and cherry trees, and a terrifying array of perennials and boxwoods unlikely to survive my tenure. Equally old houses flanked us on all sides, obsessively patrolled by the local historic preservationists. Neighbors greeted our arrival with curiosity and pies, eager to explain the provenance of the house, suss out our particulars and, occasionally, bless our hearts.

Wander or drive in any direction and dozens of historical markers compete for your peripheral vision. Here was the old headquarters of Robert E. Lee, and there lay the remains of the bridge he ordered destroyed as his troops retreated. The sign at Corling's Corner informs the reader about the spot where, every January, enslaved people ("the backbone of the city's workforce") were leased out, mainly to tobacco firms. Not fifty yards from the house, the Poplar Lawn historic sign describes the soldiers who assembled at this park for the War of 1812, and the Civil War hospital erected later.

In July of 1864, a procession of sorts would have marched right past the Pollard house into this same park. After a failed assault known as Battle of the Crater, over one thousand Union soldiers including US Colored Troops were paraded through town while Petersburg's citizens hurled spit and abuse from their streets and grand porches. Wounded Black soldiers were stripped and beaten, and a few weeks later, dozens were listed in local papers so slave owners could claim them. The Poplar Lawn marker politely omits these details.

The house held artifacts to keep its own history alive. People couldn't wait to tell us about the cannon ball that once tore through the brick and plaster of the living room. We discovered cracked brown beer jugs in cabinets, fading maps and original plans for the property, and a small fancy pair of black shoes sloughing off leather one flake at a time. Arrows scratched deep into the wooden planks of our kitchen were instructions for someone. Here, they said, the nails go here.

Upstairs, yellowed ledger pages for Pollard's accounts lined the walls, glued horizontally to insulate the attic. Their fancy script made the sale of nails and lye look like the Declaration of Independence. I spent long hours with my head cocked sideways reading these pages, hoping to find no names and ages on those lists, no prices for people.

She whispered: *Keep looking*. And then opened the door to go back downstairs.

The attic windows looked right down at the garden where, every few weeks, I battled weeds and ivy, cursing and yanking things out that desperately wanted to stay. More than once, I plunged a hand spade into the dirt to dislodge a tangled mess and hit a hard knot of something.

"Cap'n? That you?" I'd ask, demoting him to the rank of cereal captain, before unearthing what turned out to be rocks, roots, and once, a shard of ammo. But no Cap'n.

We loved the idea of Pollard seething when Black people moved into this house. We filled the yard with our friends and spicy food. We danced under the tallest tree in the neighborhood, stomping extra hard to disturb our resident dead rebel. I imagined him shaking an old, angry fist, veins popping out on either side of his neck.

"Ahhhhh knew this would happen," he would drawl.

Pollard belonged to a specific class of Virginia gentlemen, whose lives, public service, and homes were memorialized for posterity. He had a saddlery and harness shop downtown and, by 1860, recorded property and wealth of nearly $30,000, just shy of $1 million in today's terms. These "good and lawful men of the town," as court documents labeled them, were property owners, city leaders, and deciders of life, money, and truth.

Pollard's signature appeared over and over on official Petersburg records in the 1830s and 1840s, a confident sweeping P flourished with an extra swirl underneath. The signature expanded when Pollard was Mayor of Petersburg in 1844, the "r" in mayor claiming the extra space he no doubt felt he deserved. His name affirmed the truth of witnesses on matters of property. He declared how much to pay for property losses and decided who got what from estates. When called upon to compensate owners for the loss of slaves executed who struck White people, he routinely lowballed the value on their lives, keeping the government's payout to a minimum.

Then there is his service record, as a militia lieutenant, and of course, captain. This latter title came from his service to the Water Street Patrol. Such patrols proliferated across the south to capture fugitives and suppress resistance. Petersburg's went into overdrive after Nat Turner's rebellion just a few hours away in Southampton. Slaveholders and other lawful men were granted the honorific title of captain and charged with deploying and motivating slave patrols. His title and service on the Water Street Patrol are the first words on his grave marker. Before the names of his kin, before mayor. Captain John Pollard.

Below the recitation of his achievements, the granite gravestone lists the lesser Pollards, including his wife, their kids, and spouses. John's son Peyton died before him, having followed the call to invade Mexico in defense of Texas, slavery, and cotton. Three dead infants are memorialized. The Pollard family marker is fairly new, and when captured for the posterity of the internet, a small Confederate flag rests at its base.

We were long gone when we learned that Pollard's body had been removed from the backyard before we ever arrived. Once the war was over and the road to the cemetery re-opened, Pollard and others were dug up from their miscellaneous locations and reinterred in a mass grave of 30,000 Confederate dead in Blandford Cemetery. While most of those bodies and parts are unidentified, there is a list of some 2,000 persons known to be buried there. Pollard is number 1,520. There is no unit affiliation or battle next to his name. He was 79 years old when he died, not even a Civil War soldier. A true believer, and city father, he was granted the privilege to rest with his people, his glory by association.

Just past the graves stands Blandford Chapel, luminous with its stained-glass panels venerating the Confederate dead as saints, one for every rebel state. Some forty years after the war, the daughters and wives of the south commissioned the Louis Tiffany Company to create this shrine for their fallen heroes.

Bless their hearts, she says.

2. Ghosted

In the 1850s, a trader set a big price upon George Freeland, offering to buy him for $1,500. Instead, George, "a spare-built man, about twenty-five years of age," liberated himself before John Pollard could sell him off.

Between 1850 and 1860, a frenzy of speculation and greed shot through the south. The US domestic slave trade peaked during that decade. So did the yield of cotton, which doubled by 1860 to 2 billion pounds. Traders bought and sold Black bodies, and whips flayed millions of Black backs, arms, legs, and children to fuel this massive harvest.

To get enslaved people to the deep south and southwest, where the cotton was, the first stop was often the slave pen in downtown Petersburg or Lumpkin's Jail up in Richmond. From there, some were chained together in coffles and walked the million steps to Alabama or Mississippi. Traders sent others by boat to New Orleans, and from there, deeper into Louisiana, or to Georgia or Texas.

On a different boat, George fled from Petersburg to Richmond and then on to Philadelphia. Once there, he reported to the Vigilance Committee of the Underground Railroad (UGRR) that Captain John Pollard was a monster, the kind who wrung "every drop of blood" from your body, who "thought no more of his servants than if they had been dogs." George's testimony included this detail: in ten years, he was allowed "one pair of shoes," though Pollard, the saddler, had leather and money to spare.

Escaping meant George left his "mother and father, and two brothers behind." Imagine this long night of whispered goodbyes: wrenching, hopeful, terrified. Or maybe a morning when his mother awoke and George was gone, having run without warning to spare his family pain for a few hours. At dawn, instead of George, she would find only the wrath of the former Captain of the Water Street Patrol.

George didn't really have a choice. His fate would have been obvious: flogging, chains, cotton, and more cotton. Eventually, a letter back to the UGRR related that he made his way to western Canada. What a bitter triumph to be free, alive, and alone.

The 1850 Census listed eight enslaved people in the Pollard household. Whether or not they were all blood, the records suggest they had grown up and survived together at that house for decades. By 1860, two young men in their 20s were all that remained.

There are few clues for this part of the story. The other five may have been sold or traded in lieu of George for the money or out of spite. Was there a moment for goodbyes, or just a quick snatch leaving an empty space? Had anyone else breached the patrols and liberated themselves? Or did they just die there at that house?

What I do know, in my bones, is the spirit of that family stayed – or came back – to the house on Adams Street to wait.

3. Lost Souls

So many souls were brought to, owned in, sold from, left at, or last seen in Petersburg. One hundred and sixty years later, they still talk to us. Listen:

My name was George Thornton. I left my sister in the morning in the care of Henry Thornton. I left my mother in the evening at Petersburg, her name was Serlena. My father was Jasper. I was there sold to speculators…I was brought to Columbus, Miss., and sold, and I have not heard from my people since.

Mary Epps had been the mother of fifteen children, four of whom had been sold away from her; one was still held at Petersburg; the others were all dead. At the sale of one of her children she was so affected with grief that she was thrown into violent convulsions, which caused the loss of her speech for one entire month.

Do You Know Them? I desire to know the whereabouts of Beattie Giles, the mother of Susan Green. She lived in Petersburg, Va. She belonged to Billy Moody. Her husband's name was Henry Giles. She had four other children. Their names were Joshua, Rachel, Jane and Martha.

My father was named Jackson Jefferson and my mother's name was Franky Jefferson

Three sisters were sold from them at once, at Petersburg, Va.

My father Richard belonged to Mr. Frank Whiting of Gloucester, Va. and mother belonged to Mrs. Ellender Wyatt. My father was drowned and I had five sisters: Diana, Nancy, Lucinda. Ellender, and Susan Whiting, all scattered in different parts of the country. I was removed or sold to Petersburg, Va.

Elizabeth Keckley, who once lived in Petersburg and later became Mary Todd Lincoln's seamstress and companion, remembered the day a neighbor's child was sold to settle a debt:

Little Joe, the son of the cook, was selected as the victim. His mother was ordered to dress him up in his Sunday clothes and send him to the house. He came in with a bright face, was placed in the scales, and was sold, like the hogs, at so much per pound.

Keckley also recalled the whipping Joe's mother received for grieving her baby boy.

Generations of Black people held their breath, hoping it wasn't them, their child, or their husband that got disappeared next. Families were separated, left shattered, gasping for God, for their people, for a will to live or for death to come. Lying awake in empty darkness not knowing who was alive and who was dead. Day in and day out in Petersburg. And Richmond. And Alexandria. And hundreds of other cities, corners, and courthouses.

Whether or not historical markers are complete, accounts in the UGRR and other artifacts witness their yearning and grief. These stories live on in the newspaper ads families placed before, during, and after the Civil War. The ads plead for news of their people with a politeness and respect I cannot fathom. "Any information will be gratefully received," they say. One ad appeared in 1913. Nearly fifty years after the end of slavery, still looking.

4. Spirits

People get stuck for many reasons – waiting, hoping, and loving are among them. Mothers, most of all, want their families to be whole and would do anything to see their family again, to hold their hands and faces, leaning in until their foreheads touched.

Why would this be any less true for the dead than the living?

Years after fleeing that house and Petersburg, I'd lie awake, still haunted and unsettled. Stuck. "Write for your dead," Alexander Chee suggests in an essay. "Let them hold you accountable. Let them make you bolder or more modest or louder or more loving, whatever it is, but ask them in, listen, and then write."

I asked her in, the mother of this family ravaged by John Pollard.

She says: *It was like I had a phantom limb. You feel it because memory tells you it's there. You close your eyes and there's the weight of it, like a sleeve filled with flesh and not pinned to your side. The space where our people used to be is like that.*

She tells me: *We promised each other, no matter what, that we would come back and find each other there. The house was the one place we could remember who we were when we were all together. Even if it was hateful.*

She says: *How would I know who I am without them?*

I am ashamed that I fell for the obvious, the trap of white supremacy even in the afterlife. Why would Pollard stick around? He was ensconced, literally, with his confederates. His business was finished.

I say: *I'm so sorry I missed the chance when I lived there to sit with you on the porch and listen to your stories. I should have set a place for you at the table or made an altar for your family.*

I say: *Thank you for keeping my husband company.*

I think your spirit sent me down the rabbit hole to find George, to revel in his escape and freedom. You led me to the memories of husbands and mothers, of siblings and babies. You waited for me to ache with all their unknowing.

Maybe you moved on after a few years of seeing a house full of Black people. I hold tight to a vision of you all, like thousands of small stars, lifted skyward, beyond the tree line and the Appomattox. You'd head north and then east out over the Atlantic. You gather until all anyone can see is light, like a second sun rising. Carried away. Together. Finally.

I say: *I hope you found your people.*

Ben Miller

Faith Strand's Sound and Fury

Faith climbing the stairs

Meetings of the Rock Island, Illinois, Writers' Studio weren't considered official until the scribbler we all knew as Faith crested the second floor landing and arrived into the shabby meeting room.

Faith's flawed timing was perfect week after week. President Dave had always just requested the dollar dues count from Treasurer John when the door at the bottom of the stairs would bang open and clatter shut, heralding the beginning of Faith's noisy assault on the creaking stairs, carrying her canvas bag stuffed with hymns and clippings. Faith might be mysterious but her effect wasn't: The on-time fidgeters went rigid with polished agitation.

The first night she attended Writers' Studio I made the mistake of trying to assist her up the steps. Trying to play the part of the group's young buck (rickety though I felt at fifteen, a recovering anorexic), I galloped into the dim hall and looked down, sorting the stairwell shades into a figure poised at the 45-degree angle of a shopper on a stuck purgatorial escalator. Only her cat-eye frames appeared to be making progress. The lenses pitched on her brow hovered inches above a step at least six steps above the step where her pink dress shoes were digging in for the climb.

"Need help?!"

"What?"

Her voice an amok blow dryer, mine an unhinged hinge.

"The bag? Want me to take it?!"

I then learned Faith suffered from the rarest of the many forms of deafness afflicting writing club members. She heard every forth sentence perfectly.

"Yessir!"

Attempting to fling the bulging bag into my outreached

arms, Faith held the handle too long and the bag made a mid-air circle, landing behind her and tumbling away from her place on the stairs, vomiting her collected works against the lean street door.

Leg lifted, wheeze. Heel dropped, *whomp*.

The poor stairwell possessed one superior feature: acoustics. It broadcast into the meeting room every ornate decibel of her struggle with the incline's jutting steepness, its unreliable railing, its walls tear-dropped with brown paint.

Would she keel over before reaching the long folding table's spread of article drafts, stanza failures, top hat doodles, fairy tale folderol? Before burying a tan metal seat in the bulwark of her dirty dress? Would her exertions topple the frail brick building located in—to filch a phrase from Studs Terkel—the "rooming house heartland"? Could the club again survive the impact of her challenging company?

Faith's "hubbub" (as Gordon called it) hit oldest members hardest. Such behavior violated their cardinal rule of aging: *Never be a "burden" on others.* Awful as it was to think, Faith might (mightn't she?) consider "seeing the light," "doing an about face," hailing a cab, enter the nearest nursing home to preserve, with professional assistance, whatever remained of her dignity. So every Blanche Grammar or Nola Semicolon of a certain age who came to the writer's group might wish.

Yet Faith was too busy inflicting music to face it. Too blind to see light. She kept climbing in the dark. She knew what little she needed to know. She knew the way. Up!

She groaned. She grunted. She clasped her bosom and paddled like a snorkeler, the buoy of the old hat following along. And as unsettling as her ascent was, the briefest break in the bedlam intensified trepidation in eyes trained on the doorway. *Faith choking on paint chips sucked off the wall!? Faith fallen? Faith, get up! We need your spite to unite us!*

Somehow an ostensibly hapless Social Security recipient, a ragged anonymity with no car and no friends we knew of and no relatives we knew of, horrible vision, poor hearing, a made-up (must be) fiancé Dean, bursitis, sclerosis, maybe TB... contrived to confront us with a power to which no response sufficed but submission.

Congested Norm liked to say Faith "did a *sniff* number on us." Dave's chin receded into his burgundy turtleneck. For the first time that night, Phyllis the Dramatist, the very thin divorcee, ceased dwelling on what had happened last night at her favorite dive bar and with who. Tall Alabama O'Banion, the more sedate divorcee, tabulated all the hells inherent in tabletop coffee rings. Connie Glossy sat "petrified" like characters in fiction ought not do if they were to be *authentic* to a critic. Karen Gothic's lips remained typeset in a red ampersand on the pale page of her face. The brio of Roy Ribald withered as he nibbled a striped 7-11 coffee straw. Snuffling Norm Railroad Days frowned a rare frown, unhappily reminded of the roar of Engine #9, miscast star of a recent nostalgic poem. Cozie Ditty molded invisible kitten-sized prayers with cupped palms. Howard Chronometer, lemon leisure suit and white eyebrows, consulted his namesake wrist device thrice. Jack Wren, Vietnam Vet, flashed back to rice paddy helicopter landings and shot, heaving buddies. Gordon Literal envisioned his backyard woodpile tarp blowing away. Bess Rod and Reel—*Argus* outdoor life columnist—regretted not wearing her life jacket to the table. Betty Reviser repeatedly made the sign of the cross-out on a page. Shy Treasurer John's affrighted stare listed between the vintage cola machine and the splayed anatomy of the broken ceiling fan.

That's when I produced a teenage freak's smile. With Faith around I felt better about my own flailing: instantly less at risk for no longer being the most at-risk attendee. With Faith around, the question—notify Social Services?— applied most urgently to her, and so not to me.

The meeting started an hour late. But after that most meetings only started a half hour late, delayed by the vernacular of a climb that made it sound like America's most spectacular hot air machine had chosen, of all the literary havens between

City Lights Books and the Algonquin Hotel, to grace our presence in a brick tenement a half-block off the failed downtown pedestrian mall in Rock Island, Illinois.

Faith takes her seat

"Well…" Faith exclaimed, askew in the doorway, her passage from the lonesome bungalow to a Paradise of listeners complete, "…I made it!"

Hers was a stamina of constant falterings. Unmoving, timber-braced, whiskered and damp, she coughed and gathered herself. A crushed brim melted into hairnet melted into wig tufts. Rouge. Fuming couplets of her nostrils. Yellow eyes nested like swallows under the pointy rafters of 1948 frames.

"Greetings!" she warbled to us on the edges of the ledges of our chairs.

Most reasonably, Dave suggested: "Please be seated."

"Think I will!"

Girdled girth prepared, swaying, marshaling the power of embolism socks, she lifted her trail-weary saddlebag off the floorboards and embraced her own momentum. The direction depended on the physics of her mood and which hand clutched the bag.

Writers slid to free the seat nearest Faith for Faith, who inevitably pointed out the empty folding chair six or eight or ten bodies away: "That one! Over thar!"

Then members scooted in various new directions to clear paths to her chosen throne. The rectangular circle parted in three places, four, five, as she picked from many openings. Her tonnage poured eastward and westward. Her saddlebag slid the table's length, upsetting careful arrangements of Scribe paraphernalia, scraping over battle-worn binders, notepads, bookmarks, index cards. Treasurer John's ledger bumped and Alabama O'Banion's naugahyde valise nudged and Norm's sky blue rubber thimble (to aid paging) batted into the air like a tiny badminton birdie.

I held tight to the spiral notebook spelling out my fever

dreams: *At night the tree dances, ballerinas on its branches, jumping from limb to limb…*

O, the slogan mugs Faith toppled! OLDIE BUT GOODIE kaput. Smaller spills her dress absorbed; larger spills dripped into the cavern beneath the table as Karen produced napkins from her own addled bag, mopping with the tremulous genius of the third grade teacher she still was. Faith's thick wrist, flung backward, clocked Norm's tin ear. Once a Blanche ashtray butt ignited a wrinkle in Faith's dress and a second wrinkle extinguished the flickers. Regardless, Faith bulldozed on, reeking of mortality but smelling at closest range of her favorite drugstore *eau*. Lavender cocoanut, was it?

She became "a-tangled!" in sinews of reading glasses, quickly freed by the owner.

Saddlebag ephemera inched outward as she tramped with the timed expertise of a frigate cannon-tender. Table legs kicked! Toes squashed! Nearer chairs continually offered, continually rejected. *That one!* her left jab insisted. *That one thar! Pardon me!*

Betty to Blanche: *She's losing her marbles.* Blanche to Evelyn: *Batty! Not playing with a full deck.* Connie—proud publisher of her own work with her corporate husband's cash—mouthed in Latin: *Non compos menti.*

"Aye-men!"

Thud, she hit a chair, arriving in an oddly spacious corner that must have backed away from her like none of us could, forearms pinned to table to keep it from capsizing in the high tide of Faith. In front of her plump face squatted the saddlebag.

"My fiancé—he's a Protymist!"

Let it slide, let it slide, the general consensus. Begin the meeting, the general desire.

"John, could you give us the Treasurer's report?" asked Dave.

Blue-knuckling the retrieved ledger, he couldn't. Not for a minute.

"Bess, could you read the minutes of the last meeting?"

Yes, Bess, the sturgeon snagger, could. Her husband was the Moline fire chief.

"Meeting convened 8:05, July 25th…motion to accept the minutes?"

Howard always made that motion and did so again.

Faith's eyelids battened down.

For the next few hours she slumbered as the rest of us read what we had written out of confusion or pain or jubilation or oblivious fulfillment of a routine suggested by *The Writer* magazine. Written in ink, in lead, on humming Selectrics or clicking Royals, vainly striving to show not tell and avoid clichés. *Good egg…ne'r do well…* The preponderance of hooey, I suspected, was conversely equivalent to the luscious quantity of substance we were trying to reach (or in my case displace) for the sake of sanity.

Faith snoring

She produced the sounds of an Oldsmobile heard at a distance, the steady crooning of a motor on automatic save for the occasional revving hills required.

Notify Social Services tomorrow? Curl a finger, dial a number to separate Faith from her feather bed, tea cups, fiancé fantasy, scruffy scrapbooks, precious sense of a place in a community rather than a cell in it? Was this the assistance she needed? Was informer a role any of us was equipped to play? The idea kept getting tabled.

The nursing home at the apex of a winding drive: the S for *shunted aside*. These depositories for the old (not yet Orwellingly designated "assisted living centers") club members knew from painful visits to relatives and former neighbors. Hushed hallways. One-window rooms. The odor: diapers, Lysol. *No.* How could Faith be consigned to such a fate as long as she had the gumption to tackle 18 stairs? Take a bus and dress—even if it was the same dress—and stay dressed—even if shoulder pads slipped and dangled? What was the rationale for warehousing Faith as long as she had funds to maintain the salt box on the tract block, Quasar television cleverly poised near the front door, tuned to the 24-hour shopping network bark to scare off robbers and other rapscallions of the urban Midwest, a region within a region vital to fully comprehending evolving American realities of gender and class?

Distasteful to mention, it was still positive evidence to be considered—Faith sported no open sores. She was not dehydrated. She was, if anything, over-hydrated and overfed on ring bologna. Regular sink (or bird bath?) washings kept hygiene just within acceptable parameters. Alarming as the "fee-antsy" fantasy was, it was totally natural to want a future at any age—one more shot to resurrect your viability. The help Faith really needed was help maintaining her independence.

Even Blanche, though perpetually aghast at Faith's raucous meeting behavior, had no "truck" (her fastest verb) with reporting a club member to the Department of Social Services. Blanche would never interfere with anyone's inalienable right to be worthy of her truculent "ach"s, not Faith's right, not mine, not President Carter's.

"Not a whit" (Cozie-speak) of proof existed that Faith was sick—or at least not enough evidence to survive an F. Lee Bailey cross-examination. Faith had committed no crime. She just made observers feel sick at heart. Who knows? For decades she may have been living just how she lived now. She trusted in us. There existed an organization to shepherd stray writers and, considering herself a lamb in songbird's clothing, she traipsed to meetings to tender those proceeds of the heart still on offer.

Faith's old clippings

President Dave hit upon an effective strategy for dealing with Faith's presentations. She must "go" last. Once the ruckus began often the only effective method of quieting her was flicking off the lights. Awakened around 9:30 p.m. by a mantra: *your turn, your turn*, Faith opened one eye, then the other, peered through pearls of mucous. Her beige tongue flicked, pasting whiskers flat. Her eyeframes (pocked where gems used to be) jitterbugged on the abbreviated bridge of her nose. The hat-wig-hairnet conglomeration throbbed to the pulse of scratching fingers while the other set of cracked nails dredged out saddlebag souvenirs from a career of blessed creation. She rose to the surface of the room.

"Greetings!" she bellowed.

Faith proffered essentially the same material each Thursday, but never in exactly the same disordered way. Her audience had learned to be vigilant for the shifting points of transition from reverie to singing to tears.

First, fishy grin swishing, she produced corroded paper clips attached to clippings mostly not there. Her hymn lyrics had been published in previous decades. *See!*

Specks of these articles floated, joined by nebulous flakes of air vent origin. "It all telling," she assured us, squinting into the whirring flurry that called for the fuzzier faster fabulous talking in tongues—"it all telling" of her husband's church in "Lustriano"—its "goreous aleter [gorgeous alter]"—its "conogroanants [congregants]"—its "clycan suppers [??]"—its "keester sermons [Easter sermons]"—its "corer [choir]" singing her hymns and its "Whilitizer [Wurlitzer]" played by her too, and the "dahth [death]" of her husband at "thisix [thirty-six]" of "infartication [infarction]" period. His name was Dean also.

None of us were in a position to doubt. Not enough archival matter survived to confirm or deny. Triumphant inhalations guided the cloud of articles back into the saddlebag. I imagined missing paragraphs were safely archived—if forever unobtainable—in the lungs pumping out the memory-noise that made Norm wince. The old gal, she did not know the first thing about being nostalgic! She did not ah nor coo or make it easy. Norm mopped what he called his "bean" with a folded bandana.

She exhibited too well what knowing names too well for too long can do, language stealing language away, placeholders swallowed by the place held. In crashing dissonant cries, in dispersing grams of pulp, she depicted the brutal disattachments aging can inflict. A rampage of paperclips holding nothing together! *See!* Behold her adoration for empty columns of air, because a face, a story, had previously been there.

Faith's new clippings

The first addition in decades to her collection occurred in May of 1980 when Faith frisked the bag, producing her birth certificate plus FRESH columns of newsprint stapled neatly together, unraveling to the right of her delicate goatee. She read from a report describing the recent eruption of Mt. Saint Helen's in Washington State.

"Ahhhhsh!" was still settling on a hundred square mile area!

Learning this, hypochondriac John coughed, believing he tasted apocalypse too—dust on the window sill *ahhhsh*, dust on the cola machine *ahhhsh*.

Faith's hikers were "massing [missing]." Faith's governor had put the "National Gourd [National Guard]" on active duty. The name "Harry Truman" she pronounced perfectly, having seen it twice before in a voting booth. He was the most famous victim. The curmudgeon's refusal to abandon the resort he owned inspired many, including me. A smoldering mountain was his Titanic to sink with. "Bring it on!" he as much as told the national press. Now he lay under a blanket of cooling lava in his green John Deere cap.

Faith's "lava" rhymed with "love."

THE POINT! snapped Blanche's green eyes.

She finally got to it. She again waved her birth certificate, edges tattered to taffeta. Any researcher care to see—to verify the stern planet of a town seal? Her birthplace: "Awaktalka!" That great volcano had erupted on her birthday. *See!*

Gordon's partial swan dive across the table brought him within reading distance of newsprint and the certificate. May 18, 1908. May 18, 1980.

He glanced at the photograph of the Mt. St. Helen's crater.

He glanced at Faith's mouth. He drew conclusions that made him withdraw. Faith's paradigm for aging wasn't *When I am Old I Shall Wear Purple* but a volcano dormant for a century before getting down to the last hot sticky business.

Two months later, in mid-summer, Faith extracted an even more explosive new news item from the saddlebag while talking about the "Protymist!"–no longer her fiancé but now her husband. At least it looked new–a bright white fresh Kinko's copy.

Gordon snatched that column out of her hand: she wanted him to. He read the wedding announcement and passed it on.

Bess (gaze reeling) passed the clip to Dave (swallowing) who passed it to John (blushing) who passed it to Howard (numb) who passed it to Phyllis (teeth gritted) who passed it to Alabama (oh) who passed it to Blanche (*ach*-ing) who passed it to Roy (smirking) who passed it to Jack (stoned again) who passed it to Connie (blank) who passed it to Cozie (rosary out) who passed it to Karen (lipstick twisting) who returned the clip to Gordon for re-re-reading.

Now we knew Faith's last name. Strand. Faith Strand of East Moline, married to Dean Strand, a Bettendorf hypnotist.

Faith's not our problem anymore! She's Dean's! Good rid…? What a stew! Can't derive any solace from it, having never believed in him! Geez!

Blanche stabbed a filter into an ashtray's cluttered shell. *A goner on a spree! Forget the nursing home! Forget the morgue! Wire Dr. Ruth.*

Faith singing

She never burst into tune after showing off her clippings. She *blabbed* into tune, and it happened the evening of the wedding announcement, too.

Vague mumbled allusions to a delayed Las Vegas honeymoon assumed a sudden squall of octaves, the squall a brief harmonic lilt, the lilt instantly withering, submerged in a murky splurge of alto rhythmical lapses, and whilst this river of sound foamed wider and deeper, from the misbegotten saddlebag emerged crackling paper older than any yellow cell of 1936 newsperdermis, *entire* pages designed to endure. Parchment made for millenniums of pew sitters. Caffeine-stained staffs, like bridge beams, spanned the tabletop below the ringing and slurring and sparking and rhyming.

"Boulder of the Ages," her sequel to "Rock of Ages," throat secretions drowning lyrics, filling the room with what sounded like "Chowder of the Ages."

"Chowder eyeternal…!"

Some individuals had noses and others had beaks and still others schnozzes. I was certain that Faith owned a schnozz. It was ballast in any storm. It was the second mouth when she sang.

"Chowder of His sacrifice…"

She held neighing notes with both mouths. I don't think she ever finished singing some of them. Yes, some of Faith's Gs Cs Fs Qs Ps Ds sailed through my 1980s and my 1990s and far beyond—which explains how I'm hearing Faith wailing now in Cambridge in a 600 sq. foot apartment above Brattle Street, around the corner from the Ash Street address tenant T.S. Eliot once entered by a side door and blocks from Longfellow's lilac-surrounded manse—two authors Blanche did have it in her to tentatively admire.

Faith's dentures see-sawed like a pro-active ship disassembling its own hull in Atlantic froth rather than sink: maelstrom-fooling razor rudders. Shoulders, and shoulders only, tilted way-way back. Her collarbone gazed up at a Hereafter of ceiling cracks the misted eye-frames could not monitor, busy interpreting sharps and flats between wrists.

"Chowder of His sacrifice…"

It was past time to pack up notebooks highlighters pencils ballpoints and be efficient about it.

"…Chowder of the Ages!"

To the mix she added "Chrust" [Christ]—to "Chrust" "Maaaintain" [Mountain]—to "Maaintain" nuclear amounts of "Liiiiiiight"—and from light made Dylan-hard rain, embroidered hankie out, performing twin functions of fortress and bottomless reservoir.

Weeping! Like always too! *Only wetter.*

Gordon flicked off the lights.

Faith's long trip home

Descending proved easier for Faith than ascending. She sort of rolled, sort of tumbled down the stairwell—sort of slithered, sort of helicoptered toward a less-dark dark at the bottom—observed from above by Dave (tummy of a Friar) and I (childhood's bones). Both shoulder pads poised like bracket funguses on an oak trunk and that certifiable schnozz guided her to a safe landing, and then she made little noise, cried out, coughed out, wrung out.

She wore no wedding ring, I noticed. There was that to cling to, no matter the claims of the clipping.

On the buckled sidewalk Faith swayed, saddlebag dragging. Nearby club members chattered, for starters: "Good meeting!" followed by the softer "Nice meeting tonight…" then frantic whispers: "*That Dean bamboozled…*" "*At her age a newlywed! What an escapade!*" "*Gold-digger!*" "*Did he pick her up at a church social?!*"

Regardless of the season, on that bereft block, always the fickle reek of the garbage river gulls drop. I eased next to teetering Faith to steady her if she listed too far forward, too far backward. There were puddles around to fall into.

Evelyn the Petitioner, Karen's tough-minded cousin in the velour warm-up suit, stood by herself, gazing in the direction of a pay phone. An attender of meetings of every civic stripe, she gave the business (her verb) to leaders who cut social programs. A roux of cosmetics and moonlight tinted her face maroon. What was Citizen Evie's duty here? Should *she* notify the police since no airy-fairy writer had the chutzpah to? "Fiancé" claims, easiest to label a dementia symptom, had come true in a fashion. It either proved Faith was much sicker than we had let ourselves believe or, less likely, that we were the dangerously confused ones. Exploitation? *Expiation?*

Weekly the same five Wheel-less Wonders needed rides—Cozie, Blanche, Faith, John, and me—and the same pool of drivers milled between nail-studded telephone poles, every other club member save perpetually double-booked Connie (who "vamoosed"—her favorite verb—to make the next engagement.) Figuring who went with who should have been simpler, but as no Muse of Chauffeurs existed to inspire efficient solutions, a tangle of collective bargaining—consisting entirely of agreements—ensued.

Though Faith lived the farthest way and gave the most horrendous directions—as though caring less about arriving home than living forever in the back seat—interest in her shocking matrimonial news increased the roster vying to transport her. Bess's "sure" and Howard's "yep." Norm's "No (sniff) problem!" The solemn "yes" quavering on Karen's lips. Roy's daffy proposal that Faith ride home on the back of his Harley. Unshaven Jack beckoning from his banged-up pick-up truck.

Finally Dave, tests to grade in his briefcase, tugged the reigns, directing Wheel-less Wonders toward drivers most suited to them. Iowans Cozie and Blanche go with myopic Norm. Bess, best you ferry John over his raging river of dread, toward the foyer glower of a surgeon mother who tweaked hearts at Franciscan Hospital and impatiently doted on her only child. ("Late again! Are you mixed up with Beatniks?") Bess and John lived near each other. Howard—least gossipy member—take Faith and...me.

Howard, Dave's second-in-command, knew his mission, its honor: *You are the most equipped to deal with these fragile creatures.*

"Okay, folks, let's go," Howard suggested. He had given us rides before. It meant dropping off Faith first, since she lived in the opposite direction of his split-level ranch and my shadow-fanged abode. We knew we were lucky to have Howard. We would get lost only in spirit.

He settled into the town car and snapped on perforated leather gloves matching the perforated steering wheel cover.

What this galaxy of tiny holes was about I did not know. Howard's glow-in-the-dark chronometer darted like an angelfish in front of the dash. I helped Faith leverage her weight in. I slid into nice front seat scents (cologne, pipe, upholstery) and looked out across the street to see Evelyn folding herself into Karen's compact pale blue vehicle.

Police had not been contacted, could not be, in Evelyn's final estimation. Respecting Faith's right to choose to be a dupe was more vital than protecting the lady herself. Another instance when feeling sure you were making an error meant you were doing the right thing. Karen, Evelyn, heads together, bemoaned Freedom's absurd logic.

"Great meeting," I tensely chirped.

"Some meeting," Howard replied, putting an end to that little discussion. His Bettendorf home hosted the entire eccentric cast of The Who What When Where Why Writing Conference (aka the Mississippi Valley Writing Conference) one year. Over-stimulated by such luxury, I had plucked a black olive out of a salad and flung it at Dave's forehead. No one liked it. I hoped Howard had forgotten.

"Dean!" Faith sputtered. Then she fell asleep.

Faith's husband could not be. But the clipping proved it, he was.

We gazed down the block, not knowing what to hope for, and were off, bound for shingled fringes of the Quad-Cities realm, past Moline, where Dave lived in an A-frame (A for Adjective) with an adorable white poodle named Schatzi.

In new cars I kept my hands in my lap like caged animals that otherwise might poop on everything. I watched thistles of lit numbers on the dash gauges.

"How's school?" asked Howard.

"I..." was flunking Geometry and Latin, so said no more.

Snort! The third turn shook Faith awake.

"Dean! Handsome as Spencer Tracy!"

Ah, the debonair comedic genius of her talking picture youth, and my elderly adolescence. Old movies on late night TV fanned my imagination then. To have acceptable possibilities sometimes a fella had to shut out the vengeance of his 1970s for a few hours.

"Redeemer! Bless His…" Snores.

Howard steered down the off-ramp and through East Moline's long straight streets, past small square yards. Tall chain-link fences separated by a pool cue's length. Septic systems, propane tanks, garage door hubcap montages. In this "berg," as Howard called it, teenagers joined the Army or the Navy to be eligible for educational opportunities. There was a 1 ½ block stretch known as Hero Street in the next town over (Silvis) that had sent more young men to war than any other street of comparable size in America. At dawn red-eyed men in denim jackets appeared on corners to get day laborer gigs. The car slid at gondola speed down the narrow canal of open pavement between dented cars.

"Progress," Howard dryly assured himself, if not me.

To an outsider, Faith's neighborhood was less a place than a vexing rootless grid of PER MAR security signs, *MOLINE DISPATCH* newspaper delivery boxes and sooty pink flamingos, gutters stuffed with leaves though no trees were to be seen, turf pinwheels slowly revolving. Plastic siding that would last a century the color of crap after just a year. Tent-like carports in a nomadic line. Plywood decks where scant room existed for recreation's engine: the gas grill. Tilted berets of smashed trash can lids.

"Almost there!" cried Faith, conscious again, breath steaming window.

Screen-gleam-gilded stoop—indigo lawn patches—there! The bungalow with its front door propped open in the interest of safety. Otherwise the TV acting as guard dog, positioned on the rug, could not do the job. "Zirconia necklaces!" went Rover's bark.

We, and she, looked for a husband in the driveway. HYPNOIST'S LEAGUE bowling shirt, parenthetical tufts around baldness, bulge over belt buckle and the hand that once pulled out a chair for her—once held open a door like a "true gentleman."

Howard applied brakes. Faith kept looking. I powered down the window. "Zirconia necklaces! Originally $99.99 now..." Buzzers. Bells. Bids. Faith kept looking.

A local chiseler had married Faith to snag this gem? *Come off it!* tactful Howard thought instead of said—the saying saved for the second limping leg of the trip. A property worth less and less, but each day Faith left it, she stepped out hoping for more and more. Howard later wondered what had "gotten into her." I, also from a pit, did not.

It hurt to look at her house. It *was* wretched—a firetrap, a fixed-income savagery—all the more scary in that it was hope's only available anchor.

This visit proved everyone right by proving everyone wrong. The wedding announcement was not irreproachable data. Hypnotist Dean was not in residence, apparently. Club fears that Faith had been suckered justified, and Faith correct in celebrating the only genus of spouse she could abide at this late date, *absentee weight-loss guru.* It remained to be seen who would get the best of the bargain in my estimation. Whatever the con man pilfered, he had not the power to get his paws on Faith's fortune of inner resources: her patience, guile, pluck. Petty crooks don't recognize that stuff as gold.

"Here we are, Faith! Get your things together!" Howard was pleading.

She issued non-committal grunts. I got out, opened the door. She rifled the bag and rearranged its contents before rising. The newest clipping must live on top to show people fast. *SEE!* a priceless pulp handhold on tomorrow. Her face had never looked rounder. "You're home!" I quailed. She did not grab and squeeze my extended hand, but gripped the seat back with both hands and pushed. Stammering indecipherably, she pushed hard, trusting saddlebag would stick to mid-riff. It did. She abandoned town car comfort at the speed of bursitis, proclaiming to me and the galaxy:

"I'm fine! Just fine! Aye-men to that! Aye-men!" *Back in the game!*

Who were we to disagree? Actuarial Tables did and got her wrong. She faced her a-glow address, a pause, a shallow bow, and she wobbled. Sell sell sell inanity coursed from the stoop. Permanent Christmas lights blinked on a neighbor's house.

I opened my door a crack in order to exit quicker if she fell.

Saddlebag cradled by crossed arms, Faith approached the fence gate on distressed heels. She unhitched the latch and caught her 82nd second wind.

"Oh, boy," Howard said, elaborating with a *whew*.

"Do you think…" I said, and nothing else, nothing.

Was AWOL Dean snoring next to a girlfriend in Bettendorf? Huddled in a Perkins "Cake and Steak" booth, slurping carafe "java" as insomniac monkey business men called it, our local herd of joking carnival ciphers and tax-evading bunko artists?

She shoved open the gate to her "bridal sweep," as she had called it at the meeting. Entered the miniscule yard, still believing. Shuffled a Bedouin's shuffle.

This memory of this walk I would carry with me. She was showing—not telling—how it was done, how to keep becoming who you are to the finish of who you are. The effort's semi-eternal circumference. The importance of not looking down.

She looked ahead. The lawn, where not illuminated, appeared gone. "Last bid!" an auctioneer caterwauled from the door framing an interior lapped by bluish light, a surf appearing to deepen with the crush of each successive day-glo wave. Faith speeded up: moving better than at any point in the evening. Saddlebag now over one arm lady-like.

Stoop steps hardly slowed her. She did not holler "Bye!" but it was goodbye. She never attended another Thursday night meeting.

She didn't quite vanish. She resolved into an outline—fading dress, fading hat, fading wig, fading bag—as if devoured, purified of matter that did not matter, liberated from every human weight but last wild hopes.

Evidence: Ten Photographs

fig. 1: a southward view from the northern property line, 3x3 print on 126 square-format film, 1973.

A line divides the setting. Faintly purple and faintly grey, a washed-out sky dominates the upper two-thirds, gauzed in the thinnest quilt of clouds. Below, a two-acre hash of tall, golden grass Xs and bends in the wind off New Brunswick's breast. And where these two color fields collide, a line divides the setting.

This line is where our farm exists.

Reading the line from left to right, east to west: the dark steeple of a spruce, the rough pyramid of a maple, the weathered-grey gable-end of the house—two windows above, two windows below—the connected ell and barn, and set a little ways off, the remains of a collapsed outbuilding almost but not quite reaching the midpoint of the line. Past the outbuilding: an indistinct horizon ending in a copse of poplars quaking at the picture's western edge.

On the photograph's reverse, my mother's faded script: *this is the farm we're buying.*

The farm. My mother's home for thirty-five years. More than half her life. Two divorces and three children and one cataclysmic stroke on a bright September morning. Innumerable animals and arguments and summer barbecue dinners shared under the front yard maple. Her adulthood spent on a Northern Maine farm atop a blustery hill. The last house on a dead-end road. A place for hope and hope deferred.

This is the farm we're buying.

fig. 2 & 3: my sister and me, 3x5 print on 110 film, May 1983.

Winter-brown patches showing through new grass in the field behind the house. In figure 2, a nearly colorless eastern sky above a backdrop of poplars and spruce clustered across the unpaved road, a couple leafless red-twig dogwood blazing off the soft shoulder. [Not pictured: the green scent of spring-stunned grass, the tart whiff of nearby animal pasture, the lingering bite of winter on the breeze.] Nearly centered in the frame, my sister Tanya sits in the grass with her knees drawn up to her chest. Beat tennis shoes, navy shorts, white T-shirt, enormous glasses. Her left hand is raised in a visor across her forehead to shield her eyes from the sun. Her other arm forms a casual geometry: right elbow on right knee, right wrist through the crook of her left elbow, right hand relaxed in a droop. She's skinny, maybe because she's thirteen or maybe because we're poor. Or both. Dark curls tumble down her lean shoulders. The look on her face—the shape of her mouth—is disbelief verging on disgust. She is looking directly at the camera.

Before her, on my hands and knees, I clamber through the grass. Blue overalls. Red and white striped T. Blonde hair parted on the left. Brow furrowed against the sun and bottom lip in a milk-fed pout. Weeks away from my first birthday.

The second picture is likely taken moments later, vantage shifted to the northwest: the photographer has circled my sister and me. Tanya is crouching now, one knee in the grass, and we are holding one another. I am clutching her, face buried against her right shoulder, and her arms cup my body in an obvious gesture of comfort, of consoling. Her face is mostly obscured by her hair, but unmistakable is the concern in her eyes, in the shape of her brow.

I have no doubt that my father took these pictures. The evident discomfort in my sister being observed. The narrative implied by the two photos side by side. My father is who took these pictures.

In the background of figure 3: a white and black cow approaches.

fig. 4: Jaison and my father in the driveway, 3x5 print on 110 film, March 1982.

One of the few photographs I have of my father. Half-turned toward the camera in a brown flannel shirt, dark blue work jeans. Sunglasses. Bushy beard. Wind-blown hair. The photograph is almost completely white with snow, drifting to swallow a snowmobile and a tractor parked at the driveway's edge, the orchard of denuded apple trees, the leaning chicken house. Through all his hair, it is impossible to read his expression.

The same cannot be said for my brother. Dressed in a dark snowsuit, orange and blue mittens and a matching knit cap, Jaison is beaming, his mouth open wide with laughter. He's smiling so hard his eyes are all but shut. He is standing near the fender of a snow-swept Dodge Pinto. He is waving at the camera. Whatever is happening this winter morning, it is clearly enough to render Jaison insane with joy.

This might very well be the strangest piece of evidence amid what scant documentation I have of my family: my brother expressing any measure of happiness in the presence of my father.

Seeing this picture, every time, I cannot help feeling sad. I never had a chance to know my brother when he was still a laughing Buddha. I wish I could have been alive when that blissed-out child, hysterical with delight, still inhabited my brother's body and brain.

Meanwhile:

My father's slight stoop.

His unkempt ruffle of hair.

The beard engulfing his face.

This so easily could be me as an adult, unmoored from time and standing with my six-year-old brother in the snow two arctic months before I was born.

fig. 5-7: my mother, 3x5 print on 110 film, August 1982

In an obvious but effective pose, my mother sits in a throne-like wicker chair in our living room, the banister to the stairs visible over her left shoulder, a white ceramic lamp and, beyond that, the oval glass of our incongruously ornate front door unfocused beyond her right. Mum is wearing a sleeveless purple blouse with her long hair drawn in a loose ponytail. She is smiling. It's a picture-taking smile, but a smile nevertheless. I have so few pictures of my mother smiling. She looks beautiful.

Over her right breast, a lactation stain darkens a circle on her blouse. Unfortunate, maybe, but not unsurprising. Pink and ravenous, I would have been three months old.

An evident theme might be emerging. Between figures 5 and 6, Mum's expression is all that changes. Her eyes are wide. Her lips are parted. Her teeth are showing. Hers is a shock that blossoms into anger, as though the photo were taken mid-sentence: "What the fuck did you just say to me?"

Figure 7 is taken at much closer range. So close that it's barely in focus. The word that comes to mind: *encroachment.* Mum's head and face. The neckline of her blouse. A bare crescent of shoulder. Her hair has come undone. The poise and smile of figure 5 are gone. So too is the lactation stain, now outside the frame. Everything in her expression is an exhausted plea. This is the face I know. So badly, she wants to be left alone.

Again, I am certain my father took these pictures. They are exemplar of a trend I've witnessed over and over in the photos of my infanthood, in the four years between my birth and my parents' divorce. A shot of everyone smiling, followed by a shot of everyone confused or afraid, followed by a shot of anger, of disgust, of tears.

It's a trend I've seen repeated in photos of my father and his siblings, of his mother, California photographs taken by my grandfather. Everyone smiling. Everyone confused. Everyone hurt.

What was happening in the moments between the shutters' clicks?

What was being said?

Why did my male progenitors believe—what made them think—that this is how a family should appear?

After the divorce, very few pictures of the family were taken. As if the camera was an accessory to a serial crime (the complicity of documentation). As if no one anymore needed evidence of who we were, where we lived, what sorts of things were done.

fig. 8-10: three sunsets, 1973, 1977, 1999.

Three photographs sharing the same composition. Same contour of westerns hills. Same sun exploding behind the horizon. Same angle. Same aim.

The first photograph (a 3x3-inch print on 126 square-format film) is summer or early-fall—the soft shape of the skyline betrays leaves still clinging lushly to the trees—the landscape almost entirely black as the sun sinks behind the collapsed outbuilding and somnolent distant hills, liquid yellow gradating upward into smoky bluish-grey. All but the roofline of the chicken house is lost in the black below. A faint suggestion of bushes. The barest indication of an apple tree. There's a warmth to all this darkness.

The second picture—also 126 square format—is winter and only slightly less engulfed in black. You can make out the slope of lawn, the ragged thatch of the berry patch, the slump of the chicken house, the stretching fields across faraway hills. Instead of yellow, the sun and sky flare through shades of pink. The collapsed outbuilding is gone. What isn't lost in shadow is drifted in pink-tinted snow.

The third photograph—a 4x6 print from a disposable 35mm point-and-shoot camera—again, is winter. Instead of pink, the world is glossed in the coldest blue, the sun a decreasing yellow cinder behind the hills. What isn't lost in shadow is locked in a fist of blue ice.

All three pictures were taken from the exact same spot, at the end of the driveway, above the wooden platform covering the old well (a well that'd long run dry and whose cover was brittle with rot, a known danger we did nothing about, never replaced, rebuilt, shored up: a threat ever-present right outside our door). All three photos contain the same hills, the same trees, the same increasingly haggard chicken house. The same landmarks and monuments that defined our lives on the hill. Figures 8 and 9, I suspect, were taken by my mother. The first in the verdant months after she and her first husband—my siblings' father—bought the farm. The second in the final months of their marriage, before the divorce and the introduction of my father into this lonesome tree-lined world. The third photograph, I captured, in my final winter before leaving home, years after my father and sister and brother had all gone their divergent and distant ways. Our individual departures each making this lonesome world more lonely. Yet it'd be nearly ten years before I discovered this synchronicity—ten years before sifting through this spare evidence of my mother's life, a box of photographs discovered in the wake of her sudden hospital death—my mother and I hypnotized through decades by the same indelible western skyline, the same indelible flash of light lost behind the world's curve, the stark reality of where we stood versus the abounding unknown beyond the edge of what little we could see.

Given the nature of sunsets and the mechanics of photography, my mother and I were each likely trying to capture something that was already gone.

The Special Ones

We were special and we knew it, the six of us. We'd been selected to participate in a Revolutionary Educational Experiment, one that would put us several steps ahead of our classmates and most importantly, get us out of Gym three days a week. Looking around, it wasn't hard to figure out why we'd been chosen. The slate of potential candidates was grim. Dewey Vetsch was sucking on his fingers again, cramming them so far into his mouth I knew he was going to make himself puke. I really hoped he didn't because then Miss Anderson would have to call Mr. Hauser to come clean it up and there'd be a mound of sawdust right in the middle of the reading corner. Plus, Mr. Hauser gave all the girls the creeps. Last week I wore my white boots to school and he winked at me and called out in front of everyone, "Looking real good today, reeeeeal good!" Creep.

I surveyed the rest of the class. Larry Olafsen had a dull expression on his face as he stared at his left thumb, mouth open. I worried that maybe something wasn't quite right with that one. He spent much of the day drawing tornadoes in violent, spiraling swirls, pressing so hard with his pencil that his paper ripped; but he kept right on swirling, right through to the wooden desk. I sincerely hoped Miss Anderson would make a mental note to call his mother.

Then there was Carla Hogan, poor thing, who bled right through her pad at recess and now was sitting with my jean jacket tied around her waist. She tried to get cleaned up the best she could, but there was no hiding the dark stain on her corduroys. She said her mom was going to kill her, but I doubted it. Carla was the first girl in our grade to get her period and it's not like she could do anything about that.

Miss Anderson was reading aloud to the class. "To his great surprise the rain stopped. It didn't stop gradually as rains usually do. It ceased." She paused here. "Using context clues, raise your hand if you can tell me what the word *ceased* means." Several hands went up and I rolled my eyes. Ceased? Was she serious? That was a second grade word, old territory. "Yes… Kim?" Kim Baumgartner lisped badly. "Theased ith when you thtop." "That's right!" Miss Anderson beamed. "To cease is to stop, very good, Kim!" Oh, brother. I started to get antsy and looked over at Mike Torgerud, one of the boys who'd be in the special group with me. He rolled his eyes too and shook his head. I checked the clock and counted the minutes until we were taken out of class. One hour to go.

Miss Anderson was still talking. "And now I think it's a good time for us to *cease* our story so we can practice our penmanship!" She said this with a big, phony smile, trying to get us as excited as she was, but there was lots of groaning, let me tell you. Miss A. had a thing for proper cursive penmanship, but I hated it. I didn't tell anyone, but I didn't want to be that close to the other students if I could help it. At least with reading time I could keep my distance at the back of the group, but with writing practice I had to sit inches away from other kids, smelling all their doggy smells. Honestly, it was like some of these kids didn't even bother to wash their hair.

I started practicing my loops, making perfect lower case e after perfect lower case e. I was intent on showing Miss Anderson exactly why I had been chosen for the Special Revolutionary Educational Experiment, whatever it was. Kim Boettcher next to me had atrocious handwriting and her e was way too big for the space provided. She kept making the top of her loop go too high and it was secretly driving me crazy. Plus, she smelled like Alpo and shoe polish. No one would ever consider her for anything other than Hall Monitor. Or maybe Color Guard.

Laura Dahlstrom finished her exercises first and was reading a book on astronomy while she waited for everyone else to catch up. Laura with her perfect black braids and straight bangs. It was obvious she was going to be part of the special group, there was no question. Everyone knew she was the smartest because she was half Asian. Her mom was Chinese or Portuguese or something so she had a leg up in the smarts department, but no one held that against her. She was still a Lutheran.

As I finished copying my last sentence, I wondered where the six of us would be meeting. Probably Conference Room B, I thought. That's where we usually went for things like party planning or after school clubs. One time Brad Schagel snuck in there and wrote *Mrs. Berzinski is a butt face* on the blackboard and then Principal Riggs made an announcement over the intercom the next morning reminding us that that kind of behavior was not acceptable. But then I thought, maybe the Revolutionary Educational Experiment was too important for Conference Room B. Maybe there would be a special room that we knew nothing about that was saved for special things like this, and special people like us. That seemed more likely.

I tried to get Jeffrey D.'s attention to tell him my idea and see what he thought, but Jeffrey W. was in the way and he didn't see me waving. Jeffrey D. was one of us too, but he had a habit of chewing on the corner of his Cub scout scarf and his mouth was frequently stained blue. It wasn't encouraging, to be honest. It was embarrassing to be lumped in with someone like him, a scarf chewer, who probably had a lot in common with Dewey Vetsch. 10 minutes to go.

I spotted Dave across the room and when he saw me he drew a question mark in the air with his finger. I shrugged my shoulders. He'd been chosen too, but I didn't have any more information than him. Dave. I'd almost forgotten about him. He was easy to forget because he didn't really talk much anymore since his older brother was killed in a car crash last year. My parents told me I needed to be extra sensitive about Dave's situation, so I let him copy off my English test last Tuesday. It was tragic and all, but at least he still had one other brother and a baby sister at home, so that was alright. He was sitting next to Marsha, the last of us six.

Marsha was pretty cool, even if her dad was the Vice Principal. She worked harder than anyone, that's for sure. I was positive her dad must know everything, but Marsha would never spill the beans anyway, even if she did know something. I think she was afraid of her dad. For instance, yesterday we were taking turns throwing sharpened pencils at each other to see who could stay still the longest without flinching, and Heidi Weiss got the tiniest poke under her eye. Marsha got so upset, she kept saying we were all going to be sent to the office and get in big trouble. I mean, Heidi hardly even bled at all and now the lead mark in her cheek just looks like a freckle so it was no big deal. But Marsha was acting like it was the end of the world.

Just then Mr. Delmeister, the Dean of Students, popped his head in the classroom door. Mr. Delmeister had a reputation for being kind of weird and was not well-liked at school. Students called him Mr. *Dull*-meister behind his back and said that he only had two cream-colored shirts in his closet that he wore in rotation. There were rumors that he still lived with his mother even though he had to be at least 50 years old. "Excuse me, Miss Anderson? May I please have Laura, Mike Torgerud, Karen, Dave, Marsha, and Jeffrey D. come with me? Make sure they bring all their things with them." Miss Anderson nodded and signaled to us that we should get ready. The six of us looked around at each other. Did this mean we wouldn't be returning to the classroom? All eyes were on us, the special ones, as we began to pack up our pencil cases. I took a little longer than I needed to to put everything in my backpack, then closed it all up with a big zip. I could see that Mitzi Reynolds was trying her best to seem not to care because she pretended to have something wrong with her chair the whole time. But I knew she really did care. She cared a lot.

I wondered if anyone else was as excited as me. We still didn't know what we'd be doing, but we didn't care. We had been chosen, specially selected out of all of our classmates and that was the most important thing. Marsha gets a little chatty when she's nervous and she called out, "Mr. Delmeister? Mr.

Delmeister, where are we going?" Mr. Delmeister just looked back over his shoulder and smiled a little smile as he raised his eyebrows and pantomimed zipping his lips shut. Even for him, that was unsettling. The words *Revolutionary Educational Experiment* echoed in my head and suddenly my mouth was very dry. The last time I was this anxious was when Sandy Schwabenbauer and I were walking back from Trick-or-Treating and got lost out at Smoker's Pond after dark. Sandy kept saying, "Don't worry, don't worry. It'll be fine." People who tell you not to worry when you're wandering through Smoker's Pond on Halloween are the worst kind of people.

Mr. Delmeister led us two by two down the hallway and walked us right past Conference Room B. I knew it! Dave and I gave each other a thumbs up as we followed behind Mike and Jeffrey D. Then he marched us past the lunch room, past the Principal's office and the auditorium. Just after the auditorium there was a door that appeared to be locked. We waited while he took out a bunch of keys on a ring and used one marked with red paint on the end. Now we were in a long hallway in a part of the school we'd never been to before. Maybe it was where the older kids went, but I didn't see any other students anywhere. Or teachers, for that matter. There wasn't even any artwork on the walls or anything. It was absolutely quiet.

I was really starting to get a little freaked out and began to doubt this whole Revolutionary Educational Experiment business. Mr. Delmeister was acting so strangely. Mike Torgerud was a natural leader and I was relieved when he broke the silence. "Mr. Delmeister, is this an accredited extracurricular activity?" He actually said that: 'accredited extracurricular activity', and I could've kissed him for his bravery. Mr. Delmeister didn't answer.

I turned to Laura and when I saw the confusion in her eyes it suddenly occurred to me that she didn't even speak Chinese. And Dave always copied off my tests; not just last Tuesday, and not just English. Mike Torgerud's penmanship was almost as bad as Kim's, and he didn't raise his hand when Miss A. asked who knew what ceased meant. Marsha had to work super hard just to get her homework done by the bell each day. Jeffrey D. was an unapologetic scarf chewer. And I still wasn't 100% clear on the difference between a numerator and a denominator. My heart began to pound.

We reached another door, the final door, also locked. Mr. Delmeister stopped us there and said, "Alright, everyone. When you go inside just pick any chair, it doesn't really matter where you sit." The six of us, the special ones, looked at each other and Marsha gave my hand a quick squeeze. I heard Dave swallow with a tiny click in his throat. We were all breathing a bit faster, our eyes wide in anticipation of whatever lay on the other side of the door. Mr. Delmeister placed the red key in the lock, turned to us and said, "Kids, I'd like you to meet Mr. Fitzpatrick."

*

Vernon Fitzpatrick watched Kevin Richter wipe his nose on the sleeve of his jacket for the third time and shook his head in disgust. Vernon couldn't stand to look at him for one more second and finally got up from his chair, handing Kevin a tissue from the circulation desk. "Where's your mom, Kevin?" he asked, trying to hide the annoyance in his voice. Kevin looked at him dully, his sandy blonde hair already beginning to lose its summer highlights. He shrugged and went back to his coloring book, never bothering to blow his nose or even acknowledge him, really. Vernon stared at the top of Kevin's head for a full beat before noticing the mini Hulk action figure sticking out of the top of his backpack. He kept his eyes on Kevin as he deftly reached behind his back into Kevin's bag and quickly snatched the figure, slipping it under the cuff of his sleeve. *Finders keepers, you little shit,* he thought.

Back at the front desk, the books were piling up. He logged *The Mystery at Lilac Inn* and added it to the growing stack of returns. The Nancy Drew Summer Mystery Challenge was always the worst time of year at the library. A prize of $50 was awarded to the kid who managed to read the most books in the series by Labor Day. Not only were the books chronically in short supply because every girl within 10 square miles wanted to get in on the contest, but as luck would have it, the author's pseudonym, Carolyn Keane, landed her on the bottom shelf alphabetically. That meant Vernon had to kneel on the tile in order to reshelve the books, which ended up being required several times a day. At six feet, two inches, it was murder on his knees. And it was petty, he knew it, but calling it the Nancy Drew Summer Mystery Challenge was flat out stupid and wrong. It *should've* been called the Nancy Drew Mystery Summer Challenge because they were fucking *mysteries* and it was a fucking *summer* challenge. Trying to get this library's board to understand the rules of modifiers and objects was fruitless, like John von Neumann trying to teach game theory to chimpanzees.

In residency at the Iowa Writers Workshop, Vernon had made his bones in short fiction, eventually winning a Pushcart Prize for his satirical take on Pope John Paul II, *A Man and His Hat.* He'd been called 'an important voice', and 'someone to watch'; a 'promising talent who offers readers a glimpse into the human condition.' Or was it a *peek* into the human psyche? He could never remember which. Today he had to unclog the toilet because some kid had used too much toilet paper. *I wonder what the prize is for that*, he thought. He'd had some other pieces published over the years in important journals, magazines that no one around here had ever heard of. He'd even managed to secure himself a literary agent who'd been pressing him to sit down and knock out a novel or two. "I can *do* something with that, Vernon", she'd said. "You could be the next John Grisham if you really wanted to." Never mind that Grisham wrote courtroom pulp and Vernon was a serious writer, an *important* writer, someone to watch. Besides, he'd been working on his first full length novel for years. It was consequential work and that couldn't be rushed.

Vernon was 34 years old and unmarried, and although he could stand to shed a good 10-15 pounds, he hid it reasonably well on his large frame. His summers were spent right here at the local library, which was tolerable, if not preferable. He had the freedom to write when time allowed, and even better, he'd recently developed an educational program that he'd surprisingly convinced the elementary school board to adopt, despite his lack of teaching credentials. Wave around a fancy degree and a few magazine clippings and it was amazing what doors would open. Quite a few, it turned out. After Labor Day he'd be teaching a course three times a week in the school's Special Ed department. But it wasn't kids like Kevin he'd be teaching, those vacant-eyed imbeciles with limited futures and snotty noses. His kids would be special. Like him.

Vernon locked the door of the library promptly at 6:00pm. He could see Mrs. Weiss exiting her car in the parking lot, a book in her hand. He rapidly ducked behind the circulation desk to hide and he could hear her tapping on the glass, calling out "Hello? Can I just...hello?" Let her use the after-hours drop box; rules were rules. Eventually she gave up and left, and Vernon slowly peeked his head over the desk, retrieved his briefcase, and readied to leave for the day. He placed the case on the desk and ran his hands across the smooth brown leather, pausing just a moment before he unlocked it in one swift movement. He tossed the Hulk action figure inside where it landed next to a pink rhinestone key ring marked "Denise". Also contained within the briefcase were a CD of The Allman Brothers still in its plastic wrapper, two pots of unopened Carmex, a soap bubble wand, a cinnamon scented votive candle, a package of black shoelaces, a chrome drawer pull from Ace Hardware, a ladies compact mirror, a shot glass from Wisconsin Dells, a cloth dinner napkin from Giorgio's, three pairs of eyeglasses, and a small framed photo of a Pekinese named Desdemona.

Vernon's heart raced as he stared at the objects in the case, these items he'd collected without meaning to. *This'll be the last time,* he thought, as he closed the briefcase and grabbed the windbreaker from the back of his chair. Early evenings were already beginning to show hints of the cooler weather to come and Vernon liked to be prepared. On his way back to his apartment, he pulled his car over at the intersection of Wells and 7th. He got out of the car, opened his briefcase, and emptied the entire contents into the waiting garbage can. Vernon peered down into the trash and after a moment, reached inside to retrieve the package of shoe laces. He tossed them on the passenger seat of his car and drove away.

*

The phone was already ringing when Vernon entered his small apartment. He answered, laying his briefcase on the dining table which had been serving as a makeshift office. "Hello?"

"Yes, hello. Is this Vernon Fitzpatrick?"

"Speaking."

"Oh- hey, Mr.-…Vernon. It's Rudy. Rudy Delmeister from Northern Hills?"

"Of course." *Was that the insufferable one or the one with the cleft lip?* How are you?"

"I'm…reasonably well, thank you." *The insufferable one.* "Ahh, I wonder of you have a quick moment? We just received the proposed material for your first session with the students next week-"

"Wonderful!" Vernon interrupted. "I trust the slides'll be ready by then?"

There was silence on the other end of the line. Then, "Yes. Well. That's why I'm calling."

Vernon heard the hesitation in Delmeister's voice and knew something was amiss. Rudy continued. "I…well, the entire department, actually, we felt that some of the material may not be… suitable for the students."

And there it was. "Can you be more specific?" Vernon tried to keep his rising agitation under control.

"Of course. If you could take a look at reading sample number one, for example, maybe we could start there?" Delmeister sounded almost apologetic.

"Why not." Vernon was irritated as he shuffled through the papers on his table and found the packet containing his sample paragraphs with subsequent reading comprehension questions. "Shoot."

He heard Rudy inhale. "Great. Just take a second and...read that if you don't mind."

"Out loud or-"

"No, just to yourself is fine." Rudy replied. Vernon scanned the paragraph.

On the day Candace was to have had her tubes tied, the lights went out in the city. It was the sign she needed. The messy business with Ted had dragged on for far too long, all her fears of complacency, realized. She lacked the strength to move forward on her own and the universe, in its just mercy, took the reins and led her to the coolest springs while she watched, gratefully, from afar. It was done. There'd be no late night feedings, no cracked nipples or tenderly crafted booties. Those would be trophies for someone else, but not her. And not now.

Please select the most correct response:
1) How do we know Candace will not have children?
a) She's too selfish.
b) Ted has never wanted to be a father.
c) She had her tubes tied.
d) She fears feeling trapped by motherhood.

The prose was beautifully written. Elegant, even, no problem there. No typos. He read it again just to be sure. Then it dawned on him. "Ah. I think I see the issue."

Rudy exhaled in a rush, relief in his voice. "Oh, good! I was sure you'd under—"

Vernon cut him off again. "The past conditional tense may be a bit confusing for the students. I can massage that one if you like, use past perfect instead?"

"N-no, that's not the problem, Mr. Fitzpatrick."

Vernon dropped the packet on the table with a sigh. "Why

don't you just tell me, Mr. Delmeister, no sense beating around the proverbial bush."

"Mr. Fitzpatrick, are you aware these students are in the 4th grade?"

"Mm."

"When you proposed a speed reading course for these kids, I'm afraid we expected something entirely different. Does content referring to…to cracked nipples and…getting your tubes tied seem appropriate for ten year olds?" Vernon didn't respond. The gall of the man was breathtaking. In a sea of mediocrity the best learn to swim alone, and Vernon was accustomed to following his own path. Delmeister eventually broke the silence, "I guess what I'm trying to say is, maybe we could focus more on…dogs and rainbows or something? And less on…Number 7, for example."

"Remind me."

Delmeister read aloud, "*'Bertrand's face had grown pale, his hands losing sensation as Dr. Fergus picked bone fragments and bits of tissue from the exit wound.'*"

"Anything else?" Vernon asked.

"And Number 4."

"Fine."

"And perhaps…6?"

"Indeed. Until Monday, then, Mr. Delmeister."

Rudy breathed out in a rush of gratitude, "Thank you, Vernon. And please, call me Ru-"

Vernon hung up the phone.

*

It was 12:50 precisely and Vernon was perusing the spare classroom he'd been assigned, one of the new ones in the annex of the school. There wasn't much to recommend it, truth be told, but at least it was quiet. The smell of new paint was already giving him a headache as he arranged the chairs. He placed them in two rows of three with the projector in the center of the room. At the front of the classroom, where a chalkboard would ordinarily be found, there was a plain white projection screen. Vernon tested the projector to make sure it was in working order, grimacing at Slide #1, an approved slide, a slide to make the ghost of Dostoevsky weep.

Johnny and his dog, Spot, were playing in the park when it began to rain. Johnny had forgotten his umbrella and didn't want to get wet. He hid under a tree. Spot liked the rain and ran around barking and digging. His paws got very muddy as he splashed in puddles. Fortunately, it only rained for ten minutes. Then, a beautiful rainbow appeared in the sky and Johnny and Spot played and played all afternoon.

Vernon wanted to vomit. But only after first choking the life out of that pansy Johnny and his wretched dog. *Dogs and rainbows, my ass,* he thought. If he were Johnny he'd already be looking for the exit. *Please select the most correct response: When Johnny loses his middle management job to downsizing will he: A) Leave his wife and kids for the hot, young teller at his bank B) Drown his pain in Jack and benzodiazepine C) Become a Jehovah's Witness or D) Contemplate walking into the sea.* Vernon sat down at his small desk to wait. Five more minutes until the students arrived.

He rifled through his folder containing information on the six students selected for the special speed reading program: Mike, Laura, Jeffrey D., Karen, Dave, and Marsha. He'd asked, and been assured repeatedly, that these kids were special, specifically chosen to participate in this revolutionary program he'd developed; all of them scoring in the 99th percentile on standardized testing. It remained to be seen whether they could keep up, but he had high hopes for the Asian one at least. Within three months they'd be reading 700 words a minutes at 100% comprehension and accuracy. Thanks to him, Vernon Fitzpatrick, winner of the Pushcart Prize, these kids, *his* kids, would have a shot in this life; a one-way ticket out of here and on to somewhere better. They'd be spared the indignity of ordinary lives. To be merely ordinary; it was unimaginable. He could hear the kids coming down the hall now, escorted by Mr. Delmeister, no doubt. He stood and spotted something on the floor in the far corner of the room. Vernon picked it up. It appeared to be a small religious medallion of some sort, cheap pewter, probably dropped by one of the maintenance staff. He turned it over in his fingers and saw that St. Nicholas was stamped on one side. Patron saint of children. Vernon smiled, slipping the medallion into his pocket as the door began to open.

Diane Payne

Encounters

I run into an old lover I haven't seen in thirty years, and after a bit of mundane chit chat, he asks if I can still predict the future. He doesn't laugh. I don't laugh. If I could have predicted that I would have run into him, I would have gone a different direction. He waits for an answer that will never surface, while I wonder why, after all these decades, this is what he remembers of me. I want to be elsewhere, and I am elsewhere, but not sure where, and I know where I don't want to be.

Back in time.

1979. Sitting at Windmill Restaurant overhearing the detectives who have come to town to investigate a murder, saying there's a crazy girl with ESP we have to meet today. I eat my eggs and drink coffee, looking at them in the next booth. We look at the clock on the wall, and then the five of us walk across the street to the police station, and when they realize I am the crazy girl, they all laugh, and the oldest one says, *I bet you knew this would happen, didn't you? We'd be sitting at the same restaurant next to each other, then heading here?*

Their laughter hurts my ears and I regret carrying my sketch book, knowing I'll be sharing my crappy doodles, the drawings of people I may never have seen. When the oldest detective asks what I know about the murder, I admit I am not sure I know anything about the murder, but I have a feeling that more than one person is involved in the murder. He wants to know why I think this if I don't even know the dead college girl. I shake my head, embarrassed, because I don't know why I think this. I say I haven't been able to sleep since she was murdered and that I have a bad feeling that there was a group of people, people she already knew, and they were somewhere late at night not far from here.

One drawing has four numbers of a license plate number

I may never have seen in real life, numbers I wrote down another night in bed when I woke, thinking about this recent murder. The fattest detective suggests that I'm psychotic, then laughing, *oops, I mean a psychic, not psychotic. Ha. Ha.* The thinnest detective says he'd like to be a psychic so he'd know what his wife was doing while he's at work, and all the men sitting around the table laugh until someone returns to the room with info about the license plate, and they stare at me, wondering how I knew those numbers, and I say I'm not sure, but maybe it was the plates of the man I had seen jerking off by the school days before the murder, when this man kept asking me directions for streets that didn't exist, and something told me to not look at his hands, which I didn't do until I saw the kids leaving the elementary school. Then I looked at his hands as he smirked at me, jerking off. I screamed and he drove off. So maybe it was his license plate, his face in my sketch book, or someone else's that I've never seen.

The oldest detective says his daughter is also named Janet, just like the murdered girl, and they are both the same age, so maybe that's psychic also. I say that sounds more like a coincidence. The youngest detective asks if I worked at the Blue Mill Inn with Janet and wants to know if I'm holding back information. I tell them I've never been in that motel and I don't know this girl, then wonder if maybe I do know this girl since she attends the local college, and maybe I've seen her at a bar in town, she sitting at a table with her friends, me at a table with mine, and everything becomes a blur and I wonder why I offered to come to the police station to discuss this case. I flip through my sketchbook pages, and they ask if they can keep it, and I don't dare say no, so I hand it over and assure them that that there's nothing I know about her murder except I can't sleep at night thinking I know she was murdered somewhere not far from here and there should be plenty of footprints. *Great tip,* the thin detective says, and once again they all laugh.

The oldest detective says I should get help, that I'm not

normal. The fattest detective looks at his notes and asks if I am the same girl who had just found that old man by his car, the man who ended up in the hospital, the man I noticed from my upstairs apartment window looking confused, so I left to see if he needed anything, and he said he couldn't unlock the door, maybe the lock was frozen. I put the key in the lock and he started passing out, so I opened his car door and shoved him into the car seat, ran to a phone booth, and when the ambulance came, they said I should ride with him, even though the hospital was just a few blocks away, but maybe they thought I was his granddaughter, and at the hospital, a police officer asked me about my connection to this diabetic man who had a pocket filled with candy bars, this man I didn't know, and when I said I saw him through my apartment window and went to check on him, the officer said I could go home now, just like these detectives also finally release me, so I can walk home in the snow, remembering how once, long ago, I believed I was a witch, casting spells on the bogeymen I was certain hid in the closet and beneath the bed that I shared with my sister, assuring her every night that I turned these men into frogs, then sent them away into manholes, and we could sleep soundly now; but deep down, years later, I knew that wasn't possible.

After meeting with the detectives about the murder, the police circled my apartment late at night, shining their lights through my window, maybe thinking I'd come running out in my pajamas confessing I knew more about that girl's murder, or just shining their lights to let me know they had enough of my shenanigans with old diabetic men, younger masturbating men, and unknown murderers, while I thought, that's no way to treat someone you think is crazy.

And after years of dreaming of deaths that never happened, then answering that dreaded phone call about a death I never expected, I finally started breathing more deeply, feeling somewhat free of this curse of believing I knew when bad things were about to happen, untangling myself from this déjà vu of past, present, future, and elsewhere, finding comfort sitting in fields of flowers and walking next to roaring waves, far away from people who ask me questions about things that may or may not have happened decades ago.

Annette Pearson

Road Trip South

"Really, would you ever consider wearing this getup?" my sister says to me, pointing to the magazine she's been reading. A woman dressed in a floral blouse and plaid cropped pants offers a tray of drinks to guests in her glossy backyard. But it's my sister's thin hands that catch my attention. They are our mother's, small and pale.

"I wouldn't be caught dead in that," she adds, thumping the photo with a bony index finger.

That expression is our mother's, too, and when we both laugh now, it's as if the three of us are making this trip to the Valley together.

*

We're headed to Brownsville, Texas, for a look at the dead body of our father, a man others know as BL.

Brownsville has never been my home. In fact, I've made this long drive from Austin only once, for a vacation on South Padre almost twenty years ago, and that trip included no sighting of BL at all.

Now, as I partially unfold one of those giant roadmaps to chart our progress, the northernmost half of the Texas panhandle appears to be missing—a couple of inches and a few hundred miles lopped right off—until that section turns up on the back side, as if the state has folded over on itself. Even with this adjustment in cartography, you can trace nearly eight hundred miles from **AMARILLO** to **BROWNSVILLE**, located easily at the southernmost point in black letters, all caps, a wavy line of blue running between **R** and **O**. The Rio Grande might have been drawn in a shaky hand, its sole purpose to divide the United States from Mexico, where only a handful of cities are identified, suggesting that these are the only ones that exist, or matter; the beginning of an alphabetical listing of Texas cities consumes the space: *A-H. INDEX CONTINUED*

ABOVE.

Thirty years ago BL decided to build a house in Brownsville because it was a cheap place to retire and he could fish there. He once bragged to me that with the single push of a button, he could lower his boat from the dock behind his house and be out on the water in less than five minutes. I'd have to bring my sons down, he told me then, and they'd go fishing together—my father with his grandsons, an ordinary sort of family activity, if you take the words at face value. I can see myself nodding along as BL says all this with that sheepish, lop-sided grin, but however I respond, however it is that I keep up my end of the pretense that this invitation is genuine and there's a possibility of this event's occurrence, I've forgotten now how all that might have been.

I can't go any farther anyway with this half-memory, this bit of tossed-off conversation, without considering how pathetic my desire to believe that fish story must have seemed. All these years later, I still don't know what that house of his in Brownsville looks like. I can only imagine standing beside my father on a wooden dock, watching a boat slowly descend into a gray slip of water.

And in this scene, BL appears much as he always has, even before his death this past Monday: a fragmented apparition, two-dimensional and transparent, like a projection onto a wall.

With the map tilted like this on my lap, the Rio Grande River outlines the bottom of a heeled cowboy boot. El Paso is a spur on the state's western corner, Brownsville a pointed toe at the southeastern tip, poised to kick all that isn't wanted out into the improbable-blue gulf.

As we settle in for the next stretch of highway south toward Corpus, I make another fold on the roadmap near our current location just south of San Antonio. Then a hand's width due east, I find Bay City, that stunted, flat coastal town surrounded by rice fields and grass farms and ranch land. It's where I grew up, the reason I'm suspicious of all small towns. Despite its name, Bay City languishes thirty miles inland on the Colorado

River, and it is the longest half hour imaginable from the courthouse on the town square to the drawbridge across the inter-coastal canal, and another tediously slow twenty minutes alongside the muddy, snake-infested river before it merges with the gulf at a point on the peninsula known as Matagorda Beach. The line of ramshackle fish camps and bait shops and beer joints stops at that same point, the apparent end of civilization except for a few cabins squatting behind the dunes, recklessly thrown up after the latest hurricane and waiting for their inevitable destruction in the next.

The Texas Gulf Coast has its own sort of primitive beauty, if you don't expect clear water or white powdery sand, but there is a desolation to Matagorda that I've always found unsettling. It's where we went in high school to do all the things we weren't supposed to be doing, cruising the shoreline with Lynyrd Skynyrd and Fleetwood Mac and Peter Frampton blaring out the car windows. When I was much younger, I know that my mother would sometimes drive me and my sister and some of her friends down there, but I remember almost nothing of those beach trips except waiting for boats to crawl through the canal so the drawbridge could close, the heat and the stillness and the irritating whine and sting of mosquitoes. And my mother's fretting, beginning long before we got home, about all the sand in the Impala. Despite her vigorous efforts with a whisk broom, the grit on the plastic seat covers and the vinyl floor mats would vex her for weeks, while that blend of Hawaiian Tropic and salt water and seaweed so redolent of summer dissipated as soon as we arrived back at the white house on First Street.

*

My mother must not have taken photos of us on Matagorda Beach because if she had they'd have ended up in that cardboard box, the one with all the gold-and-white Kodak envelopes filed upright in precise rows. As a child, sometimes left alone at home, I might gather up the courage to open the door to the hall closet; to make a space between the wool coats hanging in plastic dry-cleaning bags from the rod above; to hold my breath and crawl down into the impenetrable darkness that smelled of moth balls and the pasts of dead people. The moment my fingers grasped hold of the box of photos, I'd propel myself backwards and shoot back out into the safety of the hallway. Then I could get lost for hours, jumbling people, places, and time inside that box of treasure.

My mother saved all photos, even the blurred, or overexposed, or not fully developed, just as she did those with precisely cut-out squares instead of faces, strange headless male torsos standing beside the more intact, familiar figures of my mother or my sister. Sometimes I came across other finds, like those rectangular black-and-whites with deckled edges, bound at the top with black cardboard in an old-fashioned sort of booklet: In these my sister is a sturdy, round-eyed child of four or five, squatting in the sand with the murky Gulf of Mexico behind her, surrounded by a group of smiling adults that includes young married versions of my mother and BL.

Years later, after my mother died and I'd sorted with impunity through her box of photographs, I located this tiny album and gave it to my sister. She identified one of BL's younger brothers and his wife; she remembered that beach outing, that afternoon with them and her parents. What caught my attention for the first time, though, in my sister's hands was the faded blue ink on the top photo, "Matagorda Island" written in my mother's tall, slanted handwriting. While there is a Matagorda Island—located south of the peninsula and accessible to birders and fishermen only by boat—this wasn't it, I knew. And I'd wondered what else my mother had mislabeled, what other information she'd relayed wrongly that I never thought to question.

And it's only just now, in remembering a place and the photographs of others' taken on a summer day years before I was born, that I consider this: How is that during all my surreptitious rifling through that box kept hidden in the dark of the hall closet, I hadn't envied my sister? And why do I still hold on to photographs of people I never knew, others' keepsakes kept safe even now, tucked into the darkness of one of my own closets?

The distance that has always existed between my father and me was captured in another photo, taken only a few days before our family imploded. A scalloped white border frames a partial view of the living room of our house on First Street, where BL perches on the edge of a couch I never knew. This BL is dark-haired and thin, much younger and more attractive than I can remember him being, and he stares down at newborn me—swaddled and propped at an awkward angle, half on his lap, half hanging from the crook of an elbow. With his downcast eyes and that oily cowlick spilling over his forehead, he looks sheepish. I've wondered if, at the very moment my mother pressed the shutter on the camera, he was planning his escape, his mind busied with lists and packing, readying to shove off and leave our family.

This photograph—the only one I have of the two of us—is part of a series. My nine-year-old sister, my mother, then my mother's mother poses with me-the-newborn. My face is obscured by the tightly wrapped blanket, but each of theirs is pointed directly at the camera; no one is smiling.

While the precise details of this joyless photo shoot are unknown to me, I can construct enough of a story from another of my mother's, one that I don't remember ever not knowing. I think I knew it even before I was born, that my body developed around this story and embedded it within my cells and tissue. This story begins with my mother's being hugely pregnant—"as big as a house with *you*"— when she makes the unfortunate discovery that my father is "seeing someone else." Since the tale was always as familiar as my own hands, I never had to ask for a retelling, or for clarification and a few more specifics (for example, how did my mother determine the identity of the other woman?); I knew how my stomach would have clenched, seeing my mother's lips thinned into a straight line of accusation aimed, it seemed, directly at me. But I didn't know what would invite my mother to insert this narrative into everyday conversation, what might make her suddenly go hurtling down memory lane toward the expected but abrupt dead end—much like the one outside our house where First Street suddenly petered out without a barrier, not even a reflective warning, into the tangle of low-hanging trees and scrubby brush alongside Cottonwood Creek.

"And there I was after all those years. On my own. With a nine-year-old little girl. And a *baby*."

My mother would punctuate this with her hands splayed in front of her, palms outstretched and empty. Mouth twisted to one side, gray eyes widened, she'd slowly shake her head to indicate how dumbfounded she remained, no matter how many years separated her from those two conjoined events: finding she was pregnant after so many years of trying for a second child, followed almost immediately by my father's betrayal and abandonment. If my mother's mystified head-turning did not signal closure, the gesture suggested resignation, perhaps, an ending to the story for her, however unsatisfying. Yet there *you* were. Here I am still, apparently, her story in my hands now as if it belongs to me.

I've examined this story a thousand times over the years, turning it over and trying to look at it with unbiased eyes. But its truth was obvious: BL had left town and taken with him the "other woman," a former Miss Texas runner-up who'd most recently been employed as my father's secretary. She'd "hooked him like a fish," as my mother put it, always sucking at her teeth, marveling at her stupidity, while I visualized a woman with silvery fishhooks for hands.

If I've entertained myself by imagining that I call up BL, or corner him at some excruciatingly awkward "family" get-together, and request a quick verification of a few of the finer points, I haven't gotten very far with those fantasies. I've never had access to the precise words necessary for asking what it is I think I want to know. How do you ask how it was when, fifteen years later, exactly—one month after I'd turned fifteen—that second wife with the fishhook hands caught another man? Now it's too late to schedule the interview. BL is gone—genuinely dead, this time.

*

My sister is napping, her mouth slightly open, her head on a pillow propped against the passenger-side window of this blood-red rental. I admire her ease in drifting off, regardless of location or conditions—such a useful skill! I've been trying to remember when I was very young and my sister and I slept in the same room, in matching white French provincial twin beds, but that was such a narrow span of years. It's easier to recall our sharing that bedroom as middle-aged women in the early spring of 2000, when our mother was dying. In the white house on First Street, we kept the days tidy and orderly to comfort our mother, but also each other, and held tightly to our familiar circle of three. Gradually, all those hours structured by the quotidian were stripped, pared down to the essential, completely emptied, finally, when, all too soon, that circle suddenly contracted and our mother let go.

*

How our mother had stayed in Bay City after the divorce, I don't know. Everything about everyone was common knowledge in that too-small town, and my family's difference was obvious. If BL had been dead, that would have been one thing, but in the early 1960s, the reasons for his perpetual absence were not common or relatable. I knew only one other kid in elementary school, Carolina Simmons, whose father was also "somewhere else," and whose mother, like mine, worked as a secretary. Carolina had no siblings, which felt much the same as my having the one sister so much older and already in college by the time I was eight. But Carolina lived with her mother and her grandparents on the outskirts of town in a ranch house filled with overstuffed chintz and painted portraits of family members; they looked like a family. Drawn together by the recognition of our otherness, our marked difference from other classmates, Carolina and I spent hours turning over the few clues we had about our fathers, until the summer I was going on ten, when BL was passing through town one hot afternoon and thought to call up and take me for a Coke. Then Carolina and I began to imagine making long distance calls to these fathers we found so mysterious. The main problem (of many) with this was that we didn't know where hers was.

It seems to me that whenever I spent the night at Carolina's—infinitely better than sleepovers at my house because her grandmother offered a staggering variety of junk food and sugary breakfast options—the reassuring figure of her grandfather was always visible, frequently astride a John Deere riding lawn mower, a cigar in his mouth. He'd drive Carolina to my house with her bike in the back of his Jeep, then return later and, with no complaints, wait until she was ready to go home; he helped with the construction of elaborate dioramas and paper mache projects for school, including a particularly impressive two-foot bright-blue whale I remember I admired immensely.

If my mother worried about my friendship with Carolina, I don't think her concern was from serious consideration of what trouble two fatherless daughters might find to get into together. That was part of a much more complicated subject that my mother and I never discussed.

At fifteen Carolina ran off with a twenty-five-year-old Vietnam vet, and I've often wondered what became of her, if she ever found out where her father was and called him up, as we'd imagined. I know Carolina's mother married twice more, and to whom—this was Bay City, after all, and for years, my mother was still there on First Street to gather news and provide updates. I'd thought I was escaping from that town when I drove off two days after my high school graduation, desperate enough to have pre-registered for college classes that summer. Even today, seeing the name of that town on the map, I can remember the visceral relief of pulling away from the white house all those years ago, the Eagles blasting from the rolled-down windows, and the old silver Impala packed with everything I thought I wanted. It was years before I wondered what my mother must have felt, standing in the driveway and watching me go, waving until I had turned the corner and was out of sight.

But I think I know why my mother stayed in Bay City in 1960, when, "overnight," she found herself a divorced woman with a whiny nine-year-old and a colicky newborn, unable to get a credit card, even, because without a husband she suddenly had no value: she had nowhere else to go. She'd settled into that small coastal town at twenty-two—a newlywed—then eleven years later, she stayed because that's where she'd made home; her displacement was not a physical one. I can close my eyes right now and effortlessly situate myself in that house on First Street: It's always summer and I'm always alone (although obviously neither can be true); my skin smells of chlorine from the public pool where I take swim lessons. The house wears that scent all its own, a blend of pork roast, pine cleaner, and my mother's White Shoulders, a bottle always on the stout mahogany dresser, its image reflected in the curved mirror. The quiet in those darkened, chilled rooms is thick and heavy, the Venetian blinds and drapes shut tight for as much protection as possible from the sun's heat and the town's gossip, and the only light in the living room comes from the flickering television and those three small rectangle windows in the front door, stair steps pointing the way of escape—out onto the front porch with its single wrought iron post, through the thick green St. Augustine, into the street. A heavy drone-like silence, never quite dissipated by the canned laughter of television reruns or the tinny country-western tunes on the kitchen radio turned low; the brass door chimes in the hallway, three dangling cylinders of varying lengths that make a cacophony of clanking brass when accidentally struck; the hollow echoes of the black rotary phone on its built-in shelf, jangling too suddenly, too loudly, jarring everyone's nerves.

*

What I didn't know until after my mother died and we

started sifting through all her things was that BL had designed that house on First Street. When the rolled-up plans were discovered in the attic, I'd immediately recognized his engineer-precise handwriting, and then, almost supernaturally, as if summoned into presence, there was BL a few days later, in the living room with us in our recently deceased mother's house, sitting in her chair. Again I unrolled the plans, offering them to him along with a university yearbook also unearthed; I'd located his photo in that year's junior class and bookmarked the page to show him who he was all those years ago.

Here's the contradiction I've always intuited, I suppose: Loss isn't always merely the regrettable absence of what's gone missing. Sometimes a shadowy but distinct presence sticks around, a thin, specious incarnation of its former self, a malingering Might-Have-Been taking up residence within some abrupt vacancy. There, the negligent Ne'er-Do-Well grows quite at home, subsisting on others' words and stories. And then loss—that shady, lazy revenant—may prove itself both surprisingly dependable and constant.

He'd learned of our whereabouts from his sister, our aunt with whom my sister stays in touch, and he wanted something from us. He looked much the same as the last time I'd seen him, almost ten years before, dressed in one of his old-man onesies, a light-blue zippered jumpsuit, with a strangely formal pair of cordovan-colored dress shoes.

He was too at ease in that living room, sprawled in my (dead) mother's chair. He took little interest in any of what we had to show him, not even the yearbook, which turned out never to have belonged to him at all but to my mother's brother who was also at the university that year. And while he remembered sitting at a kitchen table "somewhere else" and drawing out the footprint of this house to be built on First Street, he'd lost interest in this home and its contents long ago.

*

We are descending into the tornado-shaped part of the state, and the landscape flattens as mesquite and scrub replace the live oaks of the hill country we've left behind this morning. We have another five or six inches to travel on the road map.

I could say that my sister and I are dutiful daughters, trying to do the right thing after a parent's death. But we know we're making this long journey for my mother, who'll be invisible in the pew beside us at BL's viewing tomorrow, unnoticed by whoever else shows up. I'll wear that silver bracelet of hers and we'll imagine her holding her two girls firmly in her arms.

We find our way to Route 77, a straight black line on the map descending through the King Ranch. To the east and west of that vast property, the state begins to narrow, forming a long, distended triangle—a swirling funnel, I imagine, that will suck this red van into the sky and spin us southwards for another hour and a half.

Joanne Proulx

The Zoo

A little girl with a blonde pixie-cut riding a hand-me-down bike, tasselled with sparkly, blue streamers. Both of them a little scuffed up, but sturdy and fast. The girl has more energy than can rightly be contained in her little girl body; a live wire, a sprite, she can't weigh fifty pounds. She bikes all over her small-town neighbourhood. Likes her own company. Fears nothing but birds.

On a hot day in June, she bikes to the zoo alone. Skips the animals, the buffalo, the ostriches sluggish with heat, hidden away in their dusty enclosures; they often make her sad. That day she heads straight down to the river. By the easy slide of cool water, she, who is always flying, slows down. Maybe she'll drop her bike, there, on the bank, lots of shady spots beneath the trees. Maybe she'll pull off her shoes. Wade into the water. See what the pebbles are doing.

Someone calls out. She turns her head. Standing beside a car in a clearing of far-flung trees, a man waves her over. Says he wants to show her something. *Come here. You have to see this.* Obedient child circles back. Dodges a few maples and one picnic table. Stops by the rear bumper. Weird. There are never cars on the grass in the picnic area. She plants both feet on the ground.

The car is fancy, long and black, much nicer than her family's. Windows down, back door open. Shiny silver trim she'd run her finger along if the man wasn't looking. *You have to come closer*, he says. He has dark hair. A dress shirt, like her father wears for work. *You can't see from there.* He raises his eyebrows, waggles his hand into the backseat. The girl walks her bike forward, one two, one two, her sneakers slipping a little on the grass, hands squeezing the rubber grips.

Her front tire almost bumps the open door. Still, she has to lean forward, over the handlebars to see into the back of the car. There's another man in there, sitting on the black leather seat, with his pants pulled down over his knees. Odd. It takes a moment to register. He's staring at her and jiggling his penis.

She looks to the man who called her over. Hands resting loosely on the frame of the door, he smiles; this is no mistake. Finally startled, the girl pushes back, peddles spinning backwards, one catches her shin. Clear of the bumper, she flips her bike around and flies down the path by the river, too scared to look back, streamers crackling, heart a racket.

She is eight, maybe nine-years-old; she doesn't tell anyone. Because things like this don't happen. She's never heard of something like this happening. She doesn't have the words.

But whenever she thinks about those men, she feels scared. Like her parents would be upset if they found out, mad even. Like somehow it was her fault.

One evening at the table her mom reads from the paper: a story about a man being arrested for exposing himself to children in their neighbourhood. The girl's belly clenches. There's a brightness in her head, a neural sizzle. *Things like this do happen.* She pushes peas around with her fork. No one notices her quiet, she of a hundred questions, she of the constant chatter. Dinner ends. Red-faced, she helps her parents clear the table.

The girl stops riding to the zoo. Starts going places with other kids, moving in a pack. Less sure in a world capable of dark surprises, she pads her body with other bodies, draws in her borders, dims down her light. By the time she's a young woman in college no one needs to tell her to walk with her keys between her fingers when she crosses a parking lot at night. And by then so many other things have happened to her, to her body, the incident by the river has become...what? An early lesson? An initiation of sorts?

Later she often feels lucky that the men she met as a child were still sniffing around the edges, teeth at the throat but not quite ready to bite. Maybe they'd never be ready. Maybe they weren't rapists or killers, just plain old pedophile-exhibitionists.

Who knows? It would have been so easy for them to toss her into the car, toss her bike into the river.

A couple decades later, on the same hot, dreamy kind of day, the woman is on a city corner with five or six other people waiting on the light. From every vehicle, the spill of radio music; it's a good day for humming along. A car swings slow round the corner, all of its windows down. At each, a jutted elbow. The four men inside all stare hard at one spot in the small congregation, laser focused. Despite the heat, the woman feels a chill as she follows their eyes to her daughter, standing just next to her. Small for her age, years away from puberty.

That night at dinner, the woman tells her kids about the day at the zoo. Tells them that all these years later what really gets her is that there were two of them. Two men who talked it over, picked the spot, chose to spend a bright, summer day hunting down a child. Unbuckling their perversions–bold, but hidden—in the shade of old trees, by the cool of the river. Perfect shorts and t-shirt weather.

Mr. Grimsby

I woke up one morning but wished I hadn't.

My mood was no better the next day. Or the next. Someone plucked my brain out via my nostrils, like a Pharaonic embalmer. That's how it felt.

The blue devils, a cousin of mine used to call it. He suffered from the same, occasional malediction. Until he drowned himself.

I preferred to call it a visit from Mr. Grimsby, who I pictured as a stretchy Victorian gentleman with overflowing sideburns and a meerschaum pipe.

Mr. Grimsby hung about for days on end. Months, sometimes. While I languished in bed, he alternately puffed on his pipe and trimmed his sideburns.

Three weeks into his latest stay—the tobacco reek was beyond tolerance—I persuaded myself to take some air.

"I'll be back," I said to my guest as I closed the door.

Mr. Grimsby relit his meerschaum—and grinned bitterly.

*

A writer can't afford new books, so I stormed the public library and strolled out the door shouldering every self-help title I could find.

Over the next month, I read every one of them. Most of them were horribly written.

"Imagine two balls on the edge of a cliff. The balls represent ANXIETY and DESPAIR. Slowly run towards the balls. Now *kick* the balls." When I read that, I chuckled. That boosted my mood a little—but not enough. *None* of the books proved helpful in the end, so I poured them down the Return Chute and crossed the street to my doctor's office.

Dr. Aldermaston was a glum, sunburned man with one undulating eyebrow. He looked like Van Gogh's *Dr. Gachet* only less cheerful.

He leaned on his elbow while I tried to articulate my inexpressible distress.

When I finally stopped talking, my doctor stared at me for a silent minute. Then he sighed and said, “I feel the same way, sometimes.”

“I feel that way *all* the time, lately.”

“Me too,” sighed Aldermaston.

We both admired the floor for a while.

“Can you suggest a good psychiatrist?” I asked, at last.

“The good ones are usually busy.”

“I’d settle for a mediocre one.”

My physician either half-grinned or grimaced and said, “I can think of several offhand.”

We settled on Wanda Holloway. The name rolled off the tongue. She was the only psychiatrist taking patients at the time.

"When will I see her?" I asked.

"As soon as possible," said Aldermaston. "The waitlist is five or six months, at least."

"Five or six months?" I repeated.

"A *least.*"

I pictured a man laboring to hold a boulder over his head for 180 consecutive days.

"What … should I do in the meantime?" I asked, in disbelief.

Aldermaston shrugged and said, "Have you tried self-help books?"

It was my turn to sigh.

*

For *seven* months, I spent most days in bed, watching the walls blacken with tobacco smoke and Mr. Grimsby's sideburn trimmings pile up on the floor. I was close to choking on the latter when the phone rang.

It was Wanda Holloway's secretary.

"Are you free tomorrow at four?" she asked.

"Yes," I said. It was the first word I'd spoken in days.

I hung up the phone.

Then I burrowed out of the bedroom.

*

I turned right, left, and left again through a beige maze into the office of Dr. Wanda Holloway. She was sitting at a desk strewn with ceiling-scrapers of erratically stacked folders, busily writing in a blue notebook held almost to her nose and paying no attention to me whatsoever.

When I grew tired of standing, I took a seat across from her.

Eventually, she set down her notebook. Then she squinted at me and said, "How's the view from the 25th floor?"

I felt confused—and must have looked it, too.

"Aren't you the mayor?"

"I'm an author," I said, mincing words. Mayors and authors alike are paid fabricators. Though only the former are paid well.

Dr. Holloway exchanged one folder for another, shuffled through its contents and said:

"Right. The writer."

She wrote something down. Minutes later, she was still writing. I hadn't been that productive in ages.

"Would you like me to talk about my childhood?" I asked, by way of underlining my existence.

Dr. Holloway was too busy scribbling to answer. When her pen dried up, she reached for another one—and brushed a pair of manila mountains with her elbow.

Down they came, like the twin towers.

I helped her pick up every last paper. One of them was a menu for Shanghai Lily, a restaurant I'd always wanted to try.

By the time we finished, my hour was up.

"I can see you next week at the same time," said Dr. Holloway, who'd resumed writing.

I nodded doubtfully—and stood up.

"One more thing."

I turned. Dr. Holloway was squinting at me again. She took a bite out of her pen and said:

"Good luck in the election."

"Thanks," I said, as I stepped out the door.

*

"Holloway isn't working for me," I told Aldermaston, days later.

My physician sighed.

"She didn't work for me, either," he said.

"Who else can you recommend?"

"I wouldn't recommend it."

I blinked. So did Aldermaston. Then he said:

"I mean, you'll have to wait again. Just as long, probably."

"Another seven months?"

"At *least*."

Aldermaston had been leaning on his left elbow. He switched to the right and said:

"If you leave her care, you'll be taking your chances."

"I'll take my chances," I said.

Aldermaston shrugged and said, "I don't blame you."

He pulled a notebook out of a drawer. Something was scrawled on the cover. Probably *Index of Middling Head-Shrinkers.* He thumbed through it.

"I've heard mixed things about O'Dowd."

"O'Dowd it is," I said.

Aldermaston sighed.

"I'll set it up," he said.

*

For the next ten months—the time it took to get an appointment with O'Dowd—I spent most of my days at home with Mr. Grimsby, venturing out-of-doors only sporadically.

During one of those rare al fresco moments, walking downtown, I spotted an old friend crossing the street. Though I was sure he hadn't seen me, he was heading in my direction.

I ducked into an alley. And waited until he walked by.

This happened a number of times, actually. Throughout my Blue Period, I made excellent use of lampposts and mailboxes. Though talking to acquaintances would have done me a world of good, I couldn't face them.

I still don't understand why.

*

Dr. O'Dowd had wide eyes. The widest I'd ever seen. It was disconcerting.

There were no certificates on his walls. There was a painting of an owl. *That* was disconcerting, too. I've never trusted owls.

While I listed my symptoms, O'Dowd and the owl watched intently. The instant I stopped talking, the former leaped to his feet and heaved open the top drawer of his filing cabinet, which doubled as a treasure chest brimming with drug samples.

"They have some beautiful pharmaceuticals these days," he said, rooting through them. "If the first one doesn't work, there's always the next one—and the next."

He tossed me a credit card-sided box full of blue pills.

I watched astonished as his eyes grew even wider.

"You're going to *love* them," he said.

As it turned out, the blue pills, which I took for a couple months, did nothing. So O'Dowd wrote me a script for pink ones. *Those* made me dizzy, so he tagged on some octagonal cream-colored ones that resolved the dizziness but triggered hypertension. Thus the yellow pills. I passed a prescription for the latter to my pharmacist.

She frowned—checked her computer—and sternly shook her head.

"If you'd taken these with all the others," she said, "You'd be dead."

That doesn't sound so bad, I thought at the time.

*

I flushed all my medications down the toilet. They weren't helping anyway.

This was a poor idea, in hindsight. Soon I was trembling

and sweating at all hours. I had a peculiar sensation, too, of electricity bounding up and down my spine and out my hair follicles. Whenever I winced, Mr. Grimsby threw his head back and guffawed.

It took roughly a month for the withdrawal symptoms to subside. They were worse than the depression, actually.

When I went back to Aldermaston, he thumbed through his Index and sighed.

"No one's available, I'm afraid."

I wasn't sure if that was good news or bad.

"What do you suggest?" I asked.

My doctor rubbed his chin—he hadn't shaved in days—and said:

"Would you like to try any medications?"

"I'm trying to cut back," I said.

I watched his eyebrow undulate.

"If something opens up," he said, "I'll call you. I'm afraid that's all I can do."

"No problem," I said. Even though it was.

As I left Aldermaston's office, he was staring emptily at the wall.

I was really starting to worry about him.

*

I was at my wit's end with Mr. Grimsby. He never slept anymore but stayed up all night watching war documentaries and laughing uproariously. *I* stayed up watching *him*—and wondering if I should grow sideburns.

I wanted him out of my life.

But I was getting used to him, too.

That really scared the hell out of me.

*

The phone rang one morning. It was Aldermaston.

"I have good news!" he said.

I'd never known Aldermaston to use an exclamation point before. He used another one:

"I found you a psychiatrist!"

I was still waiting for the good news.

"A *competent* psychiatrist," he added.

"Really?" I said, incredulous.

"Really," he said.

I was afraid to ask how long the wait for a competent psychiatrist was. I asked anyway.

"She can see you next week!" exclaimed Aldermaston, for the third time.

"That's unbelievable," I said.

The strange new Aldermaston laughed.

"It never happens," he said. "But it happened."

I was dumbstruck.

"Thanks," I said, eventually.

When I hung up the phone, Mr. Grimsby was leering at me. I leered back. Then I crawled back into bed.

*

Dr. Beverly Shaw worked out of her home—a brick Victorian on the less-adventurous side of town.

Strolling up to the door, I noticed a ginger cat blinking in the window. A window cat—particularly a ginger one—is an excellent omen, always.

As the cat purred on my lap, I told its owner everything I could think of. I spoke more in an hour, I'm sure, than I had in years. Dr. Shaw listened quietly. But when I talked about Holloway, she stopped me.

"Please tell me you're making that up," she said.

I assured her I wasn't.

She was less doubtful about O'Dowd.

"The O'Dowds of the world," she said, shaking her head, "are all too common. I've cleaned up one or two of their messes."

"Do you think I'm clean-uppable?" I asked, hopefully.

Dr. Shaw smiled.

"Someone seems to think so," she said.

The ginger cat was licking my wrist.

A cat—particularly a ginger one—is an excellent judge of

character.

For the first time in ages, I felt hopeful.

I even smiled.

*

After seeing Beverly for a few months, I was feeling somewhat better. I was *looking* better too, and no longer dodged mirrors like a Romanian count.

The same couldn't be said for Mr. Grimsby. He hadn't trimmed his sideburns in weeks. He'd developed a tremor. Every morning, I heard the meerschaum rattling against his incisors.

When I started writing again, Grimsby withdrew to a kitchen corner and puffed away poutily. He sat there staring out the window all day.

That's where I left him one afternoon, en route to the park.

The trees have leaves on them, I almost said aloud. It had been a long time since I'd noticed.

I saw a school friend jogging on the path. Instead of jumping into a bush, I stopped to talk.

"What have you been up to?" he asked.

As I stood there wondering how to answer, I caught a glimpse of another familiar face. It was Aldermaston. He was cutting through the park with his dachshund. I didn't say anything—speaking to one's physician out-of-office is the last taboo of modern life—but we exchanged nods.

He was looking better, too.

*

I woke up one morning and was glad I had.

I stepped out of bed. I walked from one room to the next.

There was no sign of Mr. Grimsby.

His luggage was gone.

The tobacco smell was gone.

Mr. Grimsby was gone.

I took a deep breath.

I hadn't felt that good in a long time.

Ten things I would be taking to the grave had I not written them down here

1

The affair with Vivian. I'm sure Carole never guessed.

2

That finest of days I've been keeping to myself: aged 37, talking my way past police, army and special forces—with not a paper on my person—I entered a British nuclear submarine. Supposedly impregnable, the HMS Talent was freshly docked at a certain European landing stage. The crowds were marshalled, flags flew, a band was playing. Coming to the police-army-specials onion layers of security, I told the police I knew the Consul, then chatting on the other side of the cordon, and I gave him a wave. I told the army I was an international freelance journalist. (Has he got accreditation? Hm, what would international accreditation look like? No idea, let him through.) Sticking to English (I was after all a freelance international whatjamacallit), I told the special forces with their brushed-carbon-steel riot guns and body armour I was *The Press*. As the band started *God Save the Queen*, the monarch at the time, I was invited to the little gangplank and down the hatch. Not a place for claustrophobics. A political organisation detailed me to do this, to test the British navy and its claims of security. To see if these nuclear submarines really were safe from anything, terrorists, lunatics, me. I'm not supposed to tell of this—the Talent was decommissioned only this year. Keeping the details secret has kept me out of jail. But they're out now, I've confessed. If challenged it will simply be my word against mine.

3

I've aimed to take with me the number of people I've slept with. Why wait? Well, say any number—one out of a hat—and there are such judgements. The receivers of the information are so ready to make assumptions, to come out with words like *fidelity*, *trust*, *marriage*. Then there's *cheat*, *Casanova, stud.* Had I been better-looking might this modest number have been more?—*Discuss.* I have used restraint—when Debbie sat on the sofa arm in her red dress looking a blue-eyedly, blondely million dollars, pounds, definitely ready for certain moves, I wasn't going to make them. Of course I've been checked too, held back—and, equally, impetuous—how did I get wrapped up in Felicity of all people, and out there in the street? But back to the hard data. For a while I thought I would arrange for the number to be disclosed, more, for names too, in a final collection of fiction due out after my passing. On the acknowledgements page maybe. This has its problems, however. A curious feature of being dead is that you can't make sure something gets done. Logically too, there would be little difference between coming out now or later, bringing me back to my point about judgements, the cad, cheater. Wanker. Eighteen, by the way. The number doesn't mean much, not to me.

4

The extent of my masturbating. Were it not for taking this to the grave I would have liked to see a competition to guess the rate per week. A raffle at a street party, say, marking some royal jubilee. How many sweets in the jar? And how many times a week, of this? It's a puzzle why this should stay secret, I have much more unspeakable habits, far beyond the bawdy. But, dead or alive, who admits to peeing in the shower. Or the sink.

5

To take with me below the ground: the frustrations of living with idiocies for which I had no counter-arguments, no solution. Two examples. Carole thinks if you are posting something to Australia you have to find out the exchange rate so that you know the cost of postage in Australian dollars.

You then work backwards to know what the postage must be. Idiocy number two: a car boot, shocking to the eye, choked with wellingtons, trainers, beach shoes, boots, sandals, flipflops, Doc Martens, brothel creepers, boating shoes, wooden cantabrian albarcas, desert whatnots, galoshes, ostensibly ready for all eventualities (except being able to use the boot). The boot creaked open in the search for an umbrella, for our short walk to a candlelit supper. At the sight of this heap my mind turned from thoughts of love and pleasure. Instead I thought bulldozers and waste tips, and Sigmund Freud.

6

It was a Saturday in a supermarket, I was doing normal shopping in the aisles. It was a sunny day out, my trolley was good.

—Come this way, please.

Store detectives? I hadn't shoplifted since I was a student. Even then it was just a few steaks, toothpaste, razor blades. Was this about some frozen fish I slipped inside my jacket long ago? Surely not.

—Come, please, you're quite safe with us.

I was escorted down long, long tunnels, dank and echoing, probably below the Thames. Into a room underground with an enormous dark table (James Bond, war games). I was offered a cup of tea. It was tea or gin and tonic.

They asked me to join MI5.

I remember what was said.

—We know that when you were sixteen you were a first-class shot with a rifle.

One in a thousand.

—Really?

—We have the actual targets, with the holes in the centre.

—That's remarkable.

The reason I've kept this incident to myself is knowing no one would believe me. There I go again, they'd say, making things up.

7

Picture the clearout, on the same day as my funeral. No pornography, that was cleared out years ago. No correspondence with Vivian, telltale receipts, photos, hotel brochures—all shredded or deleted. However the carefully-boxed two-tone spectator shoes, as they're called, the white buckskin and brown suede oxfords—will come to light, but not their secret: for years I've tap-danced alone in rooms. He's always dead now but he wasn't always: I am in love with Fred Astaire.

8

My family know I write fiction but they don't read a word of it. That has made me immune. I've trashed my father, mother, my only brother. Mocked the family dog, huge, soppy Dino. On his fictionally first holiday in years, he ran into a field strewn with landmines. It was weeks before his remains could be recovered.

9

Ordinarily I can't say—I signed a paper—if I joined MI5. But here I will: I didn't. If challenged it will be their word corroborating mine.

10

I've had an imaginary friend for years. He's been a great support, a good listener and with none of those idiocies. His name is Otto Flake. Now by most definitions I am a writer, and may reincarnate as one again. In that event I shall try hard to return his kindness and goodwill, tell more of him, him and Miss Lumia. There are resemblances: they aren't a world away from Vivian and me, Miss Lumia and Otto Flake.

Why It's Important to Start Off Cheap

The following will come off as bad or immoral, I'm sure, but most of the key players no longer live among us, and I promise the connections will come together, probably. As a young teenager, I took up distance running. I'm talking I took off kind of like the character Forrest Gump did later in his life. I'm no psychologist, but I would bet I ran away from something: My father wanting me to work with him ten hours a day at a one-person textile supply company manufacturing something called "replacement aprons," made out of calf skin, little belts meant for spinning frames so that yarn could run without snagging on metal. Or he wanted me to plain drive around endlessly with him in his DeSoto, or his Ford Galaxie, or his VW Bug. Whatever, I took up running. I ran around the block (.6 miles) and I ran around two blocks (exactly 1mile) or I ran around the entire neighborhood (1.7 miles) or I ran to the county airport and back (4.3 miles). I ran to the airport and around the neighborhood (6 miles even). I ran and ran and ran.

Right before I turned fifteen years old, I decided I wanted to run the length of a marathon. I got up on a Saturday morning and took off, with all these mathematical distances in mind, to and from the airport, way out on highways 72 and 25, past Mr. Bratcher's Gulf station, past the Quick Way, on beyond Sunken Garden's Lounge, and the Highway 25 Drive-In movie theatre, loop after loop, past the wastewater treatment plant where I'd gone on field trips third/fifth/seventh grades. I plodded along, wearing a tank top and what would be now considered short-shorts.

I'd say I might've been five or eight miles in to my project when I heard my father's putt-putt-putting VW behind me, right there on highway 25. People honked their horns at him, seeing as I ran, at best, five miles an hour. He came up beside me and waved hard, a big smile on his face, as if saying, "Hey, in case you get hit by a car or fall over dead, I'm here." Only later on in life—after his death, when I was twenty-four—could I recognize his good-heartedness, and how he meant well.

At the time, I might've given him the finger. What an asshole, I.

I didn't make it 26.1 miles on that day. I made it 20.1 as it ended up. I came around to the end of our little driveway, knowing that I needed to get back out to the county airport and back, plus around the neighborhood, and I couldn't. It took me something like four-plus hours, as I remember. (Aside: When I was seventeen, I ran a five mile race and clocked in at 27:19, in Columbia SC, so I wasn't a pure-tee idiot, if you ask me).

Man, I rubber-legged down the driveway feeling like a loser. My father pulled the VW behind me and, again all smiles, said, "I'm proud of you, son."

I don't know if I answered. I know that I got in bed soon thereafter, and couldn't move for forty-eight hours.

And then he said, "You know, I think you might have lost too much salt in that run, from all the sweat. You need a beer." Although the notion of "carbo-loading" hadn't appeared in the southeast yet, in a way my father was correct. He said, "I think you need a beer every time you go out on a long run."

He went inside and came out with a Pabst Blue Ribbon.

Uh-oh. At the time, the legal age for buying beer in South Carolina was eighteen. Those were the days.

I started going out on long runs three or four times a day afterwards.

*

This friend of mine named Paul moved down from New Jersey during my eleventh grade year, for his chemist father got a job with Parke-Davis. Dr. Borick knew more about everything, I thought, from golf to fatherhood (two daughters, four sons). A good Catholic, he'd studied microbiology and chemistry at Le Moyne College, Syracuse, and Columbia University. He owned patents, which no one I knew could brag about. He cooked. He grab-assed and made fun of his children's friends. I loved the guy. Although Dr. Borick and my friend Paul lived in the upper middle class, neither of them acted in a better-than-thou realm often seen in the South.

Aside: The first time Paul came over to my house, he had this dog with him named Doc, a big, really stupid, friendly Irish Setter. I kind of worried about my parents meeting Paul, seeing as he had hair halfway down his back. Paul came over so we could go out and throw the Frisbee at the gigantic lawn in front of Self Memorial Hospital. My mother came out in the carport. Doc let out a fart that pretty much took over the entire neighborhood. My mom kind of gagged. Later on, throwing the Frisbee, we learned that Doc might've had some kind of vision problems, seeing as the disc hit him flat on the forehead before he jumped, stunned, doh-dee-doh, what happened?

My hometown.

Anyway, Dr. Borick bought *cases* of Pabst Blue Ribbon, and left them, stacked, in his garage, hot. I'm talking eight or ten at a time. Not Heineken, Miller High Life, Budweiser, Coors that might've been hard to get in South Carolina in 1976, the supposedly wonderful Strohs that emerged from the state of Tennessee. I'm not talking about Falstaff or Ballentine. At some point Paul and I thought, He won't ever notice a six-pack missing, or an entire twenty-four beers. We scooped them up and took them off to the trunk of my Opel, or the trunk of his Bondo-slathered Datsun. Later, we drank those hot PBRs in the woods beside his house, or the woods off to the side of my house, or while driving down the back roads around both of our houses (sorry, but it's true), or at the Auto Drive-In run by our friend George Zouras's father. Or in the parking lot of Greenwood High School before classes. Or right after Paul told his daddy that he'd go off to Catholic mass, but instead came over to my house on Sunday mornings in order to see what my blue collar father had to say about things. My parents weren't churchgoers. My parents despised most Christians, if it matters.

We drank those warm Pabst Blue Ribbons, not knowing what a cold, refreshing, normal, invigorating, non-idiotic beer could be. Well, I kind of did, what with the cold beers my dad doled over whenever I ran over ten miles, but somehow I thought it anathema to reward myself for only being able to steal beer from a friend's father's garage.

*

Right before I went off to college, a juke joint ex-train station opened up in Hodges, a place called Jackson Station, run by two gay men named Gerald Jackson and Stevie Bryant. Here's the story: Gerald bought the built-in-1870 train station for a dollar, with a promise to move it out of town. It cost thousands of dollars to relocate the building down the road a half mile, to land he owned across from his momma's house. Gerald was a Navy veteran, a college graduate, a man with a plan. In the beginning, one could bring his or her own albums to play. Then it turned into bands like the Swimming Pool Qs, Reverend Billy Wirtz, the Accelerators, Nappy Brown, Tinsley Ellis, Glenn Phillips, Widespread Panic, Love Tractor, and the Georgia Satellites playing there until five in the morning. Bikers, college kids, rednecks, preppies, Blacks and Whites, gays and straights, doctors, lawyers, and upcoming punks like me hung out at Jackson Station.

Gerald—who ended up getting hit in the head by a redneck wielding a pickax, surviving, then living in a VA hospital for a decade or so—made it a point to offer beer that most people of Greenwood County would never come across: Heineken, Grolsch, Sapporo, Asahi, Harp, San Miguel, Guinness, Peroni, Fosters lager, and so on. Hell, Coors. He kept a large chalkboard above the bar advertising the kitchen's specials, most of which involved hotdogs and cheeseburgers, but one time that I remember, the PLT, as a joke: a Placenta/Lettuce/Tomato sandwich, because a heifer out back gave birth to a baby bull, named George, after my father.

Anyway, I tried all these beers. I prided myself on the beer bottle collection I kept hidden from my mother, in the crawlspace of the house where I got brought up. Amstel, Kronenbourg, Export 33, Pilsner, Bitburger, St. Pauli's Girl,

Beck's, Carlsberg, Molson, Moosehead, and so on. Tsingtao. Carlton. Tecate. Dos Equis. I squeaked those things down, just for the bottles, but knew that I missed something.

Listen, I was eighteen, on my way to college, and ready to mesmerize my college roommate with tales of world travel, due to my Beers of the World knowledge.

But you know what? Zero of those beers matched my love for Pabst Blue Ribbon—either cold or warm. I've drunk lesser-known beers—Black Label, and a flat-out generic-named beer, Beer, come to mind, bought at a place called the Drop-In Store in Greenville—and I thought, This is close, but it doesn't quite qualify. How excited did I get when Dennis Hopper's character, Frank Booth, yells out, "Heineken? Fuck that shit! Pabst Blue Ribbon!" in the movie *Blue Velvet*?

So. Here's the thing. Hand me an IPA? Hahahahaha. Give me one of those micro-brews that's so chic and omnipresent and I'll hand it back, or pour it out into a potted plant, or go buy a BB pistol in order to use said micro-brew as a target. Or I might actually drink the thing, seeing as I'd be attending some kind of uncomfortable affair if the sponsors offered micro-brews solely. But I wouldn't be happy. No, more than likely I'd stand there hoping my tie turned into a noose. I'd look at my watch and think about the time my father offered over the first PBR, or drinking warm Pabsts in the woods as an underaged teenager. In my mind, I'd map out the closest convenience store that sold the best beer to ever come out of Milwaukee.

George Singleton

Thanksgiving

Once a week, around 7:30 in the morning, I meet up with three other ex-professors over bagels and coffee, sometimes coffee and cinnamon buns if we've given up on diets. I'm the youngster in the group, at age sixty-four. The other three men are emeritus, aged 75, 70, and 69. I think that they accept me because I'm the most liable to drive around and knock over mailboxes with a baseball bat in gated communities, then tell them about it with cream cheese covering half my upper lip.

We do not talk about the weather. We do not talk much about sports, wives, car engine repairs, house improvements, idiot colleagues of the past, obituaries, and anything else that might make us depressed or flustered. It's all how to save America, and the books we've been reading.

Two days ago, I looked across the table at the seventy-five year-old man—a guy who became an administrator after about thirty years of teaching foreign languages—and said, "Hey, tell me about that time you got hit by a car."

He should be writing this essay, by the way. I don't know if he's embarrassed about the story, or what. I'll change his name to Frank. It's a good strong name, and a wonderful adjective. Frank has cycled across Europe, and up and down the East Coast. He stands about six-two, maybe weighs 180, and keeps his head shaved. He can talk eloquently about French wines, the World Cup, bad roofers, *Don Quixote,* whatever. Most of the time I sit there thinking, Please don't ask me a question. Ten years ago he hired me for some kind of fancy endowed chair thing to teach fiction workshops and Grit Lit. I've always been scared of him.

Frank said, "Well, I was riding on a two-land road I'd ridden for twenty years. At a four-way stop, I stopped. I motioned to this woman 'Can I go first?' She waved her hand.

A mile down the road I was going about eighteen miles an hour, looking at my peddles, when I saw, peripherally, the bumper of her car."

This accident happened in 2017. He'd just retired.

Somehow I didn't know the whole story—only that Frank got in an accident, but he'd be okay. He said, "When I woke up, the police and a fire truck were there. Evidently I got my left foot out of the peddle, but then skidded across the asphalt and banged my head into a cement curb. I wore my helmet, which saved me, I guess."

Of course I said, "Damn, man."

He said, "I was in ICU for a few days because they couldn't get my heart rate down."

No broken bones. Road rash everywhere. Memory problems.

*

Now, all of this story brought on flashbacks, ones that I think about infrequently: When I was fourteen, in Greenwood, South Carolina, on highway 254, a woman hit me from behind at fifty-five miles an hour, while I rode my tragically-heavy Schwinn ten-speed. Luckily I had a friend in front of me. Evidently I flew off the bike, landed some feet up a telephone pole, and slid down. Man, I was out. I didn't regain consciousness for three days, and spent ten in Self Memorial Hospital.

This was near-dusk, and I had a flashlight attached to the handlebars.

The woman who hit me took off, but luckily the driver behind her caught the license plate. Or maybe it was the passenger, or one of the two women in the back seat—they all served food in the cafeteria of my junior high school, and came home from work late. These were women who'd scooped Lima beans, or mashed potatoes, or kerneled corn on my segmented platter in the past. They'd handed over Sloppy Joes to me and smiled.

As it ended up, I didn't have any broken bones, but

owned a couple blood clots. I still have a scar on my left upper ankle from the front sprockets of the bike. To this day I have smudge-like scars on my knees, elbows, and right upper hip.

Ten days in the hospital. Six weeks doing nothing until the blood clots dissolved or whatever. $2000 hospital bill (good god, can you believe this?) and a meeting with a judge, the woman who hit me in attendance, the judge saying that she needed to pay my parents for the hospital bill, plus a new bicycle, which I got—a really nice Raleigh ten-speed that I never rode, took to college four years later, and had stolen.

I don't remember ninth grade, if it matters. I went, I took classes, and for some reason I did really well in French I, but not much else. I remember, after I came out of a coma, that a nurse gave me an enema before I went in for a series of odd X-rays. I remember telling my mom, "They gave me an emnia and I went to the bathroom in the bed!"

Here's an aside: Greenwood's a small town. They tried to get in touch with my parents. My neighbors knew that my parents went to the drive-in movie. I have no clue what what my parents thought important to see without me. There, over the driver's side speakers, the guy in the concession stand announced, "Can the Singletons please come to the booth? There's an emergency." My father later told me that my mother became a Christian, praying from the Highway 25 Drive-In to the hospital.

Anyway, two months went past, I quit wearing pajamas over my abrasions for the entire summer, this girl named Jonie and another named Kim quit showing up to teach me how to French kiss on my parents' front porch, I went on with myself, and I took up distance running instead of riding a bike.

*

"After four months the doctor brought me in for cognitive tests," Frank said there at the coffee shop. "He had me count backwards from a hundred by sevens. He gave me that test they gave Trump, you know: Person, Woman, Man, Camera, TV."

We laughed. Then we went, "100, 93, uh, 86, um…"

Actually, of all people, I went, "100, 93, 86, 79, 72, 65, 58,"quickly, and then stopped. I didn't want to show off, understand. But, in reality, I wanted to make sure I could kind of do it.

Frank said, "He told me I was fine, that I did well."

Two men behind us at the next table started talking about warehouse jobs they had in the peach industry, back when they just got out of high school. I turned around to find two guys, maybe older than I, who looked like lawyers. I thought it necessary to say, "My first job out of college? After I graduated with really meaningful degree in philosophy? Budweiser warehouse. What a mistake on Budweiser's part! I had to take twelve-ounce longnecks out of a box, place them in six-pack cardboard containers, then put them back in the box. Then I'd put them on a pallet so they could go to grocery stores. This was some kind of test-market thing, for Greenville. About every day I'd go, 'Oops, accidentally dropped a case,' but in reality I put a case in the trunk of my old Toyota."

One of the other guys with me—not Frank—whispered, "How can you do this, just talk to strangers?"

I said, "Damn, man, how can you learn anything without talking to strangers?" but secretly I wondered if, perhaps, this was a terrible repercussion from my previous head injury. I said, "Yeah. Maybe I shouldn't've barged in like that." I thought back out how comfortable I've always been when it came to including myself to anyone's conversation.

"Anyway," Frank said. "I got an offer to run a program over in Europe for a month. I'd done work for them in the past. This guy was leaving. It was a lot of money, plus an apartment added. I said hell yes! I went for a month. And then for two months, and then for three. As it ended up, I was over there illegally, 'cause I didn't have a visa for that long. Well, my wife was there, and she went off to visit some people in Amsterdam, leaving me alone for a long weekend."

I zoned out a little. I envisioned that Schwinn bike, which got kept in my parents' crawlspace for years, the back wheel with its bumper-crater that looked like the letter C.

Frank said, "I don't know what happened. One night I woke up at three in the morning and I felt flooded with my entire life: my bad childhood, how I'd gone off to college, and then grad school, how I'd gotten a job teaching, then being an administrator—I thought, 'My life has been nothing. I've done nothing." That's all I obsessed about."

One of the other two guys said, "Goddamn, it's not true. You got a Ph.D. from Chapel Hill."

Frank shook his head. "I saw a radiator, and got up on it. I tried to open the window. I was going to jump out, but I couldn't get the window open enough."

No one said anything. We sat there for a solid minute. One of the men behind us said something about how they were growing oranges in Georgia now, that he'd seen a clip on CNN. Finally, I said, "I'm never going to ask you another question again."

Frank broke out in a smile, high-fived me, and said, "Fuck you, Singleton." He said, "I called my wife and told her about it, and she said, rightly, that we needed to get back to the United States immediately."

A psychiatrist told my friend Frank—and I might have some of this wrong—that the frontal lobe, or something, holds all the past's memories. And that it keeps those memories locked up. The rest of the brain's working hard on little things, like Breathe, Here's How to Drive, Go Take a Shower, Walk, and so on. But sometime's that frontal love releases all the old memories, and it can be devastating. With a brain injury, such things can occur. That's what happened to Frank.

So here I sit, waiting. I'm writing this on Thanksgiving Day. Earlier, I peeled three pounds of sweet potatoes that I grew and harvested this year. There's a chance it'll be my only memory, later on. I kind of hope that's the case.

Bridget Sampson

Geography

In January of 2020, we moved to Vermont from the Catskills. We were leaving Andes, New York, a Catskills town settled into a valley, for Charlotte, Vermont, a wealthy town near Burlington nestled alongside Lake Champlain. A tapestry of farmland and Vermont picturesqueness, Charlotte seemed like the town we'd been seeking our entire lives.

New York, the state where I was born, is a vast territory, and its upstate and downstate are two different worlds. Everyone not from there thinks only of Manhattan, sleek and populated by the tides of oceans of people: sinners and stars, Nobodies and Somebodies. The town we were leaving, Andes, is quiet and lonely, ruled by landscape—a meadowed and mountain-ed paradise where the sunset turned the mountains red so that winter-time walks with my dogs sometimes felt like a baptism by bloody light.

My husband, a chef, had taken a job on a 400-acre regenerative farm in Charlotte, Vermont with the intention of helping them build a restaurant program, and so we took a few trips from Andes to Charlotte in the dead of winter, moving our possessions by ourselves via U-Haul. We first drove toward the Hudson Valley, through towns we loved, Phoenicia, Shandaken, Woodstock, picking up the New York Thruway, 87, in Kingston, New York, a gritty town with a surprising food and culture scene. We loved the name of the bookstore and café there: *Rough Draft.*

My husband and I are both road trip professionals, but these relocation journeys to Vermont—driven by a brave leap into the future—felt especially freighted. We drove the route probably four times, fighting the snow and the cold, and each trip felt both heavier and lighter, as we left New York's vistas behind. My husband piloted the U-Haul, and I drove my blue CRV, so we were alone and together, the structure of our relationship most days anyway.

The highways and roads I drove led me to the past. North of the Hudson Valley, I drove up the New York Thruway, a road my father, as a young Civil Engineer, had helped to design and construct. As we neared Albany, we drove by signs for Troy, where my father had attended graduate school at RPI to study Engineering. From that gray town he'd wooed my mother, who'd lived in Utica, 98 miles away.

Wooing seemed like a thing of the past. When we'd taken a day trip together to Charlotte in the fall to check out the place, I'd made my husband listen to a DJ groan-scream into the microphone on a local station out of Troy for twenty minutes or so, the sound stopping only for the D.J. to inhale. I wanted to find out why this man was groan-screaming for such a long time, but it wouldn't end. My husband said, *Please turn that off*, and I abandoned my curiosity to the road. I changed the channel to sports radio from Baltimore, where we'd met and married and owned dogs and a restaurant together; where we'd gone practically bankrupt and drank too much to suppress our own frightening disappointments.

We stopped for gas in Saratoga Springs, the town where an old boyfriend had settled. I remained half afraid that I'd run into him at the gas station like I stumbled upon him every so often in my dreams. We drove through the area just south of Lake George, where my mother had vacationed as a young woman to cavort with her girlfriends. On those trips toward our new lives, my interior universe was so open and elastic, I could access to my mother's memories, like the cells of her joys and sadness still lingered in the places I was driving through—her life called to me across the years in the snowy, winter air of the places she'd laughed in.

We'd head east on Route 147 toward Vermont, through hardscrabble New York towns like Whitehall and Fort Anne until we crossed the state line, welcomed to Vermont by the classic green sign. It was January and snowy so we were careful, my husband rattling in front of me in a wide U-Haul truck.

Driving across the flat wide-open space of southwest Vermont, you begin to feel the clutter of humans fall off and you become solely the land and the thoughts the snowy land gives you. Houses far apart, lives carried by the natural world surrounding them, all this brought a deeper and quieter chosen aloneness than what I'd experienced in the Catskills. You can feel your heart burrow into the snow when you enter Vermont in the wintertime.

I'd been to Vermont before, had gone to graduate school at Bennington, had spent time at the Vermont Studio Center in Johnson. But driving this route at this time in our lives was like swimming there. There was a depth and slowness to my emotions as I prepared to make a new geography my home. My brain and heart would transform (just as they'd shifted to reflect the gray mountains and the intricate wildflowers of the Catskills) to mirror the furrows and waters and lines of mountains that were the Green State. The anticipation I felt was like the queasy joy you feel when you are afraid you are falling in love.

We drove east on Route 22, witnessing the outlines of self-sufficient lives in the snowy dark, and then turned left to head north up Route 7, one of the most beautiful stretches of land I've ever driven. We headed up toward Burlington, a city that seemed to look out over Lake Champlain with lively-sad memories of once being a great seaport.

We had already rented a storage unit that would hold much of what we would bring to the new place. We couldn't bring everything. We left behind an antique desk of my mother's that was blonde oak. It had sat in our living room, never used when I was a child, with an antique lamp upon it. In the Catskills, in a fantastical and abandoned farmhouse we were allowed to use, I'd cut peony and placed one on the desk. I'd write on that desk. It had a keyhole and a key that fit into it that hung from a string. I had placed beautiful books on it and looked out the window while I sat in front of it—gazing at the pond and the Catskill mountains and the reflections that settled on the pond as the sun began to set.

The desk wasn't all we left behind in Andes. We left the antique hutch that sat in our kitchen for my childhood life. Pretty useless on its spindly legs, with its silver closure and its tiny storage space up top that my mother hid random trinkets in. Its legs were uneven, and it wobbled, but it was a beautiful shade of wood, almost strawberry blond. Perhaps no one would ever use it again. Perhaps someone would chop it up and use it for kindling. But perhaps it still sits in the garage in Andes in that house where we were happy sometimes, where my husband and I sat around the firepit and talked about life, where I grew too many tomatoes and planted delphiniums and echinacea I'd eventually have to leave, where my dog of 19 years—my "buddha dog"—died in my arms; where we'd hear coyotes yipping and howling at night, sounding as close as if the coyotes were on the street in front of our house; where my husband stayed up nights with me when I couldn't sleep reading to me about Alan Watts because, in the Catskills we had the time and space to listen to books about Buddhism and to the lectures Thomas Merton gave to his novices about James Joyce. In Andes, we left behind a bartender named Stu from Florida who had demons and a handlebar mustache. We left behind a tiny church two doors away called Saint Anne's that was never locked, and sometimes—when desperate—I'd go say the rosary there. In Andes, we left behind an oil painting called *A Night Out* by Dan Keplinger, an artist from Baltimore who had cerebral palsy and painted a stick attached to his forehead. He became famous for a short time because a documentary made about him, *King Gimp*, was nominated for an Oscar. The painting was barter. We'd catered Dan's 200-person wedding in Baltimore to get the painting. We hung that painting in our restaurant, and we brought it to the Catskills in hope of I don't know what. I hope the painting ended up in one of the thrift or antique stores that surprise you in the Catskill landscape; I hope it was discovered by someone who knew. The picture, a mustard yellow rugged oil, always reminded my husband of how much of our lives we gave away back in our Baltimore days.

Mostly, what I left behind in the Catskills were the gardens I'd built and loved at the inn where my husband and I worked. I knew they would become wild and unkempt and anonymous without the kind of love I'd poured into them. I'd become a new self in that quiet greenhouse, spent time burying tubers and pressing into dirt seeds of all shapes that would become bushy seedlings and then perfectly alive beauty, flowers that would be my closest companions on the loveliest of my displaced, silent summer days.

In Charlotte, we were to stay in a suite in the Mount Philo Inn for a couple of months while we searched for a house. The Mount Philo Inn once housed a commune; it now held my husband and I and our two dogs for a commune of four. Every day, I hiked Mount Philo with my younger dog, a rescue Blue Merle border collie named Pearl. Every day, I looked out over the valley of Charlotte.

The first night we stayed at the Mount Philo Inn, the sunset lay itself orange across the Adirondacks like some kind of mink stole of light around the shoulders of the mountains. The entire sky became operatic, ethereal light. I knew that westward at around the same latitude sat Watertown, New York, where I'd been born in one of the snowiest winters in history in 1962. When I looked across the Adirondacks, I could sense both a past that went years beyond my own life as well as a future that would prove itself to be as fiery and natural as this sunset I was witnessing.

We were at the top of the country. It was a new year. We would live off the land. We found a church where we could go to mass in the early evenings. It snowed often.

Every day that early winter of 2020, from the top of Mount Philo, I could see miles across the valley to Lake Champlain laid out like a puzzle of land where the pieces fit together snug and secure, and I began to write a book in my head. It was the first book I'd ever written in my imagination that had a happy ending.

Alan Simmons

Tending Bar

I first started tending bar after college during the Recession of 1973, the worst recession since the Great Depression, a line first used to describe the Recession of '69, the one in '71 and '73, and for every recession since. I worked at The Belden Tap, corner of Lincoln Avenue and Belden Street, in Lincoln Park on the north side of Chicago. The bar was known as Johnny Weiss's Pub, before Johnny Weiss sold the bar to his two bartenders, Bobby Bright, a lazy drunk who had the money to buy a bar, and Chuck, an untrustworthy man who knew how to run a bar. I never knew Chuck's last name. I doubt if he knew mine. Chuck never asked for my Social Security Number. Bartenders were paid by the hour in cash from the register, plus tips. Bobby owned the large, multi-unit three-story apartment building across the street, commonly known as Bright Manors, where many of the regular customers at the Belden Tap lived. Bobby had been orphaned and adopted as an infant, and so the story goes, inherited Bright Manors from his adopted parents after they both died in a violent car crash. Now he was a regular at his own bar.

The Belden Tap occupied the first floor corner in one of the three story red brick buildings lined up and down Lincoln Avenue in each direction. The barroom held a mahogany L-shaped bar that ran the length of the room backed by a tall mirror, and considering how rowdy the bar became on weekend nights, it was a miracle the mirror remained in one piece all the years I worked there. The 16 foot ceiling was covered with one foot square tiles of stamped tin repainted countless times. Four medium sized round white glass fixtures the size of basketballs hung from the ceiling by dusty brown cords. The plaster walls were painted the color of sick white flesh and were cracked and stained from years of water damage. Two antlered stuffed animal heads, a moose and a deer, hung opposite the bar. Wooden stools with brown leather padded seats lined the bar. Round wooden tables and matching chairs filled the room between the bar, and the double-door entrance was guarded by the Wurlitzer juke box. A foosball and a nine ball bumper pool table nestled next to the door to the john at the back of the room. Neon signs with their jumble of tubes and wires advertising *Budweiser* and *Old Style* hung in the plate glass windows surrounding the room on two sides, offering a somewhat clear view of nightclubs, bars, and pubs that occupied the store fronts in the buildings next door and across the street in both directions.

On my first day, Jerry Dillard, a tall, dark haired veteran bartender with wild curly hair and a trill in his voice when he laughed, gave me instructions how to defend myself should someone threaten me.

"No kidding, it happens," he told me, "so, you have to know what to do."

"OK, so, what do I do?" I asked.

"You tell them, *think about it. You don't want to do this. People go to jail for shit like that. You don't want to go there.*"

Two nights later, a full-moon Friday night, I showed up at 6 pm for my first shift behind the bar. The place was already packed. Chuck gave me a quick, five minute instructional; pulled beer in a glass, $.30; pulled beer in a mug, $.40; pitcher of beer, $2.50; bottled domestic beer, $.65; foreign bottled beer, $1; mixed drinks from the speed well, $.65; and top shelf spirits a dollar a shot. If you want a blended drink, go across the street. Backup cases of bottled beer and the big aluminum barrels of beer were stored in a walk-in refrigerator in the basement.

And then Chuck told me to hold the fort, went home for dinner, and never came back.

By 9 pm, customers stood three deep at the bar. Every table and chair in the house was filled, with people lining the walls around the foosball and pool table. The jukebox played swing tunes, "In the Mood," that sort of thing. Some folks danced., Others stood at the bar calling for drinks and cussing me out because I couldn't pour fast enough.

I kept pouring drinks and hoping for the best, one eye on the door waiting for Chuck to show up. People shouted and waved empty pitchers. I kept pouring and shouted back. I could not keep up. I could feel the trouble brewing. I tried phoning Chuck at home, but got no answer. I phoned the cops every time a scuffle broke out. People stopped tipping and after a while I got tired of apologizing. More scuffles broke out. The cops never showed up. I kept pouring. The crowd got drunker.

A fist fight broke out between two guys over a woman, and then a minute later hell broke loose over a game of pool. I heard the sound of a pool stick crack and glass break. I looked up and saw a man flung backwards over a crowded table. More bodies went flying., A full-on barroom brawl erupted across the room.

An old woman sitting on a barstool by the door got taken up by the mad angry energy storm and smashed her beer bottle over the head of the young guy sitting next to her. The guy never saw it coming, unconscious and slid off his seat sinking to the floor. The old woman with no front teeth cackled and laughed out loud. I still remember her big, crazy-old-lady grin.

Women screamed and crowds rushed for the door, just like in the movies. I didn't know what to do, so I climbed up onto the bar, yelled, "Yahoo!" and leaped into the fray, arms wide, diving onto the crowded pack of brawlers leading the riot, and taking the whole pile down to the floor, just like in the movies, end of fight.

Except it wasn't. One guy, caught in the wild insurrection, dropped a thick wad of new $20 bills during the melee, and was on his hands and knees all over the floor scrambling around between and over the fallen bodies gathering up his bankroll, along with everyone else who had hands and pockets to stuff with his cash.

I may have grabbed a $20, but the guy thought I took more, and came back after it was all over and approached me outside the front door. Only now he had a carving knife in his hand. He wore a dark flannel shirt and brown eyes worked up into a murderous rage.

I went through Jerry's routine.

"You don't want to do this," I told him. "Think about it. People go to jail for shit like that. You don't want to go there," I said. "Think about it."

I kept an eye on the black handled kitchen knife he held in his right hand. The blade must have been a foot long, the perfect weapon for close quarters fighting back in the Roman Empire days. I figured him for a drug dealer out on the town celebrating a big score, too drunk or stoned or stupid to keep his money in his pocket where it belonged. He had me trapped, cornered in the doorway outside the bar with my back to the wood framed double glass doors.

He looked more heartbroken than pissed off, like any other guy who lost his dough, or I would have been dead by now.

I considered making a run for it, maybe give him a quick kick in the solar plexus, making use of my advantage but then thought better of it. I've never been much of a sprinter.

He held the knife waist high in his right hand and I watched him shuffle his feet back and forth tapping the concrete step, scraping his shoe leather searching for a reliable position. I stood perfectly still, not wanting to give him an excuse to start. I'd fight my way out if I had to, but he would have to force the issue.

"It wasn't me," I told him. "You can have all the money I have. There's not much because it wasn't me. I don't have your money."

I felt a calm come over me despite feeling my heartbeat thumping against my ribcage like a bass drum score, ba-boom. I waited and watched him weigh his will to kill me. Time bled slowly by. I followed his movements and raised my eyes to his. He must have sensed me drop my guard and faked a thrust with his knife hand to let me know I wasn't off the hook yet, and then he paused, his eyes, bloodshot and full of anguish, locked on mine, sneering, daring me to provoke him. I did not dare. I stayed quiet and remained perfectly still.

More seconds passed. He didn't move. Neither of us spoke a word. The night was warm, the air was thick and heavy, and the full moon faded off towards the south west. I heard him slowly empty his lungs, felt the tension ease, and we both began to breathe. He took another breath, called me a punk, and punched my right shoulder with his free left hand. Then he turned on a dime and dashed off to a car I hadn't noticed waiting for him at curbside, a big, black, late-model Ford Crown Victoria sedan. He jumped into the passenger side door, and the car turned left and sped away, west down Lincoln Ave.

I walked around the corner to my apartment and trudged up to my apartment. I went to the kitchen, flipped the light on, filled a rock glass with a handful of ice cubes and Jim Beam. I stirred with my index finger, took a long, deep drink, and emptied my pockets on the old oak kitchen table to count my tip and salary cash.

My breath stopped. The guy was right, I *did* have his money. There on the table were crispy $100 dollar bills, all stuck together, not $20's like I thought, a couple grand at least, not worth dying over, but enough to pay the rent and groceries for six months, or buy a car. I lit a cigarette and sat there and finished my drink, and then I had another one. I didn't move. Hours went by. The sun rose before my heart stopped pounding and I calmed down enough to finally go to bed and sleep.

The following day, when I went in to work, I heard the guy came back looking for me. I heard about it the moment I walked through the door.

"Some guy from last night was here looking for you. He threw a brick through the window because you weren't here,"

Chuck said grinning at me from behind the bar. A large sheet of plywood covered the opening where the brick came through.

I had told Chuck what happened after he finally showed up at 2 am, bleary-eyed, disheveled, and looking like he just woke up. He had taken the cash from the register and went home, leaving me to lock up the bar. Of course I didn't tell him what had happened once I got home.

"It's a tough business, bartending," said Chuck. "Take a couple of weeks off." A smile raced across his pale, bloated, shit-face, like it was all some big joke: he passed out after dinner and forgot to come back to relieve the new guy.

"Heh, heh. Trial by fire. You pasted the test," Chuck chortled over a beer back sneer. Then added, "I didn't hire you. Bobby hired you."

So, what did I expect? Bobby never showed up either.

I went on to tend bar there weekend nights for 3 more years, and no one had more fun there than me.

"You're a regular Mr. Personality," Chuck would say.

Chuck was a hard guy to like, and I never gave him any more thought than that. We worked together until he found someone to take his place, which pleased me, too. Everyone hung out at The Belden Tap. Lots of notables. Siskel and Ebert, the movie critics, were regulars. The art house Biograph Theater was right down the block. It was a cheap place to drink, located right in the middle of the action.

The incident that finally made me quit working at The Belden Tap occurred on a late Sunday night. Bob Gilbert Hennessey, "Hennessey from Tennessee" we called him, a house painter and long-time regular, stuck around until closing time and walked up close to me, pulled pulled a .38 semi-automatic from his jacket pocket and stuck it right between my eyes. I looked at his face as he held it there, a look of madness, spittle, and missing teeth amplified by twenty or so vodka tonics. He'd been waiting all night to kill me and take the till money. He must have been desperate. This was the best idea he could come up with.

"Bob," I said, "I thought we were pals?"

Hennessey snorted as only a truly drunk man can. I knew what he was thinking. I hadn't bought him a drink all night. I never did. At 65 cents a drink the house never bought, house rules, though I probably should have. But the Fucker never left a tip, either.

Still, you don't shoot people for not buying drinks.

"You don't want to do this, Bob. Think about it. People go to jail for shit like this. You don't want to go there, Bob, think about it. You don't want to do this."

He didn't. He turned, and then ran out the door, and that's when I decided I didn't want to tend bar at The Belden Tap anymore. The shit you go through for $3 an hour, plus tips. I took an extra $20 from the drawer, combat pay, came around from the register and locked the front door, then took a seat at a table by the jukebox to gather my thoughts.

Jerry Dillard, my bartender mentor, had explained to me the science behind his method. "The whole point is to make them think." Jerry said. "If you can distract them for just half a second you break their concentration. And, for them to continue, they have to reset their thoughts, rethink their will and commitment, and they can't, so they leave."

Nothing broke my concentration. I reset my thoughts.

I rethought my will and my commitment.

And I got up from the table, turned off the lights, locked the front door behind me, and went home.

William Vandegrift

The Black Dog

"What is the longest stretch of time you have been sober?"

"I do not know," is the answer I tell the doctor.

Dr. Franciosi jots down some notes in his pad. We are discussing which came first: my depression or my issues with alcohol abuse. Am I depressed, and as a result do I turn to alcohol? Or is the opposite, does my drinking lead to depression?

He does not always face me when he speaks, although I have asked him a few times to do this. I need him to look at me so I can read his lips. I was born deaf, and if a person does not face me, I cannot understand what is being said. Lipreading is a skill I've learned as a child, and I have been told I am remarkably good at it.

"Which do you think I should be treated for first?" I ask the doctor. "The drinking or the depression?"

"Both," he says, spinning his chair away from his desk to face me. He's coming to realize my need to read his lips. "I'm so sorry," he says. "I keep forgetting."

"People do," is all I say.

"So you know," the doctor continues, "you are here to get stabilized and to be detoxed from your excessive alcohol abuse. Withdrawal can be a very dangerous thing."

I am in rehab in Florida at the opposite end of the east coast from my home. I am to be here for forty-five to sixty days. I am on day two.

"You are fifty-three years old?" the doctor asks. "Am I correct?"

I nod and he continues. "You say you started drinking heavily at the end of December?"

I nod again. He dramatically counts the months using his fingers and writes it down in his notebook. "You were hospitalized in February?"

"For ten days," I tell him.

"I see," he says, and he jots down more notes. "I have something I'd like you to fill out. Take as long as you need."

He passes me a questionnaire and he waits patiently as I check off a series of boxes in response to various questions. I give him back the sheet of paper, and he does his assessments. Then he places the pad on his desk and says, "My understanding is you are not just depressed. You are severely depressed."

He hands me a worksheet on which the nine symptoms of depression are listed. He explains that I have eight symptoms out of nine. The ninth is having suicidal ideations.

The symptoms I did have include: 1) Feeling sad, empty, and hopeless. 2) A lack of interest or pleasure in activities that I once enjoyed. 3) Weight loss or weight gain. 4) Difficulty sleeping or sleeping too much. 5) Restlessness. 6) Excessive fatigue or a loss of energy. 7) Feeling worthless or guilty. 8) A lack of concentration or difficulty with decision making.

"I am not suicidal," I say, in agreement and a bit forcefully.

"Yes," the doctor affirms. "The good news is you are not a harm to yourself."

"Well," I agree with uncertainty, "I do have eight out of nine symptoms though. That can't be good."

"It's not uncommon, and it is treatable. Do not worry. You are in the right place, and we will work on these issues during your stay. I recommend you stay here as long as your insurance will allow you."

I begin to feel trapped. I shift and squirm on the oversized sofa that is decorated with bright and colorful Native American pillows. I have a pillow on my lap, and my hands are clenched on top of it.

I've battled depression throughout my life. I was moody as a child. For most of my life, I was able to function but apparently, I cannot anymore. My life has slowly unraveled over the course of a long period of time and has become unmanageable. To cope, I drank excessively.

Several months ago, I experienced a myriad of conflicting emotions in response to trauma that I had come up against in my younger years. Flashbacks plagued my nightmares and haunted me throughout nearly every moment of my day. I found solace in alcohol which not only briefly alleviated my trauma but amplified it as well. Abusing alcohol became my primary focus and I prioritized it over my health, my family and friends, and the quality of my life.

After many years of seeking treatment in various facilities close to my home, I reached the point where I decided that to get better, I needed to remove myself from my current environment. As it is said in recovery, one must avoid 'people, places, and things,' all of which might contribute to having a relapse. These triggers are always a threat and are to be avoided especially during the early stages of recovery.

I think of home, over a thousand miles away, and I miss my partner of thirty-one years, my two dogs and three cats. I long for my life as it once was, but I can no longer be there and be safe and healthy as well. I feel hopeless.

As if he could read my mind about my yearning to be back home in New Jersey, the doctor says, "You've come a long way to be down here. You clearly know you need help."

"But…" My voice trails off and feeling trapped within the clutches of withdrawal, I want to scream: "This is all bullshit!"

"You can leave anytime you want. You must want to do the work. I would not recommend you leave. But we're not forcing you to stay. You came here voluntarily."

He sips his coffee from a mug that has written above an image of a light bulb, *How Many Psychologists Does It Take to Change a Light Bulb?* And beneath the image, it says, *One, but the light bulb must want to change.*

I chuckle; he stares at me; his blank face reveals nothing. I restrain myself as he looks down and reviews the paperwork some more.

Alcoholism runs rampant in my family and throughout many branches of my family tree. During my childhood, family members and friends have made suicide attempts.

I myself have self-destructive tendencies but the idea of overdosing on pills and ending up in a coma frightens me. The notion of cutting myself with a knife freaks me out. Cutting my flesh and drawing blood repulses me, although I experimented with using a razor while in a downward spiral, after doing a massive amount of cocaine and being awake for several days and nights straight. As I wept, I only went down deep enough to draw a little blood. I have a few scars on my wrists to remind me of those moments of despair. I know I could get a gun and put a bullet into my head, but what if I survive and end up being brain dead? Suicide is futile to me. I am fearful.

I have fantasies of going the way Edna Pontellier did in Kate Chopin's novella *The Awakening*. How she swam far out into the ocean. But at the same time, this terrifies me, being in deep waters, pulled downward, and perhaps having a change of mind at the last minute. My decision having become irreversible, the shoreline now out of sight, and my long wait as I struggle until the sea finally claims me.

If I were to die, I want my death to be quick and final. See, I have no options. Yes, I am too afraid. So no, I am not suicidal. I am a coward. The doctor smiles sympathetically, seeing the stricken expression on my face. He does not ask me what I am thinking about. He pats me on the knee and reassures me that everything will be okay.

There is a lull in our conversation. The doctor spins his chair to his desk, and he takes more notes. He's evaluating me.

"Should I be saying anything else?" I ask.

He looks at me. "That's up to you. Is there anything else you want to say?"

I begin to tell him more, but I stop myself. I do not tell him about the impulsive thoughts that I sometimes have or the way I talk to myself with disparagement which I have done since I was a child. I do not tell him about my impetuousness, fortunately much rarer these days than when I was younger. I do not stand too close on the bank of a raging river such as the one that leads toward and over Niagara Falls, for I am fearful I might act upon my spontaneous, fleeting, urge to jump. That lure. The pull.

I have always had these reckless thoughts. The same goes for my avoidance of the edges of tall buildings or bridges and my staying away from the tracks of a subway as the train approaches. I still sometimes, though rarely these days, feel that urge to lunge. I have these fleeting thoughts: "What if I do it?" and "I can do it. Why not?" Or "What's going to stop me?"

I do not mention any of this. I don't want to alarm the doctor and especially my family, should there be a family session scheduled in the future. I consider the fact that I am an eight out of nine on this scale of depression. I'd rather be eight out of nine as opposed to being nine out of nine. It'll have to do.

The doctor shifts in his seat and says, "Have you ever heard of the term: the black dog?"

I shake my head.

"It is famously attributed to Winston Churchill in reference to his depression, but it goes all the way back to the philosopher Horace. Depression has lasted for centuries. Many of the greats have had it all the way to those of today. Depression is no longer a stigma and is now treatable and manageable."

I nod compliantly, not sure what to say at this point.

"You'd be surprised how widespread depression is," the doctor goes on. "Most people experience various levels of depression at some point in their lives."

Glancing at my file, he tells me that he sees I am a writer. "What do you write?" he asks.

"Short stories. Essays. And I'm working on a novel. A little of everything." I don't tell him I haven't written in months. My enthusiasm for reading and writing has vanished.

The doctor asks me if I have read any of William Styron's work.

"Of course," I say, knowing where he's going. "*Darkness Visible.*"

He nods. "And have you read Andrew Solomon's *The Noonday Demon?*"

I tell the doctor that I have Solomon's book, but I haven't read it yet; long books intimidate me.

Wanting answers, I change the subject. "Tell me what I need to do now while I am here," I say. "I'm a quick learner, and I want to get better."

"One thing at a time," the doctor advises. "Baby steps."

I acquiesce with a nod, and he hands me some pamphlets. "Here's some reading for you to do over the next couple of days." They are colorful packets with beautiful people on the covers, all radiant, smiling, jumping and dancing, and proud of their successful recoveries.

I decide that I'll review them during the quieter moments throughout the day. Since I'm not a smoker, I usually find myself alone in the lounge while everyone goes outside to smoke during breaks in between meetings. I enjoy those moments being by myself and not having people milling around or talking to me.

"Another thing," the doctor adds, and he lifts a laminated card. On it is a dark blur of black scribbles and scrawls. It reminds me of an Edward Gorey drawing or a Jackson Pollock painting. He asks in a calm voice, "What do you see?"

I struggle not to roll my eyes as I stumble through my thoughts, trying to anticipate how I am supposed to respond to this image. The doctor says in a firm voice, "There is no correct answer. Just tell me what you see."

"Chaos," is all I can muster. "I see chaos." I see my emotions and my depression, and my addictions all tied into one.

"Very well," he says as he jots more notes on his pad, which I know will go into my file. I wait for a response, and he sips his coffee. He glances at his watch. "I'm afraid our time is up," he says.

That's it? I want to say. Instead, I stand up and thank him for his time.

"I'll see you in a few days," he says, flipping through the calendar that he uses to keep track of his appointments. "I'll have the nurse find you and bring you here."

After I leave the doctor's office, I pause in the hallway that leads to the rooms where the morning groups are held. I lean against the wall and think about the word *chaos*. I do not want my assessment to be made based on a quick response to a mere image on a flash card. Then it comes to me. Is this what my life has become---Chaos?

I follow the long corridor to the end and quietly enter the room where the first group of the day has assembled. Everyone is talking at once; the counselor is trying to maintain order. I do not make eye contact. Suddenly everyone falls silent, and the meeting begins. We go around the room and name something that we are grateful for. Then we share our stories, and the chaos of everyone else's lives becomes entwined with that of my own.

Rainstorm, North Dakota

There is, in your past, a road that hugs the sea: a transcontinental highway that you can pick up or leave at any time, made not of on-ramps and off-ramps but of uncontrolled crossings and stoplights you are free to turn at, drive through, or ignore entirely.

The ocean it caresses is the Pacific, wrongly named as it is anything but: a churlish, riotous nightmare full of clicking sea monsters and tumbling currents of suspended garbage carried by the tides to Point Nemo, the farthest spot from land, where it foams so thick it almost becomes walkable. It is a human oasis in an untamable landscape. Here, though, on the coast, its fingers grope clumsily at the dunes, press themselves slowly into the rocks. This, here, is what they want: this is the biggest challenge, the unconquerable frontier, the virgin world that says no and no and no.

There is, in your present, a storm. A common storm to someone, perhaps, whose capacious thunder leaves plenty of room for meadowlarks to yaw between turrets of rain. Perhaps it comes once a month, perhaps once a day, but it is, to be clear, common.

There are, in fact, two storms: one is cold, one is warm. One rises, one sinks. When they meet, the wind turns upward to heaven. When it turns, it begins to narrow and spin.

In your present, the sky is green. In your present, the sidereal canopy of stars you'd fallen asleep to has been covered like clocks and mirrors before a funeral. In your present, you are in a tent. In your present, you are terrified.

No one expects a tornado except the people who are used to them. There are stories everywhere of relaxed Midwesterners who pull up onto their patios to watch the run-up to a storm, who listen to the sirens blare and watch the sky churl the way in yesteryear they might have parked a Chevy in front of a drive-in theater. If the blockbuster busts up the block, it's not too high a price to pay.

But you, no, you've set up a tent, a little plastic, vinyl, cheap tent that's blue and gray and nailed to the floor with thin aluminum pins. You crawled into it to fall asleep, just a few hours earlier, covered in constellations. A cool breeze nibbled off the hot evening air. A wide canyon was your only neighbor, the only clamor -such as it was- being the shuffling hooves of wild horses hundreds of feet below. The canyon was carved when the river made a wrong turn a million years before and decided, stubbornly, never to double back. You'd been there, in paradise found, since mid-morning. You'd fallen asleep, you were sure, in Eden before the apples.

When the storm comes, it comes quickly: as fast as the horses dashing into the brush below, as fast as memory. It's an ecstasy of smell: soil tilled up from miles away, all rush and brush and oil. The sky quickens into emerald. The wind begins to wrap at the flaps of your tiny plastic pyramid. The breeze turns freezing.

You are in love. Maybe. Probably. Surely. Maybe not. Who knows? You're in love and you're in Mexico, and at times it's hard to tell the difference.

You're on the transcontinental highway that hugs the Pacific, in a car that is held together only by magical mechanics: it would have been condemned in any other nation, but here it begs a premium. It functions, and that's enough. It's been a long afternoon of hot little towns and small meals, of dropping in on overhawked ruins that amount to not much more than a couple rocks or an etching that could have been left six or sixty thousand weeks ago.

You pull in, on a lark, into a half-eroded hotel built in more hopeful times, pressed into a beach that is almost inaccessible, steeply set under a rock face that's got far more kelp than footprints. Its optimistic ambition has been exceeded by vulgar reality: the paint has been lapped off by the coarse tongue of salted wind; the cement is cracked, the staff is perpetually on break. Small burn marks mar the roof; who knows how many storms have cracked lightning into it.

You are in love and it is beautiful; perhaps the only guests there, you are shown to a room with nothing outside it but five thousand miles of ocean, a little balcony hanging forward out of it and over the cliffs. You bicker to keep the doors wide open for the night and both fall asleep on top of the now-sweaty sheets.

You screw your courage to the sticking place, and decide to stay. Green sky or no, storm or no, there is no better option: the closest town is an hour away, in the dark, on an awful gutted road. You'd just trade one calamity, you think, for another.

The day before, you'd seen another tornado- a distant, lumbering wisp in another green sky, a state away, that had moments earlier flattened two grain silos. You can see why they love the theater of it: something beautiful and bad that happens to other people. You could feel the pressure change in the air- as it comes, as it goes- palpable to the mammal in you, the thing that has known for sixty million years when to scurry, when to hide.

Lightning cracks brief but bright as daylight, and you can see the whole world in blinding snaps: every inch of the canyon, the curling clouds in the distance, the funnel. The canyon is unimpressed; who knows here, too, how many storms have cracked lightning into it.

Staying, you suspect, is stupid. But stupefied, you stay. You throw a tarp over the tent and, once you're rooked back inside, immediately the wind begins to whip it violently. You clench the place where soil and rocks should be but instead is just the smooth floor of cheap plastic.

You're not scared, you tell yourself. You just need to get

away with it.

As the storm kicks up into a fury, you lie on your back, not scared, not scared, no, not scared, and marvel at how everything sounds like something else.

For starters, storm-wind sounds like waves.

With the balcony door open, it's hard to sleep. The waves roll up and slap against the rock, and it's the loudest thing you've ever heard. Worse than city wails, worse than screaming sirens. In huge heaving thuds, in and out, in and out, in even rhythm -four beats a minute- you can hear the entire Pacific breathing. The stucco walls don't seem sufficient to hold it back but, of course, they do. The ocean moans in the darkness, and the hotel's frame creaks and contracts gently in the chill.

So, when the wind begins to thrash your tiny tent around, you can try and put your fear to rest by, instead, teaching yourself to savor the sounds of things. Light rain, you can tell yourself, sounds like crackling fires- logs set up on a foggy beach, built into their own little pyramid, as families on lawn chairs circle them and warm themselves in the thick mist. When the rain gets harder and harder, listen: it's just hot steak, sizzling in the pan. A warm meal on the way.

The tree branches swing and buckle above you, but no- turn your ear to them. They're rocking chairs.

When the tent begins to shift, ignore it. As the sky begins to loosen light hail over you and your canyon, remember that it's actually just the sound of fingers tapping at a typewriter. It's just a story forming. When the hail gets larger and drops into the rain-sotted earth around you, put your ear to the ground and feel the vibrations, the way the ancestors felt the music of the earth: no, they're not weaponized sky. They are not rocks. No, they're cubes of ice, clinking into a glass full of scotch whiskey or, punctuated by the fizz of rain, a fresh, crisp glass of Coca-Cola on a summer afternoon in Mexico.

When the lightning strikes, hear instead the snap of the sails in the boats just off the Sinaloa coast. Think of the smooth seas that never made even one good sailor; think of the beautiful women lying spread across the deck, the whole world their balcony door.

When the tornado forms, you'll know. The mammal in you will feel it in his bones. You'll hear only the sound of a rumbling train but no, listen more sweetly: It's the sound of two bodies rustling in bed. It's the sound of the traffic driving down that transcontinental highway that you can pick up or leave at any time. It's the ocean, tell yourself. It's the sea. As it gets closer and closer, remind yourself: you're not scared. You just need to get away with it. And that this is not the sound of the storm. No. It's love.

Santa & Jimmy

I was six when I recognized my dad's handwriting on a note that lay waiting for me and my brother Christmas morning. The note thanked us for the milk and cookies and was unmistakably signed: *Santa Claus.*

I didn't say anything until I was 12.

For six years, I pretended to believe. Then, I finally told my parents.

"I know," I whispered.

"Know what?" Dad asked.

"About him," I replied."About you-know-who."

Dad smiled.

"I know it's you," I added. "You two."

Mom craned her neck, but only Dad spoke.

"Huh," he said flatly.

"I've known I was six."

"Six?" Mom stammered. "You've known all this time?"

I nodded.

"So you've just been pretending?" she followed.

I nodded again.

"Wow," Mom said.

I'm not sure why, but me telling Mom I knew the truth about Santa Claus seemed to bother her more than me. I wasn't sure if Mom was more upset that I figured it out or that I kept the secret and pretended to believe for as long as I had.

Something about the way Mom reacted made me wonder what else I believed that I probably shouldn't have.

*

The only public schooling I ever had was in kindergarten, and I went to three of them: Ridge for about a month when my family still lived in our old apartment; Oakdale, where I pissed my pants and got my shoes stolen twice; and finally, Pleasant Hill, where I finished the last two months of the school year.

At Pleasant Hill, I was in the p.m. group, so I took the bus home with a bunch of elementary and middle schoolers. I only really knew one kid on the bus, and he got off right away at the very first stop. My ride home from Pleasant Hill was a bit more than 40 minutes.

There was a kid on the bus—a sixth grader named Keith Harris—who'd turn his eyelids inside-out. Keith scared the shit out of me when he did that. I had bad dreams just thinking about those pink, veiny lids.

I had a lot of bad dreams.

Sometimes, I'd forget to get off the bus. When I forgot—and I did fairly often—Mom would have to pick me up at the dispatch. She'd pull up flustered and in a hurry, and I'd have to run just to keep up with her on the way out to the car.

"We've got him again," the receptionist said when she called Mom the Tuesday after Easter. "Charlie wants to know if he's slow or something." The receptionist—a heavy lady named Pam—wore so much eye shadow that her lids just kind of hung suspended like a pair of half-drawn shades. "He wants to know," she added, "if your son is retarded."

Charlie Maykeens was the bus dispatch supervisor. It bothered him that I missed my stop so often and ended up at the dispatch garage. It bothered him so much, it might've made him angry.

When Mom finally turned up at the dispatch that Tuesday, she offered excuses—the same ones she always did—about us being new and me just having trouble with the adjustment. She apologized as if she owed them something.

In June, kindergarten ended, and I didn't miss my stop ever again.

*

After kindergarten, I went to Catholic grade schools. I did 1-4 at St. Elizabeth Ann Seton, 5-8 at St. Andrew.

At both schools, believing in God was important.

Nobody talked about God at any of my kindergartens.

Believing in God seemed a whole hell of a lot like believing in Santa Claus: Nothing about it made much sense, and it felt awfully pretend.

Every Friday at St. Andrew's meant church, which was always terrible, but not because of God; church was terrible because of our principal, Sister Janice Elaine. Sister Janice played guitar and sang at mass, and she insisted that we sing and respond both loudly and clearly. If we didn't, she'd keep us afterward and force us to recite hymns and sing responses until she was satisfied that we were doing so with the spiritual intensity and fervor she deemed necessary.

"Jesus hung on a cross for you," she yelled one Friday. "The least you can do is sing— articulate clearly." Her voice rattled through the tiled alcoves and empty confessionals. "He died so that you—" she pointed, "might live."

She walked down the aisle with her guitar slung across her back as we all but screamed out songs and shouted refrains.

I hated Sister Janice Elaine.

I hated that she kept us late and made us sing, made us shout things that didn't really make sense, things I couldn't believe. But I especially hated Sister Janice Elaine during the late-spring months—May and June—when the temperatures crawled higher and the humidity rose to almost stifling levels inside the church.

No matter how loudly we sang or how intently we responded, it wasn't enough for her.

She chastised our collective efforts. "It must come from your heart. You have to believe it with your spirit."

*

One Friday in late May, shortly before the end of the school year, Sister Janice Elaine was dissatisfied with our rendition of "Sing to the Mountains." She said it wasn't believable.

She only held back my class—the 8th graders—and let the younger students go to lunch.

"There's no joy in your voices," she growled. We knelt in the pews, our backs straight as boards. She liked to make us kneel, she said, because then she knew she had our full attention.

"You're old enough," she continued, "to understand the power in this song, to understand why it's important. And," she added, "you're an example to the younger students. They watch you, and they learn," she snarled. "You need to believe," she paused. "You need to make them believe."

She was about to continue, to say who knows what about "Sing to the Mountains" when Jeffrey Phillips groaned and wavered. His eyes rolled up into his head, and he tumbled down, suddenly and immediately, and passed out exactly where he knelt. His head smashed off the pew, hammered the tile floor, and he began to convulse. I shouted for Ms. Darten, our eighth-grade teacher.

"Help!" I yelled. "Help!" I repeated. Panic leaked from my mouth. "Jeffrey!"

There was a flurry of movement behind and around me, and I remember Ms. Darten as she squeezed into the thin pew. She smelled of coffee and chalk, and her half-moon readers dangled from a thin chain that hung around her neck. Mr. Lietsig entered through the other aisle as Jeffrey continued to writhe and shift on the hard floor. Spit came from his mouth, and he gasped for air. I stared at him. I wanted to do something, to try and help him, but I couldn't do a goddamned thing.

Kids moved out of my pew, out of the pews in front and behind me, and at some point, the paramedics arrived. I just sat there. Somehow, I never moved. Finally, Ms. Darten's hand fell upon my shoulder, her readers suddenly perched on the edge of her nose. The silver chain swayed in a gentle *U* just above my head, and she nodded. I followed her down the aisle, out of the church, and back to our classroom. Neither one of us said a word.

That afternoon, I worried about Jeffrey; we all did. Ms. Darten had us say a prayer for him. She made the prayer up, and it was really short. We stood in a circle and held hands while she spoke. After that, the classroom stayed mostly quiet, and at 3:15, I went home a little different.

Maybe we all did.

The following Monday, I rode the bus to school. I waited outside with my friends and classmates until the morning bell rang. I tried not to feel different, but I did.

Jeffrey Philips never came back to school.

There were a whole bunch of things Jeffrey Philips never did again. And there were so many things Jeffrey Philips never did at all.

A few weeks later, I got up in the middle of the night and made a list of all the things Jeffrey Phillips would never do again. Then, I made a list of all the things Jeffrey Phillips would never do at all.

I'm not exactly sure why I made the list, but I know that for a while it made me feel better. I didn't feel good, but I felt better, as if writing down the things Jeffrey wouldn't ever do again somehow gave shape and substance to who he was. But then I kept writing and writing. I wrote things I hardly understood, and the list made me feel worse.

*

When I told Mom about Santa and how I didn't believe anymore since I knew it was her and Dad, she told me that beliefs were only as strong as the person who believed them. Back then, I didn't understand what she meant.

*

A few years ago, a friend of mine was killed in the Syrian desert. Some deranged terrorists cut his head off. They made a video of it, a video they put on the internet. They forced my friend, Jimmy, to say a whole host of things on the video—things I know he didn't, couldn't believe—before they beheaded him. I've never seen the video, and I never will. But I wonder about that video quite a bit. I wonder why they made it. I wonder if they were actually deranged or if they just did deranged things because of what they believed. Or maybe they did deranged things because of what they didn't believe.

I think it might work both ways.

When I found out about Jimmy, I couldn't believe it. He'd been missing for a while, and I think I knew something bad might've happened, but I don't think I or anyone believed that something as fucked up as him getting beheaded on video could ever have happened.

I thought about making a list for Jimmy like I did for Jeffrey Phillips. Only Jimmy's list would've been different; it would've been a list of all the things he believed. At first, I felt like I had to make a list of the things he believed since the people who killed him made him use his last words to say such terrible things. I thought that maybe I owed it to Jimmy to write down the things believed. But I never wrote that list.

*

It's been eight years since Jimmy got killed, and it's still hard for me to believe I live in a world where something like that can happen.

My mom was wrong: Beliefs don't have anything to do with the strength of the person believing them. Beliefs are what we hold onto until experience tells us different. Beliefs are hopes, and they might not mean a goddamned thing. Then again, they might mean everything.

Defying the Gods

Taxonomy

Near a stand of quaking aspens on the Kenai peninsula, my sister Shannon and I run through fields that, our father tells us, are home to over two thousand varieties of wildflowers that have yet to be named. We pause to catch our breath in thickets of dazzling purples and shameless yellows that reach our six- and seven-year-old shoulders while Daddy crouches nearby and snaps photo after photo of Mama and us.

"But everything has a name," Shannon insists.

"Not until someone says it. Shannon," Daddy answers, between the whirs and snaps of the shutter on his second-hand Nikon.

We drive back to our duplex where the windows are covered in foil to block the perpetual daylight of Alaskan summer. Shannon and I fall into bed, exhausted from hiding and seeking in the fields, and from chasing butterflies as wildly colored as the flowers they lit upon. Despite the crackling of the speakers on the record player, the needle popping and skipping on a Ray Charles album Mama borrowed from the library, sleep overtakes us as it always does—suddenly and with no regard for our intentions. We surrender, mid-sentence, wearing on our lips the half-articulated attempts to name all those flowers about whose anonymity we are still incredulous: Purple Babies of the Valley, Don't You Dare Delilahs, Am-I-Bluer-Than-Thunders, and Glory Hallelujah Sunshines. Our nomenclature is not based in Latin, but in the language we've adopted from the Blues, country music, stories we love, and from the Sunday School lessons for which we've found no better use.

The next morning, Shannon and I wake to find a plain white envelope, the kind our parents mail the rent check in every month, beside a pie tin full of melted candle wax on the coffee table. The envelope is addressed to "Genevieve," the name Daddy never calls her. She is always "baby" or "honey" or "darlin" whenever he addresses her directly. Only outside her presence and in speaking about her to third parties does he call her by her given name. Her name in Daddy's blocky script renders the contents of the envelope irresistible. Mama has a proper name, like any wildflower deserves, and here is proof: Genevieve.

"You open it, Mary," Shannon says.

"No, you," I say.

We tacitly grant each other permission to breach our parents' privacy, an offense made easier because the envelope is unsealed. Shannon pulls from the envelope a single sheet of nearly transparent airmail stationery, fragile as dragonfly wings.

We read the note together, silently at first, embarrassed by its simple, first line in blue Bic ink: "Dear Genevieve, I'll love you til the day I die." The note is signed, simply, "Liam." At the bottom of the page is a second, shorter sentence: "p.s. You are beautiful." We puzzle over what "p.s." might mean: "pretty sure"? or "please see"? or "probably sometimes"? We tuck the note into the envelope and leave it as we found it—flap open, leaning against the wax-filled tin.

Daddy's post-script is the truth—Mama is beautiful. Her shiny black hair falls to the small of her back. Her impossibly green eyes can set you on your way, or pull you in and draw from you a confession for crimes you have not yet even contemplated. Her features make of us a lesson in the contrasts in any family, human proof of the genetic recipes Mendel found in his flowers. Mama is dark, and the sun never offends her with so much as a freckle after she has worked or played all day in its light. My siblings and I sunburn easily and our hair is various shades of blonde.

We grow up hearing Daddy invoke the post-script of his airmail love note. He tells us often and emphatically that Mama is the "most beautiful woman (he has) ever seen."

Baby-darlin honey-love sweetheart-sugar.

Well into our adulthoods, Genevieve is a name we hardly ever hear, though she deserves the taxonomy owed any rare flower: Genevieve-ceae, Genevieve-oidea Genevieve, Genevieve speciosa.

You Are Dying

"How did I get here?" Mom asks.

Her faltering mental state compels me to wonder whether this is an existential question or if she has forgotten, literally, how she came to be at my house. She spent Thanksgiving weekend talking with family and playing with my toddlers. Now she is so tired, she rarely leaves the sofa except to go back to bed.

"You drove down, Mama. With Daddy, remember?"

"No, Mary, I mean, how did this happen?" she asks.

She wants facts, it seems. So, I give her a clinical answer. I talk about bilirubin counts and clotting factors and liver function. I explain her diagnosis, as I understand it, and the underlying causes as they've been explained to me. I rely heavily upon my own research and phone calls with her doctors to encourage and inform my family. A lot of times, I'm full of shit. I either rage against the inequities of the organ sharing network and transplant criteria, or I dispense sunshine and hope, depending on what my family needs to hear from the battlefront.

"But, I mean, what is going to happen?" she asks. She has cause for worry. She was diagnosed two years ago and has begun the sudden and rapid decline her doctors warned her about. I give her the best possible clinical scenario. I restrict my answers to the medical facts as I understand them, and avoid conversation about the future.

"You have to be so sick you're dying, Mama, but you must be healthy enough that you could withstand what the surgery will do to you." And it sounds like doubletalk.

"But, honey, what's next?" she presses.

I offer her another anecdote from a medical journal. I

report numbers and survival rates. She looks away from me, out the window at my toddlers playing in the sandbox that is a kind of redundancy here in the New Mexican desert. They wave at her. She waves back. This exchange registers on her face as worry. Mom's impatience with me seems to grow with every kiss the kids blow to her from their muddy hands.

"Just. Tell. Me," she says.

And then I realize she wants the narrative. She is, after all, the woman who taught us to love stories, the woman who wove plot as she spoke, told tales that scared the crackers out of us or left us awake late into the night, aching to know what happened next. The storyteller isn't asking for clinical data. The closet novelist could care less about percentages and statistics. And the Halloween fortuneteller doesn't seek a prognosis. She wants a narrative, a story—even if it is scary.

The story recorded only in my notebook, the story I'll never tell her, goes like this:

"The insidious thing about liver disease, Mama, is that it leaves your beautiful face and body intact for months, maybe even years, while it ravages your insides and drains you so gradually of your will and energy that, at first, you hardly notice the loss. Then, the transformation from someone who is "sick, but looks so well" to someone who is "dying, I hear" is almost overnight. Primary Sclerosing Cholangitis (PSC), a string of words and their tidy acronym you never heard before, slowly take over your life before finally taking your life.

One morning, you walk out of your bedroom a little wobbly, and you might feel like you have the flu. Your real friends will observe to you how jaundiced your eyes and skin have become, and offer to drive you to the ER. Eventually, foundation and lipstick only make you look like a scary clown. Your cheek bones, one of the features about which you were always so proud, jut from your face. The whites of your eyes are no longer that—they are a mad yellow and, combined with your impossibly green irises, give your gaunt face a startled, alien look.

Suddenly, your pants won't stay up, and a belt only makes it impossible for you to take yourself seriously. Your skirts and blouses hang on you like you've raided your own mother's closet to play dress-up. Even your feet seem to have been diminished by your liver's failure. They swim in the high heels you will soon have to exchange for the flats and sneakers you've always called "tacky."

When the downhill slide becomes a full-on plummet and the only thing longer than the list of things you didn't get to do is the list of people ahead of you on the transplant registry, then your mind goes. This is a state called encephalopathy, a kind of intoxication—what you might compare to being drunk, if only you'd ever experienced it. Your daddy was an alcoholic and so were all his brothers, so you never drank. Not a drop, you cautioned us. But your liver is as quit as it can be, and oh well, here you are, drunk as a skunk, confused and a little combative, like most of the people you spent a childhood avoiding.

You had plans, remember? You imagined learning Italian or Spanish. Instead, mi amor, you will learn the language of evasion from your physicians and surgeons. Your doctors speak in passive voice about your condition, and they tell you that although your disease has developed slowly, your deterioration is now rapid and advanced.

You dreamed of travel with Daddy, somewhere "far away but affordable," now that your children are mostly grown. But you won't need a passport where you're going—which is only from your home in northern Arizona to any transplant center that will take you, if you're lucky, where you will wait for a donor organ to become available and where, if you're even luckier, you will receive the surgery that will damn near kill you in a gods-defying effort to save your life.

I'm so sorry, Mama. This is how you came to be here. And this is what will happen. It's happening now, only sometimes you forget."

Careful What You Wish For

The long-awaited phone call comes after Mom's physicians at Baylor have told us to take her home in the morning. Make her comfortable. Say our goodbyes. Instead, after a call that they've found a matching donor organ, we prepare Mom for surgery and reassure her against the shock of this news. Shannon's calm, quiet nature is steadying, and sometimes the antidote for toxic levels of smartass from our younger sister Liz and me. Shannon keeps us from straying into sleep-deprived nonsense or the wilderness of doubt.

Three hours after they've taken Mom for surgery, Dad walks into her hospital room. His smile is almost polite, a little shy. He wears his work clothes—Wranglers and work boots, a heavy cotton button-down, and a windbreaker that is not enough against the Dallas winter. His six-foot frame is leaner than usual. His eyes are more tired than blue, and he wears a couple days' growth of his sandy beard that is beginning to gray. We jump up from our chairs to hug him. He smells of motor oil and Old Spice aftershave.

The brim of his baseball cap is pulled low over his face until Liz reaches up and removes it. Baby sister is allowed these moments of instruction. "We can't see you, Daddy," she says.

"How is she?" he asks. He looks around the room, questions all over his face.

"The surgery will take about eight hours, but they'll let us know how she's doing," I say.

"What do you mean, surgery? Where the hell is she?" he asks.

Liz takes his arm, says, "She's in surgery, Daddy."

"What? What do you mean?" Dad seems confused.

"Transplant surgery. Right now, Daddy. They found a donor for her this morning. Everything is going to be fine," I tell him.

He turns to me, his face hard. His stance is tense, his arms at his sides. His hands are in tights fists, fairly shaking. "Why'd you let 'em take her?" he says through clenched teeth. "Why didn't you wait?!"

Somewhere between our relieved greetings and Dad's accusing questions, I have regressed to my ten-year-old old self, defensive about chores done wrong or a colicky horse we didn't know what to do with or young trees we lost to the wind. Or about the mother who took care of us during his long weeks away, and who now needs our care in his absence.

"Hey," I say, "how bout, thanks for taking care of your Mother. Thanks for looking after my wife. How bout that, huh?"

"You should've waited! This isn't right. It isn't right, got-damnit."

"Really, Daddy? Not right? But it's right for us to make decisions when you're not around, but now you want to criticize?"

"Don't talk to me like that," he says.

"Two years of waiting, and bake sales and car washes and selling every damn thing we could to get her here. But we shoulda waited? And oh, by the way, Daddy, I left my own kids to be here, so—"

Dad turns to Shannon. "What's going on? Where is your Mom?"

"She's dying, Daddy—you know this," I say. "There's finally an organ available, but we shoulda said, 'Hey, y'all Baylor surgeons, let's hold off a little while?'"

"I said don't talk to me like that," he yells.

"That's easy. How bout I don't talk at all," I yell right back.

Liz takes Daddy to a chair by the window. Shannon throws an arm around my shoulders.

"Okay, let's calm down," Shannon says. "Mary, come with me."

We walk past the nurses station and down the hall to the little alcove of vending machines where Shannon speaks her mind. "Try to put yourself in Daddy's shoes."

"Are you kidding me? We've been in his shoes for months—years. I'm tired of it."

"You don't mean that," Shannon says. "Come on."

Shannon's face is lit by the soft glow from the soda machine. The Coca Cola- sponsored illumination of her face reveals dark circles under those fire-and-ice blue eyes.

"I didn't mean it," I say. "I'm sorry. But what the hell's he mad about? Makes no sense."

"He's scared is all," Shannon says. "He crossed a picket line, and he's been sleeping in his truck just to keep that job in Phoenix. You gotta give him a break."

Shannon and I walk the halls of the transplant floor where we've stayed with Mom during the four days since her last collapse. By the time we return to her room, I am chastened by the stories I've gleaned from other rooms and by the burdens borne by spouses and lovers. After walking a turn or two around the fourteenth floor, I realize I should take a few steps in Dad's worn out work boots.

Back in Mom's room, I try to take in the scene as Dad might've when he arrived. The room is empty, except for the bedside table and a few chairs against the wall. Next to the table, some socks, pajamas, makeup, and a notebook spill from Mom's small overnight bag, as though she left in a hurry. Her shoes, the sensible flats she hates, are crossed over each other as though she kicked them off only moments ago. The most conspicuous feature of the room is its emptiness where her hospital bed should be. Every piece of furniture and equipment is oriented toward that blank space. Walking in on that scene would strike panic and fear, and subsequently even anger, in the heart of a man who had tried mightily to get here before his wife was taken away for a procedure that could be the end of everything or the beginning of a precious second chance.

*

All the deep and heavy conversations have been had, it seems, or successfully avoided. We pass the next few hours with small talk, until we discover the book cart in the room down the hall where no families ever lounge.

I look up from a Mary Karr memoir to see a surgeon approach the nurses station. And I hear him speak our name—

"Dailey." His surgeon's cap is pushed back on his head a bit, and his surgical gown gently flutters at his sides like delicate wings when he strides quickly toward us. He turns to enter Mom's room, and I'm not sure whether we should sit down or remain standing.

He introduces himself. "I'm Doctor Klintmalm. Am I addressing the family of Genevieve Dailey?"

"You are," I say.

All of us "kids" stand and cluster around the doctor. Dad stands, too, but he remains in his spot near the window, with his head slightly bowed and his hands in his pockets.

"May I know to whom I am speaking?" Doctor Klintmalm asks. His singsong, Swedish-accented English is pleasant, and his voice is reassuring.

We all quickly say our names. Dad is quiet.

"Genevieve is responding well. Wait a minute. Can I get you all to step back a moment?" the doctor asks. He parts us with his extended arms, creating a wide space before himself.

We step away from him. I'm worried now about what he has to say.

"Come, Papa," the doctor says, and motions for Dad to come forward.

Dad touches his own chest, raises his eyebrows.

"Yes, Papa, come."

Dad crosses the room and accepts Doctor Klintmalm's extended hand.

"I'm Liam Dailey, sir," Dad says.

"Liam, your wife is doing very well, as I was telling—your children, yes? The surgery is going to take a little longer than we had anticipated. We have encountered a complication, and it's serious."

Dad shoves his hands deep into his pockets and bows his head. "Is this…common?"

"Well, it's not uncommon, but it is an unexpected difficulty. So, the surgery will take much longer than we'd anticipated. But I wanted you to know. Do you have any questions?"

Dad's silence is unnerving. Finally, he says, "No, not now. Thank you for telling us, Doctor." They shake hands again, and the doctor strides out of the room. Dad watches his departure. We hear the doctor's surgical gown swishing at his sides until he steps into the elevator.

The news we heard is hard, but Dad seems calmer and somehow more resolute. He took to Doctor Klintmalm. Dad returns to his post at the window, and stares out at the Dallas night.

*

We pace and read and talk. And pace and read and talk. The last five hours have been the most difficult. We're in that twilight space now, between expectations, not yet transitioned from one hope to another.

Around 10pm, Doctor Klintmalm returns to tell us that the surgery is complete and Mom has been moved to recovery for observation. After a short time there, she will be moved to the transplant ICU, where she will stay for at least 24 hours. We will be permitted short visits, two at a time, when she is awake.

"Now, a word of caution. This is a critical time, the next day or so," Doctor Klintmalm says. "Papa, Genevieve did great. She's strong. But she will need quiet, calm interactions and reassurance when you speak with her. Her body has been through a lot, and she has quite a lot of recovery ahead."

The doctor looks like he, too, has been through a lot tonight. He has lost some of the energy he had earlier. His eyes are tired, and he seems fairly slumped inside the gown that hangs off his shoulders now. But his smile is sincere, and his tone is bright. "Take good care of your mother," he says to my siblings and me. "And your father."

"Thank you, sir. Thank you so much," Dad says. They shake hands again and smile big at each other.

"You're quite welcome, Papa. Quite welcome."

*

Around eleven o'clock, Mom's nurse Rachel steps into the room to tell us we can visit Mom in the transplant-dedicated

ICU. She warns us that Mom is sedated but conscious. We all take a silent ride on the elevator.

As if on cue, my brother Seamus walks around the corner to find us all gathered in the hallway outside the ICU. His Stetson is cocked on his head, and he looks tired, but his half smile is comforting beyond belief. He is the one among us who can comfort Mom on one of those dark days when motherhood seems like some sort of test she has failed. They're of a kind, Seamus and Mom.

Seamus removes his hat, looks around at all of us and, after we embrace him, he says, "Well, where is she?"

"Let's go," Dad says. "They'll buzz us through two at a time, but we have to be real quiet."

Dad is first through the doors, and Seamus follows closely behind. The rest of us stand in the hallway, making small talk, lighter in mood now, but only a little. I'm anxious to see Mom, but mostly I am anticipating Dad's face—I'll know more about how I should feel and what to hope for when he walks back through those doors.

We're seated on the floor, leaning against the wall, when Dad returns about twenty minutes later. His eyes are lit up. He smiles at all of us, and says, "Your mother is doing great."

Seamus pushes through the ICU doors behind Dad. Seamus sets his hat back on his head, pulls the brim down low over his face, and strides straight down the hall to the elevator. I haven't seen him cry since he was a little boy—and I can't pretend to recall the occasion that, even then, was so uncommon as to be unsettling.

Shannon and Liz visit Mom together. When they return, their relief is a thing to behold. Liz is temporarily and uncharacteristically speechless. A few minutes at Mom's bedside and Liz has gone from twenty-two to twelve. Pain and worry never make her cry, but happiness gets her every time.

Shannon says, "She made it. She made it. She made it." And then she sighs long and hard.

It's my turn now, but I don't want to go in alone. "C'mon,

Daddy," I say. And he eagerly accepts my invitation.

Dad leads me through chirping and hissing pumps and monitors that make an obstacle course of this specialized ICU. We take seats at Mom's bedside. She appears to be sleeping.

He speaks to her. "Honey, can you hear me? Mary is here."

Mom's face is swollen and a little bruised. She can't speak, because her larynx was roughed up during the surgery. Her wrists are tethered to the bed rails.

I lean over her, so she can see me. "Hey, Mama. You're doing great. Everything's okay."

She moans something unintelligible at us. She grows a little agitated, trying to speak. Dad asks one of the ICU nurses for a pen and paper. The nurse brings him a stubby pencil and some scrap paper. Dad places the pencil in Mom's right hand, and holds the paper for her.

"OK?" she writes.

"I'm okay, honey, I'm okay. We are all fine. Don't worry, baby."

Then she writes, "Love". The short messages in her unsteady hand look like a first grader's attempt at passing notes. Dad takes the note back to write a response, though it's clear she can hear him. The pencil and torn graph paper are the voice Dad needs right now, and where he must meet Mom for this conversation. I shouldn't be here for this exchange, but I'm trapped between Dad's chair and the wall in this cramped space between monitors and IV poles.

Dad's right fist is closed over the pencil stub pressed against the paper on his knee. He holds the note before her. The only word he has written this time is, "Genevieve."

Mom reads her name, looks over at Daddy. She stares hard at the paper, as though that last word is inscrutable or might disappear altogether. She half-coughs. Her eyes want to cry but her body won't let her.

"You okay, hon?" a nurse asks Mom, and scowls at us.

I want to reassure the nurse that we haven't said anything scary or brought bad news into the ICU. But how could I explain the importance of that note? Who would believe more information is contained in this single word than can be read in all these monitors reporting even the slightest of changes in Mom's every vital sign?

Mom manages a nod. This gesture, its own language in specialized intensive care, satisfies the nurse. She walks away.

Dad again presses the note against his knee. "I love you. Always," he writes.

Mom nods. He stands up, leans over to kiss her forehead. "Genevieve," he whispers. When he sits back in his chair again, I'm relieved and embarrassed.

Mom tries to point up at us, or at something behind us, but the tether on her wrist restricts her motion. Then I see the clock, high on the wall above Dad's head.

"Hey, yeah, Daddy, look—it's almost midnight," I say. "Happy New Year, Mama."

'14-yo Female'

After two days in ICU, Mom returns to her hospital room on the transplant floor. She is in pain, and we watch her closely. Rachel returns to take Mom's vitals; when she leaves the room, I notice a new chart hanging on the wall, just inside the door. My eyes are drawn to a cryptic line on the new chart: "Donor organ: 14yo Caucasian female", whose other organs were also harvested, the chart seems to suggest.

All of our veiled and passive language about this gift, the way we've avoided the truth that was always in our peripheral view—the fact that Mom's survival depends upon someone's death—is glaringly inadequate and seems a little dishonest now. "When a donor organ becomes available;" "when an organ is located;" "when there is a match for you."

We gather at a nearby hotel room, and I tell Dad what I read about the donor organ. This information seems to weigh heavily on him. He wears it in his shoulders, slouched over a book he's not reading, and it's on his face as he stands at the window, again, staring into the darkness. He calls us together, and doesn't make eye contact as he tells us to kneel for prayer. We are awkward and quiet, assuming the postures of childhood and a faith most of us have abandoned. But we do it for him. And for Mom. He mentions the donor's family in his prayer, calls them, "those generous people" and asks God to bless and keep their "little girl." We don't speak of it again, but I hear Dad crying long after we turn off the lights.

Defiance

Scott McCartney's *Defying the Gods* was an important reference for my family during my mother's wait on the transplant list. McCartney's research is a mix of the clinical and anecdotal, the physiological and the spiritual. He addresses the cost of transplant surgery and the inequities in organ distribution. His accounts of unprecedented access to the organ allocation system, transplant surgical teams, and patient recovery at Baylor University Medical Center are riveting and harrowing.

In all the years since Mom's transplant, my tattered copy of *Defying the Gods* has occupied a spot on my bookshelf, less for its clinical and programmatic data than for McCartney's reflection on a post-operative condition that has persisted since Mom's recovery: our family's seeming and inexplicable ingratitude. Our response is not uncommon, and has basis in the psychology of the process and in the sheer magnitude of the donor's gift. McCartney observes:

"If there is a curious footnote, it is that none of the (organ recipients chronicled in the book) has been able to sit down and write a letter of thanks to the families of their donors. The words do not come easily; the emotions overwhelm the pen. Transplantation has allowed this unique charity to become standard operating procedure in our society, and yet those touched by it struggle to find ways to show gratitude. How do you thank someone for your life? How do you tell a family still grieving over the tragic loss of a daughter or son, a husband or wife, that you are thrilled to be alive…? How can you possibly explain why you got a second chance and they didn't? How can we deal with such irony, such tragedy? Why do some win, and some lose?" (McCartney, Defying the Gods: Inside the New Frontier of Organ Transplants. Port Townsend, WA: Copper Canyon Press p.278).

McCartney's interviews reveal that the gift of life is so truly awesome as to be almost incomprehensible. And that's how we all felt: grateful beyond our capacity to express it. We were as unsophisticated and uneducated as any patient's family could be about the system from which we directly benefited. And Mom herself can still hardly speak of it. But I can't help wondering if the real defiance against the gods, the one "sin" I might be persuaded to believe in, is unexpressed gratitude.

As I witness now the aging of my parents and watch my own children enter adulthood, I feel a greater sense of urgency about expressing our gratitude—and condolences—to the family of "K", a fourteen-year-old girl we never knew, but will never forget. Mom has drafted many letters to K's family, and the organ donor organization between our two families has agreed to pass them along. But Mom has never sent any of those letters. And in the years since her transplant, social media could only make finding and connecting with K's family so much easier. But Mom cannot be persuaded. She has a drawer full of drafts, notebooks with starts and re-starts. "It doesn't seem near enough," she says. "How could it ever be enough?"

Another Mother's Day approaches, the holiday when my gratitude to K and her family is most acute, and I begin, again, a letter of my own; the delinquency is more shameful every year. I start with condolences and an attempt to account for the "good" my mother has done with her life. I tell K's mother we've all tried to earn this gift—though our family is dysfunctional and scattered, and perfect only at being imperfect. But even in this, even in expressing sorrow for her loss, in offering explanations and making introductions, I am so remiss.

I start over. Again.

Because the first words to say, maybe the only words, are *Thank you.*

Corina Zappia

Five Boxes

My mother started to price cemetery plots around the time my father began to lose his way back from the bathroom. He had been diagnosed with Alzheimer's eight years prior, but it was only in the last two that he would grab votive candles off tables at restaurants, mistaking them for glasses of water. We would wrench them away before he burnt his tongue. It was then when she began contemplating where she and my father would be buried, even though she had never thought of herself as old before. That's the reality of this kind of preplanning; it forces you to mentally pre-bury yourself next to your spouse.

Refusing to be bested by any industry that overcharges, much less one that takes advantage of the grieving, she started bargain hunting for a plot early. A few weeks after she started looking, we went out to lunch at a Japanese restaurant. She waited till the ramen soup arrived to make her an announcement.

"Corina, I bought boxes for all five of us."

"Boxes?" I said. "What kind of boxes?"

"Cremation boxes."

I almost spat out a pork chunk. "What, there was a 5-for-1 sale at the local cemetery?"

"Well, I wanted your sister Angelina to come with me, because if you bought a plot by February you could get $1,000 off. But she thought it was too grim."

"$1,000 off? What the hell is that—the Valentine's Day special?"

"Well, that's if your father and I were buried at the Catholic cemetery close to the house. Or we could be buried at the military cemetery in Kent. The military cemetery would be for free, because he was a Vietnam vet, but it's so far away, and only one of you can come with us."

"Come with you?"

"Yes, be buried with us. The V.A. cemetery isn't as nice, but it's free. Completely free. I want you and Angelina to come with me to see both, but she doesn't want to discuss it."

Usually my older sister Angelina was the family member my mother relied on most, the one who became a physician like both of our parents, the one who spoke my mother's medical language of stethoscopes and ventilators—the one who, if it came down to it, could change my father's diaper.

"Sure, I'll come," I said, though I knew contemplating funeral plans with my mother would mean considering my own as well. I mean, there were boxes already, and only one of us "could come with them," although who wanted to go to Kent, WA, the onetime Lettuce Capitol of the World.

"To be honest, Mom, I don't know what's happening with me. I'm single, I don't have any kids, I don't know if I'm going to stay in Seattle.... It's a little hard for me to think even three months ahead. Who knows where my life is going?"

"Don't worry, Corina." She patted me on the arm. "At least you'll have a box."

Fifteen or twenty years ago, I would have never connected the aging of my parents with my own fears of getting older, but perhaps back then I imagined I would be more of an adult by now with a partner and kids and home of my own, instead of a junior one bedroom and bus pass.

About 10 years ago, my mother retired and bought a house just outside Seattle, about a half hour away from my older sister and me. I visited them a couple times a week, sometimes catching a ride with a colleague after work and letting myself in with the key my mother proudly presented to me after they closed on the house.

"Hey. Anyone up there? It's me, Corina." My voice would float up the stairs to the dining room where my parents sat. It was a funny house, three narrow floors connected by an elevator and stairs. They bought it because my father fell in love with the top floor's views of the Puget Sound at sunset, streaks of lavender and pink painted onto the water every night and dotted with tiny white ferries and sailboats.

I heard my mother's voice, drifting back down from upstairs. "Oh it's you, Corina. Come join us. We're just having dinner."

I ran up the stairs, and before I could set my bag down, before asking for a greeting herself, my mother said, "Kiss your father hello."

I gave my father a quick peck on the cheek, and he smiled at me sweetly, looking up from the plate of food my mother cut up for him. "Aww…hello there, beautiful daughter."

"Hello there, beautiful father." He chuckled at this.

When do we realize who the more resilient parent is? Before we even know what resilient means, I think. Even when I was child, the fear of my father dying early kept me up nights, but my mother's death is something I have only begun to consider. She's always been the kind of parent who would live forever and then haunt her children into the afterlife, coming back in specter form just to remind me to sit up straight at dinner.

In my father's defense, he only appeared weaker next to my mother because, well, we all did. When she broke her toe ramming it into a door once, my mother just reached down, straightened the bones out herself, and went about her day. Instead of vacationing back home in the Philippines, she would plan medical missions there, lending her physician's expertise to small mountain villages. Many of the towns lacked electricity, and she hauled IVs and medicines over from the States, packed on ice.

"When Armageddon comes," a friend of mine said, "your mother will be the one pulling bodies out of the river."

With my father, it was different. Certainly hardy enough when it came to his job, he could oversee the entire ICU unit by himself and drive to the hospital several times a night for emergencies, and yet his weaker constitution and gentler personality made him seem much more vulnerable. Oddly it was when he was at his kindest that I feared for him the most, as there was always something a little heartbreaking about his generosity, a guilelessness about it, as if too honest and innocent to last. It didn't help that he always suffered from some bodily ailment or another: kidney stones, high cholesterol, arthritis, a sour stomach weakened by overeating.

When I was younger, I feared he would suffer a heart attack because heart disease ran in the family and my father was already overweight. He loved his ice cream, just like his father did. When we visited his side of the family in Yonkers, at some point my grandfather would make a not-so-secret retreat to the freezer on the second floor of the apartment, to dip into what seemed to be a magically replenishing tub of vanilla ice cream. Amazing, the pleasure my grandfather and my father took in just a simple scoop of plain vanilla—no sprinkles, no hot fudge on top, no cake or pie nestled next to it. At home my father had his own private stash in our second fridge, his shrunken down to a more reasonably sized pint of Haagen-Dazs. He would visit it around 10pm and then between the hours of 3am and 4am, as his own personal reward for a dinner of Slimfast shakes or Lean Cuisine lasagnas.

"You know it doesn't work that way," I said, "this losing-weight thing, if you follow it up with ice cream."

"It's for my heartburn," he would reply, his eyes never leaving the bowl, his spoon scooping up every last melted puddle. When there was ice cream in front of him, my father could concentrate on nothing else.

He still consumed it that same way, scooping out the puddles that the rest of us would let the dishwasher clean off later, eating with the glee of an 8-year-old. It was a vision as charming as it was painful. He now had the mental capacity of a child; his love of ice cream was one of the few things he retained. For a man who had no problem eating anything and everything all his life, it's surprising how difficult it is to make him eat now. This must be the smallest he's been in decades—

too small, I think. We beg him to drink Carnation shakes; we supplement them with protein powder, call them milkshakes. We tell him if he doesn't finish his vegetables or take his pills there will be no ice cream after. Sometimes we just give him the ice cream anyway, because it's the only thing he will eat.

My father knows that I am his daughter but can no longer remember my name. I visit on Sunday nights for dinner and head back to work on Monday, thinking too much.

I had lied to my mom about not thinking about my own funeral. I'd been planning it since I was a teenager, at least the more fashionable aspects of it, dreaming about it the way some girls imagine what they want their wedding or bachelorette party to look like. Sounds a bit macabre, but I'm a firm believer that one should never leave any major life events to chance or to others. I had been to enough bachelorette parties, weddings and funerals to know that poor planning gets you penis rings and suck-for-a buck t-shirts, games where the bride-to-be must guess the name of her fiancé's first dog, dry wedding receptions with the Electric Slide, honeymooners in public hot tubs, and when I start to believe there might be an afterlife, funerals where the deceased have had no say.

I don't think you can be raised Catholic like I was and not start thinking of death early, what with the whole ashes to ashes bit, the body and blood of Christ, all those hours looking at the Son of God dying on a cross. How primed we young Catholics are to contemplate mortality from First Communion on, the flimsiness of life and the human body stressed and underlined when Sister Aquinas informs us in middle school that Christ was actually nailed to the cross at the wrist and not in the middle of the hand, as is often rendered in paintings and sculptures—for if that had been the case, the weight of his body would have ripped the nail straight through.

I couldn't have been the only Catholic kid planning her funeral by 6th grade. I debated who would speak at the ceremony—sisters or best friends?—and what reflections they would share in this ultimate toast to dead me. Sometimes I made mental notes on headstone trends: When walking past more modern markers in cemeteries, I would notice how the polished, almost reflective facades etched with head-to-shoulder images of the deceased were reminiscent of the smooth coating of a Sweetheart candy. If I had my wish and a bigger bank account, I would swing for the rough-hewn slabs I'd seen sticking up at odd angles at Pere Lachaise in Paris, half-hidden by weeds and grass. Those were the Cadillacs of headstones. While I could never afford the original, I would settle for a shabby-chic reissue with ersatz wearing around the corners.

As soon as my mother and I returned home from lunch, I called my little sister Gabriella in New York to tell her the news.

"I've actually thought of how I want to be buried," she replied.

"Oh yeah, me too."

"No, Corina." She sighed. "I've thought about how I actually want to be buried, not what I want my *party* to be like. Cremate me, and I don't need no box. Just toss my ashes into the nearest body of water. Boom. Done."

"You say that, Gabriella, but you don't know what happens. It ain't neat, perfect, ashy powder that flies away in the wind. There are shards. Sometimes, the wind blows. *Blowback*."

"Damn, I hadn't thought about that."

"Who does? It's all good until you're cleaning Aunt Bertha out from under your fingernails."

"Oh god. Well, maybe you can just put me in a compostable bag and drop me into the water."

I put my hand over the receiver. "Mom," I said, calling out across the room, "when Gabriella dies she wants to be cremated, thrown in a compostable bag, and dropped into the ocean."

My mother glanced up briefly from her iPhone. "Like dog shit?"

When my father's parents passed away, we buried them whole in a Catholic cemetery, one of those cinematically perfect graveyards near where they'd lived in Yonkers, New York, with sloping hills and valleys dotted by headstones crammed into every last patch of grass, clunky hearses winding their way up narrow pebbled paths, and somber men in black suits and dark shades emerging from town cars with tinted windows. During my grandfather's burial, my sisters and I liked to pretend that the men were part of a mafia funeral instead of just another boring Italian-Catholic family from down the street like us.

That was a cemetery mostly for coffins. Cremation was forbidden until 1985 by the Catholic Church out of reverence for the body as a temple of Christ and the Holy Spirit; the ban eventually had to be lifted because of space concerns. Cremation now appears to be all the rage among environmentally concerned Catholics of the Pacific Northwest, at least if the Catholic cemetery near my parents' home in Washington were any proof. Flatter and far emptier than my grandparents' graveyard, it featured few of the massive, intricately etched headstones I associated with cemeteries, which were replaced instead by foot-long plaques squeezed so close together that a full human body could never fit in between—just a condensed, cremated one.

A week or two after lunch at the Japanese restaurant, my mother scheduled a meeting with the cemetery's funeral director. Persuaded by further prodding, my older sister and I joined her.

Though I'd never met a funeral director in person before, I always pictured them as some kind of sleazy real-estate agent, preying on my sense of obligation to hawk a 24K gold super casket. The portly thirtysomething guy with thick black-rimmed glasses who greeted us at the door of the cemetery's business office looked more like a stand-up comedian, but his voice was too gentle and unctuous for open-mike night. After a brief introduction, he drove us to the mausoleum on the far edge of the grounds, a minimalist gray building that could have doubled as a small library.

Mausoleums always seem to have doors like bank vaults, as if the souls and smells of the dearly departed might escape through anything thinner; this one was no different. Heaving the mausoleum door open with a hefty push, the director led us a few steps into the vestibule.

"This is actually a great gift your parents are giving you," he said, his eyes shifting toward my sister and me. "So when the worst day in the world comes, you'll know what to do."

I resisted the urge to roll my eyes. Yes, it's the worst day in the world, but those lines rolled off his lips a bit too easily. On the other hand, why shouldn't he have lines he uses? His 9 to 5, at the end of the day, must be just as rote as the rest of ours.

Following the director into the mausoleum's center room, we found ourselves facing an altar surrounded by rows of chairs, as if mass was about to begin. Two crypts off to each side held walls of metal drawers—niches, they called them—which resembled safety deposit boxes until you walked close enough to make out the names of the deceased. The director headed toward the crypt on the left, and we followed.

"Those are ours?" my mother asked, gesturing at one of the rows of niches about halfway down the wall.

"You have those four, and that one below it," the director said, pointing to another niche on the row below the rest.

He said it so nonchalantly, that it took me a minute to realize what we were looking at: my family's final resting place. No transition, no lead in, just boom: Here's the wall you're going to be stuffed into someday.

I didn't know that my mother had already purchased space, but when you think about it, who the hell buys free-floating cremation boxes? And yet when she had first mentioned them, that was exactly what I had pictured: five cardboard cubes a little larger than shoeboxes, shrink-wrapped together like a Costco bulk-pak that we could stash in the garage until needed.

Each of the five spaces was less than a foot long, and half a foot wide. It was amazing what the body could be reduced to. There was nothing exceptional about our niches, other than that one of the five was on a row below the rest. I didn't want to hurt my mom's feelings, but the cemetery seriously jacked her on that one; it looked like where you stuck your estranged second cousin. Some of the other niches above and below us had been decorated with three-inch oval photos of their occupants in plastic frames, images from when they were still alive.

"These photos are grim, man," I whispered to Angelina. "We are not doing that. Our names up there are enough; I don't need to be staring at some fridge magnet of you." She nodded silently.

Two feet away, my mother busied herself examining some of the niches' short, two-line inscriptions. "Huh, not much room to write 'Devoted, Fabulous Mother,' eh?" she asked the director.

"No," the director chuckled. "Not too much room, I'm afraid." He proceeded to lead us out of the crypt, cutting short any further pondering of our mortality. I wondered if it was an unspoken rule in the funeral business: Don't let clients gaze upon their final resting place for more than five minutes. Really, is there anything more awkward than showing people to their graves?

Back in the center hall, I noticed a few short glass-covered bookcases between the front door and the altar. "Jesus, what is that?" I said, pointing to a few urns in the bookcase. "It's like you're a high school trophy." I thumbed my finger back toward the walls of metal drawers. "I'm more into this gym locker vibe, myself."

Sigmund Freud once described gallows humor as a triumph of the pleasure principle over life's more depressing reality; he left out what acting like a brat at the family mausoleum meant. And yet I couldn't stop myself. I was okay with hashing out funeral contemplations on the surface: what I would do for a toast, who would be invited, but the actual purchase of post-mortem property felt like a step further than I was ready to take. I knew that my generation were getting married and having children later, if at all, and meanwhile our parents were not getting any younger. I knew that because of this, it was far more likely for someone my age to be single, childless, and already tending to their aging or dying parents, or in this case, watching as they tended to each other. It was even more likely in my sisters' and my case, because my parents married and had us relatively later in life. Knowing and telling myself these things didn't change the feeling that it was still happening too fast. My father wasn't supposed to get diagnosed with Alzheimer's when I was 30, and I wasn't supposed to be picking out his grave and my own a few years later. Certain adult milestones were playing hopscotch with other adult milestones, when the linear progression of it all was one of the few securities I had unknowingly relied upon all these years. Why were they dying before I had even had a chance to become a proper adult, whatever that was supposed to be? I hadn't even bought my first house yet.

Weirdly enough, shopping around for a burial plot did seem a little like house hunting.

After the mausoleum, the director drove us around on a guided tour of the rest of the grounds.

It began to feel less like we were driving around a cemetery and more like we were checking out a new neighborhood with an estate agent, peering into people's driveways to cast judgment on their crabgrass.

Along a slight dip in the road, he pointed out the window to a shrine with a statue of the Virgin Mary, where other Filipinx families were buried. "This is Our Lady of Antipolo," he said.

My mother dismissed the area with a wave of her hand. "No, no, the feng shui's no good here, can't you see?" Our Lady of Antipolo was tucked behind a columbarium behind the main road. I had no idea when or where she had studied up on cemetery feng shui, although it did appear that our people had been buried in the least attractive part of the cemetery.

The funeral director continued his 5-mph drive around the grounds. Peering out of the passenger-side window, my mother spotted a few flat, rectangular metal plaques bolted into the earth, gravestone markers so small and close together that they resembled bricks in a paved road. "Wow, how much are those?"

"Those are our lowest price option," he replied.

"Wouldn't someone step on you all the time though," I asked, "mistaking you for the path?"

We drove on. As the road started to slope upward again, our eyes drifted to the highest point of the cemetery, where two walls of niches in gleaming gray granite stood just beyond a wrought iron arch bearing the title "Resurrection Walkway."

"Resurrection Walkway is our most expensive space," the director said. "*Completely* full."

The walkway overlooked a majestic view of a nearby lake, like something out of a tourism ad for the Pacific Northwest. We continued onto "The City of God," a few modest walls of niches that reminded me fondly of the book stacks in my old college library, so I inquired about them.

"Nazareth is full," the director said, "but there's still some availability in Mount Sinai, there in the top right."

Availability. The word made me feel queasy, but an odd queasiness mixed with hope, the hope that comes with learning there's still some real estate left on the market and you have a chance to get in there, literally. Just beyond Nazareth, I spotted a few small freestanding granite blocks, each holding a single shelf with a permanent flower vase.

"I like these little guys," I said. "How many fit in one of those?"

After the tour, the funeral director drove us back to his office, so my mother could sign the final papers. Right before signing, she looked up at my sisters and me.

"No open casket for my wake," she ordered. "I mean, what

a time to be vain, you know?"

I nodded at this last attempt at humor but couldn't muster a laugh. While we needed to secure a space for my father, did we have to decide everyone's final resting place today?

"Listen Mom," I said, "while I appreciate having the option, what if I don't want to be cremated? Or what if when I am cremated, I want to spread my ashes somewhere like Gabriella? Or what if I get married and want to be buried next to my spouse?"

"You can always sell your space," the director piped up from across his desk. "People sell them on Craigslist all the time."

This guy again.

"Really? Craigslist? I had no idea."

"You could also consider a cenotaph, a memorial marker even though your remains are buried elsewhere."

"Isn't that a fakeout though?"

"Well, with this *fakeout*, as you call it, for some people who are married twice, they might want to be buried with their children, but they love their second wife.... These are tough decisions."

I was starting to annoy him, I could tell. But I hate being sold to, especially when it comes to something as sensitive as a funeral, and I loathed the idea of someone trying to sell to my mother, although Lord knows the woman could take care of herself. And anyway, why treat death so delicately? Why not jokes? I like how Mark Twain put it, humor being the "kindly veil" we drop over the hard and sordid things of life "to blur the craggy outlines and make the thorns less sharp and the cruelties less malignant." Humor is one of the few shields we have, our only release against the inevitability of our mortality.

I wasn't sure if humor had become some elaborately weaponized shelter of sarcasm I was hiding under today or my own way of confronting death. Maybe it was both. Maybe I needed it to do more.

I used to think I was fairly good at accepting the concept of death because I wasn't afraid to let conversations grow dark, because I could read about decaying corpses and find some descriptions of the dead and dying beautiful even—intestines that "bunched out in a thick white cluster like the congested petals of a sea flower," as Norman Mailer wrote in one of my favorite passages from *The Naked and The Dead*. In contemplating my own funeral or affecting a macabre sense of humor, I liked to imagine that I was more comfortable with the concept of death than others. This is what an unwavering love of goth music and Victorian cemeteries does to you. My thoughts about death had never involved the act itself, just the pageantry.

I was initially startled by my mother's no-nonsense approach to funeral planning—real, actual funeral planning, not just lofty ways to decorate one's grave. Deep down, I had to admit there was part of me that respected it. She was trying to accept the idea of death through preparation, and in buying graves for the family, she was relieving my sisters and me of one more financial burden in an age of ever-escalating healthcare costs. My sisters and I would pay for nothing in the end: not my parents' healthcare in their elderly years, not their burial—hell, if we wanted, not even our own burial. It was as if, in building a home for us, my parents had paid to have it taken down as well, slat by slat, stone by stone, sweeping and cleaning up the dust behind them, to make room for the next family that would take our space. It was a generosity I could never repay. I couldn't help but feel that the roles should have been reversed by now, that I should have been taking on more of the financial planning and caretaking at this point. She was the adult nearing 80 and I was still the child, nearing 40. My father had become an additional child for her to take care of, now that his body and mind were destroyed by dementia and cancer.

When my father had been healthy, he was jolly and rotund:

a more patient Fred Flintstone, a younger Santa. It was hard to believe that he was the same person even, and often I tried not to, because it was easier to accept that he was slowly dying if I fooled myself that the man I once knew was not the man in the sick bed. To connect him to the same person who retired early to sit by my own bedside for years when I was sick, this was a reality too horrible to be realized straight on. It was a reality that I never returned in kind. I spent more time helping out my mother in the kitchen because I could not assist my mother or the caregiver with my father. I was too afraid of seeing him naked; of the excrement, blood, and vomit; of his tunneled bed sore they stuffed with gauze. When I was with my father, one eye was always aimed at the clock, waiting for the moment when I could escape the room and resume my life: dress for work, go to the movies, meet up with friends for a drink. It was as if life outside sped up the instant I entered his room, and I was reminded of what I had not yet done that day, that week, those past few years; and while life flew by outside, it stood still within that room, as I patted my father's hand, and smoothed his hair, and waited for him to die, in that useless dance of those who cannot be helped and those who cannot give it.

I had been told by others that the end would be harder to accept, if I remained this detached. But long illnesses offer these little moments of reprieve, I like to think, that small bench to rest at before the end, when you're handed a box filled with your father's ashes. Until then, there needed to be snarky comments about high school trophies and fakeouts and stupid Resurrection Walkway. Humor removed the reality of my father, at least for a minute.

I could make jokes at the cemetery that day because we were still debating metal boxes versus limestone gravestones, and I had asked my mother not to bring him that day, to have a nurse watch over him at home instead. I didn't have to talk around him on the car ride over, or pretend that we were on a big family trip to nowhere. I didn't have to picture him waiting in the car while the rest of us went to look at the mausoleum, where he would be buried first. He would have sat in the car and wondered where everyone had gone, and he would have complained, as he always did now, about how cold it was, and why the invisible mosquitos were biting him, and when we were coming back.

POETRY

Sean Cho A.

Act Three/Sonnet +1 #36

Sure fine.

i want the sun bear to be happy too.

the days are always the same amount of too long

and there is either too much to do or what there is

is not exciting. but of course he's happy to return

to his cubs watch the game and have something

to talk about. when the cubs win the world series

it's a great story. cubs grow up because that's what

they do. you shouldn't look into that still river. the moon

will be here soon. if the air doesn't feel like being wind

the sun bear can see himself in the still river. or. he could

return home and use his closet mirror. all the advancements

are too helpful and present to be noticed. the sun bear's

neck ties are all the wrong shade of green. turn the lights

back off. can't you see the sun bear's wife is trying to sleep

Act Three/Sonnet #37

Okay you got me. i cheated. the last poem was
too long.i didn't think you were paying attention. i am
glad you're paying attention. isn't that what we both want.
the sun bear reads books on bear traps so he can feel
empowered. the trap expert paid the ghost writer
because he likes to be listened to but isn't good with
words. and the ghost writer is on a plane to malaysia.
the sun bear isn't sure what the opposite of
a zero sum game is. he hasn't read the theory. yet.
he still believes in the good of it all. he plants
the seeds and waits till spring. see there's been
star fruits all along. why bother convincing
the sun bear of anything else. there's a cub being born
in the san diego zoo today. we do not choose the definition of home.

Act Three/Sonnet #42

Of course there's a sun bear in birmingham that knows
about mars. but everyone seems really happy and he
is good at keeping secrets. today the sun bear is searching
for land. there's a marble in his pocket. since this is a poem
we get to know this marble is *earth* and that the bear
works as a public relations director for the sun bear
space program. this sun bear knows that visuals are more
effective than words alone. it is difficult to find seven
square miles of open land. sun bears keep secrets from
each other. it's for the best we're told. yes from a far enough
distance the sun bear world is small but it's best if we don't think
about that. the sun bears come home and kiss each other. then.
back to their possibly fulfilling jobs in the morning. all at once this happens
on the sun bear plant. many times over. the sun bears eventually fall asleep.

Anthony Aguero

Warlike

I keep your name on the spot of my tongue
you've touched —

you no longer see the world I see, do you?
The carousel moving;

your finger moving, too, in circles around me,
around the muscle of the hip-

bone, against the trellis of my ribcage
caging the only warm thing

I have left. I compliment the meth escaping
your mouth in thick-wisps

of smoke and then I want to kiss you, again;
always *again* with you and I,

isn't it? You tell me *Stop scratching your neck*
and I tell you *Find me before*

I can no longer recover from this damage.
This damage is all that I, too, have

left, and while I was living, I hadn't imagined
it would come to this: you and I

so brute and warlike, but it had. It had stayed
like this for years: the incarnadine

morning where you jabbed both of my wrists
as I spilled salted tears on your lips —

you never once look up from that small sky
and ask *Are you doing okay?*

As I never look down from my own small sky
and ask *Do you feel the same horror*

I feel? Years later, I would learn that you had
spent the mornings flecked with pain

inside of a lonely body I had touched, had missed,
for the longest time — a hidden wound.

My Lover

My lover with the abscess in the left side
of his musculature build. My lover not working
any longer because passion is down or fleeting
(anything to help us sleep at night). My lover
not sleeping — day 8 now. My lover pulls out
Death from the tarot deck and lights go out.
My lover is cooking me a PB&J (I've never
understood the relationship between drugs
and sweet foods). My lover pointing to his dead
ex-lover below the balcony where an acacia tree
obstructs the view to the ground. It's beautiful,
light refracted off green. My lover is squeamish
with needles and pulls the one out and falls back.
My lover is kissing a disbarred lawyer on the bathroom
floor and I find it unsettling. My lover lost his mom
and is pointing to her up the stairs in the hallway,
again (I'm not superstitious). My lover with his blot
it starts on his arms from the drug use. My lover,
so beautiful and lost in his residency — just like I.

Meditation at a County Rehabilitation Center

You come outside in your county-slippers,
the sun is bright, orange and daring,
so I don't look into it, but, instead, to you
in your county-slippers and a loose t-shirt
and your cock resting beneath too-large pants,
and you sit beside me — cracked hand resting
atop of my hand — and I could never tell you
where I find this act of safety. You come outside
to tell me *Don't leave*, dry spit around your mouth,
the meth almost out, and I'm excited for beauty
to enter into you once again, or, better, to show
itself once again. You say *Don't leave* nearly crying
but stop yourself moments away from tears,
but I want it. I want to watch you fall apart,
and I want to watch it all burn as I have
burned down but you stop yourself moments away
from the bravest thing you've ever done, and,
instead, say *Be safe* with a stoic look —
unflinching and coming close to beauty again —
and I place my cracked hand atop of your hand
and almost say *I don't know what I'm doing,*
but instead, I say *Ok* and, moment by moment,
I fall apart in front of you too early in the morning.

My Obsessions, I Have Them

I'm dreaming, again, of Christian.
His lips aren't blue but berry-red
and full of water — full of a burst
of living that the living ought to do.

Once again, I want to scream at him
We have to leave from here, otherwise,
there is no returning. And I do not
scream at him. I kiss him and again

against, aghast, a gasp, the brown
tower of dirt in this desert place
before we are incapable of loving
because the drugs disturb the most

of us. I dig and howl my nails into him,
into his pricked and prodded flesh,
and water falls, leaving a trail of mud,
slowing us down. *It's unreasonable*

I think *having to leave this world, again.*
Nevertheless, a body through the wind-
shield. The white lines blown away.

Darius Atefat-Peckham

The Patient Stone

The Wi-Fi is banned indefinitely. And so
she wants to send the letter of her body

home. *Nastaliq shekasteh.* Broken handwriting.
She wants to join the protests, burn

her hijab. I would forbid it if I could: her
leaving me. I wish to be the patient stone.

The patient stone listens. Absorbs
the sorrows of those who confide

in it. When two beings are inseparable, *and*
is pronounced *o.* Layla o Majnun,

Gol o morg, Khosrow o Shirin, my Bibi
o her country. Séance of my ear harboring

secrets, dribbling like a mouth
at a fountain. Our voices cling to one another.

Our eyes distend, bursting. As I wait
to board my train, she asks how

my Persian is *doing* as if it is a sick relative
or a child in trouble at school. The man in me

grovels his sorrows in the desert basin,
his memory making mud from the dirt.

*Even I—Even I—Even I—*I say and she listens,
eyes downcast, waiting for her turn to speak.

Heathcliffs

There is a woman carved
into helmet shell, now haunting
the space just below my knuckle.
Useless, I slip her in my pocket
and take a watering can by its wing.
I wear a new ring for every day of my life.
I do this with most things, making them
permanent. The face of a moon peaks
out from beneath Isabella's shirt-sleeve.
She holds her dress at either side. Is it
raining there? Is there mud? Born
from the soil, dusted clean, put to
my lips. I plan to have many. They will know
who I am, accrued across my fingers,
hung down hollows of my neck, waiting to be
lost back. How do I mean? I am not meant
for this. I stand in the rain, dumfounded
and searching, wiping myself from my eyes.
I wait for the right conditions to put my self
to practice. I am told to express myself
this way, just nothing permanent, *please*.
I am obsessed with myself. Like
a planet, I long for something I can't
slip off at night and forget to wear
in the morning. I want to make it all wuthering,
whatever that means. I want to be clothed, fed,
taken care of. The hands of my love. Tomatoes
so sweet my eyes flutter and moan.
The accidental salt of fingertips, like an ocean
at my lips, teaching me something
about worship. That question there, sealing me
shut: if she was too good for this world,

as they say, what does that make me,
still standing here, gathering myself
at the gate?

Haunt

~for Tahereh—poet, activist, martyr

When the Eyes open, finally,

they won't yield

to touch. Like ice-

flowers reaching to catch the soil. To blossom,

the mystics wrote, is to open

her smile. A man sits, head

wrapped, holding conversation

with a parking meter. A real poet haunts, her mouth

full of white silk, singing quiet

*Ta-da*s*!* to take *our* breath

away. *Ta* meaning: so that, up to, until

then, rather than—sometimes, even,

when. Is translation the least we can offer?

Is there even less? What remains

down the well that terrify us

so. That

we offer pebble and coin

to bury it. Some men learn

to be ghosts before they ever

learn to die.

Patchwork

The needle occasionally punched through her finger and nail / so a smear of red remained on whatever she was making. She seemed to elongate as she worked, growing wide / as an ocean, big and tall as Paul Bunyan with his ax. Confidently and forever / the story of a wedding dress, The Boy's / mother, the thousands upon thousands of pearls inlaid, glinting like eyes. How it came to life beneath her / fingers. To sew is to see stitched / to an end. He watched her rings, wishing he could wear them. Everything came from her, even The Boy, even her own name. A name she stitched / together from The Boy's pronunciation / of the cardinal considering Him on the balcony as He sat in His high-chair one summer's day. *Birbie… Birbie…Bibi!* He clapped at the bright winged / thing alighting on the railing, light as the feathers that made it. She dropped / the tool she'd been using to feed Him (startled the cardinal, who disappeared into the burning, unblinking eye above, making The Boy frown) and ran inside, yelling with elation to no one, to anyone / who would listen, *He said His first word! He said His first / word, and His first word was / me!* At the end of the night, she rested / her ruined, arthritic fingers against the table, her foot lingering at the pedal. Una corda / sostenuto / damper. The Boy watched—it was all He could do—her foot slowly rising / winged, letting go the sound.

I Am Not Disappearing

To be a Boy, there are rules. Chief
among them is that I must not
die, even when the words escape me
like lightning bugs
dying in my jar, making their short lives
shorter. I must tell no one
about the ghosts of them fluttering up against
the glass. Flickering gray
then grayer. Must act as though they
never happened, hold
my hands cuffed as I wait in line
for security, surrendering my Real
ID. A woman just ahead of me
says to her child, over and over,
her hand held tight to her ear
like some body's small chest:
I'm not disappearing.
I'm not disappearing. She is
saying. Is sung. My mother once
snuck her pet gerbil through
like a fugitive tucked in a barrel,
a toilet paper roll squeezed between
her legs. All that, just so the secret
body could travel a bit further
and die, later and alone, taken
apart in the strong maw
of her husband's boyhood
pet. What can be
done? My father used to laugh
until he cried. The dog was trained
to keep out pests and she was
old and blind and miserable,
anyhow. It's the natural order

of things. A story always comes
to mind, knocking like a chick
to be let back in
its shell, prodding the membrane
of my eye: my mother
once mourned. Now, I
walk past every officer, the after-lives
of wriggling animals tucked
between my legs like a suspicious
lotion or IM hip rod or family
curse. I can never quite
depart. I feel their evil
eyes sown across my shoulders
like wings, just like my grandma
warned, their tired lids
are shut. But I think it may be harder to admit
that when the TSA agent doesn't order me
step aside, when I glide
through the gate—known
traveler, transparent as Ghost—I miss
those hands patting me down
like earth. Halving me. Reminding me
that what the crow does
on the side of the hot dirt road
is a kindness. To untie a body
from itself, a kindness. Assuring me
of my held breath. I'm there,
in a body of delayed
light—light
that hasn't happened yet—reaching
me in the welling look
of people I long
ago survived.

Darnell Arnoult

Pickup

Grinning altar of twenty years warbling
variations of thriving light.
Hear that powdery sound of ashes.
Hear that crackling sound of unfired absolution.

Hear the warbling neighbors and grinning
children, nervous and amiable, a clashing
band of flames dancing at the threshold.
Invalid tongues split reason.

The thing is, deep gentle reason shows
nothing called meaning. Dying levels
out. Still, imagine a hummingbird.
Those two wings curving a thousand

breathless cymbals. Imagine tongues split
and hear lungs ring the dying dance.
Sock-footed nothing. Dark matter.
Breathe in the traveling music.

Invention

Put on the wheels of bird armor
until the shade of Heaven

confronts your breastbone.
Motionless metal mosaics

feature chariots and dog
faces blinking in the dazzling

eyepiece of rattling man.
Your weight threatens

my limbs. Cobblestones
curve and crown the silenced

mouth ablaze and shooting
cindery fevers to flower

the strange gaunt hand
and the beam of nailed wood.

Reclamation

Huddled deep-rooted in darkness
a cancer steadily speaks its office.

Hear with your eyes! Death changes
flesh to sparkle, bodies to forest.

Changes. Your song yet to drift
beyond its window, yet to turn

grasping secrets into hovering
voices of light waking the sleeping

source of the unclasped world.
Open your palm and the grave.

Mouth and fingers plant the army
of light trees yet alive

in that ultimate told and magical wood
beyond the sun's Easter choir.

Passing

Perceptive enough, the human gaze licks itself
with the fascination of sorrow.

Line and curve glitter, and still
unearthly arms require neither

bird nor bush. Home holds the slack taste
of changing leaves. A son still intently watches

the cold dust drift earthward. Barns and graves
shift and graze, confident the essence of fields

will hold fixed in harmony beside churches
and bejeweled branches. But love shifts in midair,

itself not bitter or uneasy, forgetting
the heart and the body, requiring no farewell.

Widowhood

Peer passed vibrant stalks of rain. Think of his absent face
now uncaught by earth, light among stars. The man

is now stardust. His voice like the riddle of dreams.
Whoever unfailingly loves a cowboy, truly loves him,

meets him hand-to-hand and head-to-head, a connection
like home until falling is the only tangible move. The love

allotted hurtles like raging stars to some tough and poetic parting.

It waits forward unobstructed amongst the stringy sawgrass
somewhere in the dead of winter, somewhere past the speed of light.

Christine Barkley

Threshing

The starlings are nesting
in the walls and the harvest is
half-finished. I have not
lost my mind. What wakes
me now is not the reaping
but the threshing. The starlings
have only just started to nest.
The fields have not finished
with me yet. My mind fills
with the threshing, or thrashing;
some sound of fear or frenzy
or feeding. The distinction
won't be made unless
I go mad, or until.
I do not call for help
but men will still come,
bearing solutions in
the shape of threats. Sickles
and pitchforks, claw traps
and snares. Surely something
must be done;
with the overfarmed fallows,
with the life
in the walls. When they say *cultivation*
I hear *culling*. When their fixing is
finished the crops will fail.
When the evening
ends the fledglings will be dead.
When something dies
in the walls
it dies in the fields it dies
in my mind. I can still hear the thrashing.

Or threshing. It makes no difference,
unless or until.
If new seeds are sown
this spring I know
that nothing will
grow. If children
are born this year
they will never be safe.
The machines have finished
off the fields.
The exterminators have started
on the nests.
I have boarded up my own home
and locked myself
outside.
I have not lost
my mind.
Something in me
has overgrown and
if it is a child
I will never be safe.

Prey Naivety

The doe moved through the underbrush
with such calm that she was close enough
to touch before I knew that I was not
alone. If she saw me, she did not see me
as a threat. She did not behave as though

she was fragile. I stayed very still as my fears
found root in her vulnerability, though
I knew that fear could not save her;
though even terror had never
saved me. I flinched at the snapping

of twigs while she grazed, my heart
the only prey thudding and thrashing in the
bracken. When she stretched I caught the pulse
at her neck, steady. When she grew tired
she lay down among the cornflowers

and cottonwood fluff, unconcerned.
In the sunlight her fur seemed the same
shade as my own hair, and for a moment I felt
crosshairs settling on my throat; a distance
and a safety removed. I wondered if

she had ever felt it too. I wondered if
she had ever felt herself inside of her skin
and understood that men might watch her,
wondering only when they could take
a clean shot. That her body would glow

in their thermal sights, begging to be called
a target. That they would be willing
to sit in wait, already cutting
their teeth on tender thoughts
of how she might taste.

Apparent Death

In this meadow the only doe is
a nursing rabbit; still prey enough to
give me pause, to pull the hairpin
of fight-flight-freeze. I know that
in fear of predation a mother might
eat her children. I know that then my
heartbeat would limp ragged for
a day or two, that forever my chest
would echo echo empty and bloodied
as a nest abandoned just after
birth. I can't watch a soft animal
without waiting for the gunshot.
I can see that somewhere in the flowers
is a snare. Beyond the treeline a set of
teeth. Across my own flesh a flinch,
an understanding that softness always
ends in pelt or meat or trophy.
Just as my body has been worn
or consumed in victory; unlucky
rabbit feet becoming soft little
trophies. Likely they never even
sensed a threat, just like every time
I bared my throat instead of teeth.
I've learned that some victims are seen
as more sympathetic but I haven't yet
found the magic, the trick. If I had been
born a witch and my mother had never
felt this type of fear I could have turned
all of the rabbits into rats and they might
have kept their feet if not their lives.
Of course then all that would be said
is that they deserved it, and I would be

burned, or drowned. Regardless, all things
feral know know that sometimes the only spell
against death is to eat the young. When I sense
a threat I remember fight-flight-freeze, forget
fawn. When any animal enters a meadow
the human instinct should be to beg
for something far worse
than forgiveness,
and less soft
than death

Ace Bogguss

Notes for My Autobiographer

I did. I didn't. I did nothing.
I did what I was told.
I did wrong but in the right way,

a master assassin strong in his craft
from a distance. I did their bidding.
I didn't know who they were

or why they wanted the child's lunchbox
with a sandwich in it. I did little
to prevent brutality of the war.

I did my best. I did my worst.
I didn't understand there was a difference.
I did the deed. I didn't get caught,

but confessed to anyone who'd listen.
I did dance in the moonlight once,
a long time ago when I cared

not a whit for what night's eyes might see.
I didn't go into the woman's apartment
or the man's cigar box of a house,

although of course I did &
there, found places to hide
from cameras & paparazzi.

I didn't disabuse them of their stories
about what I did & didn't do,
letting them build better myths of me.

I did step into this new religion.
I didn't believe, but didn't want
to know if it were true.

Apologies If You Hear Me Cuss

the plumber says, gauging the coming struggle:
six inches between two walls behind the tub:
room for an arm, no line of sight.

I tell him, *I wouldn't trust you if you didn't*,
same as I'd promise anyone,
because sometimes shouting *Fuck!*

is the only answer to whatever question
the Absurd throws at us. The plumber
says, *We're a Christian company.*

We're not supposed to.
I hold back quips about wine
flowing through the pipes or practice-

walking over the tide of a soapy tub.
Sure, my god gets my sense of humor
(has a pretty twisted one as well),

but this man won't, prepared to work in shit,
not say it, mapping the Infernal maze
builders of the house created.

He reaches, wrenching in blind faith
while my god & I are grinning,
the joke having turned on us at last.

There will remain a part of me

that wishes I had been less ethical,
not read Buber a month before we met &
sought to practice Thou-

speak, bliss-inducing like opium sap,
enlightenment by dullness;
that would've said *yes* rather than *be careful.*

To think how well our bodies might have fit.
To imagine the un-undoable. Too,
part of me sees friendship as the kiss.

Possible to hold both views
when the past snaps its fingers
as if to get my attention

while I'm observing a woodpecker mining a tree
or two jeweled fawns rocketing through the yard
faster than legs should carry them toward the future.

Hannah Bonner

The Prize

When I became a single woman,
the men swarmed all around me.

It seemed the more I was,
the more they multiplied

with their prophecies,
and their payments, and their wagging,

tepid tongues.
Their attention, it angered me.

How they told me not to
worry. How they told me

they'd be back.
The worst ones

I let do whatever they want.
My body—a glass

or liquid—
submitting to their heat.

(I have loved
three men in my life.

I have held one
up to the light.)

Fast

Shot in the dark,
out like an arrow:

I pull my underwear
down, while standing up.

I keep my mouth shut,
except when you're in it.

Shock of skin like an animal
going frantic, fast.

I fuck with you, and love
shakes its salt

lick into me.

Eyes level, hackles raised.
Pink on the inside,

pink on the inside,

tell me I'm not
someone's daughter you'd praise.

Once You've Left

October light pierces possibility
right out of the air. Tree trunks

unmoved as a haunting. Birds darken
with worry in a crushing

autumn wind, and a barge cleaves
the Mississippi, smooth as repetition

with no difference. Everything hushes
before the worst of it—

how a doctor tells you to relax
before administering pain.

Keep my heart, you can't cure it. Tonight,
I'll lie down with the ear of another.

At every hour
the river wheels and eddies.

Promise me
the song always comes back.

In Spite Of

and when you told me you loved
your wife

it didn't matter

and when you sent for me
in another state

it didn't matter

and when you told me to leave
the next morning

it didn't matter

and when you said you wouldn't touch me
(and you touched me)

it didn't matter

and when I wept, swore,
had other men (again and again)

it didn't matter

and when I finally made haste
like a heroine

it didn't matter

I did it all
(and then some)

to speak achingly
and to live.

Still Life with Citrus in February

This morning I look at the wedding
ring I never wore, the lemons limning

the wooden bowl, furred
white from age and heat.

There is snow again. There is morning
again. There is the predictable

deer print tracking
the perimeter around the house.

Last year I let a love go,
then lost another.

What this is
it is, no matter

where you edge.

There is sun again.
There is luck again.

Relief across a blameless ground,
a bright light,

no longer begging.

Wendy BoodeGraaff

Beer City

My first sip of beer, on a picnic
table, next to my sister: Labatt

Blue, sour, puckered my face.
I was seven, eight, twelve—she

six years plus mine. My next
taste, on my boyfriend's tongue, slick

metallic ferment. Living in Ontario,
Hail to the Beer Store, brown glassed

cathedral of Molson or some other long
necked bottle held by teenage

boys around the fire. In college, kegs
meted into red plastic cups. Yeasty

humidity. I snuck in mickies of tequila,
Kahlua, vodka. Church told us parties

were sinful, but all those people packed
in, closer than hymn sings, had to be holy.

Grand Rapids crafts Founders, Perrin, Brewery
Vivant. I've cozied up along counters, bar

tenders saying you'll like this
one. They hand me Rubaeus, red

as a daquiri, watching to be proven right. I sip
and smile, hops curling my tongue inward

down toward the guts of memory
when I first decided I didn't like beer.

Jacob Boyd

Remember that Your Life Belongs to Others as Well. Do Not Endanger It Frivolously

Even if our father did—after slipping at home and hitting his head—
wander out of the hospital and fall
fifteen feet off an embankment, whatever spirit

he did it in, it was not
frivolous. Not him who had always
wanted to dip

into the wild. It was an inexpressible wish
granted. Rain dripped
from the beak of an eagle to her nest. You slept

on two chairs pushed together. I told him
it was time. Drive
carefully, sister, but fast. Guide us out of Kentucky, away

from cremation. There isn't a mortician alive
who can force us to that table again—the forlorn meeting room
where Stewart "I-don't-know-about-you

but-I'm-a-Christian-Man" Throgmorton told us he'd
get a hold of your husband
as if a woman can't decide for herself whether to buy

the necklace of ash. Maybe he was only hoping
his own daughter will collapse
stupid with grief when he dies. The complete

and total opposite of what our father
who art on fire
desired. Our dad knew what he wanted and

what we wanted did not always need
to converge. He believed
in his own ignorance, it rankled him, and still he seethed

at the false convictions of smaller men. Better to be clueless. If,
when I stand outside at night, I say thank you,
I am equally as estranged by stars or clouds or the surprise of surviving

as I was by the fires of Ethiopian music and the slideshow of children—
bellies distended, beset by flies—
when I was tucked between you and mom in the golden pews at
Bethlehem Lutheran

and he was at home stealing what sleep he could
before hunting again
men so desperate for something to cling to they smashed

windows and crawled through. He'd seen enough. Forgiveness,
he told me once—
we were driving along the Ohio River
in the gray, purgatorial light of early spring on a kind of pilgrimage—

forgiveness is not justice. Some things
are best left unforgiven.
Hominid, sister of a common ancestor, weren't we just now

crossing the living room in our ring-shaped walkers
like the riverine peoples of old Babylon
in their coracles—stirring no wake, frontless, backless, beautifully

afloat? If we get lost along the way, it's only
an hour. Guide us
over these gargoyle hills. Get us out of here, well

north of this place that ate him, these people with their eighty-five
dollar Ark Encounter
and its five-hundred-foot-long shadow.

And Never Endanger the Life of Another

Tell that to the tourist feeding Cheetos
to black bears at the campground. Tell it
to our housebound dead. They never meant
to venture but off they went, bending
no branches. Tell it to the singer singing
Que He Sacado Con Quererte: Natalia,
gardener of dark, your voice pulls me to cliffs.
When I hear you, I haven't left home in years.

My love has decided this summer
she wants us to face a grizzly bear on its
own ground; she wants us to fight it
if we must. Are you sure you want this
I ask. She does. To brave the corridors and creeks
where it breeds. We must make exceptions
in love and art. Exceptions only. Okay,
I will deliver her to the bear.

Reduce Your Use of First Person

Does anyone else here—entering your own dark
apartment after jogging three blocks, walking four,
jogging two, walking five—leave the lights out
and keep the earbuds in so the hallway feels
like some kind of gauntlet? Do you not
imagine a stabber hiding behind the curtain,
and get just a little excited, for a second,
thinking there's a human snooping around?
Maybe you did once and that was the moment
you decided it was time to get married. Smart.
Some people fly right past those warning signs—
nothing in their head but Sarah McLachlan's voice
saying *hold on to yourself* and *this is going to hurt
like hell.* Some people have a playlist on Spotify
they titled "90's Movie," and it feels like
the soft rock soundtrack to a horror film, like
Jeff Buckley climbing onto your boat or Billy
Corgan coming to tuck you in. To be fair,
that Pumpkins sound is stronger than nostalgia.
It's not Billy's fault if you refused to get married
and now that last, long decade of your youth
terrifies you. Leviathan of possibility.
God goes 'mong the world blackberrying, Stubb says,
implying we ripen and get plucked. Does anyone
else here sometimes catch sight of a burglar
padding to the kitchen in pajamas for cinnamon rolls
at midnight and think *That bastard better not
eat the last one*? You aren't the only one living with
burglars. It's a rush, letting them in like this.

Live Memorably

This is a little like watching nature
on tv, he thought, sitting cross-legged
on the gravel shoulder, listening
first to a shy French child and her
father teach Katie the word *ours*
en peluche—for teddy bear—
then to a ranger saying *she's kind of*
an ideal mother, all while focusing
the field glass on a scruffy cinnamon
black bear. She was busting open
a rotting log and snuffling up grubs.
Down from the lodgepole pine
where she had treed them to get
a little time to herself, two cubs
bumbled. They lived like any other
bears. They had their routines, their
indulgences. A pint of creamed huckleberry
honey. Why was it important to live
memorably? Whose memory? The cubs
loved their mother's ways and would
remember when the berries were where.
Not much more mattered than that.
Nor needed remembering.

Catherine Pritchard Childress

Wife to Wife

My father admonished me
to remember you.
He couldn't have known
how I would heed
his warning. I don't
condemn your trespass,
I commend you,
don't blame you
for wanting to stay
behind in a place
where you had friends,
unstained clothes,
a name.
I imagine your skeptical exit
from the gates of Sodom,
walking toward your life,
the view stinging
your eyes like desert sand.
A clouded image of Lot,
who didn't fill your needs,
but satisfied his greed
when he pitched his tents.
Looking back was better
than blindly following
a father who offered
your daughters' virtue,
kept his honor
locked behind doors,
conspired with angels
who lauded his intentions,
grieved his union
with an impure wife.

My father warned me
of the wrath
that changed you
to a pillar, scattered you
throughout that razed city,
but he didn't know you
were the one
with power to cleanse,
couldn't fathom teaching me
to remember
just how much you are worth.

Queen Mother

When I stepped from the scalding water onto my roof,
I knew you would make me queen, would watch the Mikveh
wash me pure, ready for the seed your smile promised.

I didn't know you would ordain Uriah's death, that your god
would smite our firstborn son (retribution for the so-called sin
that made me finally your wife, secured my place in the bed

where I conceived a king, watched you die) but not before
I contrived your last wish, removed Adonijah from his throne,
his mother from my palace, secured my place in the legacy,

made Solomon your heir. Our fourth son, not our first
whose birthright was usurped by whom Jeremiah calls
your son, twenty-eight generations removed,

King of the Jews, descendant of my tainted line.

Salome's Ghazal

I left my veils in the laps of men for whom I danced,
'Round their necks, wrists—in this silken costume, I danced.

At the birthday celebration befitting a lascivious king—
Planned by my mother, a gift for her groom, I danced.

Your guests witnessed you pledge your solemn oath
To grant my wish, so in your reception room, I danced.

Terracotta firelight flickered off my jeweled breasts,
Kindling improper desire—perfumed, I danced.

Thinking of John who spurned my incessant advances,
Swaying to the suggestion of his coming doom, I danced.

Gratified by my performance, you promised to make good.
To sate the desire that leaves me consumed, I danced.

Reluctantly you delivered his head on a bloody tray,
Dressed his body, buried him, and at his tomb, I danced.

Sarah

I only wanted Hagar to bear my son.
How could I have known she would love
My husband, that when I asked him
To send her and Ishmael away, his face
Would reveal he loved her too,
That I was right when I guessed
He was in her bed (long after she conceived),
That he was thinking of her
When he hummed in the fields,
When I caught his distracted gaze,
When he kissed me goodnight.

My barren body cannot compete
With the thrill he must feel
When the soft curves of her youth
Respond again and again to his touch,
Cannot elicit his body's firm response
With only the light pressure of an ankle
Against his calf, the brush of a hand
On his forearm, a probing tongue—
Cannot bear to see his eyes follow her
As she braids her hair, nurses their son,
Cannot watch her become my husband's wife.

Grant Clauser

Have you reckon'd a thousand acres much?

—Walt Whitman

Today from a ridge top I can see a thousand
acres ripened with maples and chestnut oak.

The last road an hour out of sight. Rain
a season old still draining from spring cricks.

Is this what we save the soul for? Losing
grip on a cliff edge, a river still remembers

what it was like to carry coal dust,
the occasional body, over white rapids.

Still a million raptors navigate the pass
every year, chasing summer into hollows

and gorging on sparrows. Four sharptails
just now cartwheeled in the wind. A bridge

is falling somewhere. There are protests
in Tehran and Prague and a furniture sale

at the home goods store. I'm tired
of walking today, but the sky is blue

crayon blue, and the ridgetop haired
by low blueberry bushes stained russet

by October, so I'll settle for a solo
of meditation while fewer birds migrate

south again, some music in the wind I can't
put a name to, stuck in my head like hunger

One Mountain Seen Through the Trees of Another Mountain

Maps never show a view like this,
yellow blazes on trees leading
to a ridge, the trail so close
to the edge just walking feels
like falling. A five-day trip away
from towns or news of the world
brings me to moments so sublime
I forget myself. Anthropologist say
joy in landscapes is burned into our DNA,
distance a factor of dreams. Below,
the lake is starting to ice over, a cold
that's been building for years. And this
mountain loop I'm walking could go
on too. In the next county there's a hill
called Hope, and here one called
Sanctuary. I'm walking down it now
to a lake the settlers used to feed
their families. Its feeder creek
powered the old iron forge also
called Hope. So many things named
for what we want. Or is it what
we have? My legs grow sore
on the rocky trails I climb
to get home. This path called
Daybreak might be the one.

Pheasant Court

It's been years since I thought about
the ring-necked pheasants that came down
from the woods and into my yard
when I was a boy. My mother
woke me one Christmas morning
to tell me they were here, their heads
and necks shimmering like tree tinsel,
their long tail feathers bright
as new copper pipes. They waltzed
among our frost-covered garden,
dipping and strutting over the furrows,
then disappeared at the first sight
of our young collie Caesar.
My father said the game warden
stocked the woods for hunters
and sometimes strays survived
nested in the trees near the dying farmer's
fields. His children sold the land
for housing tracts, named the new roads
after grace that passes so quickly
in and out of our lives.

Last Mint

Even at the dry hinge that closes
summer into fall, when the mower
cuts down the last surviving mint,
its bright scent lingers
like a spiderweb after rain
the way some lives do, thriving
even when all signs say otherwise.
This mother of bees through summer,
accent to tea and gin, is even
now preparing roots for winter
as our transitory geese announce
their night flights, leaving
behind a season's dead weight
and long evenings with firelight.
Still, a fresh green shoot
is trying to hold out
alongside red rose haw
and pumpkin, creeping
along the ground, something
new to wrap your hand around.

Lily Greenberg

Mrs. God

When the Father and the Son reach agreement,
she appears—eyes open as a snake
in dead noon, head grooving side to side.

The message: *There are three of me.*
We are bodies, not men. We dance
to break each other.

Suckling at the clouds is not her business.
She is the drool the dog drops. The miracle—
she spills on her shirt. When you hear

the schoolbell and hightops streaking,
she is the open hallway after, the half-cracked
locker, tipped bin, plastic bottle dribbling.

She speaks through prophets disguised
as people asleep in the park—her speech,
Should you outlive your life? wanders

to the backyard where devil's ivy
vines the gutter grates. In rain, she is that
which pours. In drought, she is the river's

drop to creek. What I'm telling you
is that she empties herself. She empties herself
until she becomes power.

Mrs. God Goes to Church

People all buttoned up on the kneelers bow
going breadbreadbreadbreadbread
and Mrs. God stands at the back wall

arms over chest like a principal catching kids
red in the act of poorly drawn genitalia
on the girls' bathroom mirror. "Ave Maria"—

who? "Maria." *Who? Who coughs*
the stars into light? Who is dark matter?
Who's the bird to your left wing, right wing?

The priest pours wine that tastes like
courtly gestures. People bow
and the black heart of church lights up.

Who stood the tornado up? Who knows
why you're here? Take the wheel,
you said, but who took it?

Rattling legos in a plastic bag
a boy gathers himself under a pew
and does not stand, sit, kneel, and

it is music to Mrs. God's ears.
You who bow to the flies
kissing the choir, the holy water

slurped by a bat, the subsequent burp,
the robe sweat and light up sneakers
ripping through the prayer aisle—

you who start the ceremony with
"I do not know what to do" and end
"I do not know what to do"—please,

you belong to Mrs. God. Come backward.

Mrs. God Exercises the Right to Refuse Deliverance

It all started with yoga women
preaching the emptiness of being

in their thousand-dollar voices
smelling of lavender wearing lavender

Lululemon and Mrs. God stood up
and said, *I won't with them.* And

then the computers going *Human?*
Human? Prove it! with a mosaic

of blurry boats and which one is a
sailboat? Mrs. God is not human

by way of motorbus. The bicycles
do not know who she is. *Jesus,*

she said, *this is the last cookie*
I will accept. The final horizon

was a help line oaked with options
all dead-ending in: *how*

can I help you? It was here on hold
that Mrs. God said to the Lord, *Not*

everyone is coming to the land
of hush. They who will not be led

are plastic streets on which
I will not be driving.

You're Trying to Grasp Mrs. God

but she is not graspable. The lucky
stand under her

as under a ferris wheel
whose baskets drip old rain and
scattered voices that call to you in

your first language—
you lost it, didn't you

when the holes appeared
in your ears, when you filled them
with metal, when your whole mouth
became magnetic.

If only you
or your mother
or her mother
understood.

What is there to understand
about a large animal passing in the night?

What is there to know about elk
absorbed in fog, then there, grazing—
so physical you can almost taste
their grass, almost feel the cricket

wings coming apart in your teeth.

She has nothing to do with you.
She could kill you. Without her
you would die.

Vanilla

The word "vanilla" comes from the Spanish word "vainilla" (meaning "little pod") which itself is descended from the Latin word for "sheath": "vagina."

a silver teaspoon
of Pure Bourbon Madagascar Vanilla

not a lot
but enough
to lift my mind
from my American kitchen
and wrap my senses
in its African island sweetness

enough for its heady orchid fragrance
to cling to that spoon
hours later
and carry me back
to the memory of you
and your body
spooned with my body

the frames of our flesh
bending and fitting themselves
to fill and fulfill
each other's need

you me us
two seeds of vanilla
in our own little pod
pressed together
until we yield and spill
our own hypnotic pleasures
too sweet
for our bodies
to contain

Butter Pecan

smooth confluence
of sugar butter
nuts cream
this delectable dream
churned into real-life lusciousness

salty sweet delicious
chunky pecan crunch
milky mound that enters frozen
into my mouth
then melts in a pool
of liquid pleasure

ambrosial marriage of flavors
tangy sweetness so exquisite
that with each taste
all my body rejoices
even my tongue
speaks in tongues

Pot Au Chocolat

"Chocolate pots are distinguished by a hole in the lid
where a stirring rod could be inserted."
~ Taylor Newby, Metropolitan Museum of Art

Some nights
like this night

an invisible flint
sparks a kindling
between us
that sends our bodies
beyond words
shapes them
into symbols
and poetry itself

My hips
my behind
my belly and thighs
paired with the exquisite
almost unbearable
nearness of you
become a feminine
French metaphor
replicating the curves
and silver sheen
of a chocolate pot
whose hidden sweetness
melts at your touch
and the lush
lean length
of your phallus
and your physique
become my stirring rod

most welcome agitator
rising, gravity-defying
flesh stick
aimed and sliding
into me

pulsing churning spinning
a delicious liquefaction
of pleasure
greater than even the sum
of our poetic selves
can express

Mocha Brown

for Sam

He called
the color of my voice
mocha brown

Deeper than caramel,
he said,
but richer and sweeter
than coffee

A voice
whose liquid-like earthiness
can be imbibed
and savored
and linger
in a listener's mind
long after its sound
has left his ear

How then could I not delight
in such a description
from such a man
who used his own voice,
the soft silvery dark
of dew on a morning glory,
to call forth magic and light
from something of mine
so familiar
that, until him,
I dismissed it
as ordinary

Christen Noel Kauffman

Never Close a Knife Someone Else Has Opened

my father hands me the knife, says look
into the eyes before you take them,

there where we sit on the front porch with
my mother eager for me to step out of girlhood

and into a well-pressed dress. my father
says take god with the blade and cut

along the bone, careful not to spoil
the good meat grown from my mother's

pumpkin pie we offer on paper plates.
a man learns to hunt while a woman gives

birth, sets her babies in the windowsill to cool
like cherry tarts and asks how god could

leave her at the first sight of blood.
wind chimes call the dead when we least

expect to hear them, stomp of hooves
on a gravel road until it's almost here,

almost to my father where he asks me
to remove the skin with my hands,

pull from the fur until I feel a hollow pop.
I don't want to hold death like this, follow

god into a carcass we bled from a tree
as if it were nothing, were me, disposable

as any meat we suck from a severed rib.
tell me, whose god would make it so.

As Someone Must Have Made Me

god finds me in a public restroom
with my hair pulled back from my face, hand
against the toilet to keep me from falling to
the other side where nothing exists unless
I want it to, unless I ask for it to make a home
in my body, the way my mother spoke me
into cinder spark from an apartment downtown.
it's the answer I want to hear at the clinic
to keep me from disappearing
like the ghosts my mother sees at night, flashes
of yellow and white where the curtains pull together
just so, cat's eye of moonlight a sliver in the dark
and no one sees me standing there, featherless bird
as someone must have made me.
I turned this god away when I was born
and again when the crop circles staggered
their spiraled prints as if carried on the wings of bees,
but always someone brings him to my feet,
covers my eyes with a shroud and there I am
unfurrowing myself in the shadow of a 7-Eleven.
even in this restroom where the walls could be pearl,
dust catching the sun's gaze like tiny crystals
someone tossed into the air, almost beautiful,
how I'd imagine god's breath to flicker before
it's gone, before I release it.

I'm Open to the Concept of an Afterlife

and in it I smell the sweet fruit of what comes after,
persimmon painted the halo of a flame, not sun
or sunset as someone may have claimed it was
before there was fire. if you sit with me long enough,
I'll touch your hand with the soft of my wrist, how
veins color me into blues and greens like the ocean
where I lost my best pair of shoes and isn't that
like saying goodbye to a friend, watching them
float into the unknown without you. the truth is I've lost
myself, not in the water but the earth, the time sheet
punched into little perfect spheres. my name
becomes the grocery list left stuck to an empty cart.
if you sit with me long enough, I'll write you a list
of tastes, personify your unmade bread until it walks
through the door, doughy and delighted to see your teeth.
once I made a baby with nothing more than hope
and see how she turned out fine, sparked into the room
all sinew and tangled kelp. it isn't enough
to replicate yourself, send your cells into the sea
and wait for sharks, a body to return—there's blood to be spilled
on the floor, in the car, on the windowsill smeared
but I always forget to clean it. if you sit with me long enough,

I'll bite into your cheek as if you could be fruit, as if
the list was you and not me, dangling from the hood
of Hera's open eye.

Shilpa Kamat

The Fires Are Not Yet Contained

When one hits the bridge
near Richmond, we pack
two days' worth of clothes
and a few of everyone's
sentimental objects. I
pull goddesses and
gods from my altar
leaving stones as
place holders, pack
photographs, books
necklaces, steel plates
from Vile Parle, arrange
them in a blue suitcase
knowing if the fire
hits the refinery
we may return
to nothing.

We take refuge
at an adopted grandma's
friend's apartment in
San Francisco that is
saturated with scented
candles, upsetting my
sinuses. It's Diwali. I
wear a salwar kameez
as a token new year's
gesture. When the smoke
clears, I walk to the park
with a journal and no
writing implement. My
sister meets me, buys
me a golden pen.

After returning
the things we packed
remain in suitcases
waiting in stacks
to be put back on
walls or tables—
at first as precaution
and then as habit. I
talk to a friend
in my old countryside
neighborhood who
evacuated her home
for weeks. *I keep*
looking at the things
around my place now
she says. *It's*
remarkable how
little they matter
How few I need.

It is that way
afterwards, soothing
as an intact home
might be;
most things
are just things
that do or don't
complement the reds
and purples painted
on the walls.

Rainstorm / the Calm before the Fires

lightning sears periwinkle sky
above palms and other trees

crows fly into a thick willow
leave the shelter of the willow

it is 10:59 in the morning; the
morning glories are wide open

pausing in the novelty of thunder
storm after a two-day heat wave

the Bay Area feels like Miami
like Atlanta like Mumbai

humidity thick on my skin
the day cracked wide open

my homelands
merging into one

Evacuation #4

Speak of displacement. Speak
of where you go when the smoke thickens
and enters even through double-paned windows
even through masks. Speak of the way you try
to frame leaving, how you handle the perpetual
tremors of uncertainty through arms, back, chest
belly. Speak of how your forms slowly unravel
of how everyone is unraveling, how making space
for work while the children are fighting grows harder
and harder, how it feels when the family sleeps
in a car, how packing out in the mornings every day
never grows easier, how you switch between smoke
masks and pandemic masks and how not everyone
around you wears masks. Speak of how even when
facing red cedars or Douglas firs or Japanese maples
or wisps of cirrus clouds over lilting estuaries as tides
rise, your page stays blank even when you have a pen
poised, not knowing anymore what meaning to make
or when it will be over or whether it will be over
in a way that will let you be still again.

Evacuation #5

June 2021

This time, we are aloft
between two Douglas firs
in a treehouse with a loft
bed and we are talking
while the children sleep
in structures below, talking
as the heat presses our skin
despite the dark. I pull open
a window to cool our skin
despite our fears of the bats
who, we've been told, live
in the branches. The bats
swoop swiftly past us at dusk
as we sit below, reminding me
of when I used to walk at dusk
back when I lived in this valley
tracing its curves with my feet
on both sides of Green Valley
Road, back when I lived with
my old roommate for whom we
are treehouse sitting now. With-
in seconds, my partner worries
she smells smoke, so I shut the
window without any worries
despite the drought, wondering
why anyone would make a fire
in the dry midsummer, wondering
but not worrying until the light
of a vehicle crosses the ceiling–
We search for clothes and light
as we hear a man shout: Fire!
We climb down two ladders, wake

the children and tell them: Fire
We call our friends, search
in vain for their shy cats, pack
our important items, search
and find our friend's truck keys
load the dog into the trunk and
figure out how to use those keys–
My partner drives, and I navigate
down the dirt road, show her where
to curve past the old oak, navigate
around the pond, emerging to open
gate after gate and staring each time
at the Milky Way, which rakes open
my memory of this place where I
walked countless times through mist
or through puddles of stars, where I
still feel at home, the fields and night
sky suffusing me with familiar wonder
as we evacuate from the smoky night.

Reflection

I am inclusive
like the fires, but

rather than singeing
or consuming

I allow everything
into and through me

turning me to ashes
from the inside.

Broken Hallelujah

I walk beneath a sky full of holes,
among brittle stalks in the field,
trees raining leaves like tongues of fire.
Praise in minor keys rises from the plains,
my home in wind, each face,
each eave, a new octave.
The twinkling distant farmhouse
flickers life in the night
when the ransacking bandit plunders cat food,
when the feral dog drags my hen
home to her ravenous pups,
night owls call, respond.
A wandering stream scores
the pasture in ragged hoof-print hieroglyphics.
Shadows loom in the gloaming, true trunk of pear,
arthritic magnolia,
dry-eyed susans, shrunken bodies of clover,
milkweed, thistle.
The huffing wind seals rain
beneath a crisp skin of ice
sends chickens burrowing into their deep down.
I stumble upon the altar of an ancient steel plow
left last century, in the wood where it collapsed,
returning bit by rusty bit to its beginning.
cruel mercy, unrelenting,
amen & again.

Rural Missive

up on the old highway
near the curve that veers south
at the top of a hill
sits a farmhouse
where a widower lives
next to a graveyard
back off the road
behind a wooden gate,
a gate that swings wide
on a hinge, through which
a pasture rolls towards listing
granite markers gathered
at the end of wheel ruts
harbored beneath the oaks.

along that worn path
an ancient tree drapes weary arms
low branches spread wide,
heavy on the ground,
next to the graveyard where
a widower lives among barns & bins
chock with plows, combines,
tools to plant and harvest
each year's crop, to husband
a small herd of cattle penned
out back, behind wire panels,
steel tube gates bought
from the guy who canvases
these parts in summer, his large
flatbed truck piled with red steel,
all sizes, peddled to farmers
because buying a gate off a guy
is easier than hauling one from town.

through his gate the farmer
drives a row-crop with a 3-point hitch
to impale round bales of clover
and prairie grass planted, mowed
raked and baled from the pasture
that fronts the graveyard with the closed
white gate out by the road,
the road that curves at the top of the hill
where an old widower makes his life
wife and kids now gone
(Olathe, Atlanta, Raleigh, the grave).

the hay is for a feedlot full
of cattle, stuck in January mud, heavy heifers,
girls he calls them, with their yearlings,
who've trampled the hay, shat
indiscriminately, piss brewing
a rain and snow-soup muck the cows
don't seem to mind. the farmer hauls
another ton of hay to the lot
where the girls ruminate, circle cud
over flat wide teeth, process
of process and elimination, spoiling
their food as they ruin each bale
and the farmer heaves another
onto the growing pile of excrement and mud
in the middle of a lot behind an old farmhouse
in the dead of winter where a low white sky
hovers over fallow fields
stretches to horizon, under a gray sun,
that makes no heat.

I pass the farmhouse
where cows stand like cutouts jammed in mud,
one lone steer from last spring's

calving stands atop the waste mountain
head and shoulders above the others,
unchallenged, still-life, as if snapshot,
as if having just arrived the moment I drive again
past the old farmhouse up on the highway,
near the pasture that fronts an old graveyard
where etched in listing tombstones
are the names of nobody I know.

A Galaxy of Silence

the song of the wood thrush
trilling hidden among the trees, falls silent

season's last clutch
of swallows & phoebes fledges
indistinct into the blue.

spring's last blossom falls
spent. earth leans into
its slow aft tilt, sun slipping
low off her shoulder.

milkweed,
goldenrod, nodding onion huff
their slow exhale.

the last monarch
unfurls her wings uplifted
as arms, flutters, disappears.

one
last sip before hummingbirds
wing it south.

purple harvest moon spills
lamplight down the long gravel
road, shimmering over an ocean of grain
to here where you remain
only leaving on your mind.

Matthew Landrum / Rannva Holm Mortensen

Suntaste

Suntaste 14.

today the sky is gunmetal gray
cold steel fallen
to the seabed
the surface of the sea hardened
to a tarnished mirror
and wanderlust pours
from my body
like smoke

i walk on the sea
a mirror carrying me
past the tip of the island
the foghorn's frequency matches
that of my bloodstream
i ache and my shadow
hovers over the deep

Suntaste 17.

everything is salt
the salt of the sea
the salt in the blood
you and me
me and you
the salt sweat
i licked off your body
tears
saline feeding an iv line
the drip drip drip
into the drop chamber
down the tube
through the needle
into the body

salt oozes from my body
coats my skin
i kneel
and crush tiny grains of salt
they stick to my lashes
the salt taste of the sea
the salt of oyster shells
salty fingers
salty memory

Suntaste 30.

when did i first consider the sound
was it always there
that note
that vibrates through everything
the sound of eternity

was it born
in a storm beyond the stars
or in the light
that burst between my fingers
while i was fishing for trout

glass green
trout leap like arcs of electricity
beneath the seaweed
her braids are dripping
skinny bare legs
clunky mary janes
a red bucket
today's haul
of magical sea creatures
blue white membrane
iridescent intestines
bake on bedrock
a strange concord
of eye and sex
straining to comprehend a foreign universe

Suntaste 33.

give me a canvas
subconsciousness worlds
comforting brushstrokes

as i wait
i can feel you breathe

as i wait
for the day to wake
i rest in darkness
i let go
sink endlessly
to the sea bed

days come
like schools of fish
in greenish light
they caress my face
with their soft fins
a gently fluttering radiance

as i wait for
blood to swell my breasts
for milk
to flow
and overflow

Jennifer LoveGrove

We are all touch-me-nots now, exploding at the slightest provocation

Impatiens, named without irony or
wit. Ripe pods burst when touched, buckshot seed spray,
shotgun wedding. Tastes like walnuts, can float
for weeks. I'm a strong swimmer, I have a
good job, it's embarrassing to still hope
to be loved. Hollow stems. Weak, succulent,
juicing when broken. Sour like bile. Treats hives,
rashes, measles, fever, ringworm and warts.
How did you break your collarbone so young?
Mix with alum, orchids to dye hair, nails.
Our lady's eardrops, wild lady's slipper,
slipperweed, snapweed, Busy Lizzie, touch-
me-not, kiss-me-on-the-mountain, quick-in-
the-hand, policeman's helmet. Runaway.

Ruby-throated hummingbirds' favourite.
Prefers marshes, swamps, damp woods. Shallow roots
cause erosion, choke out competition.
See? I told you some asphyxiation
would be fun. No floral scent. Maintenance:
low. Symbolizes maternal love. Crush
the petals to ease anxiety. R—
sleeps in soft sputters, pulsing mouthfuls of
puffballs, like he can't stop kissing what is
already drifting out of reach. I sit
vigil, rigid, watching his lips twitch, purse.
All I want to do is just stop thinking.
At dawn, he curls a leg over mine. Sighs.
Orange ones crowd around the banks of the creek.

Topaz ordeals like waltzes, always packed
yet too scared to leave. Same old suffix hoax.
Invasive weed or meritocracy?
Fiction, torn narrations. Spraying selves for
yes-men. *You're kind of freaking me out now.*
Cuckold the phallus to grant forgiveness.
Ecclesiastical apologies,
each more ulcer and put-down than the last.
Compliance chorus, keep swiping for change!
Good job. It's embarrassing to still hope
for pollinators. Self-compatible,
self-cleaning, no need to decapitate.
Motherly love or revenge fantasy?
When mature, splits into violent valves.

Winged euonymus, on fire but never burning

Haven't torn out my lower lashes in
decades but today is all pinprick rage,
eggshell kid, tiny scar assembly line.
Outside, I press my ear to dead leaves. Roots
writhe in dirt, ancient cello strings straining
into song: if he dreams of me in rain,
in his coastal hometown, does it mean that
I'm a person? Or still the soft sludge trees
burrow into? The burning bush pulses
at its most crimson. I shield my eyes from
its glare. No one needs to be that honest.
Maple, poplar, oak all rumble then thrash.
Copse in chorus, chanting their secret names.
Shaking loose remaining leaves. Defiant.

Look. I'm no prophet, no role model, no
birds' nest or symphony, just the swampland
no one can build on. Office kitchen, the
Finance gals fruit flied around me, stirring
coffees, buzzing, *You look so good, you lost*
so much weight! My guts all quartz scrap, acid
clench, and threatening voice notes. It's been years
since I've seen a ghost or those severed hands
on the bannister. Now I'm the ghosts, those
kids left alone in cornfields by angry
fathers, their favourite t-shirts first torn
off. Mine was yellow. New, with a bronze horse
ironed on. No one ever liked horse-girls.

It wasn't a depressing dream. At the
end we even saw a rainbow. I hope
Edgar is better. Someone's behind that
tree, scratching their initials into bark

with my torn nails, gluing my eyelashes
onto branches like leaves. My real parents
were trees, they held the canopies up high
for me, silent and still and calm, smoothing
over the edges of the jagged sky.
Only they know what I call myself in
sleep. Celastraceae, flying spindle:
can invade the forest understory.
My eyelids twitch and ruffle, forcing out
fresh shoots, antennae, to block out the dirt.

Amber: resting place of departed souls

Pine tree resin, fossilized. Urine-hued.
Draws disease from the body. Balances
left and right brain. Bitter lipids dissolve
to acrid spit. Mustard tongue. We're all so
preoccupied with mouths. Teething necklace,
natural pain reliever, jaws rattling
like a child's toy. Female fear – always the
finest entertainment! I swallowed the
first bead after he ripped the strand from my
throat. Attracts good luck. Eliminates fear.
The sun's sweat dripped on shore, dragged away by
tides. Washed up. There are beautiful cities
where it is mandatory to hug your
opponents. He kissed me. Then bit my face.

Now less fashionable for jewelry,
amber melds to golden mouthpieces for
glassblowing, for smoking. Preserved insects
glint the ghosts of our kin. That beetle knew
about freeze and appease. Fuck fight or flight.
We fawn. Try to remember, to forget,
pour it in a pendant, a belt buckle,
a lager. He leapt into the taxi
I tried to leave in. Claimed it was unsafe
for me to ride alone. Scaffold, tunnel.
Mined in open bell pits, prone to flooding
and collapse. Words. Necklines. Try not to drown.
All Ambers lighthouse. Compass to swansong.
Ballet the ballast, tune the antennae.

There is counterfeit amber, phonies forged
from Bakelite, polyesters, vinyl
polymers. Amber alerts are fake news.

All Ambers lie. Especially about
men. I lurched lucky. Heavy door, locked. In.
Scar above my lip. Scarab. Pour myself
into trance. Jackpot chant, sweepstakes tempo.
Morning scorch, hungover, scanned the sidewalk,
the fences, the trees. Sometimes they don't leave.
Draws dismay from the bomb. Believes only
those encased in gold at their most fertile,
silent. Hush, swish, don't bother to disclose.
Believe algorithms. Lipstick benchmarks.
Alibi fallacy, truth myth, my word—

John C. Mannone

Intersection

Across Balter Beerworks at the corner
of Jackson & Broadway, Knoxville, TN

Patio twilight subdues the golden
backdrop of a glass of pale ale,
each bubble lifting through the silk glow
as if reaching for the stars.

Beer slips past my lips that are momentarily
silent but questions still effervesce
without answers. Sometimes, in the quiet
lull of a waning summer day, philosophy

merges with that silence and creates
its own music ... or cacophony. Across
the street, between the hush of cars
I hear the haunts of a repossessed building,

its brick no longer in the agony of neglect
but quickened from deep piles, dusty
with crumbled history along with busted
plaster and rotting lumber—a warehouse

of memories that once lit up the downtown
sidewalk with its collage of tiffany lamps
imputing character to the hundred-year-old
building. And now, reprieved, its eyes

literally windows to its soul, reflecting
assurance in the afterglow of the sun—
glass on fire breathing hope.
I take another sip, my glass

bathed in the same radiant light
full of intoxicating promise, glints
into the mirror of my own eyes,
my own philosophies whispering

partial answers to those rising
questions
of mortality
and resurrection.

Jude Marr

Moving Continents

boxes become three-dimensional, their joints taped
and double-taped, their corners crisp: open mouths agape, they stand ready
to receive needed objects—

[hats: bubble-wrapped but mis-matched
plates: books by friends
and strangers, rubbing covers under rolled-up shirts: yellow-handled
knives in newsprint: pillows
and picture frames: a bronze hare with her blind
eyes fixed on ceiling cracks: boxers and cotton
balls: a folder of old photographs]

meanwhile, half a year away, the boxes' future selves—torn and misshapen
but otherwise intact—sag against a sack truck's rigid back: after seven
months contained, hostage to sick, sequestered trades, packed
objects have settled into new shapes: their corners
crushed: their pages warped: their fabric frayed—

[there is risk in filling any box: belongings, once devoured, reemerge
as scat: buried items fall apart when disinterred: needed
objects, lost to time and transit, leave a scar]

and when, half an epilogue away, my future self—forlorn and mistaken
but otherwise abstract—drags a duffle and a fat backpack off a baggage
carousel [our fabric torn, our corners frayed] my boxes
and their objects have, without my knowledge or consent, become quintessence
of uncertainty, both position and momentum
unknown quantities—

[until we reconnect: when our dimensions may be altered but our scratched
and dented bodies recognize their former shape: when we still pass
as needed objects]

so, today and yesterday, in an old / new world of hurricanes and summer
haze, I tape my boxes closed against all doubt: stack them, hope

on rage, next to the dresser and the bed frame and the bookshelves
and the lamps: all shabbiness disguised by movers' wrap—

and tomorrow or today, in a new / old world of frigid rain and memories
that sap, I straighten aching shoulders: tear old tape away: unpack.

Uncertainty Principle

contained by our skins and our skulls, we are discrete
microclimates ruled by our blood's temperature

our body-maps' coordinates are not fixed: our borders
shift and our rivers divert: our topographies

are both known and not known: our cells secret
caves: our synapses bridges and ravines: we are tree

and storm: like countless shards of glass
in a kaleidoscope, our patterns shake loose whenever

we move, startling upwards to become sun-dazzled
murmurations: we are infinities of suns: together

a universe: fellow human, how should I praise
your countless shards?

Space and the Body: Fragments From a Mind Museum

this building appears known: a space
that is body: my brain but infinity

someone has daubed an intervention
on the bathroom wall: space
should not talk: to not think is ecstatic

inhabit or exist: museum and afraid
connect: exhibit limits petty

make words angry, teenage
painted: a sign/space dispute: people
as noisy signs

imagine noise: more image than matter

small different wants: head games
free floating: touching outside the heart

to be old in the museum: play
death as an installation: space
alone changes

space when connected is always
burnished: not space, bodies

this body looks metal: fingers don't
find comfortable spaces

the body is inside me: I am myself
a habitable space: genderless

what wall is appropriate for my art?

Jennifer Stewart Miller

The Orange Blues

With a few words drawn from "Ghazal of Oranges," by Jan-Henry Gray, and all the oranges changed to blues.

I know well
the *faraway scent of* blues,

know the exact shade
of *warning* blue, am still

astonished by the strange fruits
in my *wheelbarrow full of* blues.

I have packed roomy
wicker *baskets with* blues,

or *mostly* blues—
mandarin blue,

this crop of blues,
expensive blues,

messy blues,
blood[y] blues.

Those days, months,
years, *peeling* blues …

I still love all the orange
blues: azure, indigo,

lapis lazuli, periwinkle, peacock,
midnight, Nile, electric,

Prussian, Wedgewood, navy,
sapphire, sky…

But not cobalt, not
cyan or cerulean—I'm

done with cold.
And I've squeezed

every last drop of juice
out of steel and pewter.

Fistfuls of Green

Scrub pine—not a tree anyone wants
to plant, but a runty one, a scrapper

scrabbling out of miserable soil, windswept
coastal lands. The kind of tree that

even when young tends to be gnarled, if maybe
a little beautiful in moonlight. A paltry

shade maker. Pugilist. Porcupine. Thrusting
fistfuls of green into the needling wind.

A tree in which a starling preens his black.
Backbreaking work, to endure

in scrub lands—gripping the sandy earth, maybe
over a lifetime making the dirt a tad less poor.

Come spring, its seed cones have gone grey,
plain enough beauty for even the old Puritans,

that ancestral branch that tugs at my roots—
a faint guilt at the occasional scarlet-painted toes

or choice of wine over milk.
But if you are pine, you don't grieve overmuch

about what can't be helped—ancestors, bad soil,
whether you have the spine to be scrub—

you are here to impede the wind, you are here
to take your time.

Red-breasted Merganser

The winter sky this morning
is an old grey sheet spread out
for the mind's animal `to curl on,
and the tide is a liquid

battering ram heaving itself
higher up the marsh each surge.
A thousand thousand times we say,
how the time goes by—as when

you're flying subsonic through clouds
and don't feel a thing.
Yesterday's black-tufted waterbird,
which eyed me as it floated alone

near the shore—absurd and beautiful
as a plume-helmeted soldier—
is this morning's bone bird.
Was it dreaming in moon pull

in the marsh last night,
head tucked under a wing?
Mind and body—one day
you are many years married,

the next you are married
but not. In the beach wrack,
the bird-body is still mostly feathered
in black and white.

Stretched out like a thin rope,
its excarnated neck
ends in a thin pink beak baring
the tiniest sharpest pink teeth.

And above the missing eye, yesterday's
jaunty black head-tuft
still flutters like a thought—
'til death do us part.

Naomi Shihab Nye

All the Details Followed by Silence

For years, my friend cared for her father.
Delivered snug, knee-high socks,
tugged rug to artful angle on his floor.

She arranged his paintings,
refreshed the fruit
in his bowl.

They attended every
traveling musical
at the Majestic

because her father
loved showtunes so much.
He took a guest to each,

sometimes sharing a meal
before the trek downtown.
She called him

more than once a day.
And now they are both dead.
Even her husband

who was sick the whole time
yet assisted everybody,
is dead.

All these people
who traded so much care
are dead. Their dog

is still living though,
sniffing old friends curiously
as if we each became

an unspoken language,
vaguely familiar but who?
Some invisible force girding

all our days.
A wave we count on
returning to shore

but with none of them
here anymore, where is it?
Could this be the mystery we feel

walking outside
just before dawn,
softening sky,

breath of wings
rising from ancient cypress,
a crane called into the air?

Beacon

The teacher who sends her tiny students
to the front of the room, saying,

You will speak without mumbling,
and never swallow the end of a line,

believes in you
before you do.

Calmly she sits, hands folded,
golden bracelets glistening with light from the window

which falls exactly onto the middle of her desk.
As she will dwell forever in the middle

of your mind, listening
for a lifetime.

There might be a stage and you could stand on it.
Really? Corners of bookstores,

basements of libraries. someone might come to listen.
Really? Someone believed you could.

*

We didn't want much.
A circle of people unlike one another
with similar quietudes,
smiling around questions.

After such evenings
it was hard to sleep. The lamps

along the hallways of old hotels
kept throbbing yellow,
impressing themselves
on your closed eyes,
worrying you awake,
maybe there would have been
something better to say.

*

Finally, we went to our friend's lighthouse.
Slept in a perfect gray-shingled house at the foot of the lighthouse.
The children kept climbing to the top of the lighthouse,
but I was happy at the bottom
waving up at them. They said they could see forever.
Fishing boats glided past on the channel,
the pirate tourist ship and party barges would come later, all passing
at a distance. At the lighthouse we felt safe, never locked
a door, crabs dozing under the stairs, soft air lifting us
from silvery dawn, we had many days coming.

How could we be better people after knowing the lighthouse,
casting out calm reassurance the way it did, hoping for the best,
letting others know they might find their ways, staying rooted by
the ever-changing shore? For years it wasn't lit. No one could find
a certain lens. It was a quest. And now, every evening at sundown,
the strong golden light comes on automatically, long beam reaching
out across sand and rocks and your future and mine.

"Keep Up Your Joyous Practices"

My mom saved letters for fifty years
addressing her as
Dearest Immortal Self.

Devotees welcomed her
to communes,
urged her to stay strong

in yogic devotion,
"Don't miss a day."
Soon she would be a great sage

shining forth as blessed sunbeam!
I loved her hope.
My mother's hope girded her life.

I don't think she ever visited
that holy Connecticut commune though.
I did. It wasn't fun.

Guinea Pig

My mother and her friends wanted to visit the clairvoyant they'd heard about.
So they sent me to test her out.

A humble wooden home, on a street named for a tree. I didn't drive yet.
I asked my friend to drive me. This was not a new thing for my mother.

She'd also sent me to the Hindu breathing swami, the Filipino faith healers.
Always first, as her personal guinea pig.

My friend waited in the darkened living room. I was escorted to another parlor
by a man in a sleeveless undershirt, then seated in an upholstered chair.

The clairvoyant, who charged 5 dollars, said, "I'd like to talk about your friend out there."
"Yes?" She was a plump grandmotherly woman in a printed dress.

"Her mother just died and she's grieving terribly. She was asked to drive her mother
across the border for treatment, and it didn't work. Tell her she did

everything she could. Her mother is fine. Her mother is with her all the time.
You must promise to tell her the moment you leave. Right now, she has

many more problems than you." I was stunned. The facts of this were true.
She stared at me somewhat disinterestedly. "I see books coming out of your hands.

What does this mean? Do you love books? I see your grandmother
across the ocean in a long dress. She can't read and she loves you very much.

Take time for her. She's important. And don't marry that professor everyone likes.
Something's not right about him. You'll find your way."

An hour of details later, I staggered back to the living room, notes I scribbled
gripped in my hand – to find my friend nearly comatose on the couch.

I told her the moment we drove away. "This is good news! Your mother is here!"
My friend dropped out of college after that freshman year and has let the
angels guide her all her life.

Hiss

Good thing you said
the iron's soft breath
was your favorite sound
of childhood.

You'd lie on the rug
next to me
reading out loud
as I flattened the tablecloths,
your daddy's shirtsleeves,
pants legs,
afternoon light steaming us
on. It felt cozy, you said,
like a song you feel better
just hearing.

Good thing you told me
because now that you're gone
what other reason would I have
to make anything smooth?

Door

If you open the door to happiness
what comes through?

Friends come through.
Cool breezes lift your hair.
Words relax around the page.

For seventy days after you died
I watched your basketballs
deflating under the tree.

They were fire now, I couldn't touch them.
Couldn't sit, couldn't rest, couldn't dream.

Is it possible to be every age at once?
Return to a time before you left,
hold it longer, say something
that might help you stay?

Leave the door open.

Okwudili Nebeolisa

It's Never a Ghost

It's just the trees swaying to the breeze,
The confetti of their leaves falling.

It's someone walking home, counting steps
So he doesn't fall asleep, starting again

At every hundredth step, at every
Streetlight he passes. It's just the glow

Of a cat's eyes, it's surprised at the length
of your shadow. It's just two dogs

Looking for a suitable place to mate.
It's never a ghost; it's nothing spiritual.

Everything seems sacred at this time,
Everything has a leg. Everything's walking.

First Weed

I wanted the greed to slice me like the need
sheaving through my belly, this brilliant scythe
edges twice-sharpened, glinting, ricocheting
the angry rays of the afternoon sun. I thought
I was the mice scuttling through the room,
hoping to make it to the hole in the wall.
On second thought, there was no hole in the wall.
At one moment I thought I would bleed
through all the orifices of my body;
I thought I had already started bleeding,
dark red spots blooming on my purple shirt,
spots that, when I bent my head, patterned
the ominous brown of the paneled floor.

To be a lynx in her own thicket
was what I wanted. To be a raven
perching from tree to tree was what I wanted.
I opened my mouth and screamed but nothing
poured forth. Had I lost my hearing?
I struck my head on the concrete wall,
hoping to open the orb of my skull
but there was no wall. Can you imagine
the whole room was dark but all I saw
was this continuously burning light,
that I believed I slept with multitudes
when I was alone in the room all night long?

Loner

Too late for coffee. Too cold for linen.
There was rain. Now a teal light in the sky.

Lacerta has crawled out of her tree.
The dog downstairs will not stop crying.

Nostalgia has lain her head in the clouds —
I can't stop thinking about the years I spent

Away from my family and not cry.
I hide my face from the window, burying

It in the damask of the curtain;
When I'm done, I blow my nose into it.

I'm writing a letter no one will read
Because, after writing it, I will burn it.

Carolyn Oliver

Deep Learning

In another life, I am a voice for hire. Nights
in a blanketed back room I give you names,
side effects, animals, hours, kinks,
colors, formulas, phonemes in tone
permutations from even to enthusiastic.

(I would like to talk to you about *dolorous*,
a word no one has ever asked me to produce.)

Frost. I pass houses full of opera playing out.
You could identify this rustle in the leaves.
Between rainfall and ten thousand monarchs
in a forest, thawed and taking flight,
you would know the difference.

(*Know*: I mean you would commit the process
of knowing. Recognition. Knowing again.)

I try not to imagine the uses for my voice.
Instead I wonder when I say *blue*
which version the listener imagines:
cerulean slate sky soft baby.
Which hexadecimal you call up.

(There is a smell to *morning*, opposite
to the lights always coming on.)

One day they run out of patience, or sounds
for me to make. You, voice clone, begin
to synthesize my speech. Unsupervised,
how uncomplaining your architecture,
requiring only power.

(*Consolation*: the room was leaking anyhow,
sirens breaking through.)

Tell me your instinct toward prayer.
Tell me how to figure *home*. Tell me
where to look when the call comes
in our own voice: someone has taken
a four-day-old baby, butterfly on her back.

Manifestation

In another life I'm a ghost interpreter, gleaning
intention from images the desirous whisper:

Tulips puckered in shadow, expecting
daylight's long lick. Quilts made

of looking glass, maps from long
unfolding creased greasy silver.

When they pretend they don't like
to be overheard, I eavesdrop, I sample

the aftertastes of shame and pride
(blush-warped valleys, plastic wolves).

It's tricky work, like plucking lyrics
from a car stereo blowing by at ninety.

The pay is good, but the clients—well.
Impatient. They want justice, or lost

duchesses, assurance of their flag's
heroic snap in every gale. Who wants

sunburnt snow, nettle welts,
contour maps of empty houses?

But you—I can tell you about the pleasure
of warm water coursing over my hands

after I peeled tonight's potatoes,
and it can mean nothing else

except what you remember.
When you say—I'm paraphrasing—

I want for you rain budding on locusts
I don't need to explain

here the hills are always gilded and dying
and our echoes beg for higher ground.

Devonian

In another life I am a fossil slick of agate,
once honeycomb coral, clustered. Crushed
in pressure's fist, I ache for your chisel's kiss,
I crave the sting of your hog-bristle brush.

Strange Attractor

In another life I am a sea witch,
you the tidepool I'm afraid to lose

little cosmos I could wrap my arms around
little chaos I would keep whole.

Even as fractal coastlines unspool
like light I tremble to touch your every surface

to know your rock of mottled flounder's skin
your urchins and anemones, fish and fronds.

For you I'd forsake my lair
I'd sacrifice my tentacles to turn

every shorebound ship shark and ever gone.
From the boundary where air and water meet

I'd draw a thread, sew for you a net of fixity.
With my voice and the velella's sail I'd conjure

a shield over your exposure—because rain is coming
always it comes to sweeten what should be salt.

But all my spells would fail.
For who and where and how you are converge

against permanence
and in your name my power is unmade:

the sea the seathe seathe sea the sea

David B. Prather

Migration

Brown bird in the apple tree,
let's switch it up. You be the watcher,
and I'll be the singer. I want you

to know the kind of loneliness
you can't fly out of. I want you to
wander from room to room
and look at the world from windows.

For just a moment, I want you to listen
for the sound of distant machinery
as it screeches like an animal in pain.

The train leaves town, follows the river.
If you stayed here long enough,
you'd know. Let me be the one
in the branches, the one with more

feathers than foresight. Let me find
my way in the wind, a force invisible
as hope. But, no, you are gone.

There will be no bloom on this tree
for months.

Myth of Men

Twang of men's voices
next door, they gather
to work on a car engine,
power tools exultant
with effort. My father
taught me how to change
a tire, oil and filter,
taught me to get my hands dirty,
show the world I am a man.
Yesterday, two boys walked
down the street, palm to palm.
They could have been brothers,
one the caretaker, the other at risk
of running right out into the street.
They could have been lovers,
showing affection in a way
I've always wanted.
The men next door laugh.
And because my thoughts are
a flock of birds, I know
they are laughing at me.
Because I know nothing
of automotive repair.
Because they scorn me
for whom I love. Because
my hands are clean.

Cockchafer Beetle

—Melolontha melolontha

Sometimes ancient
 meanings get lost.
Words crawl around in the mouth
and in the mind, scuttle under
stray thoughts, no more than leaves

 fallen to the forest floor.
 I think lustfully.
I cast nouns and verbs aslant
as shadows of themselves.
I make the world

 lascivious, even this beetle
 with a name that denotes
a large, plant-gnawing pest.
But that was centuries before now,
when children used to tie

 a string to a bug's jagged leg,
 then watch it fly, trapped,
in circles above them.
There are days I only feel
this way, all my inklings

 tethered and buzzing over me,
 a swarm of unquiet sorrows.
I know I shouldn't ascribe emotions
to a bug, but those ebony eyes
look too wise, adorned

with anemone lashes. I imagine
this creature a hazard to men,
sneaking in at night,
doing unspeakable things,
laying eggs within their privates.

Or another word for an STD, or
an addiction to sex. Or, worse yet,
an ugly epithet that just can't be
shaken loose, like the past.
It's always there, even if

we remember it wrong. How it slips
through trees at night, enters dark fields,
and eats tender foliage. When we wake,
we know something is different,
and there has to be a word for it.

Executioner Wasp

—Polistes carnifex

I remember the Wong-Baker FACES
pain scale from smile to frown, from joy
to agony, but I find it impossible
to match my suffering to the correct countenance.
Sometimes, my body hides how it really feels.
Hot peppers are measured by spiciness
on the Scoville scale—jalapeno, habanero,
ghost, and reaper.
When you chew on the flesh of demons,
even your lips will burn. For far too long,
I've described pain according to weapons—
stabbing, piercing, burning.
When my back broke, the hive of my flesh
swarmed with bees, all that venom
numb in my legs, arduous in my eyes.
An executioner wasp
has golden eyes, amber wings, and a sunset body.
Where it stings, a wound swells then leaves
a hole like a bullet. I've seen movies
where the condemned is offered a last
cigarette, a blindfold
always refused, a chance to repent
Rifles are raised, triggers pulled, and a hail
of hornets flies through the torso. Lord
help the soul that angers this vespid.
The hurt with last a lifetime. It will
be indescribable.

Jane Sasser

There's no telling

my aunt would say,
meaning, of course,
the outcome of the subject

was anyone's guess:
a field of knee-high grass
on a sky-blue summer day

might conceal a hidden well;
a dip in the lovely pond,
cool and sweet on your young back,

might end in your lonely drowning;
any minute walking this earth
could be your last.

I loved the way *no telling* hinted
how nothing existed
before spoken into life:

in the beginning was the word,
that silver-tongued sword,
as though birdsong

emerged from lyrics,
as though even this poem
could push you—

stunned and blinking—
into the light.

Scar Tissue

There's no predicting where it will go,
the physical therapist says. *All those photos*
of beautiful muscles in textbooks—
no one really looks like that.

We are pushing my knee, newly released
from tightening webs, trying to outpace
any new spread of healing gone wrong.
Outside the walls of this room

the world reels from pandemic and hate,
all ills that won't heal unscathed—
every Garden of Eden riven and divided
by its snake, imperfection's patchwork

stitched snug, callus and keloid
pocked over beauty's terrain.

Ode to My First Mother-in-Law

who attacked a world full of pending hurt
with scrub brushes, down on her knees,
purging dirt and germs from every surface,
pushing back black worry that dogged

her days: the aquarium stand pinned
to the floor so the baby couldn't topple
weight of water and glass. The cookie tin
she ruined, convinced the dark coating

was baked-on fat she punished
with oven cleaner, stripped to bare shine.
The endless calls we had to make
so she could sleep, assuring her

we continued intact. The way she claimed us
as hers to protect, every dog and cat
we ever owned knowing the sound
of her car coming up our street, bearing

their grandma, too, her arms weighed down
with cans of tuna and meaty bones.

Ceri Savage

Beers in Berlin with Lionel

I'm not lost. Just trust me. I lead Lionel down concrete steps
to a featureless door, tiny neon humming. I feel smug. Inside

is bright and not-cold with long, shared tables like we're in Munich
or something. I drink Panke Gold, a citrusy kick, he, a Roter Wedding

that's boring. Red beers are boring; fight me. The next bar is
named after vagabonds. He sips a Schwarzfahrer, some dark stout,

talks about Ireland, jumping in a freezing Loch Lomond at 3am
that I don't remind him is Scottish. I, a bittersweet DIPA, and

talk about Canada, the time we did Centurion with Blue Buck shots
and I kissed Mae as soon as we got to the party, on the stairs, her knee

between my legs. We sneak Flensburger bottles onto the bus.
They have flip-top lids that *plop* open and fit the inner pocket of a

Levi's jacket. Me and Lionel both like no-nonsense north German
beers; we like to think ourselves stony-faced fishermen on harsh

Baltic Sea beaches. Next, in a twenty-on-tap kind of place, I take
a smoked beer that reminds me of cheese and the firepit at Kath and

David's, and how I hope they have kids soon. He takes a frothy
Belgian Dubbel that any Englishman would ask to be filled to the rim.

Our last is a something-or-other on a corner doorstep. We watch
some poor bastards head to work. A white puppy sniffs our feet.

Yellow trams jangle. Laughter comes from black-clothed shapes over
there. We cheers and clink and talk of nonsense til the bus arrives.

Claudia M. Stanek

Do Sheep Dream of Other Sheep

In a pasture far
from the hearing of others
a sheep lifts its head from grazing.
The edible greenery is sparse
yet somehow barely adequate
and the sheep isn't hungry enough
to wander little or far.
The sheep does not know
it is alone, that miles away
there is a lushness to a land
beyond its vision, a fragrant land
of sweet nourishment beyond
its sense of smell. Unaware
that the fence is no longer intact,
the sheep bumps against rotting rails,
the animal's vision poor.

O for one step over a rail,
to journey toward a flock
it does not conceive of existing
where a shepherd cares,
and the call of the wolf
is silenced by the bark of a dog.
But this sheep stays, ill kept,
close to the pricker bush
it can just feel, knowing only
what it has always known
to be its thorny truth.

Eclipse

Everything we see hides another thing, we always want to see what is hidden by what we see. — Rene Magritte

Because you cannot look at the sun
even as the moon would hide
the light in near totality
you look instead through
special glasses if you look at all.
Because you are tempted to look
at the sun directly, your eyes
make you look away for their own sake.
The needs of your future sight
outweigh the desire of your mind's eye.
Because your curiosity hasn't
killed you thus far you persist
in looking for light in darkness,
unlike Job wishing that light had
not entered the day of his birth.
Because you hold to the light
of one star still in the night
holding onto you in a covenant of love,
you wake in the morning no more
the countenance of joy but alive,
brave enough for one more day
of love eclipsed by sunken wounds
you do not need special glasses to see
though no one chances to view
the wounds you wear.

See

What do you see everywhere, everywhen, as you consider the stars?
Do you see Sirius in need of petting, as I do, or do you view this sky
through the reflection of artificial light as on my dog's widened eyes,
in the same way as I gaze upon the Milky Way veil of your glory?

O to see each atom and all the stars at once, knowing
that to do so is an act of grace, beyond my visual field.
Perhaps for you there is the simple want of a slight blindness—
to see yourself as I do, through my imperfection and hunger.

O to be seen by you, as carbon in your image, atoms and molecules
you touched with the same spark of intent which burns
as intensely as the thought of a dog star or the drop of a dog's tear.
I would dare to touch the stars with my tears in your scarred hand.

Note to a Dog

I want you to look down, now, not thinking
about the ground. I want you to look
at the dry blade of grass and the dirt around it,
how the soil absorbs all the light that touches it,
warming it the way you warm my lap.

Please look at all the grass, both dead and living,
even not comprehending that dead grass
once lived and covered the dirt beneath your feet.
Would you want an uplifted vision—to be able
to look at yourself as I do, knowing life and death?

Please look at me as more than giver and taker,
more than a version of yourself who pets you
with a not-so-different purpose, with the same
desire as you have. I would hope to give you more
than the earth offers, hold onto you for life.

Annie Woodford

Clearing the Hands

Lord I miss my dog,
he said, his smile collapsed
by missing teeth,
old blue tattoos
of blurred wings and words
circling the sinewed arm
he reached out to my lab,
who paid him no mind,
intent on my fries.

The only way I could stop
that dog from begging
was to show him my hands
like a blackjack dealer,

palm wiped against palm,
then both palms shown,
hands all skin no secrets,
the first and second
fingers on the right one
stained yellow from smoking.

No more, Buddy.
No more, Boss.

We all laughed.
We all sipped our beer.
We all tried the honest
gesture on for size.

He used to root me
out of my chair.
I gave him his own recliner.

The February afternoon
melted the unmelted
snow edging the weeds
edging the bar's grimy deck.
We all imagined
a big dog stretched out
in his own recliner—
like a god of happiness and appetite—
and then we laughed
some more and got pretty drunk
for it to still be daylight.

Let Down Thy Milk

Cushy Cow bonny, let down your milk,
& I will give you a gown of silk,
A gown of silk & a silver tee,
If you'll let down your milk to me.
—*nursery rhyme*

All the winnowing world
is rain-blind
& blurred with mist.
Let it be said:

the dead are missed.

The neighbors sold
their late father's
herd last week,
a plan promised
since spring.
I did not have to hear
the cattle cry.
They were just gone
on my last walk.
My child & I
have loved
their black shapes
blending into dusk,
their large heads
slowly lifting
 to observe us,
a shifting
of planes & deep
eyes, a light thrown
back from the shadows,
calves bedded down
in the grass,
one wild & leggy,

willing to lope
right through the fence
& graze unbounded,
while the others tried
to call it back.
Their blue vowels
wove the tree-lines,
the pasture-breast.
The lamed bull
dragged his hoof.
Now only one
mother & her calf
are left to watch
for dogs & coyotes
alone, a vigil
of senses all night.
All the flies go to her now,
her sides shivering
with their welter.
Otherwise she is smooth
& many shades & silvers
of black, a massive heat
radiating off her
flanks, her gaze
taking us in
as we approach
the fence with melon rinds
she will not take
from our hands,
preferring
to eat them
off the ground,
her big flat teeth
a patience of grinding,
a sound like the way
the earth will
one day take us in.

The Latest Name of Our Beloveds

Our town's only laundromat shifted to accept
a dipperful of pale winter sun,
its plate glass windows, fluttering
with rain-curled flyers, open
to the yellow asphodel glow
& jake brakes honking like geese on the steep road in front.

We sat outside with our backs against the glass.
A girl with long green fingernails scratched
my timid dog on the head,
gave him little bones at my request,
understanding how we're trying
to make him believe in goodness.

A man in the parking lot buffed his black truck
though it already shone back the sky,
the clouds tongue-kissing as they slid by
& I worried over the human contact necessary
to wash our comforters & to comfort
us as well. The proximity

of a girl rolling her towels
on a table, a woman folding stacks of baby clothes,
the neighborly wash sloshing the portholes,
the back & forth from dryer to metal laundry basket on casters,
the scent of all our different soaps
strung between us like flowers,
like a beating of wings,
some change in the temperature & current of the air,
like the melody of "Dark Eyes"—
a melody so old no one knows
where it came from & that,
my Love, is just its latest name.

Endling

Soon the Red Wolf will be but a series
of genetic code stored in metal drawers.

They are hunted in the pocosin swamps,
in the Weyerhaeuser stands drained & dried

to tinder, a uniformity no
forest, but crop of pulp, monoculture

naves presaging a vast human absence.
Come spring, though, half-coyote pups will be

snout deep in warm fawn meat—wolf-tall, rough coats
burnished by a touch of rust, infantile

bellies gorged with blood, ignoring sprayers
programmed to crawl the loblollies, fine mist

of fungicide rainbowing the carpet
of needles, breathed in by the wind, the pups

& their mother. In our book of holy
days, in the catalog of our errata,

record this survival.

Luke Wortley

Ouroboros

I find myself in a political debate with a timber rattlesnake slithering out of the fescue. It asks me if I believe human beings should be afforded special privileges and rights based on their perceived sense of superior consciousness. I say I've never considered the question before, which is not true. I've contemplated many permutations of this question, just never in relation to snakes. The snake rears up pensively and shows its fangs. I can see a gossamer droplet glimmering on the tip of one of them. I don't recall now if it was the left or the right. Of course you haven't, says the snake. Its voice uncannily similar to my father's. So I ask him if he believes snakes are ultimately destined to eat their own tails. That's a wicked stereotype, he says, and I confess I can't answer his question without looking too much like an idiot. Just so, the snake turns and slithers away into the grass as I feel my jaw unhinge and my body contort toward my feet.

Conversation

The father says, *You're my best friend. You know that, right?*
The son says, *Yeah, I know. You're mine, too.*
The father says, *I love you.*
The son says, *I love you, too.*
The father says, *More than anything in this world.*
The son says, *I know. Me too.*
The father says, *I need to tell you something.*
The son says, *Okay. What is it?*
The father says, *Please, just hear me out. I need you to know this isn't your fault.*
The son says, *I know.*
The father says, *I don't know what to do about it.*
The son says, *Me neither.*
The father says, *What would you do?*
The son says, *Don't ask me that.*
The father says, *Why not?*
The son says, *Because I'm not you.*
The father says, *Aren't you?*

Comprehension

One night I looked at my cat and found I had the ability to comprehend language the way it was intended instead of what was actually said. In meows I could tell he was saying, *I care not for your existence.* When my wife said, *It's fine,* I knew what she meant was, *I need more help.* I texted my best friend, *I miss you*, and he sent me back *Same, bro,* which I somehow knew meant *I want to say I love you but can't without too much consternation on my part…It's just the way I was raised.* I tried to apply my newfound power retroactively to the things my father used to say, and I came to some startling conclusions. I found that his words were untranslatable, that the memories of his utterances defied my power and I had to make up what he meant based on what he said, which meant that I had to inhabit his mind, which meant that I had to get progressively drunker and meaner. And I didn't want to do that. My power, as it turned out, was short-lived.

Mercy

Inside my father's safe there is a forest of broken pines. Inside the forest of broken pines there is a letter written to me. Inside the letter written to me there is a wet heart. Inside the wet heart there is an orchid. Inside the orchid there is a grasping hand. Inside the grasping hand there is a shot of bourbon. Inside the shot of bourbon there is a concrete goose wearing a bonnet. Inside the concrete goose wearing a bonnet there is my only memory of my grandfather. Inside the only memory of my grandfather there is a plastic tumbler. Inside the plastic tumbler there is a solitary frog. Inside the solitary frog there is a headlamp. Inside the headlamp there is an urn. Inside the urn there is a mattress laying by the creek. Inside the mattress laying by the creek there is my father's pistol. Inside my father's pistol there is a flip flop covered in sand. Inside the flip flop covered in sand there is a fractured tibia. Inside the fractured tibia there is a gallon of milk. Inside the gallon of milk there is my son's toy truck. Inside my son's toy truck there is forgiveness.

FICTION

Amber Wheeler Bacon

Another Time Could Be Different

It was July, and Eli was eight weeks old. Shelly and Frank had moved to South Carolina a month before, finding positions at the same college. His was adjunct; hers was tenure track. Every morning since they'd arrived, she took her four-year-old Adam and baby Eli on a walk around the lake in the center of the neighborhood. She'd always lived in the South, but delighted in the maritime forest plants like loblolly pines, magnolias and palmettos, which were new to her. There was color everywhere.

Something about the forest and the new baby filled her mind with sex. She saw a vagina in every flower. The bright green ferns at the base of the American hollies unrolled and stretched like erections. She walked deeper into the woods, blushing, and remembered a boy from high school, her first stirrings of desire. She couldn't remember his name, only that she'd never felt longing in her body before. In that room, on the boy's futon, there had been so much possibility. She wasn't yet locked in by the choices she'd made.

Halfway through their walks, Eli always needed to eat, and she nursed and walked at the same time so Adam didn't get bored. Her triceps were sore from holding the baby, who weighed over ten pounds at birth. Now that he was large enough, she could strap him to her chest in a carrier and just pop out her boob. He usually fell asleep after nursing, a puddle of sweat where his cheek smashed against her, his hot breath releasing a soft tang. The walks were peaceful. They rarely saw another soul.

When they reached a certain spot where the lake met a creek and opened up, they saw an alligator, his snout and back poking out of the green water. Shelly didn't mind the alligator. They rarely attacked and were often afraid of humans.

Adam stumbled. He sometimes became overzealous in his

running, like a puppy, whose exuberance ended in a tumble. The boy—in blue shorts and shirt, *locally grown* written in cursive across the front—held a stick out. "I'm going to get it!" he said, baring his teeth and heading toward the water where the alligator floated.

The sun overhead was so bright it was bleak. Shelly's armpits were slick. Behind the canvas carrier, Eli rooted for her breast. She reached for Adam's hand to pull him to safety, trying to keep him on the path to put distance between him and the alligator.

He whined. "I hate alligators. I want to see a shark! Remember when the shark killed the alligator?"

"That was a crocodile," she said, regretting she'd shown him the YouTube video: Who Would Win? Shark or Croc.

"He's small," Adam said, pointing. "Is he a baby like Eli?"

"I'm not sure. You know as much about alligators as I do."

She tried to remember the boy on the futon. Was it Eric? She'd never been to a house like his before. They had a monkey they kept caged in the den. It was her first realization that families could have different tastes and values.

In some places the trail was exposed, and in some, forested. They entered a shaded section where the soil beneath them was a mix of sand and dark organic matter. She couldn't walk this trail without thinking of all that had died in the world. She wondered if she'd always be morbid now that she'd lost her father the year before from a heart attack. Since then, she couldn't walk anywhere without thinking of her life as a trail of dead things under foot—flakes of skin, dried up animal feces, trampled leaves, the seconds passing by on a microwave.

Eli began to root more frantically and she gave him her right boob. It was stupid, she knew, to be modest, but she never felt comfortable feeding Eli in front of Adam. In front of anyone, really, even her husband. It was something she wanted to do alone, something that involved only her and Eli. It was impossible not to hold her child against her breast, to feel the sucking at her nipple and not think how she would someday dry up. How Eli would, and Adam. And Frank, of course, already well on his way. Or maybe not him, but what had once been their love for one another. It wasn't exactly gone. Just parched.

In front of them, a man approached with his dog, a white freckled collie-looking breed. The man's hand slid into the satchel resting against his hip. He pulled out something black and pointed it in Shelly's direction. Shelly saw a gun in the man's hand. She grabbed Adam and held him close. The beat of her heart pulsed in her breast as Eli sucked. The steady thump of pumping milk and blood filled her. It seemed fitting somehow that they'd go together, these small beings who'd been born of her.

But the man held a camera, not a gun, and when they got closer, she recognized him from flyers they'd received in the mailbox from the neighborhood beautification committee. He was taking photos of the flowers in bloom along the trail.

The man's dog barked. Adam jumped up, landing in a fighting pose with his stick out. "Who's there?" he shouted.

"Adam, please let the man pass." Shelly moved her arm to shield any part of her breast exposed beneath the carrier, though she knew the man could see nothing. Seconds earlier, she'd thought they were to be shot and left dead in the forest. She inhaled to calm herself. "Sorry. My son has a vivid imagination."

"Who do you think would win?" Adam said to the man. "A shark or a croc?"

The man put away the camera and squatted by his dog, one arm draped over the animal's neck. He brought his hand to his chin and rubbed his stubble thoughtfully. "No contest, really. You'd have to go with the shark, right?"

Adam seemed pleased by the man and his taking the question seriously. When Adam had asked his father the same question after seeing the video, Frank had said, "That sounds a bit violent, bud."

Something about the man's willingness to engage struck Shelly. She imagined unbuckling the canvas carrier and letting it drop in front of her like an apron, then removing Eli from her chest, lying him in a bed of leaves at her feet. She wanted to expose herself in some way to the man with the dog—the softness in her postpartum stomach, her swollen and reddened nipples. She wanted to give him every part of her that had been damaged by motherhood.

The boy on the futon—Eric—had slipped his hand so easily into her underwear from the leg hole of her shorts. She remembered a coldness down there she'd never felt before, as if he'd exposed her vagina to a cool breeze, but it was only his cold fingers, moving in and out of her. She'd sucked in her breath at the sensation. A part of her had wanted to turn away from this side of her. Her childhood best friend always talked about embracing herself as a "sexual being," but Shelly had been afraid.

Now that she had so much more to lose—children, a husband who tried to be good to her, a tenured teaching position—she wondered what she'd been scared of.

"Mommy thought the croc." Adam's hand lingered on the dog's ear, rubbing his small fingers over the soft fur. The mother felt a pull of desire in her breast like she'd felt just before Eli latched, like an invisible thread of desire being tugged.

She wasn't the sort of mother to obsess over her children. The need asserted itself to let the man know that she was *more* than a mother. She pondered how to casually mention her new position at the university. Something about him, about this trail, the child pressed against her and the one caressing the dog made her want the man. Or maybe she just wanted him to want her. She giggled, moving a sweaty clump of hair to behind her ear.

Past the man, a collection of flatwood pines stood, scraggly and thin. There were palms and live oaks lining the trail along with some jagged bushes. Shelly tried to think of something to say to the man. Were their words to express what she wanted from him?

She hadn't even had sex with her husband since the birth. The doctor had said to wait six weeks, and it had been eight. Frank hadn't mentioned it, so she hadn't either. She wanted to see how long she could get away with not having sex with her husband, even though when they *did* have it, she always wished they did it more often.

Before, with the boy Eric, it had been about fear. With her husband, it was about giving away too much. How much of her was left for him?

"He looks like a shepherd of some kind," she said.

The dog licked Adam's palm, the tongue around his fingers, and Shelly thought his hands must still be sticky from the yogurt and banana he'd eaten for snack.

The man moved closer and held out his hand. "I'm Drake. This is Augustine. Auggie. He's a rescue. We think he might have some border collie."

She felt slighted by his wedding band and use of the word "we." Shelly held on to Drake's hand, feeling the need to overcompensate or exert control. He allowed himself to be pulled closer. Their bodies were less than a foot apart now if you counted Eli pooching out of her abdomen. "Named after the saint?" she said.

Disliking losing the man's attention, Adam turned around and ran toward the baby alligator, with what action in mind, Shelly didn't know.

"He's just a baby, but he'd kill us if he could!" Adam yelled.

She called his name, moving toward him as she had earlier, but her limbs ached. There was a hesitancy to let go of the man's hand. It seemed unfair Adam had ruined this moment.

Drake, sensing danger, pulled away and ran after Adam. The man's concern snapped Shelly out of her reverie, and she moved faster, but then stumbled on a tree root. In order to protect Eli, she twisted in mid-fall, so that she landed on her side, cradling him. She turned on her back, and Eli's body went rigid. He let out a wail. From the ground, she saw Drake scoop Adam away from the pond's edge. He carried him back with one arm. Beside him, the dog's tail wagged.

The alligator scuttled away after its own prey—a blue crab somewhat camouflaged by the greyish dead grasses.

"We're okay," Drake said.

Adam beamed at him, unfazed, clutching the man's shoulder, a fist full of his shirt.

When Shelly righted herself, she saw Eli's head plopped to the side, angled toward the earth. It reminded her of the time in third grade she'd let her hamster run around the floor while she took a bath. Getting out of the tub, she'd stepped on it accidentally, breaking its neck. She took a deep breath and cupped Eli's skull, unlatching the front of the carrier and peeling him from her abdomen. His onesie and her tank top were soaked in sweat.

He was okay, just shaken from the fall, red-faced and whimpering.

"Shhh, shhh," she said, bouncing him as he lay across her forearms. He looked up at her, blinking his cloudy eyes—which she hoped would turn hazel—finally quieting. She saw that her child trusted her to take care of him and wondered if she deserved it.

"Mommy!" Adam pointed at her chest.

Shelly had pulled the collar of her shirt underneath her breast to feed Eli. It hung out in an odd and unattractive way. Her engorged nipple, covered in Eli's saliva, dripped milk. Drake's eyes met hers. He put Adam down, then looked away, kneeling once again to pet his dog.

Shifting Eli to her left arm, Shelly slipped her boob back inside her nursing bra and tank top. "I'm so sorry," she called, still adjusting.

With Drake kneeling, he and Adam were close to the same height. Adam seemed to have forgotten the intensity of the last few moments, speaking to Drake as a peer, someone interested in similar pursuits. "The shark grabbed the croc by the stomach and shook him like this." Adam acted out the shark biting into the crocodile's stomach and shaking it, adding sound effects.

Drake stood, brushing off his knees, pressing his shirt flat where Adam's grip had wrinkled it. "Well, I can't say I'm surprised," he said. "Sharks are at the top of the food chain. They're called apex predators. Everything's below them. Though I do wonder how they came across one another. They live in different habitats."

The man suddenly seemed like a know-it-all. Like someone humoring her son only to flaunt his knowledge of sea creatures. And who could even say if anything he said was right? There was no one to challenge him except a four-year-old and a tired mother. She strapped Eli back into the carrier and reached for Adam. "It's time to leave. Say goodbye."

After the initial excitement of Eric's hand in her underwear, she'd realized he didn't really know what he was doing. She lay back on the tie-dye fabric draped across the futon, bored. He told her he loved her. The words seemed ridiculous breathed in her ear, but pleasing, too. She liked that he loved her without having to love him back.

Shelly turned from Drake, retracing her steps on the trail. Adam followed for a moment, then ran back toward the lake, yelling, "Bye! I love your dog."

Her son could be brash one moment and so generous the next. She was both awakened and exhausted by him.

At home, Adam skipped up to his father reading in the den and said, "The man was right! Drake. The man at the lake. He was right and Mommy was wrong. The shark killed the crocodile. It's stomach was too soft. It didn't have enough scales."

Frank closed his book and put it down slowly. "It was one video," he said. "You never know. Another time could be different. The croc might win." Her husband had an annoying habit of playing devil's advocate with Adam. He liked to be instructive. Usually, Shelly argued Adam's side, but today, she was silent.

When she fed Eli that night, she closed her eyes and

fantasized about the man by the lake. The memory on the trail with the man and her boys was another death, like Eric and the futon, like her father, like the dried out grass around the creek. So much of the world was imagined anyway, why not try to make something come alive again inside her head.

Finally, the children were asleep. Shelly was empty. She'd run out of the ability to give.

In the den, a soccer game flashed on the television. European playoffs. Outside, someone set off fireworks, which happened almost nightly. When they'd first moved there, she was afraid the noise would wake the children, but they'd already grown used to it. She turned off the television and sat next to her husband on the couch, then lay down with her legs across his lap. His hand fell against her ankle, then slowly moved toward the thigh, underneath the shorts, and finally, past the elastic of her underwear.

Frank was right that another time, the crocodile might win. The shark in the video was almost beaten. Bleeding from its eye, clouds of pink erupted from its flesh. But in the final seconds, the crocodile needed air. Seeing its last chance, the shark ripped into the belly of the croc as it swam to the surface for a breath. Like the tender abdomen of a new mother, its soft belly, with no scales, no armor, didn't have a chance. As soon as the shark's teeth lodged itself into the smooth underside of the crocodile, everything went silent and still. There wasn't any twisting or trying to get away. Knowing its weaknesses, the crocodile had given itself up.

Matt Barrett

The Bright Green Door

We found ourselves in Pennsylvania, our boxes scattered across empty rooms, my father and mother sweating. For some reason, my father liked to move us in the summer time.

Our new neighbor sat on his porch. He was short and plump like a teapot, *here is my handle, here is my rump* which he covered in denim jeans, held by checkered suspenders and a big brass belt. He called himself Jasper the Friendly Jost, since that was his name, Jasper Jost, JJ Jr, and if it weren't for his little Yorkshire Terrier with its bedazzled pink collar, I might have been scared of the man. He watched me through a cloudy eye and hiked his pants up higher, and when my parents went back to unpacking, he asked if I knew what cancer looked like.

Jasper loosened his suspenders and lifted his shirt.

On his big white belly, he had what looked like a giant hand pressed up against his skin.

"Used to be an itty-bitty hand," he said. "But it clawed and grew and now look at it, you'd think it could palm a basketball."

I bent over to give it a real close look.

"You sure that's cancer?"

"Sure is," he said, lowering his shirt. "It tickles me at night. Its index finger," he raised his own, "tries opening the knot in my stomach, I swear to God I saw its nail poking through and part of me thought just let it out. *Come on out cancer, show yourself, let me see your ugly face.*" He picked his little dog up off the porch and placed it in his lap. He stroked its head. "Anyway. Doctors gave me six months to live a decade ago, but what none of them knows is this cancer don't wanna kill me from inside, no, it's gonna find its way out and kill me then, what's the point of dying in there with me?"

Then Jasper leaned in toward me, his big belly practically swallowing his dog.

"But when it finds its way out, I'll be ready, too. I got a

plan," he whispered. "For how to face it."

"What's that?"

He held a finger to his lips. "Shh," he said. "It's listening. But it knows it's getting a fight. So, it keeps growing and I keep letting it, giving each other a fair chance, you know. Man to man, pick on someone its own size."

My mother stepped out of our new house across the street. From Jasper's porch, you could see it all. It was painted yellow with a bright green door and red shutters around each window. A pink rose bush hid most of the porch, which was navy blue on one side, orange on the other, and whoever owned it before us, my mother said, must have had quite the imagination.

Jasper shook his head. "No one owned it before you."

"No one?" my mother asked.

"No. Someone came by and built it and then went on his way."

Other than Jasper's house and ours, the street split farmland as far as you could see.

"Before that man came by, I could sit here and see those mountains way off and drink my beer with the stars above my head, but you know what that man did? He set every light to turn on at dusk so those stars no longer shined."

My mother shook her head. "And he wasn't even living there?"

"Nuh-uh. He came through one day with a truckload of wood and nails and took his hammer and saw and put a sign out front saying, *Under Construction,* and the only time he said a word to me was on the very last day, when he nailed that final shingle above the attic window. He nodded his cap, and I swear to God, he looked at me and said, *Enjoy.*"

"And then he left?"

Jasper put a hand over his heart and raised the other. His dog sniffed his scraggly chin.

"You think you got the world in your hands and someone'll come and hide it from you." He stared across the road at our bright green door and all that nothing in between. "For a while

I thought the man would come back. I kind of wanted him to, you know? He didn't make sense to me, but maybe if we were neighbors, I'd understand him more. See eye-to-eye. But I got the feeling that was the point—he built that house to confuse me. Why me, I don't know, but for ten years I've been staring at it, not knowing why it's there, and now you folks are in it."

My mother lit a cigarette. She didn't smoke except for the days we moved.

"Doesn't make sense," she said. "Building something not to fill it."

Jasper shrugged. He put the dog down at his feet and stroked its head. "As a warning, you ever see Moxie peeing on your door, I'm sorry. Trained her to do her business over there." He breathed so I could hear the air enter his lungs. He leaned way back in his chair. He kept his eyes on our door. "When I can't sleep, I ask *why me?* You know? I think everybody asks that. Why build that house right in front of me? But maybe I'm missing the big picture."

"What's that?" my mother asked.

"Maybe it wasn't about me. Maybe that man didn't even see me here. All that time he was working, he didn't look my way. Then he hammers the final nail, and there I am, materializing before his eyes." Jasper's one good eye was green just like the door. "He builds that house and then sees me. And what I can't figure out is if all that time, he thought he was building me, too."

*

A week after we moved into the yellow house across the street, Jasper came over for dinner. My mother insisted. We sat around the dinner table, a family heirloom we'd moved from town to town, a cherry slab my grandfather cut and stained the year he met my grandma. I ate on the side where the wood sloped like a crashing wave and placed my plate on a little black knot, raised in the middle, which made me think the wood could see me as well as I saw it.

When we led him up the porch, Jasper tapped his cane

around the entrance, feeling the floorboards like a blind man. He didn't trust it, he said, with just one eye alone.

My father poured him wine. Across the street, Moxie yapped. If we paused a moment in conversation, there she was, reminding us she still had more to say.

Jasper cleared his throat. "It's a pattern," he said. He tapped his cane in rhythm with her yapping. "Sooner you know the pattern, the better off you'll be."

He counted it with us, each high-pitched bark, followed by a pause, just long enough to know she was starting again from the top.

Jasper surveyed the walls of our dining room and finished his wine. "You know something? Everything I've ever seen, I've walked to. The mountains in the distance, I've walked to them. The cluster of spruce trees two miles west, I've packed my lunch and eaten in their shade. Anything I can see from my window, I've stood on, or at least beneath. Orion's Belt—I've walked to a place where I could gaze straight up at it. Every speck on the horizon, I've also seen up close. But not here." From where I sat, Jasper's cloudy eye moved from each picture my mother hung. "Houses are funny, you know, 'cause they kind of got a face. The two top windows are eyes. The shingles, its hair, the porch, its chin and mouth. And ever since this place rose from the ground, that face has been watching me. Everything I do, it watches. And it's hard 'cause a house is just a head—you don't get to see its neck or shoulders. You can't read it other than what's in its eyes, there's no body language. You don't see if its arms tighten. You're looking at it, but you don't really see anything. And now I'm here." He looked around.

My mom waited for him to finish.

"So," she said in that quiet moment between Moxie's barking. "What do you make of it?"

*

It was the summer, like I said. A hot summer, too. But not just hot, sticky. The kind where sweat pools in your armpits. The kind that feels all right until a drop rolls down your side, and you feel your mother's fingers tracing bones beneath your skin.

When that sweat journeys on down, you wonder how much of this is memory and what parts you're making up, but still, you feel it: her nails working down the same small path the drop carves out on your skin.

"Roman," you remember her asking. "You ever get scared you'll stay like this forever?"

You know that's what she said but aren't sure if these things are connected, that question about who you are and her finger working its way along your side.

"Like what?"

"Like this. Hungry, scared."

You remember following her finger from rung to rung, down the scaffolding of your side, how her nails felt more like teeth.

"Well?" she asked.

You remember a steady ticking outside, rain dripping from the gutters. One-two-three. Drip. One-two-three. You remember counting them.

Drip-drip-drip.

You breathed in rhythm with the drips.

"Well?" she asked again.

It was raining. You know that. But the sun was shining, too. You remember following your ribs down to her finger prodding the bones you thought she could remove with a single pull.

What's the question? you wanted to ask, but that little drop of sweat completes its path, and you're here again, in this big yellow house, standing in the foyer behind the bright green door.

*

There was a sawing across the street. Across meaning across from Jasper's porch. I spent most of my days there. There wasn't anything else to do, or places to be. The nearest store was six miles east. A convenience store—convenient for I don't know whom. It sold everything you didn't need: chips, but only the spicy kind, and sodas, but only the knock-off kind, and papers, I swear to God, as Jasper liked to say, they were three days old. Plus, the store was down a long dirt path covered in apple trees, and if you didn't know where you were headed, you'd have thought you made a wrong turn despite the fact there were no turns at all.

For weeks, the sawing went on. Sawing and hammering, and one day, when Jasper and I were sitting on his porch, Moxie got up off his lap and crossed the street to our house. Only this time, when she crouched by our door to pee, my father was hammering so loud, she ran. Where she was going, Jasper wished he knew. She hadn't ever left this place, he said. Her whole world was no wider than a classroom—from the foot of his bed to our front door.

When Jasper and I drove to the convenience store, we asked the man behind the counter if he'd seen a little Yorkshire Terrier come this way.

"A what?" he asked.

"A dog," said Jasper.

"Oh," said the man, glancing out the window. "What'd you say it was called?"

*

There was no barking the next time Jasper came over for dinner. Just that sawing behind us, my father in the backyard sweating.

My mother poured Jasper wine.

"You think she'll ever come back?" she asked.

Jasper shrugged, sipped his wine.

"What's she know about where she is?" He pushed the wine aside, then thought better of it and allowed himself to drink more. "I used to think her barking was white noise, you know? Something you could just tune out. But I can't hear anything anymore. Can't hear myself think. Can't hear the birds outside, can't even hear my own footsteps when I walk. I look at my feet, and it's like they're not even meeting the ground. I tap my cane on the floor, and I don't hear it. It's just that sawing," he said. He opened his mouth to say more, but thought better of it and scratched around his bellybutton like something inside him was starting to tickle.

*

For one week straight, it rained. Not every minute but enough to think it wouldn't stop. Some days you woke to the sound of rain and some days you could see it coming. Some nights the clouds sunk so low, you could feel them hold you like heavy wool, and a part of you thought you were drowning.

Jasper said the rain had to do with the mountains. Something about the clouds getting stuck on their peaks.

When the rain stopped, so did the sawing. Then my father started digging on the left side of our house. Jasper and I watched him from the porch.

"You know what he's digging?" he asked.

"No," I said.

He winced when he touched his stomach.

"The cancer?" I asked.

He lifted his shirt. His belly was hard and round. He scratched it. "Look." The hand beneath his skin had grown. Its fingers were bigger than his own.

"You think it'll come out soon?" I asked.

Jasper watched my father dig. "I don't know," he said.

And his eyes moved up and down, up and down, in rhythm with my father's shovel.

*

I've never heard my father speak. When I dream of his voice, it sounds like the work he does. Out comes hammering or sawing or digging. In my dreams, I understand what those sounds mean. Sometimes when I watch him work, I wonder if he's trying to tell me something. Maybe it's in the patterns. How fast his shovel hits the dirt. Or how many boards he lays on a sawhorse.

I've asked my mother how she could fall in love with someone who cannot speak. But what I really mean to say is, "How do you know he loves you back?"

He doesn't speak to us with his hands. His face doesn't change when he's mad. I do not know if he feels anger or sadness or pain. But there was one time I saw him cry.

We were living on the coast of Maine. Our home overlooked a crowded port of fishing boats. My father stood by our living room window. He must have thought he was alone. In the port, two fishermen had just come back from a long day's work. A girl, no more than seven years old, stood on the dock waiting for them. The men helped her onto the boat, and the girl in turn helped them clean it. And they all just stood there, the boat rocking back and forth.

And then my father cried.

"Dad," I said. But he pretended he was still alone. Even when he turned to look at me, he carried on like I hadn't seen a thing.

*

Two weeks after Moxie left, a rusted Honda Civic pulled up between our homes. The man who worked the convenience store rolled his window down.

"Hey," he said. He signaled Jasper to come closer. "I found this on my way to work." He handed him the pink bedazzled collar. "This your dog's?"

Jasper cradled it in his hands. "Where'd you find this?" he asked.

"About fifty feet from the store."

"And she wasn't there?"

"No."

"No signs of—" Jasper almost couldn't say it. "Bones or fur?"

"No bones, no fur. Just this."

When they finished talking, Jasper sat back down beside me. He stared across at the bright green door. To the left of my house, the hole my father dug was so deep, all you could see was the top of his head bobbing up and down. Up and down as the shovel rose. One-two-shovel, one-two-shovel. My mother stepped out of our home.

"Morning," she said.

Jasper looked past her at the hole.

"What's your husband building?" he asked.

My mother stopped in the middle of the street.

"I don't know."

"That's what Roman said."

"Well, it's true, we don't." My mother noticed the collar in his lap.

"But how can you not know?"

"I mean he's still figuring it out. Sometimes he never figures it out."

"What?"

My mother sighed. "If you're asking me to guess, I'd say he's probably gonna build a market. I mean, where do you even get your food around here? Either that or a little diner."

"A diner?"

"Maybe."

Jasper shook his head. "I don't get it."

"That's 'cause we're talking about the future, honey. And the future's all about getting people what they want." She smiled. "Listen—when he's finished, you're gonna thank us. When you can just walk across the street and eat something fresh."

Jasper tightened the collar around his fingers.

"Was he the one who built that house?"

"Him? God no. But I thank whoever did. That man knew someone would want to stop here someday. Settle down, figure the place out. We're still talking about the future. Only that future's now."

"I don't want a market," said Jasper. "I don't want more buildings, I don't want—"

"Shh. Not everything's about you, Jasper. You said it yourself. *Why me?* Maybe this is for someone else."

"Who?"

"Look." My mother turned to face the mountains. "You can still see them to the right. And the stars above, listen—we'll make sure the lights go out at dark. How's that? It'll close each night at six, and anyone who works here, they'll know to turn the lights off."

She smiled.

Jasper shook his head. "I used to be alone."

"Is that what you want, to be alone?"

His shoulders tightened, back arched forward.

"I mean I had Moxie."

"*Moxie*," my mother laughed. "Listen to yourself. We're the ones with moxie! We're the ones with drive! We're the ones who are changing things!"

Up and down the shovel rose. On-two-shovel, one-two-shovel.

And calmly, in rhythm with my father's bobbing head, Jasper crossed the street.

Maybe because my father liked pretending he was alone so much, he didn't feel like turning when Jasper eased himself down into the hole, the pink bedazzled collar wrapped around his fist. Maybe he just didn't hear him. Or maybe because my father had lulled himself into the rhythm of his digging, the world seemed all right to him, at peace. When my father screamed, I thought, *So that's what his voice sounds like.* It wasn't the way I pictured. Wasn't as strong as the sound of digging or as steady as his sawing. It was too human for that. I didn't know what that meant, for my father to sound human, scared. But that's what it was. The scared cry of someone who hadn't been paying attention, hadn't noticed the barking gone missing or the stars dimming above his head. He screamed, then stopped, and my mother ran down into the hole.

Jasper tapped his cane back across the street. He sank into the chair beside me.

"Shit." He breathed. "Where'd you say you folks were from?"

I shook my head. "Where do I start?"

"Name some."

"Parts of Florida. California. Both of the Portlands and

everywhere in between."

"I've only ever been here."

He looked around, at all the places he'd ever walked to.

"Man." He took the collar off his fist and laid it on his porch. I followed his eyes to that bright green door. "It's really just another house, isn't it?"

"Yeah."

"Not that ugly, not that great."

"Just a little bright."

"Yeah, that's it. A little too bright."

He smiled.

"How's the hand?" I asked.

He rubbed his knuckles.

"No, I mean—" I nodded to his belly.

He lifted his shirt. The fingers had grown so large they covered his ribs. He pulled the shirt back down. "You think I stand a chance?"

"Of course."

He motioned for me to come closer. "I don't want it to hear this," he whispered. "But I don't really have a plan." He smiled and looked back across the road, first to the left of my house, then to the right. For a moment, that's all he did. First to the left, then to the right.

Then he made up his mind and stood.

Alaska, 1951

The plane circled the lake over the trees and Daniel David Benton smothered the ember of the fire with the heel of his boot. He kicked dirt over the ashes and then walked to the edge of the water.

The plane came down past the dark, green trees and landed its pontoons hard on the still water. A fish jumped twenty yards from the plane's landing and two sets of waves spread out over the blue lake.

The propeller whirred loudly as the plane turned towards Daniel and then approached him on the small, rocky beach. The pilot accelerated and then cut the engine. After a few moments, wood frogs broke the silence on the far side of the lake. The plane drifted towards the beach and then the pilot set anchor. The waves from the plane's landing pushed on, farther and farther up the shore.

"Jim," Daniel said, his voice hoarse.

"Dan," Jim said and stepped from his plane into the shallow water.

Jim pulled the plane around its pivot on the anchor so that the passenger's side faced the beach. He opened the door and lifted a sack out of the plane and brought it over to Daniel.

"You modify the rations like I asked?" Daniel said.

"No canned cigarettes, no canned chocolate, and no canned biscuits. Added two Hershey's bars and a pack of Lucky Strikes."

Daniel nodded and rooted around in the pack.

"Your voice," Jim said. "It's hoarse. You all right?"

"Hurts, but I haven't spoken in two weeks."

"Huh, yeah. Guess I didn't think about that."

Daniel smiled. "Yeah."

"So—"

Daniel pulled a .38 Special from the canvas bag. "And this?"

"Captain Falks thinks it's a good idea for you to have one in the field."

"For what? In case I run into the Russians?"

"No, for self-defense, for animals."

"Jim, a .38's not going to stop a bear, a big cat, or a wolf. I'm not taking this," he said and held out the gun. "It's dead weight."

"Captain said for you to keep it. Use it for game, if you like."

"If I had wanted to hunt, I'd have taken a rifle. Game takes too much time, and I can't survey much if I'm tracking, butchering, and cooking my meat."

"Hell, I don't know, Dan. Do whatever you want, but if I head back to base with that gun,

it's my ass—and I'm not having that."

"Bullets too?"

"Bottom of the bag."

Daniel put the gun back and found two boxes of bullets next to the matches and the pack of Lucky Strikes. He took out both the matches and the cigarettes and then opened the pack. He watched two ducks land on the water at the far end of the lake. "Anything else from the Captain?" He placed a cigarette between his lips.

"Just that you did a great job with the last map. Says you're the best."

"Yeah. I bet," Daniel said and lit the cigarette.

Jim smiled.

Daniel pulled on the cigarette and took some papers from his pocket. "This isn't going to be what he wants," he said and unfolded the two charts. He set them side by side on the beach. Jim kneeled down beside him, and Daniel waved his free hand at the map on the left. "The ravine's no good. It's all granite and shale and the grading's too steep. It's an eight percent incline." Daniel flicked the ash from the cigarette over the rocks. "Here," Daniel pointed to the map on the right. "We have a creek, but it's small, and there's fifty feet of flat land to the right of it.

The grading is six and a half percent and there's hardly any shale. It's got a good foundation but we could, if we had to, make a road."

"You weren't supposed to map that route."

"Yeah," Daniel said and pulled on his cigarette.

"You were supposed to try the valley over to the east."

"I looked at it. It's all swamp."

Jim shook his head. "The hell they want to put a road through this?"

Daniel shrugged. "It'll come, one day or another."

"I don't see it. There's no reason to be here." Jim looked out across the lake.

"Maybe," Daniel said, "but people are coming, one way or another."

"I don't see it."

"Well, I guess we're lucky that the U.S. government didn't order you to chart the terrain and survey the road."

"Guess so," Jim said and stood up. "Besides, nothing happens out here."

Daniel watched a red-tailed hawk circling above the trees. "Guess so."

Daniel gathered the charts, stood up, and handed them to Jim. Jim took the old charts and pulled out several new ones from his pocket and opened one.

"Basically, the same as the last assignment. Just you and the woods and no one for hundreds of miles. The cover is the same, about ninety miles in a straight line, but probably a hundred and fifty or a hundred and sixty with all the up and down." Jim pointed along the hills on the aerial chart. "Around here," Jim tapped the map with his index finger, "you'll run into some long patches of what almost looks like prairie, about eight days in or so. Once you've passed them, change your direction and head southwest. You'll come to a lake about twice the size of this one, and that's where I've picked for the next rendezvous in two weeks. Looks a little bit like a quarter moon from above, has a beach along the northern edge."

"If I'm not there, you know I'm dead."

"You say that as if you're doing something like living out here."

Daniel laughed.

Jim folded the newly mapped charts he had taken from Daniel and waded into the water. He swung the plane in the direction of the open lake and then pulled the anchor. By the time he had started the engine, Daniel was back at his campsite. His watch read 7:08. He turned back to wave at the plane, and as it passed out of sight, the hum of the engine faded as it pushed into the sky.

Daniel added the new supplies, minus the pistol and the ammunition, to his pack and left the empty bag beside the campfire. He turned the gun over in his hand and checked it to make sure the chambers were empty. He threw the gun on top of the smoldering fire and then walked to the edge of the water with the boxes of bullets. He threw the first box into the lake and watched it splash into the water. As he threw the second, it opened in mid-air, cascading bullets across the surface of the water.

"Dead weight," he whispered and walked back to the campsite.

He pulled the pack on and walked south into the woods. The sun disappeared under the pine, spruce, and cedar trees, and a soft, green glow covered the forest floor. He walked through the fern covered underbrush and felt the weight of the pack sink into his shoulders and pull against his back. Descending slowly, the ground fell away into the trees. He walked at an even pace and listened to the sound of his own breath and the brush beneath his feet.

After he had been walking for a few miles, he came to the bottom of the hill and saw that it ended in a shallow, three-foot ravine. Daniel stopped short before the edge. His heart pounded. He took the pack off. Two squirrels watched as he took a compass and an altimeter from his bag. He watched them dig around the pine needles at the bottom of the ravine and then they ran into the trees.

Daniel looked at the compass, the altimeter, and his watch, and then wrote down his measurements on the back of one of the charts. He put the equipment back and then looked at his watch again. 11:12. He looked down the path of the ravine and watched it curve slightly. He took the pack from the ground and pulled it up and over his shoulders onto his sweat-drenched back. When he had reached the other side of the ravine, he looked up the steady incline. He paused and then began climbing up the hill as he listened to the sound of his breath and watched the shadows among the green.

Miles up, the trees broke into a clearing a hundred yards from a rock face set into the side of the hill. The forest opened in a wide ring around the cliff, the hill sloping up evenly on each side. Daniel followed the hill through the trees and then walked out over the ledge. Cedar and spruce lined the overhang and a single spruce stood out at an angle over the drop. Daniel guessed the cliff was maybe eighty feet wide and seventy-five feet high. Set back from the trees further down the hill, he could see over their tops to the north. He took the pack off and peered at his watch. 14:18.

Taking a can of vegetables and beef from his rations, he opened it with calm, even motions. He sat on the ledge and poured the contents of the can back into his mouth. The soft, cooked vegetables blended with the thick, fatty taste of the meat. Three golden eagles circled the forest before him and he watched a fourth come up from the grass in the clearing. Gray clouds pushed over the landscape from the west. They drew a steady line across the horizon going from north to south. The mountains rose high in the distance to the east. Daniel scooped the rations at the bottom of the can with his first two fingers and then licked them clean. He picked up his canteen. Two of the birds had moved north from the group, two had remained. He took a long drink. He placed the empty can on the ledge and then looked at it against the pale stone. After a moment, he took some measurements with his instruments and wrote them down on the back of his chart. Studying the rough chart, he looked at his compass and adjusted his course.

At the top of the next hill, he took more measurements and looked up into the canopy. The sky had clouded over and had begun to gray. He glanced at his watch. 16:23. He shook his head and descended into the trees.

Four miles down the other side of the hill, Daniel heard a soft rushing further into the woods. After another mile, the sound had grown into a hum and then a rumble, at which point he found himself at the edge of a dark-colored, quick-moving stream. He dropped his pack, pushed his hat back on his head, got down onto his hands and knees and stuck his face into the ice-cold water. He waited until he needed to breathe and then he pulled his face up and gasped. Putting his lips against the water again, he drank. When he was finished, he pulled water from the stream over his head and neck and let it pour down the center of his back. He sat back on his knees, breathed deeply, and grinned. His breath settled as he watched the stream. Looking up, he saw the canopy completely covered the width of the stream. Sunlight caught the water only at odd angles between the shade. He checked his chart, saw that the stream was not there, and penciled in its location. He took a few other measurements and then refilled his canteens. After he had taken his equipment and supplies and bundled them up, he found a fallen branch the width of his wrist and about ten feet long. He took it to the edge of the water and lowered it into the stream. He was almost in to his shoulder when the branch touched bottom. He set the stick aside and looked at the eleven or twelve feet of deep, fast-moving water that separated him and the other side. He listened to the calls of the robins and the chickadees and then he looked up and down the stream. After he placed the pack on his shoulders, he moved east.

A mile away, he saw a thick, moss covered spruce log crossing the length of the stream. When he got to the tree, he ran his hand over the moss and felt the wood chip into thin, brittle chunks as it fell away. He kicked his foot into the trunk a few times and watched a half-inch of splintered wood drop away. Kicking the wood in the same place a few more times, he saw only dust float to the ground. The color of the wood beneath the rotting bark was still a honey brown. He climbed up onto the log and stood carefully. Hands out, he side-stepped over the water an inch at a time, the carpet softness of the wood giving ground as he followed the dark line of the moss over the quick-moving water. Halfway across, his left foot slipped out and he bit his lip hard as he reeled to keep from falling. He jerked to the right and then to the left and then ran slipshod nearly stumbling forward. As he made the other end of the log, he grabbed one of its dead branches that snapped under the pressure and pivot-jumped for the other side. Landing on his feet, he fell forward—face in the dirt and laughed. His heart was racing. The dead branch was still in his hand. He sat up slowly and looked at the log. Then he inspected the branch while the earthy, metallic flavor of blood filled his mouth and he licked his lip. Standing back up, he brought his hand to the tear and measured its length against his fingertips. The cut was a finger-width-long and shallow to the touch. In the light beneath the trees, the blood was a dark red. He washed his hand in the water and then washed his face. He continued to move south. The terrain leveled out as he lost the sound of the stream. The tops of the trees swayed in the wind and he saw green in the distance, green beneath him, and green above.

When the shade from the trees had become dark, Daniel stopped and looked about. The trunks nearest to him were a deep burgundy, and the ones a little ways on were almost black. He looked at the time. 21:38. He set the pack down between two trees and then lifted his arms over his head. As he stretched his fingers towards the sky, he felt the muscles from his neck to his calves. He felt them move, twist, grind, and ache. He felt them become warm and sore. He dropped his arms to his side and rolled his shoulders forward and back. He stood and stared into the fading light, feeling his body heavy and dull. Leaning over his pack, he took out his tent, the stakes, and a thin rope.

He strung the rope between two trees, arranged the tent, and staked its sides. Beneath the brush, he scavenged dead wood and gathered it in a pile beside the tent.

Pulling up the ferns in an area around the pile, he threw them out into the blackening forest. He laid down beside the wood, took a match from his pocket, and lit the brittle kindling. The small flame pushed against the twigs, climbing over the yellowed pine needles, and smoking into a dim light. He blew on the embers with steady breaths. The fire took, and he pulled out two cans of ham, eggs, and potatoes. He ate them cold while he listened to a boreal owl call to another boreal owl who called to another boreal owl who called to the first one. The birds formed a chorus stretching into the distance. The fire popped and hissed.

The taste of blood mixed with the eggs, meat, and potatoes. The salt stung in the wound. When he had finished, he poured water into one of the cans. He swirled it around and gathered the food around the sides of the can, then he repeated the process with the other two. He drank the contents of the last rinse and then filled the can to the brim with fresh water. He poured instant coffee into the makeshift mug. He set the can against the edge of the fire and waited. The smoke from the pine bark and twigs smelled peaty and sweet. The forest was dark beyond a few steps. The coffee began to steam and Daniel took a shirt from his pack. He wrapped it around the can and drew it away from the fire. He sipped the black coffee boiling hot.

Taking a chart, a pencil, and an eraser, he went over his math. He played with a few numbers and then notated and mapped his findings. The fire shifted forward and fell onto itself. It scattered cinders and thick smoke into the air. Daniel erased almost everything, leaving only his final figures and the course he had walked. As he was putting his figures away, rain began to fall through the canopy. Drops landed on his hand, his leg, and the chart still beside the fire. He re-folded the heavy paper and stuck it into his back pocket. The rain became a drizzle as he placed the pencil and eraser back in his bag. Looking up into the darkness, unable to see sky or cloud, he listened to the rain fall around him, and then he looked back into his coffee. He sipped and watched the rain hit the fire. The light flickered and the embers hissed. He could no longer hear the owls. When he finished his coffee, he picked up his pack and climbed into the tent. He took two blankets from the bottom of the bag and wrapped them around himself. He laid down with his head against the earth and listened to the raindrops falling softly on the tent. He drifted into the space between sleeping and awake.

The light through the tent was yellowish as Daniel opened his eyes. The wind was pushing hard against the canopy. After crawling out of the tent, he looked up through the trees. He waited for the wind to stop blowing long enough to see through the branches. When it eased, he saw the sky was pale and clear. He looked at the time. 5:58. His hands moved slowly as he took the tent down. Numb and stiff, they warmed gradually, gripping his things lightly, then tighter and tighter. He opened a can of ham and lima beans. The thick, savory paste was chewy and heavy in his mouth. When he was done, he lit a cigarette and watched the end flare bright as he inhaled. He listened to the sound of the wind through the trees. Beneath the upper story, the air was cool and still. He knocked the ashes of the cigarette into his empty can. The smoke rose towards the wind and he looked as far as he could into the woods. The angles of the branches, the roll of the ground, the limitless number of trees. As he exhaled the last of his cigarette, he dropped the stub into the can and tossed it towards the burned out fire. He stood up and pulled his pack on. He felt its weight settle on his hips, and then his knees, and then his ankles. As he walked into the forest, he listened to the sound of his breath and stepped into the rows of trees.

A few miles from the campsite, the forest opened onto a wide ring lined at one end by dead trees. As he entered the clearing, ravens called overhead. Two flew from one dead tree to another. Their calls carried in the now windless sky. As he walked into the tall grass, the long blades brushed against his body. He counted eighteen dead trees. The sun was hot. Near the middle of the clearing, he saw three caribou at the far end opposite the dead trees. None of them lifted their heads from grazing as he stopped and watched their long antlers rising and falling over the makeshift prairie. When he reached the other side of the meadow, he saw that the land sloped down into the trees. He pulled his equipment from his pack and charted his position.

Half a mile from the clearing, he stopped still. He felt his breath in his chest. He placed his hand over his heart and then, gradually, kneeled down and placed his hand to the ground. He felt it move. In the distance, he heard a rumbling that turned into a churning that broke into a roar. Thousands of caribou drove through the trees and down the hill. The brown mass moved as a whole less than fifteen feet from where he stood. Moments passed like eons and Daniel was still. When the last of the caribou had crossed before him, he reached out with a shaking hand and leaned against a tree.

He heard a loud snort behind him. He turned and saw a bull thirty feet away—antlers hanging in a six-foot arc, nose dripping wet, eyes fixed on the spot he stood. He barely saw the caribou lower its head before it charged. Daniel dove behind a tree and felt the animal's hot breath on his arm as it passed. It ran down the hill to where the other caribou had been, then turned and followed them away.

His heart felt still as it raced in his chest. He slipped the pack from his shoulders and pulled his cigarettes from the bag. He sat with shaking hands while he tried to light a match. When he had the cigarette lit in his mouth, he began to cry. He sat for an hour, then for two hours, and then he got up. He slowly pulled the pack up. He started walking and watched the hill fall away.

When he came to the bottom, he found a wide, shallow river. Small stones lined the bottom of the stream and boulders punctuated the surface of the water. Light caught on the scales of the whitefish in the pools beside the boulders. On the far side, the trees thinned and he could see sunlight on the forest floor. He looked at his watch. 10:17. He pulled his gear from his back and untied his boots. He took his socks off first, then his pants, then his hat and shirt. He took his three canteens and a bar of soap to a boulder beside the shore. The water was cool and the stones were sharp beneath his feet. He poured the contents of one of the canteens over his head and body, and then he lathered his head, limbs, and torso. Taking the rest of the water from the canteens, he managed to rinse half the soap away. He filled all three containers in the stream and then doused them, one after another, over his body again. The water was cold against his skin in the open air and his body prickled with the shock. When he had finished, he stood breathing quickly in the stream and then filled the canteens with fresh water. He brought them back to the shore and packed them away. He sat in the sun and mapped the distance he had covered over the last few hours. When he was dry, he put his clothes back on and carried his boots, socks, and pack across the water. The stream was slow-moving and quiet. On the other side, he dropped his pack, sat down and put on his socks. He looked out across the water and then he checked his watch again. 10:48. He scooted up against the nearest pine and laid his head against the trunk. He watched the dense trees on the other side of the river until he fell asleep.

When he woke, the sky was cloudless and without a wind. He looked at his watch. 11:18.] He put his boots back on and started up the hill. The sunlight in the gaps between the trees made his skin hot and sweat began to form on his limbs. After walking a mile up the hill, he saw the outline of a hawk as it flew over the trees. He looked up and then pointed his forefinger and his thumb in the shape of a gun. He followed the bird in the sky, and then he shook his head and smiled. He dropped his hand to his side and started to climb up the hill again. To the west, he heard a gunshot. He turned his head in the direction of the sound and then he heard it again.

Matt Cashion

Love Song for the Headless

Maria had been waiting for an hour in the Pain Management Clinic waiting room, eager for a refill, hopeful for a higher dose, still bundled in her coat, scarf, gloves and hat because it was minus forty degrees in Wisconsin, which meant every time someone came shuffling or rolling or crawling through the door, the polar vortex smacked the bull's-eye painted on her face, and she cursed them. If she had to wait much longer, she'd have to strangle someone. Was chronic pain the leading cause of crime? She didn't want to go to prison. She had a five-year-old son to take care of and a sick husband to nurse back to health and a shit-job to avoid being fired from, all while cringing from back spasms that made her want to murder anyone who said (or looked like they *could* say) something agreeable about any of the stupid political leaders who advocated for increased stupidity. Her incompetent doctor said she should simply learn to live with pain. So she got a second opinion. And here she was, in this waiting room that resembled the purgatory she was no doubt headed toward.

From the wall-mounted television, giggling newscasters from Fox News tortured her. Beneath the TV, a two-year-old screamed her little lungs out like a tormented Joplin (Janis, not Scott), while standing on her mother's lap, flapping her arms as if her diaper were on fire. Maria wanted to get in before the kid. She'd arrived first. Were her pain less excruciating—were she not on a time-crunch to pick up Miles—she'd say, "No, please, let the child in ahead of me; I'm happy to suffer longer for her sake." But no, she wanted in first.

An older man sat two seats away, wearing an orange duck-hunting hat, flaps over ears, beard drooping to his chest, newspaper two inches from his eyes. He grunted when he turned the pages. Because they were too heavy? Two elderly women sat across from him wearing matching Green Bay Packer Jackets, both eating from bags of popcorn they'd scooped from the machine next to the empty fish tank, talking of yesterday's playoff collapse and dumbass coaches. They'd come in together, sisters probably, twins maybe, faces blank as tombstones. They kept looking at the screaming baby, kept saying, "Poor baby." The poor baby's mother kept rocking the poor baby; dark eyes set in a ghostly face. Closer to the door, a skinny guy, mid-twenties, couldn't keep still—clenched jaw, bouncing knees. He scratched his face with one hand, held his phone in front of his eyes with the other, squeezed it as if had insulted him.

Maria thought of her mother in Jacksonville, Florida, who one month ago had undergone what was supposed to be a simple kidney procedure to remove a benign tumor—so simple her mother insisted that Maria didn't need to come home. So she didn't. Her mother had said, "Don't worry about *me*, honey, you have enough to worry about. If you need to feel guilty, feel guilty about some of the other things in your life. You need to take care of yourself."

So she didn't go. She focused her guilt on being a bad mom and bad wife, a failing teacher and cold colleague, an apathetic neighbor, passive citizen, and pill addict. And sure, she also felt guilty for being a selfish only child who couldn't fly home to hold her mother's hand before she went into surgery—to say comforting things and assure her that she'd be there to see her when they wheeled her back out.

Today, she'd canceled her afternoon music class, then felt guilty for feeling good about it. She hated the gen-ed students who hated the music they were required to appreciate, and she hated herself for being mean to them for hating it. She wanted to stop her colleagues in the hall, explain that her back pain made it difficult to smile these days, ask them what sort of pain they were living with and how did they manage? Her mother told her last month, via telephone, to "offer it up," which was what she'd told Maria in her youth every time she fell out of a tree, or off a bike, or got whacked in the head with a softball she was supposed to catch. Marty too had been saying, "Please.

Find a therapist." And just this morning, finally, to herself, she'd said, *okay, okay, yes.* Following her Pain Management appointment, she'd step next door and make an appointment with Dr. R. Angle, PhD., certified psychologist.

But it was already 4:30, and she had to pick up Miles from his new preschool before five and didn't want to embarrass him by being late. He'd gotten kicked out of his last preschool for punching three other kids on three separate days, allegedly unprovoked, and with no explanation afterward from Miles, which led to weekly appointments with a child therapist who was having no better luck getting him to talk than Maria and Marty were having. Potential medications were being discussed, debated, fought over.

The bearded man said, "Fake news," turned a page, grunted.

The baby's screams were operatic, amplified, off key. One of the Packer sisters said, again, "Poor baby."

It'd be easier to live with pain if she still lived in Florida, away from a landlocked state and its bland food and grey skies. She'd prefer an occasional hurricane over living inside a freezer. And she'd prefer not to summarize her life every time she said hello and revealed her accent and got the inevitable "Where are *you* from?"

Over the screaming baby, one Packer sister told the other, "Ted Stein has been brain-dead for a month yet after slipping on the ice, still hooked to the machines, poor thing, and his children never call him."

"Poor thing," her sister said.

With a dose of stronger meds, Maria might manage a good night's sleep. She might wake up restored, might return to the treadmill for a mile, might enter the campus-wide meeting addressing budget cuts and layoffs without a sense of panic, even as she knew the music department would be the first to go. And following that meeting, she might very well find the old spring in her step and waltz, as she once did, into the auditorium to greet one hundred hearing-impaired sophomores whose collective angst was difficult to pierce, even last week when she veered from the syllabus and played Hendrix playing the Star-Spangled Banner, at which point students grimaced and poked fingers into their ears. One said, "But wasn't he on drugs?" And just like that, she veered again, suggesting *they* try drugs. Then she riffed through a lecture on the history of psychedelic music, played a sample of the fifth movement of Hector Berlioz' Symphonie Fantastique (1830), written while Hector enjoyed opium, then she sped through the heroin-infused jazz of the '20's, trying, before class ended, to reach the Beatles, then the Merry Pranksters and the cultural conditions of those times that fed the music and fueled rebellion. The students grew sleepy, despite all the Red Bull in the room. After an hour, and still with twenty minutes to go, she said, "Fuck it," and let them go, which cued the cacophonous unzipping and re-zipping of backpacks, sounds that made Maria's brain dance with apoplectic rage.

The office phone kept ringing, an old-timey bell-ringing rotary phone, circa 1976, that bounced off the hollow walls, which, even on a good day, would give Maria a migraine. At the first meeting with the pain management specialist, she'd said, "I also have chronic misophonia." He typed that into his records, said, "What's that?" She explained it was a strong sensitivity to certain sounds that might, if severe enough, trigger a desire to kill whatever's making the noise. When Miles attacked his cereal bowl with his spoon, for example, or when people ate popcorn with their mouths open, or men grunted while reading newspapers, or kids shook the walls because they bounced their heels, or loud-mouth pedantic pundits praised a racist devil, making babies scream. She looked at her phone again. Nothing. She inhaled deeply. She closed her eyes.

She'd hurt her back shoveling too much snow too fast because she was late for work and needed to dig out her car. Since then, a year ago, she'd twice fallen on ice, spraining her back. She hated to think she'd grow old while walking over ice, breaking arms, hips, necks. Marty kept saying, "It could be worse." Before he got exhausted from being sick, he stayed exhausted from mediating conflicts with parents and children, foster parents and bureaucrats, removing children from their homes and placing them with strangers. When Maria complained about her job, he said, "What do you do again? Listen to music? Talk about music?"

Worse than the ringing phone was the overly-chipper tone-deaf receptionist just home from the set of *Fargo* with her vowels that pierced her script like ice picks: "It's A *beau-tee*-ful *more*-ning at Weee-Care pAIn clin*ic*, h*ow* can we ease *your* pain today?"

The baby screamed. The baby's mother looked toward the ringing phone. A Packer sister said, "Sounds like she's being tortured, poor thing."

The bearded man flapped his paper. "Torture?" he said. "You want to talk about torture?"

Maria didn't want to talk about torture. She stared at her silent phone, looking through it all the way to her mother's incision.

"I'll tell you about torture," said the man. He lowered his paper, looked at Maria as if *she'd* made the comment. "Every six weeks, I get a shot in each eye because I got doused with napalm in Vietnam. I've had a headache since 1965. But them's the breaks when you fight for freedom. I knew what I was signing up for."

Maria laughed, a reflex as quick as a hammer to the knee. She had pictured him carrying a machine gun through a Vietnamese jungle while wearing his orange duck-hunting hat. The man looked at her, and she looked away. She knew engaging him would lead to greater pain, a kind of torture. She knew better than to engage him.

"Aren't you angry," she said, "that you were sent into an unwinnable war?"

"The media lost that war," he said, and flapped his small-town daily to illustrate what the media looked like. He looked at the Packer sisters for affirmation, and they nodded while chewing, though Maria wasn't sure they'd heard him over the screaming baby. She wanted to yank the newspaper out of his hands and rip it into shreds. She decided to say nothing else. Anything else would create more tension that would escalate, turn hostile. She stared through the front glass door and into the freezer outside that waited for her.

She wanted to call Marty, say, "I'm sorry." She wanted to call her dead father in purgatory, say, "Sorry I didn't call you more often. See you soon." She wanted to call her mother, say, "Sorry, sorry, sorry," one thousand times in a row.

A worker in white stepped out with a clipboard. She was in her twenties, but prematurely old, more exhausted and dead-eyed than anyone in the waiting room. For one second Maria saw the toll it took to deal with people in pain, and she wanted to apologize to her too.

The worker called the mother with the screaming baby.

"I was here first," Maria said, more of a mumble, really.

"Here's what I want to know," the bearded man announced. "What with all the beheadings going on over there, what are we doing for the people who have had their heads cut off?"

Maria laughed again, more explosively.

The man stared at her, like, "What's wrong with you?" The Packer sisters looked curious too. She wanted to ask whether first aid for the headless had ever done much. She wanted to ask if he knew the success rates for head-reattachment procedures.

The man said, "You're not from around here are you? Got you an accent, sounds like." He narrowed his eyes to get a better look at the affliction around Maria's mouth. Sometimes it was a harmless "Where are you from?" conversation-starter. Other times, the passive aggressive MO of the Midwest announced itself like the shadow of a shark fin and all Maria heard was: "You're not one of us." She'd heard it from real estate agents, neighbors, bankers, dentists, even professors. Professors sneered, sometimes, with smug assumptions about every individual who resided in a red state.

Maria said, "You have an accent too."

He cocked his head like a confused chicken. The Packer sisters watched, awaiting escalation. Maria needed to retreat, soften up, disarm, or the teaching moment was lost.

"I'm from a small town in Florida," she said. "I came here for work five years ago. It's a pretty place." To pacify a native anywhere, Maria knew, compliment their home. The office phone went off again and the receptionist recited her script. Maria cringed.

"You people," the man said. "You're still fighting the Civil War down there."

The Packer sisters eyed Maria, looking for her musket. The guy in the corner looked up too, in case the musket was concealed. And the truth—the *sad* truth, (a truth she'd confess to Dr. R. Angle, certified) was this: she wanted to retrieve the hatchet-handle she kept beneath her driver's seat. She'd learned this from her grandfather, who kept a handle beneath his truck seat, which he called his n-word knocker, a phrase that nauseated her then and filled her with great shame now. But he was indiscriminate—he waved it at anyone who pulled too far past red lights or stop signs. She'd lifted her own handle only once, while cursing a driver who rolled through a four way stop. Miles had been with her, so she made it a teaching moment. "Be courteous of other drivers," she had said. "Be kind," she said.

The bearded man said, "You people never surrendered."

Maria imagined waving her hatchet-handle around the waiting room, first at the man, then at the receptionist and her phone. But she surrendered. She leaned forward, stretched her back, closed her eyes and inhaled deeply.

"I went to Disney World thirty years ago," the man said. "Stopped at a gas station in Georgia, confederate flags waving everywhere, then I went inside, saw these old men standing around talking, so I said hello and they asked me, said did I know the difference between a damned yankee and a goddamned yankee, and they told me, said it's one who's visiting versus one who's staying. So I said to my wife, so much for that southern hospitality you hear about."

The Packer sisters looked at Maria so she could answer for this crime, maybe make reparations. And she *wanted* to apologize, to say that unkindness wasn't right there or anywhere. Instead, she retaliated with her own story, said, "Last Sunday, I was shoveling snow, and this guy stopped by with a snow-blower, offered to do my sidewalk for ten bucks. I asked him if he wouldn't rather be watching the Packers, and he said, 'No, I don't care nothing about watching a bunch of—and then he used the n-word. I told him to leave." This wasn't completely true. She'd waited for him to finish the sidewalk, gave him ten bucks, and spent a sleepless night preparing the lengthy lecture she would excoriate him with next time.

"You know what the guy said?" Maria said. "He said, 'You're not from around here are you?'" That part was true.

"Was he driving a green truck?" the man said.

"He didn't care about the Packers?" one woman said.

"If it was a green truck, it was Karl. He's not hitting on all cylinders."

The office phone rang.

"I wish he'd come by *our* house," her sister said.

"Not if he's a Bears fan," the other said.

The phone rang again.

The worker in white stepped out and called the guy in the corner who limped across the room, head down.

"Here first," Maria mumbled.

"Karl's from Missouri," the man said. "A southern state."

It's a beautiful morning

"Isn't Missouri in the Midwest?" one woman said.

at We-care Pain Management clinic.

"Missouri's the south," the man said. "They owned slaves there. Ask Mark Twain."

How can we ease your pain today?

"Missouri's in the Southeastern Conference," the other woman said. "With Alabama, Florida, Georgia. Teams like that."

"But," her sister said, "that arch-looking thing in St. Louis—you're supposed to go through that thing to head west—what's it called?"

"Excuse me," Maria said. She stood and stepped toward the door. Was she really going to fetch her hatchet? The worker in white stepped out again and called the bearded man. He got up slowly, made a show of shaking his head (*some people*, his head said) while he gathered his coat, grimaced and grunted and left Maria alone with the Packer sisters, who looked away. It was 4:45. The TV talking heads talked more loudly about the dangerous things inside the heads of pro-immigrant people.

"The arch," a Packer-sister said. "It's called the arch. In St. Louis."

"That's right," her sister said. "You go through that to go west."

The worker in white came back, called the name of one woman, so both women rose and went in together, one for support, no doubt, a good listener who was going to take notes, a team, which suddenly made Maria deeply sad and jealous. She turned off the TV.

A minute later, the mother came out carrying her baby, who wasn't crying. The baby's head was propped on her mother's shoulder, eyes closed, having gotten a shot of the good stuff. They went through the door, letting in cold air. The younger guy came out, stared at his phone while marching toward the door and through it, letting in cold air. It was 4:55. The bearded man came out, limped to the door without acknowledging Maria, face like cement, and went through the door, letting in cold air. To her aunt: *everybody ok*? The Packer sisters came next, zipped their coats and walked out, talking of their efficient visit. The receptionist turned off the lights.

"Hey," Maria said.

She turned the lights back on.

"Oh," she said. "Didn't see you there."

Maria approached the window, gave her name. "I was here

at 3:30, for my 3:30 appointment that was scheduled today *for 3:30*."

The lady looked at her calendar. "Did you check in?"

She hadn't checked in.

"I'm sorry," the lady said. "There must've been a mix up."

"Yes, obviously, there was a mix-up." Clearly *their* mix-up.

She flipped a page. "I see you *here*, one week from *today* at four o'clock."

That couldn't be right. She was out of pills. "I'm out of pills," she said.

"I'm sorry. I'll leave a note and we can—"

"Can we call—I'm sure you have a cell number for someone."

"No," she said. "I can't do that." She'd replaced her chipper telephone voice with the disciplinarian-voice she must've once used on her children. She stared at Maria with jail-warden eyes. Maria squeezed the ledge outside the lady's window. She wanted to release the ledge and grab a chair she could throw. She'd thrown lots of things in her mother's house while she went through high school, and her mother came home to find her house in shambles, a single mom working her ass off at jobs she hated to pay for a house Maria wanted to destroy. Dr. R. Angle said, *Is that where your guilt begins?* and Maria said, *Shut up*. R. Angle said *Where was your father? Tell me about your father*, and Maria said, *shut up*.

She'd have to get through the night with something else, call first thing in the morning. Her brain made a strange noise. She smelled mold, or mildew, or swamp gas. Her stomach lining burned. She turned away, went out into the dark night and let the cold air punch her face. Her car was a cold casket. But there were seat warmers, and she'd have Miles' seat warm for him before he climbed in. She'd gone in debt for seat warmers. She'd bought a new SUV to get through unplowed alleys, her first-ever new car, which she felt guilty for admiring. She inspected it daily to make sure the doors weren't dinged.

It was 5:11. Miles stood outside, waiting. They'd locked the doors at five, he said, and left because he'd sworn his mother was coming.

"Those assholes couldn't wait with you for five minutes?" He'd stop shivering soon, she knew—the car was warm, his seat was warm.

Miles slumped and sulked, deepened his silent treatment. Once they got to the grocery store, she'd tell him to get whatever he wanted. Another pizza for dinner? More beer for her? She called her mother.

The car ahead of her stopped so a hundred-year-old man could hobble by. Another car sat on her bumper, waiting for her and the car ahead. Her mother's phone was ringing. Miles said, "Uh-O." To their right, moving backwards out of a parking space toward Miles's door: a Buick. Maria tapped her horn. The person ahead of her raised a middle finger. Her mother's phone was still ringing. The Buick kept coming. Maria held her horn for a four count, loud enough for a deaf person in the next county to hear. The Buick was going to hit her new car. She was going to have to stand in the cold and argue over blame, wait for a cop. She held the horn. Miles scooted toward the middle to escape injury.

The Buick hit Miles' door and made a thunk louder than Maria had expected. Miles yelped like a little girl and Maria hung up her phone, turned off her car, reached beneath her seat for her hatchet-handle. It wasn't there. All at once, she put it together—Miles had told his father about it, and he'd taken it, put it in his divorce file. This pissed her off more than the deaf Buick driver. She reached behind her for Miles' big plastic bat. It'd been there for six months, the fat end of it big as a cartoon bat, which made it hard to miss a ball, though Miles managed to miss every time, and the last time they'd gone to the park, Maria had grown impatient at Miles' consistent whiffs from five feet until Miles finally said, "I hate you."

She grabbed the bat and went out and around her car, through the headlights of the car behind her. She raised the bat over her head with both hands and slammed it on the Buick's trunk six consecutive times, feeling no pain. So she did it again. Then again. Then she carried it to the driver's door, waiting for it to open so she could start swinging. She crouched into the batter's stance of a right-handed power-hitter, teeth clinched, ready to send a human head as far as she could send a softball. Behind Maria, the car that had been on her bumper sped away. When the Buick door opened, finally, slowly, the tip of a cane came poking out. A skinny leg followed it. A second skinny leg followed the first, two skinny legs now straddling the skinny cane held by a 90 year-old woman.

Maria lowered her bat, feeling sick to her stomach. An elderly woman pulled herself out of the car and leaned on her cane. She was the height of Maria's mother, who was 5'-1. They had the same grey hair—a short tight perm her mother got done every Wednesday at nine a.m. The parking spot the woman had tried to pull back into was a handicapped space she'd missed again. The woman looked into Maria's eyes. She didn't mention the terrible noise Maria had made on her trunk. She didn't mention how her car had backed into Maria's. Her eyes were milky grey, like Maria's mother's eyes when she was tired. The old woman didn't acknowledge Maria's bat or ask what she planned to do with it. She pointed toward her open door.

"It's my husband's car," she said. "Do you know how to raise those seats? He died last month and I'm out of bologna."

"I'm so sorry," Maria said, thinking of what she had come so close to doing.

"He was older than Methuselah. One must go on though, mustn't one?"

She wanted to hug the old lady, to cry into her shoulder, to ask forgiveness, to take her home, to *help* her in some small way. She sat in the lady's car, fiddled with the manual adjustments, moved the seat backwards and forwards, backwards and forwards, backwards and forwards, but not *up*. There was no way to move it *up*. She tried until her hands grew too cold to work. She got out and faced her, still holding her bat. She said,

"I'm sorry. I can't—I don't know."

"My daughter will fix it," the woman said. "She stops by every day after work to check on me. Such a good girl." Then she walked away, leaving her car door open. Maria closed it for her, returned to her car, placed the bat in the back seat. Miles was deeply silent. Maria knew he would forever remember the time he watched his mother behave like a deranged lunatic. Maybe he'd grow up to repeat the story to therapists and friends: "The day my mother almost killed an elderly woman." She imagined then a scenario where the driver had been a man with a gun who would've shoot her dead while Miles watched. Her back hurt now, more than it had all day, and her hands were dumb blocks of wood, shaking. She rested her forehead on the wheel, and tried to start the car. Miles reached over, held her hand and helped her turn the keys.

"We're okay," she said. "I'm sorry. I just need to call Grandma." She was crying now as she stopped to wave one car ahead of her. She said, "Siri, call Mom."

"Mom?" Miles said.

She felt Miles staring at her. She kept driving and didn't wipe her face. Her mother's phone was ringing. Maria would quit the pills cold-turkey. She'd learn to live with pain, like her first doctor said she should. She'd offer it up, as her mother said she should.

"We're okay," she told Miles.

New snow had started falling, which she hated to see, because it meant more shoveling. She waited for her mother to answer.

"Mom," Miles said. "But Gramma died last month."

She looked at Miles to see how serious he was. He seemed to know. She remembered then, and laughed while crying. She laughed at the logic of forgetting. She saw herself sitting in the front row of her mother's ancient church, Miles next to her, too young for a funeral, Marty on her other side, squeezing her hand. It was the church where Maria had received her first communion, given her first (and last) confession, had been confirmed in. She saw them sitting in the first pew, facing the ten-foot wax figure of Jesus stretched out on real wood, thorny crown-capped head hanging to one side, sword-wound to the ribs, naked but for a skinny towel, knobby knees and all, hanging there front and center as a favor for the visually (and spiritually) impaired. She remembered the old organ in the balcony hitting fat chords that floated over the church and hummed inside her bones.

She was crying so hard now she had to stop at the edge of the parking lot. She cried until five year-old Miles said what he said next.

"Would you like me to drive?" he said.

He found a Kleenex and passed it to her. She laughed and cried. She said, "Yes. Yes, I would like you to drive."

She moved slowly through the falling snow toward home, thinking she'd warm some soup for dinner, take a bowl to Marty and place it outside his door. She turned up the Berlioz softly now, and drove slowly, both hands on the wheel, eyes fixed where her headlights stopped. She heard something new in the final movement then, as if an eleven-fingered pianist were reaching new ghost notes, as feint as wind from a conductor's wand, as necessary as the tiny space between heartbeats.

"Listen to that," Maria told Miles.

He was listening.

She knew he could hear it too.

They listened together.

Nancy Cook

Out of My Depth

In the dream I am coming from a gathering of women. The streets are dark but for the faded light of a lonely streetlamp on a far corner. I approach the pay lot where I'd left my car. A Ford Fairlane, Acapulco blue, with vertically stacked dual headlights.

The meeting has left me depleted. Women I know only casually: smart, competent, underpaid in their non-union jobs. Talking without real direction, mouthing phrases they've heard on TV or from their husbands.

The parking lot is empty. My car is not to be seen. There is no attendant on site, no attendant's booth. I look for a posted sign that might display hours, rates, or maybe threaten towing. The brick walls of the two adjacent buildings are blank. I see no sign.

Acar passes on the street behind me, its tires swooshing on wet pavement. A muted siren in a distant neighborhood announces *emergency*. I stand on the sidewalk gazing stupidly at the emptiness in front of me. It's like I'm at the edge of the stone quarry at Wildwood Lake, and if I can just will myself to dive in, I'll be all right.

*

Hot town, summer in the city. It was the summer of love, and I was in love.

Marty drove. I snuggled close against his scent, a mixture of light sweat, freshly bleached tee, and English Leather. It would be hours until dark, skin to skin, mouths hungry. For now, there was the peace of summer heat coming through the open window, easy weekend traffic to the Wildwood Lake quarry, Lovin' Spoonful on the radio.

In the back seat, Angie was singing to Greg. She got the

words wrong, like always.

We did everything together, the four of us. Best friends and best friends.

First love.

*

The first time I ventured from the grassy knoll, leaving my beach towel behind, and strode to the stony cliff edge above the quarry – now a spring fed lake – my eyes met the sky, my gaze rose above the trees across the water. A slight breeze ruffled my long hair. I was not afraid to look down. Not afraid to take the dive. Not afraid to go deep.

*

Drew's room at the frat house was cramped, the dresser blocking half the window, a desk not more than a foot in front of the closet. A twin-size mattress atop a two-foot platform squeezed into a corner against the far wall. The bed was always messy. Drew complained it was too difficult to change the sheets. We often slept on top of the corduroy bedspread.

On Valentine's Day I was visiting from St Louis, a thousand miles away. It was early Saturday morning and we hadn't yet made love. We hadn't made love the night before either. What we'd managed after my arrival on Thursday couldn't really be classified as making love.

Drew rose and, barely awake, I watched him go to the dresser where a huge pile of records was stacked beside a turntable. He flicked on the stereo, gently lifted the stylus and even more gently placed it on a rotating album. *Lay lady lay, lay across my big brass bed.* Dylan, as Dylan had never been heard before. A boy from Duluth, pretending to be country.

Valentine's Day, visions of a big brass bed, Dylan singing Nashville twang. A study in irony.

*

I'm very good at making beds. The secret is in the way the sheets are folded: top end to bottom end first, then side to side. That way, the sheet can easily be flapped into position. Then it's just a matter of tucking corners into place.

I learned this skill as a nurse's aide at a long-term care facility. I got a job there shortly after dropping out of college and I stayed two years. I had a great fondness for the residents. But even more I loved the women I worked with, who made beds, gave baths, cut toenails, changed catheters, cleaned up after unexpected bowel movements, fed and clothed and comforted. At minimum wage, many of them. For many years, with few perks or benefits.

Sometimes I was reminded of Angie, who was in nursing school and still my best friend.

Where did they get their courage, these unrecognized heroes? This was years before Donna Summers' *She Works Hard for the Money,* before Cher's *Working Girl*, even before Helen Reddy's *I Am Woman*, which didn't really resonate with these women who never considered themselves feminists. All they asked for was a little R-E-S-P-E-C-T.

They all thought Dylan was self-indulgent.

*

Some day I'd like to find out what happened to them, the women who worked beside me. I can imagine walking into a bar and finding Louise and Cadie and Sheila and Gayle seated at an oversized booth sharing a couple of pitchers. They'll maybe only vaguely remember me but will readily offer a seat and let me into the conversation, which will have no real direction and be filled with phrases they've heard on TV or from their grandchildren.

Some day. For now, though, the best I can do is think fondly of the person that I was and forgive myself for the person I've become.

*

In the dream I am lost and confused. Unsettled by an awareness of women's lack of awareness. I'm in the dark, I'm in deep. But I know a dream even as I'm dreaming. I know I can wake myself. And I'm very good at making my own bed.

Blink Book

In a list on a website Jim had never heard of before, number six instructed grieving partners to "carry on with usual activities." So, one night, he showered, put on his black jeans and boots, buttoned his denim shirt with the milky pearl buttons, let his sister watch Owen, grabbed his guitar, and drove down to The Barrel. He sat in the parking lot for a while, watching neon signs shining on snow banks. Smokers huddled beneath their dense clouds. Couples, so many of them, walking up and down the sidewalk, arms hooked. Laughing. Laughter was a tonal language, the kind you have to immerse yourself in if you ever hope to understand it. Through the window, Jim saw the mic stand in the corner.

A crowd of wool hats and fingerless gloves, skirts and boots in the hazy glow of Christmas lights. Jim put his name on the list and pointed to one of the taps. The bartender slid a beer across the bar. She squinted at him. He left five bucks and moved to a high table against the wall. He sipped. A woman was talking to him. He watched her until she stopped, until she scrunched her face and walked away. A man in a backwards baseball hat stepped up to the mic and started telling jokes about celebrities Jim never heard of. A group of women in their early twenties got up next and sang "Santa Claus is Coming to Town," holding on to each other and laughing uncontrollably.

When it was Jim's turn, he carried his guitar up to the mic and faced the crowd. He felt his mouth open slightly. Red faces staring at him. A cough. A laugh buried in a gloved hand. *Let's go!* someone shouted. Jim looked down at the strings: tight ropes taught across a dark hole. He squinted at the crowd, and just before he got to the door, the amp cord resisted for a moment, then ripped free.

*

The next morning, Owen sat in his high chair smearing pureed apples and sweet potato across his tray in wide pukey rainbows. He sucked his fingers, then dipped them in again. Jim had only had a few sips of beer, but he felt hungover. When he turned his head, the kitchen slipped at the edges, then righted itself. Behind Owen was the pile of papers Jim moved from room to room. Most of Leslie's things were in storage – clothes, jewelry. Her presence reduced to paper. Stacks of it. The mail keeps coming. Circulars. Coupons to a fried chicken place they'd never been to. Ads for an online MBA claiming it's never too late.

A lifetime ago – which isn't an exaggeration in terms of Owen's life – Jim and Leslie would get drunk and watch "Where Are They Now?" on VH1. The show was mostly about one-hit wonders, rock and pop stars whose skyrocket to fame lasted about as long as the Space Shuttle Challenger. Bands the average idiot couldn't name, but whose lyrics they knew by heart, artists who wrote the soundtrack to so many of their aimless teenage drives, their basement parties, their losing-their-virginity-on-the-bottom-bunk-in-someone's-kid-brother's-bedroom memories. A few beers in and Jim was talking loudly about all the ungrateful people who *consumed* this music, who *lived* by it, in it, and then moved on to the next fad, the next gimmicky pop song. And what was left? A group of flabby, middle-aged white dudes sitting in folding chairs on a TV show, talking about their sad, post-stardom lives. It scared the hell out of him.

Leslie always took care of everything behind the scenes. Oil changes and water filter replacements and dentist appointments. Jim never had to think about any of it; they were all just neatly-printed notes on the refrigerator calendar. It reminded him of an interview with someone he watched late one night after Leslie died, a musician, not one of the Jackson 5, but someone similar, someone who'd been famous longer than they hadn't, and he was saying something about how it had been so long since he handled money that he forgot a transaction of any kind had to take place. He got used to walking into a room and everything was just *there.* No wonder these people don't write their own songs, Jim almost said out loud. How could they?

Now the weight of minutiae pressed on his skull like a steel-toed boot. Pediatrician appointments and kitty litter and recycling; watering plants and paying the heating bill; planning meals and food shopping. It wasn't that he never helped with that stuff before, but somehow knowing he was the only one left to do it all, that if he skipped one thing it would never get done, made each task crucial. Writing a check or running the dishwasher became load-bearing beams. Perched on top of Jim's flimsy structure, like a weather vane, was Owen, cooing and smearing.

*

Stand in a room of 467 people. 467 beating hearts. 467 pulsing brains. 934 lungs inhaling, exhaling. 467 soon-to-be mothers smiling and glowing, petting their stomachs, sharing baby names and breast-feeding tips. 467 partners massaging the smalls of 467 backs. All of them thinking of paint colors and crib models and sleep machines. Not a moment, not a single thought wasted on bacterial infection. Not a second. Not a blink.

The doctors called it puerperal sepsis. One of those narrow percentages you don't worry about until they include you. Then you find out how spacious that percentage really is. Big enough for online communities. Support groups. Underfunded nonprofits. They comfort you, initially, because no one else understands. But after a few months, you begin to wonder if your partner's death is your new identity. You worry if any of this is seeping into your child. You change course. You retreat.

For months after Leslie's death, Jim and Owen spent their nights watching YouTube clips of old concerts. Joe Cocker. Aretha Franklin. The Who. Owen was mesmerized by Keith Moon's drum solos, or at least that's how Jim interpreted the boy's rocking and kicking. They watched the sweaty kid in a white t-shirt, stringy black hair stuck to his cheeks and forehead, flailing like a free-falling octopus, pushing harder and harder until the beat teetered on the edge of chaos then snapped back. No matter how many times they watched the same clips, Jim was certain this time Moon would lose it. But he never did. He always landed.

What really got Owen kicking was the end, when Moon stood up, grabbed his high-hat and swung it down like an ax across his bass drum. He drove his fist into the top of his snare, then picked it up by the stand and threw it at the crowd. Then he threw his bass drum and cymbals, and as he started kicking his toms off the stage, the crowd threw pieces back at him. Moon stomped and bashed and screamed. He quickly looked behind him, snatched his stool, and smashed the remaining pieces of his drum kit. Whatever song they were playing was reduced to echoing feedback.

Owen started making sounds. "Mmmaaah, mmmaaah."

Jim decided he was trying to say "Moon."

*

Before Owen, before Leslie, Jim kept his guitar in his bedroom. He didn't have a choice. His studio apartment jammed everything into one room – stove, futon, television – with only a thin door separating the bathroom. In the mornings, as the coffee pot gurgled, he sat in that cramped bathroom, knees nearly touching the door.

Living in the studio made him understand why cats hide under beds or crawl behind the couch the first few nights in a new home. Comfort in confinement. If a giant kicked his apartment building down a hill, Jim could probably tumble a few times before falling off the toilet. The sink and tub and door fit around him like a custom mold. He sat and flipped through the paper, glancing at photo captions. Jim was living that "struggling artist" act of his future biopic – those scenes when the musician is poor but brimming with integrity. When he's still working nights at a gas station or bussing tables or mopping floors at a porno theater. When he's wearing his one pair of jeans, his one leather jacket, his scuffed boots.

The scenes of him walking by an iconic venue on his way to work, some hotshot band blaring out to a packed house, the same venue that will one day spell out his name in black letters on the marquee. The scenes where he walks anonymously through the city that will eventually list him on Wikipedia as one of its notable people, will refer to him as the "warehouse worker turned rocker." All he needs now is that eureka scene, the moment when someone at the restaurant or gas station or theater makes an off-handed comment: "Jim, you a dime a dozen" or "Plenty of talent out there, not much endurance." And then one night, Jim stays up late, takes his guitar onto the fire escape, strums one slow chord, and the lyrics to "Dime a Dozen" or "Ya Gotta Endure" come pouring out and that's all she wrote. Rocket to fame.

Jim flipped the newspaper. The full-spread of the Challenger explosion, in blazing color, held his attention. A tunnel of thick white smoke streaking across the sky, forking at the end. In the middle, a lumpy red tumor of an explosion. Jim hadn't been following the story, but the story followed him. Followed everybody. Weeks after the explosion, the death of the story followed everyone, too. Fished out wreckage off the coast of Cape Canaveral to be studied, preserved, and displayed. That band of astronauts and one school teacher reduced to fire and smoke above a screaming crowd. What would they have seen? What would the teacher have shared with her students if she returned? How would a civilian describe space to a child?

Jim folded the paper in half and tucked it between the toilet tank and the wall. It remained there for weeks, the last photo of seven lives sandwich between car ads and the funny pages.

*

Jim traced Owen's eyebrow, over and over, slowing down just a little each time, until the boy's breathing steadied. His mouth slightly open, his head sunk deep in the pillow. He looked like a brand-new boy in his original packaging. Jim was trapped. Owen's crib – sheets and blanket tucked with military precision, pillow full and cold as marble – was in his room across the hall. Jim's bed was the only one Owen would sleep in. And he would only nap if Jim was in the bed with him. Once Owen fell asleep, if Jim so much as scratched his chin, Owen's eyes would peel open like a frog's, blink vacantly once or twice before returning, full bore, to the waking world.

The Who's *Live at Leeds.* Otis Redding at The Monterey Pop Festival. Hendrix at Fillmore East. While Owen slept, Jim stuck in his earbuds and time traveled. Sweaty, sweetly stoned, his internal temperature the same as the air around him. The womb of the crowd. Even though he's from the future and knows that this moment will be etched in stone, he's there, he is completely there, so when the singer delivers a call to action, Jim has to bite his lip. When the drummer claps and the crowd obeys, Jim has to restrain his hands under his thighs. And when the band slows down, leads the audience through a long and winding ballad, Jim's eyes pool with tears.

Sometimes the music warbles, amps sink into an ocean and fade to whale songs. Jim on stage, Leslie the only one in the audience. But she doesn't act like she's alone. She sways with her eyes closed, thick folds in her leather jacket as she sips from the little red straw in her gin and tonic. She drinks with her eyes closed and never stops swaying. Bleached jeans just below her hips. Red boots. Her lips moving around Jim's lyrics.

He never knows what song he's singing in these visions. He's not so much performing as he is transmitting. Brain wave synced to brain wave. A feedback loop. They could be in Boston or New York, Nashville or New Orleans. That night in Chicago when he used the house's beat-up acoustic and cut his finger on a frayed string and his thin blood mixed with sweat and ran down the guitar in streaks. Those day beers at The Barrel after his meeting with the record company, pitcher after pitcher on an empty stomach and the best pool game of his life and the stumbling, hooked-arm walk to the diner and how the month after felt like their entire lives were perched on the tip of a rumbling spaceship in perpetual countdown. And then the months turned to years and the countdown froze on "1." Their focus shifted inward. Nesting, she called it, even before she was pregnant. And though Jim entertained hazy snapshots of fatherhood, as Leslie's due date approached, his anticipation faded to dread, the volume of everything turning down, down, down.

"Daaa-daaa?"

*

Years vanished. Frozen dinners. Life insurance claims. Unemployment checks. Owen at Jim's sister's house twice a week, then three. Jim tried on personalities, identities. Gardened for a while and gave up. Renovated half of the basement and gave up. His bedroom wall a rash of different colors, tiny sample paint cans with dusty lids underneath his dresser.

Would he even know if he was crazy?

He imagined the eye of a hidden camera capturing him in a sleeveless shirt and sweatpants, sitting on a stool, hunched over his guitar, big black headphones clamped on his head. The cord snaking behind him, the amp's glowing red light. A steaming cup of coffee. A granola bar with its wrapper peeled back like a banana. The camera doesn't see what Jim sees, what he's trying to see. All the camera finds are Jim's fingers slowly plucking up and down the strings.

More like letting go than holding on. More like gripping a rock in a river until his arms ache, and then surrendering to the current. That's what it was. Not a giving up, but a giving in. Without understanding how, Jim's curling fingers and tapping foot and nodding head pulled him down stream. Astronauts describe zero gravity the same way: weightless, how once the push/pull of the Earth is gone, it's difficult to sense the position of your limbs, to even feel them at all.

The creaking floorboard. The sniffling. The door between the garage and the house squeaked. Opened.

"Daaa-daaa?"

Rage. Molten anger gurgling in Jim's chest each time Owen disturbed his mornings. If the playing was going well, Jim could temper his response. If he got in a good hour or two, he had the strength to smile at Owen honestly, put away his guitar, and start making pancakes. After those moments, he sometimes imagined Owen decades into the future, maybe long after Jim was dead, answering interview questions for a music magazine, Owen referencing those pancake mornings, the vision of his father hunched on the stool, strumming. The interviewer presses Owen. Owen gets choked up, says something like, "That's when I knew. That's when I knew I'd devote my life to music."

That's if the playing was going well.

When it wasn't, Jim teetered on the stool like a mangy circus bear. Every note do or die, could save or kill. When the *Daaa-daaa?* came, Owen, whether he understood it or not, was stealing food from a gobbling dog.

Jim stared at Owen. Five years old now. Blonde wiry curls that have never been cut. Two green gems for eyes. He dragged the plastic feet of his dump truck pajamas along the cement floor, clutching Joy by the throat. A stuffed unicorn he named himself. The kid's quick, can read books most kids two or three years older can't, uses words like "literally" and "peculiar" correctly.

"What's up, bud?"

Owen looked down at the cement. His eyes followed the crack in the foundation to the middle of the garage, where it branched out in oily tributaries. The same crack Jim noticed every time he walked in, the one that reminded him of that Bruce line from "Hungry Heart" about a river taking a wrong turn.

Owen's pajamas *slip-slapped* across the concrete. He curled up into a little ball on the deflated leather couch, bear-hugging Joy. Jim shook out the camouflage blanket and draped it over him. Owen cooed and snuggled deeper. His breath settled into a rhythm. Each exhale parted his lips gently. His eyes wide open. Somewhere – a documentary or a book – Owen learned that the average person blinks about 20,000 times a day. If you add up the amount of time spent blinking over a lifetime, it comes out to years, *years* of waking hours with our eyes closed. Combine that with sleep and we're blind for a long time. Owen began slowly reducing his blinks each day. He counted them. He kept a notebook. A Blink Book. Little prison notches in chicken scratch handwriting. Like most obsessions, it was impressive and worrisome.

Dr. McNally called it a "coping mechanism," something kids do to feel in control, which was kind of funny to Jim because if you want to talk about power, Owen is supernatural. Most kids are. Jim couldn't think of another person in his life who could walk into a room and make everyone else stop what they're doing and serve them. One time a mother at the playground was talking Jim's ear off and referred to her son as her "little prince." It was creepy, and that term lodged itself in Jim's brain like a jingle. Sometimes his brain repeated it so many times he had to mouth the words or whisper them quietly to himself, just to scratch the itch – *little prince, little prince, little prince.*

*

When Owen was an infant, Jim set up the white noise machine Leslie had bought a couple of weeks before the day he was born. The day she died. Owen slept soundly until he was about three years old, then one night he woke screaming. Jim rushed in and found him sitting up in bed, palms squeezing his head like a vice. *Too loud! Too loud!* Owen fought for air, his breath sucking and slurping like a clogged kitchen sink, and when Jim reached out to rub his back Owen jerked away. Jim ran into the hallway, fumbled with the switch in the dark, Owen's screams devolving to a primal octave, grabbed the sound machine by the cord and swung it to the floor, shattering it in one blow. Owen kept screaming, gasping. Jim eased one of Owen's hands away from his ears and let the silence in.

*

Days go on and on. Disturbing thoughts. Questions trespass through his brain as he's making coffee or tying the kitchen garbage: *Would I think this much about Leslie if she had lived?* If they were simply divorced, would her face appear each time he closed his eyes? Would her expressions flash behind Owen's – the curve of a lip, the wrinkle of an eyebrow? If she had left him, would she still be trapped inside his head?

People tell him it gets easier, but what if it doesn't? What if the next forty years are exactly the same?

*

One night, Jim stays up late, sticks his earbuds in, and lets YouTube lead the way. He gets up for another beer, then another, and on the last trip grabs the rest of the twelve-pack and drops it on the couch beside him. When he drinks the last one, it's still cold.

A clip of Keith Moon throwing his sticks leads to Moon filling his bass drum with dynamite leads to an interview days after the explosion, cymbal shrapnel buried in Moon's arm. Jim types in "explosion challenger" and watches the space shuttle burst from multiple angles. Then "mother die child birth" and he's in what he assumes is an African country as a white doctor walks through a village spouting statistics about maternal mortality. It isn't until Jim looks up and sees Owen standing in the hallway that he realizes he's been holding his breath.

He shuts the laptop, takes out his earbuds, and waves him over. Owen slides the twelve-pack box out of the way and lays across Jim's lap. They don't talk. For a few moments, they just breathe together. Then with an urgency that surprises him, Jim tells Owen about his last concert before Mom died, then he tells him about Moon's exploding drumkit, then he's rambling about auto-destructive art, that these musicians destroying their instruments aren't just defiant punks, but intentional artists and by wrecking their equipment they're gifting the audience a singular experience, a moment that can never be re-created. And though Owen nods, it's impossible for Jim to know how much he understands and even twelve beers in, he has the sense not to say it out loud, not to show Owen the dots and connect them for him. Jim can't talk about "legacy" and "myth" without talking about death, so he stops and hopes when Owen unwraps his thin arms from Jim's neck, takes his tiny steps back up the dark hallway, that the right words are ringing in his ears.

John Duffy

The Second Saw

Jeremy closed the choke. The whine of his chainsaw's motor faded to an echo in the wooded valley. "Well, shit." He pulled off his work gloves one by one, and tucked them into the rear pocket of his bibs before reaching up to pluck bright orange plugs from his ears. In his palm, they slowly expanded to their original marshmallow shape, and these he pushed way down into his hip pocket. He stood looking at the chainsaw trapped sidelong in the old lady's black walnut. He had been an arborist for a long time. Knowing how to notch a tree to guide its fall was instinctual. Bar pinch was rare, catching him only when rot in the heartwood veiled a tension in the trunk. Off the driver's side mirror his well worn Carhartt jacket hung by its hood. He fished in the pockets for his cigarettes, only to withdraw the Camel soft pack and find it empty. He pulled the dented door open with a metallic clang and squeal, crumpled the soft pack, and tossed it on the floor. The interior of the F-150 was rank with stale cigarette smoke, mildew, and bar oil. The smell of another job, another day cutting wood in southern Indiana. He climbed up behind the wheel and sat with his hands clutching the keys. Staring out the windshield, his head still swimming in the fog of last night's alcohol, he was fighting the urge to cry.

*

Usually it's the older brother who looks out for the younger, but Jason was only ever looking out for himself, and failing most of the time even at that. Jeremy was two years younger than Jason, but by twelve he was taller and stronger, and that trend never reversed. As kids, Jeremy could see that his older brother lacked a sense of self preservation. Whether it was climbing too high in a tree, holding a bottle rocket too long in his hand, or mouthing off to too large a classmate, Jason always acted as though his body wasn't made of a very vulnerable combination of flesh and bone.

Their father always said that Jason thought he was invincible, but over time, Jeremy developed a more nuanced understanding of his brother. It wasn't that Jason believed that he *couldn't* be hurt, but rather, that he *wouldn't* be, and there was a difference. Jason believed in fate, even if he never spoke that word, and this meant that nothing could harm him but those things that were supposed to. If he was supposed to break a leg jumping off the detached garage, he would have, but he didn't. If he was supposed to drown swimming in Lake Michigan during a storm when they visited the dunes, he would have, but he didn't. If he was supposed to sever his spinal column and suffer severe brain damage after falling from the railroad trestle spanning Lake Lemon as he tried to drunkenly walk across it, he would have. And he did. And Jeremy was there to witness it, terrified, having pleaded with his brother not to walk out onto the beams hanging seventy feet over the shallow water. One minute he was screaming himself hoarse, cursing his brother's stupidity as Jason walked the steel rail like a tightrope. The next minute Jeremy was sucking wind, bounding down the hillside as briars tore at his face, his eyes fixed on the motionless body floating in the brown lagoon.

Jeremy should have left for college that summer to pursue his wrestling scholarship at the University of Illinois. Standing in a hospital hallway, his father yelled how foolish he would be to throw away such an opportunity. That was back when they had just been given the good news. Jason was going to survive. But he would require round-the-clock care. Jeremy assured his father that he would only delay college for one semester, until they had Jason back home and comfortable. Then it was just one more semester, until they secured Jason's disability money and a nurse. By the third year, his father stopped mentioning college, and Jeremy was no longer of any interest to Illinois' wrestling program. Without the scholarship, college was out of the question.

When his dad was diagnosed with stomach cancer, Jeremy

was twenty-two , and he tried never to think about how he would have finished his degree by then, how he should have been beginning his adult life, going anywhere he wanted to go, doing whatever he wanted to do. Those thoughts were the gift wrap on a box full of resentment that Jeremy never wanted to open.

*

Dropping the tailgate, Jeremy instantly remembered that his other saw was in the shed. He left it there after bucking the ash that fell in last week's storm, and this morning when he loaded up, he was too hungover to think of it. Over the ribbed truck bed, he dragged a red milk crate towards himself, and drew from it two plastic, yellow wedges. With the wedges in one hand and an eight pound maul in the other, he walked back to the tree that had captured his saw. He set to inserting the thin end of a wedge into the tight mouth of the cut he'd made in the walnut. He tapped the wedge with the fat side of the maul until it refused to penetrate any deeper. Doing the same with the second wedge, the mouth of the cut began to slowly part like a clam preparing to spit, until the first wedge popped out under the pressure, and the weight of the tree sat back down.

He picked up the wedge that had been ejected onto the grass, and tried to hammer it back into the recalcitrant tree trunk, only to watch in utter frustration as the second wedge shot out laterally and landed on the lawn.

"Fuck!" He forcefully struck the remaining wedge with the maul. He planted a boot against the black walnut bark, and with his whole body he yanked on the saw's bright orange handle. It didn't budge. Howling another obscenity skyward, he pulled and pulled, his bootheel driving into the tree, his upper body twisting and jerking with pathetic impotence. He let go. The saw was stuck, and there wasn't a damn thing he could do about it. And it was beginning to rain.

*

Sitting at the bar with a cold bottle of Coors, Jeremy was just passing a little time, catching up on the college basketball rankings before heading home. The nurse's shift ended at seven sharp, and then it would be his turn to bring the straw to his brother's lips. To roll his body. To change his diaper. Swallowing a mouthful of his beer, someone called his name, and Jeremy immediately recognized the voice.

"Hey, Travis." He turned on his stool, forcing enthusiasm.

"It's been a while man, how've you been?"

"Can't complain."

"How's your brother?" Travis asked, using the same concerned tone that everyone summoned when asking about Jason.

Jeremy never knew what to do with this question. His brother was never going to uncripple, his brain would never undamage. People wanted him to say "fine," so that's what he said.

"He's fine."

"Good, man. Good." And then it got awkward, which Jeremy knew it would. It had to. Travis was Taryn's brother. Jeremy and Travis had presumed that one day they would be brothers-in-law, but that ended almost two years ago when Taryn took a nursing job in Minneapolis.

"So. How's your sister?" Jeremy didn't want to ask it. He wanted to leave, but the question was blocking the door like a stone golem.

"Oh, she's good man. She's doing really good. She loves it up there. I think she's nuts. Minnesota winters? No thanks man, I would not want to deal with that!"

Jeremy nodded. He gulped his Coors and wished he would have stopped for a six pack instead.

"Listen man, I don't want to upset you or anything, but I figure it's best if you hear it from me."

"What's that?" Jeremy's heart was already falling to the floor.

"Taryn's engaged. I'm sorry, man. I know how much you loved her."

Loved. Past tense. Everything about Jeremy was made past

tense by somebody else. Three words whispered past the lump in Jeremy's throat. "Who's the guy?"

"Some prick doctor."

"Wow." Jeremy looked at the boot-scuffed floor. His heart had already been mopped up and dumped out back.

"Shit. Actually, he's not a prick. He's a pretty decent guy, really. You'll never believe this, he wrestled for Minnesota!"

Jeremy nodded the way the condemned nod when a judge announces their sentence. "That's good for her. That's real good. Tell her I said congratulations." Jeremy drained his Coors and set the bottle atop a five-dollar bill. "Take care, Travis."

*

Heavy drops pelted Jeremy's windshield. The worn wiper blades squeaked with every pass. A rainbow smear of water remained undisturbed by the driver's side wiper, so he leaned to his right to find a dry patch of glass. What should have been a quick job was now going to take all afternoon. Having surrendered to that fact, he didn't see any harm in taking a detour to buy cigarettes. With two fresh soft packs in his pocket, he cranked his window down an inch. The drumming of the rain grew louder against the metal roof. He lit a cigarette. He wondered if Taryn still smoked. He always thought it was strange that a nurse would smoke, and when he told her that, she laughed and said she felt the same way about the son of a man who died from cancer. Now she was marrying a doctor. Of course she didn't smoke anymore. She had moved on. She lived in a big city. She probably jogged and did yoga.

Jeremy's head throbbed. After his run in with Travis at the bar last night, he'd stopped at the liquor store for a case of beer. When the nurse closed the front door behind her at exactly seven, he cracked the lid on the first can. By the time he turned off the T.V. in the living room where Jason slept, Jeremy had finished six beers. Before going to bed himself, he'd drunk six more, and with each new can, he lit a fresh cigarette. For several hours, he moved between the sickly yellow light of the kitchen where he would take the first cold sip of each new beer, and the silver moonlit porch where he would take the first warm drag of each new cigarette, hunched on the concrete step, refusing to look up at the stars. After sending the last bright red cherry arcing into the black night, and with the last beer can crushed flat and tossed in the bin, he had stumbled back into the house.

Turning the key, he silenced the rumbling truck engine and sat listening to the cascading rain, staring at the wall of water between himself and the shed. All morning, he tried to pretend it hadn't happened, that he never let such darkness overtake him, but as he watched steam rise from the warm hood of the truck, his memory came flooding back. Last night, between the front porch and his bedroom, he stood in the still black surrounding his brother. His heart full of acid, he looked down on Jason's face, and silently cursed the mouth that hung agape, choking lightly on every breath. Staring at the enfeebled arms long bereft of function, he wanted to snap them over his knee like kindling. Years of vitriol that had remained encased in his body like prehistoric beasts flash-frozen in ice, began to thaw. Forbidden feelings raged in his mind like an overdue prison riot, and as he stood beside his brother's slowly rising and falling body, Jeremy had imagined Jason carted out of the house one last time, a coroner's sheet pulled up over his head. He'd imagined a FOR SALE sign shifting in the wind in front of the house, another that read "Now Leaving Indiana" somewhere along the interstate beyond Terre Haute, and a red dawn laid out before him. He'd imagined the saws, and chains, and chaps, and jugs of bar oil and gasoline all cleared forever from the bed of his truck, and in their place, suitcases. He saw the Mississippi River, the Rocky Mountains, the Sonoran Desert, and against all of them he saw himself, a man entirely unencumbered, a man bound only to his own hysterical whims and ambitions, loosed on the world with no tether, no name ringing in his ears to call him home against the desires of his pleading heart. He saw the town of Bedford in flames and himself witnessing it from some impossible rise with a look of complete dispassion, no, with joy! With celebration! With the applause of a madman who watches the lion eat the lion tamer.

In the big dark of that room, with no sound but his half-dead brother's wheezing, he knew there was no God who would grant his prayer that his brother just fucking die already. In his knowing, he had looked at the extra pillow behind Jason's head. Staring deep into its stitching, he considered that pillow. It was right there. Right there. So easy.

And then he'd turned and gone to bed.

The truck door opened with its clang and squeal. He slammed it shut and ran across the yard to the shed. Rain beat on him, and by the time he pulled back the heavy wooden doors and ducked inside, his clothes were drenched. Sitting on the table that ran against the back wall was his second saw. He grabbed it by the black handle that ran horizontally over its crown. From the darkness of the shed, he looked out into the gray blur of the world. Rain fell in sheets. He thought of his other saw, stuck sideways in the old lady's tree. The rain would be soaking it. It was going to rust.

Nick Rees Gardner

Psychedelicious

By the time Allen fired up the grill at The Great Midwest Beer Fest, we were already food truck experts, smash burger virtuosos, burrito hotshots, savants of kimchi slaw. When I glanced up through the service window, the crooked queue of beer enthusiasts stretched out past the kegerator tents, proving *Psychedelicious Street Food's* weird allure. Allen told me, Who doesn't like beer and greasy grub? What could go wrong? A culmination of his batshit dreams and our grueling effort, of nights where Allen killed his beer and hit the hay, leaving me to soak and scrub the dishes alone. This was success, and we shared the pride between us. What could go wrong, I wondered, when Allen always won? A question I, the loser, was too caught up in his shadow to properly ponder.

We traded food for sample pours from Dad Bod Beer, the festival's host, names like Double Dry-Hopped Terpene Dream. Live bands droned from the stage in the meadow and heads swarmed with woozy vibes. I told the customers twenty minute wait. Twenty five. Thirty. Allen said: Catch-up. I mangled a name barely audible above the psych rock background din and passed the paper tray to the appropriate hungry hands. My mouth was dry so I tipped the last sip of beer foam and felt wings fumble around my mouth before the stinger pierced my tongue. I screamed and the wasp missiled out, undamaged. The taco tray hit the ceiling and I lurched into Allen. His palm sizzled on the grill. We spun, tumbled, collided, the space too tight to dance out of one another's way.

He said, What the fuck?

I said, Mfhfmblfth.

The swinging slapbox of Allen's hands. The dodge and mumble of my swelling face.

*

The plan for the summer was to stuff myself in a space too

hot, too cramped to think. A relief. My philosophy was that if I kept busy I could clear my head, but my thoughts continued to reel. I'd been listless since April, before I defended my thesis and graduated with a masters and a mountain of debt. PhD rejections piled on and my partner, Callie, signed up for a doctorate out west, said we should take time to ourselves. I was hesitant and lacked focus. I broke my lease, drove the six-hours from DC to Ohio, and took up residence with the wolf spiders in my parents' basement. Academia was a ladder, but what happens when you run out of rungs? The answer: I laid in bed for a week. No clear direction, no definite point. I'd put so much effort into drawing a line between my promising future and my more troublesome past. New number, no social media, a jumble of addresses without forwarded mail. I'd never considered my mom handing me the cordless, another relic. I didn't expect Allen's voice in the receiver, my best friend from a life forgotten. I answered with a frown. He said, Welcome home Billy Boy! Good timing. I had a dream!

I sat up. Riveted. I said, What?

He said, Listen. We gotta act fast. Come by.

Sure, I said. I had nothing better to do.

We formulated a plan. Two days later, he pulled out the Hide-A-Bed in his spare room and offered me a place to stay.

Allen said he was better now, a changed man. A few drinks per day and a bit of pot. He looked clean. This fresh incarnation with his tight haircut and button down, long sleeves that sheathed his stick-and-pokes. He'd lost two fingers since I last saw him. I noticed when he held up the envelope of food truck seed cash. He explained: Outback Steakhouse meat slicer. Grease-slicked floors. A wake up call. A boost forward. A settlement. Ambition. Cash. He shook the envelope, fingerless, in my face.

I backed my car out of the drive and he explained his success. He said, I listened to this podcast. All about putting your plan out there. Speak it. Write it. The universe will respond. He said that the plan for the food truck came to him while he slept, the night before the meat slicer accident proved it a reality. Luck. Fate. All you had to do was pay attention, keep your eyes peeled for a sign.

Hokey, I said. I didn't want to be a dick, just reasonable. I rebutted that it wasn't that way for all of us. I said some people work hard all their lives and never get an answer.

He said, It's not about you. Don't force it. The universe is saying something right now. Roll down your window. Take a hit. Breathe in the air.

He reached his vaporizer toward me, but I waved it away. Clean for seven years except the occasional drink. All I saw was sunshine, the sprigs of knee-high corn, the wind's judder through the cab. I merged from farmland into downtown Westinghouse, Ohio: Derelict banks and offices, the boarded up Worlinger Department Store. The same city, same abandoned buildings I'd explored with Allen back when we were delinquents, drug heads. The same bent signpost where we'd practiced boardslides and the rooftops where we'd stargaze, stoned, awed by the cosmos. As I took a left onto Main Street, though, I noticed the meters were replaced by a single kiosk. The fire escapes repainted or gone. Westinghouse, a city we knew from brick to rumor, now featured coffee shops, galleries, a microbrewery in the refurbished space that used to be a mortuary. The sign over the beer garden depicted a phoenix emerging from its pile of ash. Renewal. A message too blatant to be mine.

We were supposed to pick up a retired FedEx truck from Hillbilly Oz, a neglected company town once hailed as the *heart of the opioid epidemic*. At the time it was a thrill to be at the throbbing center of anything at all, but as I entered the old park, I looked down at the trap homes from my eco-friendly ivory tower and my stomach turned.

I said, You promise no drugs, right?

I cornered past one old dealer's house, spinners on a Caddy parked in the dirt yard.

He shook his head. I told you, man. I've changed. We all

have.

The road broke down to gravel, signs that threatened Beware of Dog and Trespassers Will Be Shot, the words Rusts Recks spraypainted onto plywood without the apostrophe or the W. Pitbulls paced my Prius. Familiar hope and dread. I was tickled with the hot blood promise of fresh painkillers, giddy with the rekindled fire of expectation that's adjacent to the high itself. I barked the tires and shook my head to clear out the past, but it lingered, nostalgia and trauma in the same dose. The dogs squatted, straight-edge teens in between songs, panting, ready at any moment to mosh.

Allen was telling the truth: Rust wasn't any longer the scrawny pit-eyed thug who'd funded carpools to Florida pill mills. He banged out of his trailer to meet us, belly slung up in a tucked-in tank top stained with Doritos crumbs. When we hugged, he slapped the wind from my lungs, but there was comfort in his hairy arms, his greeting: Missed you, bub. There was comfort in the lazy way he recounted the peaks and valleys of his career: His drug ring busted, followed by a battle to scrape by above the board. He said, When Allen told me about this investment, I figured a second venture couldn't hurt.

We passed a row of dismantled Jeeps, not enough parts between them to piece together a full Wrangler.

I said, Investment? Venture? I turned to Allen for an explanation, but Allen changed the subject. He said, Look at us! Business owners. Who would've known?

The vehicle heaped in a lonely spot of yard. A retired FedEx truck in all its mud-smeared glory. It was as Rust described it: A fixer upper with a wasp problem. One hell of a deal.

He handed us each a can of RAID and we braced ourselves. The mad buzz rushed my ears as Rust rolled up the door. We opened fire.

*

My summer dove into a muggy Midwest slog, but I took the oppressive heat as my penance, learned to see the sweat of my brow as liberation. Our schedule was packed with visits to farmers and butchers, buying organic, local, and in bulk. Our fingers ached throughout days of dicing, adjusting recipes and prep time. Our fare skewed towards adventurous palates, multicultural delicacies blended with working-class American flare. Allen had the idea to add alcohol to every dish, so there was a shot of mezcal in our guacamole and local rice lager toned the bulgogi marinade, a quirk, a niche. We sampled, wordless. Nodded or shook our heads. Weird. Delicious. Fresh. Other days I scoured crannies of the truck for secret wasp nests while Allen Sawzalled windows into the walls. We followed YouTube tutorials on electric and gas, bolted coolers to the floor. When it came time to sandblast the exterior, we rented the machine and blew through the layers to the original dull shine. Blank space. Stripped down to nothing, it was easy to rebuild.

Despite my better judgment, Allen tripped mushrooms and we jammed The Flaming Lips, went wild with the paint. He said he'd be fine. A couple caps, not a spiral. Inspiration, he explained as the name, *Psychedelicious* bloomed large along the paneling, psychotropic splashes of color against black rims and bumpers. Mistakes turned freeform sprawl, unrestricted, wild.

Allen said, Pretty good for an art school dropout, yeah?

And I had to agree. I stepped back, took it in. Impressive. A business to be proud of. Our own.

A drum solo beat arrhythmically at the fog that late May morning. Angels and Demons at Play. When the paint hardened, we parked the truck in the driveway for all to see and shuttled serving trays to the front yard: pulled pork sliders with kimchi slaw, tacos with chicken, bacon, ranch. At first I argued about regulations, inspections, licenses to serve, but I gave in when the money began to flow. Day two we backed up traffic for a block. We passed fries to the nurses of Westinghouse general, dipped cups of pickle potato salad for shift change cops. Day three, overwhelmed, Allen talked me into taking a hit from his weed pen on a trip between the folding table and the grill. One tiny puff, for medicinal reasons, a celebratory buzz, and as I wadded patties and pressed them into the grill, I popped each bubble of worry that floated through my head. We tipped the health inspector with cupcakes. The mayor tweeted our photo: Westinghouse's own!

The day that the truck passed inspection, we walked to The G&T Bar to celebrate. Both of us broke from our investment, but I offered my credit card to start a tab and ordered shots of Patron. Allen thunked his finger stub gavel on the bar and ordered another shot and I thought about how far we'd come. On our own terms. He added a drink to my tab for the woman beside him. Didn't ask me, but we weren't the type of people obsessed with money. I didn't pay rent. We shared. I said, I got you. As long as we did what we loved. As long as our business scraped by. Another shot and I met the bartender's gaze, aware that I was overdrinking. Drunk. She winked. Another round. A celebration. I met her eyes and smiled into my beer. A corner turned. Let's try this again.

What? Allen asked. He texted furiously and slammed the phone into the bar.

Her, I said, The bartender with the tattoo.

Allen was back to muttering curses into his phone. I said, Should I tell her I dig the tattoo?

It was a bird on her bicep adorned with a crown and I had an inkling of the folklore it referenced, but I'd forgotten how to flirt. Allen thumped the phone back down. Distracted. Yeah, He said. Hit that shit.

He said, Let's have a smoke. Come on.

He bummed two cigarettes from a couple on the patio and stuck them both in his mouth to light. I didn't smoke anymore, but he waved me away, plugged the Newport into my mouth. For old time's sake. Needles of menthol, fire and ice. My head floated.

I said, About that bartender.

Allen clawed my shoulder. This is serious, He said, If Rust comes around, you need to call the cops.

He held his phone in his right hand and it lit up with text after text. It was going so well. We'd see profit in a matter of weeks.

Seriously, Billy Boy. He's trying to fuck us.

How? I remembered Rust's words: Investment, venture, *our*. I said, You cut corners, yeah? What did you do?

He said, Jesus, dude. You're so uptight.

So, we owe him? What?

The patio lurched and my stomach barrel-rolled, the booze catching up. I hit the cigarette which drew the heat from belly to head, but only for a moment. Allen said every time he tries, it's like there's something there to fuck him up. Something out there to get him. Everything he does, there's someone who wants to bust his balls. But it was hard for me to listen. My stomach crawled up my throat. I mumbled and wove off to find the bathroom, slipped inside and bolted the door, bowed to the toilet, and all the pressure poured out, each doubt and hesitation purged, flushed away. I stayed there for a time, waiting, sobering, spilling my guts. Someone knocked, but the knocker moved on. I puked again, waited till I was sure I was empty. I couldn't remember the last time I was drunk.

When I returned to the patio, Allen wasn't there. He wasn't at the bar when I sat at my stool and the Deadhead owner returned with my tab. He said my friend had taken off with the other bartender. Inconvenient, Her leaving him alone. A damn shame.

From the parking lot, I saw the sky splurged with stars. So little light pollution, traffic so many miles away that time itself was reduced to a plod. I couldn't any longer claim this town. I had no name here. Little to call my own. It's not like I'd asked the bartender out. I never asked Allen to wait. My fault: I'd been to drunk, to unsure, to act on my desires. Of course she chose Allen, confidence over indecision. It wasn't so awful to wander home alone, too busy, I decided, to bother with falling in love.

*

The Midwest Beer Fest was in July and *Psychedelicious* scored a coveted invite. Mad respect. Our name was known. It appeared to me that the business was flourishing but Allen grumbled that we weren't making shit.

The morning of the beer fest, he woke up late, but I drove fast and hustled with the set-up and we were parked, windows wide, meat on the grill just in time. While I shuffled orders around, he complained about the heat, his headache. He cursed and drank as he shuffled meat around the flat top. All the vibes from the month before had swiveled. This was the old Allen, grubby, angry, bored. I did my best to pick up the slack, to keep the fervor flowing towards our future.

I sipped my beer and was wasp-stung, Allen-smacked. Swollen-tongued, languageless, I stumbled off the truck alone, pitched past the line of hungry zythophiles and Cicerones, past the booths of Malty Mother Brewing and Humble Raccoon. The heady beer humidity carried me to the first aid tent where Lilly, the volunteer nurse, fed me cubes of ice until the swelling went down. She dropped two Ibuprofen in one hand and set an IPA in the other. Take this, She said. You'll survive.

She had purple hair and a gentle touch that fluttered my heart. My tongue was too beefy to speak, so she filled in the next half hour of my silence. The hoppy beer she passed me was West coast, the only style she drank because the brewing world was oversaturated with hazies. It was a recipe she'd experimented with while at med school and perfected when she was kicked out of the dorms. Now it was the flagship at Dad Bod Beer who hosted the festival each year.

A touch of honey, She said. In your case, it's a bit ironic.

I must have looked confused, because she said, Yes. A woman. A brewer. But part of me used to want to be a nurse.

I nodded, beamed apologies on brain waves from inside my head to hers. I didn't know what to do with my hands, how to respond, but she refilled my fist with a fresh drink, and carried on. She pointed at my shirt, the *Psychedelicious* logo, and said she'd heard positive reviews. She said, Heard the owner's an asshole.

I laughed around my tongue, but the swelling was diminished.

She pulled a joint from behind her ear and fired it up, a shrug like, What are they gonna do? Fire me? She explained, No one ever signs up to volunteer at these things. It's generally just me.

I imagined the two of us in the future, my chef to her brewer, at subsequent beer fests, volunteering at the first aid tent, curing hydration with Gatorade, food for those who overpoured and wound up drunk. Beer and Advil for the pain. She offered me the joint and I was too afraid of fucking up all our possibilities to decline. I didn't inhale, though, only swished the smoke and when the taste grew faint, released it.

She said, Come on. You gotta really hit it, and before I could make up my mind to ask her out, she drew deeply and kissed me. College party, shotgun, kidshit, the smoke shared between our open lips. When she pulled away, I coughed. Bubble-worries busted before impact. My tongue loosened and I talked. It all came out. The wasted degrees, the failure. Allen's warnings about Rust. The food truck had been fun, had been magic, but as I sat with Lilly, I realized I didn't want to go back.

But you love it, right? She said, If you're doing what you love.

I nodded, but I wasn't really sure if it was my love or Allen's, if it was the food itself, or the truck itself, or that over the last few years of disappointment I'd outsourced my joy, glued it to other people's plans. Before I went to school, I wanted to be a gangster like Rust and Allen. But that path was untenable for a scrawny confused white boy. Now I was onto something new.

What do you love? She said as she lifted a finger and guided the cup to my lips, a marriage of Riwaka and Nelson Sauvin hops. My body hovered, divine as her kiss.

Beer! I said, holding up my cup. I was only half joking. I said, I don't know. I used to think I was a writer.

*

The sun was hot, but not as high as when I'd entered the tent. The air outside wasn't so stuffy as the live music wailed and growled. Voices carried, indistinguishable and across the lot and *Psychedelicious* squatted, lonely, shuttered, without a line. Allen had given up. I crossed the lot and lunged aboard, ready to open back up and finish out the day, but the flat top was scraped clean, the prep table shut, everything bungeed, resecured. Allen was hitting his hash in the back corner. He said, Fuck this shit. I'm tired. Let's go.

The truck spat gravel as we exited the lot, bouldered onto the open road. The dream was in its death throes. But my phone vibrated in my pocket: Lilly. It would all work out. Each vibration was a piece of my ever-evolving plan. Allen cornered too hard and the truck tipped, so he slammed on the brakes and we swayed, righted. Fucked up. Restless. Filled with rage. I offered to take the wheel. The least I could do was get us home alive, but Allen thumped his finger on the wheel, that confidence remerging. He said, I'll get your ass there. Trust me.

I didn't. Another sharp curve. Up ahead, the road Y-ed off with a stop sign coming the other direction at which no one ever stopped. The sightline was awful. The place was known for accidents. Allen sped up. He asked how much we'd get from the insurance? Twenty, thirty thousand? The name, the recipes, all those adjustments and repairs.

I said, You better fucking not.

I read and reread Lilly's text, a mantra.

More work than it's worth, Allen said. Barely any time to sleep, and for what? We give Rust his cut just to sit around?

Stop.

But he went on. All the problems that money alone could solve. Allen treated words as currency: as if he could throw enough out there to right any wrong. He talked too much and didn't listen to the buzz, too tuned in to his excuses to see the whirlwind of wasps around his head. A nest I must've missed. A swarm.

He punched the headliner, said, Sometimes, you listen to the universe and you think you've heard it right, but you really heard it wrong. Listen harder! He slapped at the insect cloud around his face.

I said, Stop! Pull over.

But Allen wasn't done. He barreled us towards the intersection. He said, I know I haven't been straight with you about all of this, but we'll get our money. We'll make it right.

This was the old Allen.

I said, Stop!

He cursed and slapped. His eyes bulged in recognition. The first sting. He swerved, stomped the brakes, and the truck swayed, implements crashed in the back. We skidded sideways and I saw all of it, a vision of the end.

Years later, Lilly and I would tour the breweries of Virginia together, myself as a reviewer and Lilly as a beer rep. And though we would break off our engagement after half a dozen years of life together, our relationship wouldn't be wasted and eventually we'd move on and eventually Lilly would call me from Westinghouse, Ohio, where she now worked as head brewer for a micro specializing in sours. I'd be in Colorado at the time, writing, savoring my beer, and she'd tell me Allen passed away. No cause listed, only *in the night,* which at only forty five years of age rings nefarious. And I'd know what I knew all along: That the fervor can't last forever. That you can't make meaning by glomming onto other people's dreams. I would thank Lilly for letting me know. I'd worry that I might cry. But I wouldn't let myself cry.

Instead, I'd think back on the summer when I started a food truck with my best friend because it made him so happy and because he wanted me there and I didn't know what else to do. I'd think back to the moment when the swarm descended on us, skidding sideways along Ohio backroads, and how I hesitated, afraid to make the jump. Afraid to leave Allen alone. But he shouted another fact about the universe, another platitude or mantra, like if we went with the flow it'd all work out. He said, Trust me. A stupid thing to say. I didn't. I chose. The truck was still careening, but I pulled and the door slid open. I flung my body out.

Natalya

MEDICAL EXAMINER REPORT
GROSS DESCRIPTION:

The autopsy is performed approximately 26 hours after death. Permission is by the mother of the deceased. When I read your name on the toe tag, I don't believe it right away. Then I see your ankle tattoo, faded but still the same shape.

It's late and I am alone in the morgue. I lean in close to you. I open one eye with a blue-gloved hand and stare at the dilated pupil. I press my fingers into your inflated cheeks. Through the excess tissue, I feel the familiar shape of your face in my hand.

"You can't choose the things you remember," my mother told me one afternoon, while she cleaned and gutted a fish in the white mouth of my grandmother's kitchen sink. "The important things will find you."

I remember this: the sharp scent of raw fish that stuck to my mother's hands for the rest of the evening; the seaside town in rain, smelling rotten and alive at the same time; the smudges in your eyeliner as we stood under the awning of a shuttered convenience store; me with the bag of onions my mother forgot, and the slimmest cigarette I'd ever seen like a lollipop stick between your lips.

You knew I wanted to kiss you. That's what I heard in the crackle of paper and dry tobacco each time our eyes met in that small space. A cold wind swept in from the coast and the coming winter cut its teeth on our ears. We didn't know each other yet. Between us there was still the strangeness of a stranger's body trapped near your own. We didn't know each other yet but you closed the space between us and blew smoke too close to my face. I couldn't speak, only stare at your cracked lips, plaster skin and that round, graspable chin.

When the rain eased, you stepped back onto the sidewalk, but I stayed so I could watch you toss the cigarette butt into a puddle and walk away.

I never thought I would find you so many years later and so many miles from where we met. Yet here you are, unexpected and fruit-flesh pale. I have forgotten many things from that year. My mind smoothed out what my skin couldn't. Despite this, your dark bun and the pinkness behind your knees clings to my mind.

CLINICAL SUMMARY:

You, the patient, are a 41-year-old female with a medical history significant for diabetes, chronic tobacco use, COPD, and teaching me how to coax an orgasm with my tongue. For several days prior to the event that took your life, you complained of dyspnea. Your mother found you only hours after your death, lying on the carpet in the apartment where you lived alone.

Our history began in the last summer of high school. I came to your town because my grandmother died, though I never told you this. That lakeside colonial you dropped me off at was hers. My father had grown up there. He learned to swim in that lake and spent summers cycling through those neighborhoods. Throughout my childhood, I visited my grandmother, between summer camps and over long weekends, but only after her death did we spend so long in that house. It brimmed with my grandparents' long, full life. My parents didn't know what to do with its remains and had to spend a month carefully sorting, discarding. They brought me not because I was too young to be unattended, but because a few months prior, I had been sent to inpatient care for cutting myself. No one dared to leave me alone.

I saw you for the second time on a Sunday morning, as I tried to swim across the tiny lake between my grandmother's house and yours, bored and taken with its smallness. My long limbs, which had come in a sudden growth spurt the previous year, were still new to me. I thought I could catch anything within my new wingspan's breadth. Barely halfway, I grew tired.

I stopped to tread water, panting, and wondered if I could drown in that shallow lake. How many minutes until I stopped fighting for the surface. How many hours until my parents noticed I had not come home. How many years before people stopped thinking about me, dead or alive.

This is when you, skinny as a carving knife, emerged from the trees on the opposite bank. I recognized you immediately by the shape of your limbs and the lines your arm made as you dropped the cigarette from your mouth to your side, flicking ash. A nymph-thing masked in smoke. You looked my age but there was something animal about the way you leaned against the tree, like you were listening. Did you see me swimming or were you looking at something beyond my bobbing head?

Because I couldn't bring myself to drown in front of you, I swam back to my side of the lake. But I searched for you everywhere: the paths in the woods, the kitschy town center, the mall in the next suburb. You were nowhere until you were walking across a parking lot towards me, no longer fantastical. Just another teenager, like me.

EVIDENCE OF INJURY:

Your body is entirely unscathed. No bruises, no wounds. Not so much as a bit of peeling around your fingernails. There are some new creases and stretch marks but the texture of your skin is exactly as I remember. I always envied it.

In medical school, I discovered that suicide is contagious, especially with teenagers, and this filled me with dread. I could have been the first link, dragging a chain of unknowable length into an unknowable non-existence. I remembered you then, your mouth around the phrase, "You have to be afraid to live."

EXTERNAL EXAMINATION:

You, the subject, are 62 inches tall and weigh 140 pounds. Your body is well-developed, well-nourished, albeit slightly overweight for your stated age. You have a blue-gray tattoo on your ankle: blurred Cyrillic letters. I can't read them but I still remember how you spoke his name out loud as you sat naked before me.

There is dependent lividity, algor mortis, and rigor mortis that keeps your arms open. I try to fold them against your sides but they keep springing back out, your tendons unwilling to release their last pose. Once, your hand flies out and almost slaps my face. My startled gasp echoes through the morgue. Before I can stop myself, I say your name out loud. I plead with you to be still. My voice sounds strange, ricocheting between walls that never hold tenderness. Fluorescent bulbs buzz through the following silence like summer insects.

"You don't live here," was the first thing you said to me, a statement rather than a question. I had just unlocked my bike outside the grocery store in the town center. I couldn't identify your accent, though I could guess something Slavic in your name. When I replied that I didn't, and I didn't know anyone, you seemed to sparkle with home field advantage. We exchanged names. I thought the Capri Light you pulled from its pink-and-white box was a piece of candy until you lit it. You offered me one, but I declined because I had never smoked before we met.

I was nervous for our walk, palms sweating as I dragged my bike along with us. I hardly paid attention as you pointed out places you liked amongst the storefronts, until you stopped at the little one-screen movie theatre and pointed at the marquee. "I love this place the most."

I listed moderately artistic movies I knew, hoping to impress you, even though some of them lulled me to sleep. I was reluctant to admit I had never seen your favorite, *Coffee & Cigarettes.*

You offered to watch it with me, and I caught your ash-and-soap smell for the first time as you stepped closer and said, "Come over."

I replied, "Sure," but I meant *yes yes please yes.*

Your head is not deformed and you have no scars. Your sclerae, cornea, and lenses are clear. Your nose and external ears are beautiful, petite and pale like the imperfect end of a half-molten candle, but unremarkable, their passages clear. Your lips and gums show no lesions. Your neck is symmetrical and has no unusual masses. Your clavicle, breasts, protruding abdomen, all of your flesh is unremarkable, unlike mine.

I pull up a sleeve to show you how well my scars faded. It has been years since I made the most recent one.

INTERNAL EXAMINATION (BODY CAVITIES):

On the strip of balcony outside your mother's third floor apartment, I pretended I was having trouble with the lighter so that you would lean in close. The scrape of the wheel striking flint was crisp in our ears and contained between our cheekbones. You offered me the flame, cupped like a fluttering insect in your waxy rose lotion. I liked how your apartment faced away from the lake, towards the sea. Over your shoulder I saw the broken Maine coast, beach-less and wooded, a series of lakes widening out into the Atlantic. The smoke tasted barely bitter, faint enough to keep puffing as you watched.

Inside, we played the film on your computer monitor, sitting on the bed with a screw-top bottle of red blend. At first I joined you each time you opened the window and lit another Capri, dangling one arm out into the evening, but past the third I couldn't keep up.

I remember that the film was black and white and there was a lot of talking, mostly about nothing. It appears this way in my head: a few images, one or two lines of dialogue. Wrinkled faces and checkered tables, ceramic cups and ashtrays blooming with cigarette butts. I didn't like it very much, and after a while, I gave up on paying attention.

The sky blackened slowly as the sun dipped into the opposite horizon. Your room filled with cool air. There was still about a quarter left in the movie when you tossed your shirt aside and unclasped your bra. The rest of the evening is a blur of fingers and teeth. On the brink of your second orgasm I realized the film was ending because it was silent and completely dark, your breath caught in that hitch of anticipation before you came.

As you smoked again afterwards, limbs dribbling into the moon-wet night, I noticed the black lettering on your ankle. When I asked what it was, you turned from the misty window. Your tongue flicked Artur's name in a way mine never could. The love of your life, an older man from your hometown. I grew anxious as you told the story and began to gather my clothing quickly. I had never been on any side of unfaithfulness. I felt naive when you laughed and said, "Don't worry, he lets me fool around."

I wonder what happened with Artur. All I know about your relationship is that photo you showed me decades ago, the two of you on a rooftop in Moscow, a place you promised you'd return to. Your file cites you as a US citizen with an address in the city, unmarried. As I make the first incision, your hand finds my waist. Your fingers brush my hip like you're reaching for me. I hold your arm down with my elbow and push the blade deeper.

The standard thoracic incisions are made. Your pleural cavities contain a moderate amount of clear yellow fluid which I must measure, reduce what's inside you to cc's. I unravel you on the cold table. I split a seam through your center, tug and rearrange the jeweled yellow fat. Everything within is slick, threatening to slip from my grasp. I catalog every centimeter of you, weigh each organ with equal care. Your skeletal muscles are dark red-brown, of normal firmness and bulk. Your ribcage is intact. There are many things I never asked you. Even with my hands around your heart, my fingers tracing your vertebrae, you are a stranger.

HEART: I first saw my wife from afar, too. On a blinding January afternoon, I passed her alone in a classroom on the way to my advisor's office. The tight, tumbling chaos of her hair writhed in the sunlight. She flipped a page in her book and didn't look up to notice how long I watched her before walking along. I never told anyone this story until now, how mythical she looked then with dark eyelashes, thick eyebrows, a round face like a thumbprint in her curls. We met later, in the same study abroad group. She introduced herself as Emma, and though I had never heard her name, my heart rioted in my chest, *I know I know I know I know you.*

Emma doesn't know about you. I never thought she would need to. I recount all this because it was nothing like when you told me your name in front of the grocery store. My whole being stilled at the sound of your voice—muscles, organs, mind. Rigor mortis. You finally understand how it feels.

With its fat peeled off, your heart weighs 296 grams, heavier than average. The walls are thickened by calcified yellow plaques. The myocardium, in contrast, is soft and mottled. I describe you with words I've written countless times. Smooth. Moderate. Transparent. Yet you were never any of these things.

GENITOURINARY SYSTEM: After we started hanging out, I told my parents I'd befriended a few local kids and they were happy to drop me off wherever to meet up with them. Really, it was just you, but they didn't ask questions. They were relieved to have me out of the house, where they listened to my every step and tensed each time they heard silence.

My mother and I kept a strict routine when I returned home each evening. I stripped down to my underwear and she checked every inch of me for fresh cuts. When she was done we spent the rest of the night in front of the television. My father joined us to watch a late night talk show. They asked about my day, but each question felt heavy with the big unanswerable ones they never voiced. My father placed one hand on my shoulder and left it there for a long time. My mother watched me the way she must have watched my mouth open and close when I first lay beside her. Each act of affection was a small humiliation.

Your right kidney weighs 111 grams and the left weighs 120. Your bladder and uterus are normal. You have never carried a child.

GASTROINTESTINAL SYSTEM: Most afternoons I

spent with you seem indistinguishable now—hotboxing your mother's SUV, driving aimlessly while the trees sipped and swallowed the sun. I saw every shade of your face on those roads, the painted yellow and white lines ticking past your sunglasses. While my parents emptied my grandmother's house, stripped all the places touched by our family's fingertips, I catalogued your features white and gold and pink and blue, then flickering in and out of the dark with each passing streetlight.

In sparse towns we found quiet streets to park and fold down the rear seats. The nearest houses glimmered faintly between the trees. The windows fogged up from our bodies, sticky and panting in the air conditioning. On clear days, the crickets were deafening, and on others we listened to the rain. Curled together in the back of your mother's car in pitch black, you traced your fingers over the ridges on my thigh.

"I knew a girl in Moscow who did this kind of thing," you whispered one evening, tapping the marred tissue. Click, hiss; your cheek and lips came up in quivering snatches of yellow and gold, then disappeared. "I don't get it. Why?"

I could have told you about each scar then. How the first cut was an accident. While helping with dinner, I was careless with my mother's sharpest kitchen knife. I didn't recall how it slipped, only that when the crisp mark swelled with blood, my heart suddenly returned to my chest: *I know I know I know.*

"It feels good," I said, unable to explain anything more. I followed the cherry in an arc from your mouth to the gap in the back window. I imagined Artur lying like this by your knee in the cinder block apartment complex where you met. My nostrils filled with smoke.

You switched on the car light and climbed to the front seat, skin sallow under the tiny bulb. The glove box fell open with a *thunk*. You returned with your mother's Swiss army knife, and I held my breath as you sat cross-legged and slit the inside of your leg. A tiny red streak appeared, bubbling until a thin line slid down your thigh. I had an impulse to lick it up, tease the opening with my tongue.

"It stings," you said.

I pressed one finger next to the wound to find that it barely cracked. "You didn't go deep enough."

You lay down and rested your head on my leg. "I'm afraid of blood. I can't look at it any longer. It makes me sick."

I wasn't sure if it was the blood that made you sick, or me. My skin gave away how many times I had done this, how much more blood I'd drawn. "You didn't have to do that," I said.

If you had asked, I might have explained how I stole one of the X-Acto knives from the art studio at school and tucked it under my mattress. I started out very careful. I enjoyed the power of counting secret wounds for several months, though the nights I made them were murky. My game ended one evening when my mother returned home from work early. I stood before her in my towel, damp and exposed, and she looked me up and down with her house keys still clutched in one hand. She slapped me and began to cry.

Instead, you asked, "What are you afraid of?"

I thought of the lake. The green water turned my scars to ripples and my limbs into disappearing things, unrecognizable. "Nothing," I said.

You laughed. "That's stupid."

"Why?" I took a napkin from the center console and wiped up your blood.

"You have to be afraid to live."

You sat up. I realized it was almost ten, and you called Artur at eleven each day. We dressed and you drove me home, the Swiss army knife rattling in the glove box each time you turned.

Your gall bladder is surgically absent, a no-show to our reunion. All the parts of you that could have once been sick are what we call grossly normal and unremarkable, no tumors or ulcers to be found. I check your thigh for that cut but it was so shallow, it didn't leave a mark.

ENDOCRINE SYSTEM: I can't examine your thyroid because of the limitations of this autopsy so I will just write this: when I'm asked why, I remember being fourteen at a fitness class in school when I saw myself in the mirror, working the candy-bright dumbbells up and down, my sneakers squeaking off the hardwood, thudding onto the plastic step, and staring right into my sweat-polished face, I thought, what am I doing here, and then, what am I, and suddenly the clapperboard hit my throat and my blood screamed *cut, cut, cut* and the whole scene was reduced to a tick-marked screen behind a long, fat lens and I squinted, trying to make out where the set ended or what lay beyond it but I couldn't, the lights were too bright and I didn't know who I was outside the script and the dumbbells slipped from my grip and hit the ground and there is still a dent on that floor and I haven't been able to forget my own eyes since.

RETICULOENDOTHELIAL SYSTEM: Your spleen has substance, slightly enlarged and firm, which I find ironic. I never moved or upset you. I never even heard you raise your voice.

The first time Emma saw me naked, she stopped everything to stare. She ran her hands along the marks just like you did once. "If I ever see a fresh one, this is over," she said with a hard edge to her voice, and I nodded, assuring her, "I'm past it." Like this, we lied into each other's mouths for the rest of our lives.

The temptation never left me. I'm in my best years now. I see a therapist once a week and nothing bad happens if I skip a session. Still, sometimes I think about every kitchen knife we have, black handles jutting out of their wooden block.

Emma, fierce heels and unflinching cerise mouth, never has patience for finicky painters and catty art dealers. Despite this, she gives me chance after chance, because we all have to be weak to something.

An incision in your spleen reveals a small imperfection: an area of infarction, pale as a pink moon.

LUNGS: The rest of that summer passed in a swift daze. My parents cleared out my grandmother's house. Rugs rolled up, furniture and antiques sold, the books, clothing, and kitchenware picked off from the lawn during several tag sales. Everything else in a bin at the nearest Goodwill. We filled a rented van with the important things: photo albums, family heirlooms, my grandfather's glasses. Soon the house was empty.

I can no longer pinpoint the last evening you and I spent together, but I remember taking one last dip in the lake before we drove home. The water in Maine is never warm, even at the end of summer. I stared up at the stretch of flat blue, strands of clouds like scar tissue across it, and wondered if I should tell you I was leaving, whether you would care. I tried to imagine what you would say, but I could only picture you sitting cross-legged on the balcony, shrugging, taking a drag and not looking at me. Staring out at the sea that separated you from someone else. Fear, colder than lake water, slithered into my veins. My body came alive at something so petty. I pulled my head underwater. Bubbles flew from my mouth and nose, but I couldn't ignore the ache in my chest as the last of my breath left me. I surfaced into the creamy sky coughing.

I received your text the week later, *Hey, are you around?* I wasn't so I didn't reply and you never contacted me again.

Your lungs have a combined weight of 723 grams. They are the usual shape, but full of carbon and plaques. You must have switched from Capri Lights to something harsh and heavy, even though you told me that thick, stubby cigarettes looked ugly in a woman's fingers. I imagine you felt death come for you. I picture you lighting a cigarette on some balcony in the city, waiting. Instead of traffic, you heard pines chatter in the wind and tides lap the soil.

I'm sorry I never said goodbye.

EXTREMITIES: I pull back your skin looking for everything I never understood about you. I put my fingers in your mouth, feel around your teeth. Your tongue is dry. You don't even twitch when I prod your uvula. Your nipples, soft and wide, won't bead up if I pinch them. If I pluck your ribcage, you won't recoil. No matter how I touch you, you remain still, peeled apart like pithy citrus.

I seal the fissures and wipe the smears from your skin. I try to arrange your body symmetrically, but your limbs and breasts keep falling askew. There is so much more to you — stomach folds and dimpled thighs. The girl from that summer was only a sliver of the person you became. I lean in and hold your round face in both my hands, your earlobes' familiar fit in the crook between my thumb and forefinger. Obscenely, I still want to kiss you. I want to bite your cheek to see if it tastes the same. Instead I release you, and pull the sheet back over your face. This is the last time I see you.

CLINICOPATHOLOGIC CORRELATION:

Emma and I spent a semester in Italy. We spoke the language better than our classmates, so while they were in Rome and Florence, we stayed alone in a small town with a university that only offered classes in Italian. We often had coffee before class, dinner on pleasant evenings. My host family had a beautiful garden and patio where we would sit with wine, a soda can ashtray, and a Marlboro between my fingertips, talking for hours after everyone had gone to sleep. One hot night, our faces barely lit by the splatter of yellow windows and sickle moon, I kissed her.

"I was wondering how long it would take," she said as I pulled back. I thought of you then, how you cornered me between the movie and your window. You never waited.

You died naturally, of acute myocardial infarction. After I shut you away in a drawer, I wonder if I was trying to recreate my evenings with you that first summer with Emma. Hold a mirror to the last time I wanted to devour someone cheek first.

SUMMARY AND REFLECTION:

I still don't know if I loved you, yet you linger within me like an apparition. I carved my deepest cut right before I took the MCAT. I still have a slanted seam across my forearm. It needed many stitches and the doctors told me I was lucky my hand remained steady after it healed. That night, with the shower running, the tiles turning red all around me, I thought of the tiny slit on your leg and how much that hair-thin wound hurt you. As I fainted, the sound of water became the engine of your mother's SUV, the rush of the highway, and then your breath in my ear.

Kathleen Gibbons

I'm On Highway 1

"Start from the beginning," Audrey said, and Walter's story tumbled out. He jumped ahead of himself, then circled back again, but she managed to piece it together. Early that morning, while he stood in line at the town pharmacy, the elderly woman ahead of him chatted up the pharmacist. On and on they nattered at the counter, without as much as a glance toward Walter. The longer he waited, the angrier he became, until he'd had enough, he told Audrey from his hospital bed. She imagined her eighty-one-year-old father's fury—his fierce scowl, the way his pink cheeks turned a bright, flaming red. She knew that face too well.

"She blathered on about every grandchild within a fifty mile radius," Walter said.

Finally, when it was Walter's turn, the pharmacist said the co-pay was five dollars for his blood pressure medication.

"Five dollars?" Walter asked. "I used to pay a dollar!"

In the seconds it took the pharmacist to check the price, Walter swiped the pills from the counter and ran for the exit. A hefty security guard lumbered through the greeting card aisle and tackled Walter to the ground, bringing on a heart attack. Soon after, an ambulance transported him to the emergency room.

Audrey was mulching her garden when the hospital called with the news. The previous day she'd submitted her students' final grades at the community college in San Luis Obispo and was looking forward to a relaxing summer. Realizing she might be staying at Walter's house for a few weeks, she packed her bags and drove the forty miles north to his small town on California's central coast.

She wasn't prepared for Walter's appearance in the hospital room: hooked up to an IV and oxygen, tubes twisting every which way, his white hair in matted strips across his scalp. A heart monitor made persistent beeping noises. His skin had turned a pallid gray. Seeing him this way reminded Audrey of her mother in the hospital two years ago, when she'd been admitted with pneumonia.

The bed sagged when she sat on the edge of it, waking Walter. He seemed perplexed and scanned the room, his eyes flitting back and forth. They landed on Audrey. He stared at her for several seconds.

"Helen?" Walter asked.

Audrey paused before answering. Helen was her mother, the one he ran out on when Audrey was a teenager.

"No, Walter, it's Audrey," she said.

"Oh Audrey, I'm sorry," he said. "You look just like your mother."

They sat quietly for a few minutes and Audrey wondered if the heart attack had worsened her father's memory, whether he understood her mother had passed away two years ago. She decided not to remind him just yet.

Walter put a finger to his lips and pointed to the door.

"Not too loud," he said. "He can hear us."

"Who?" she asked.

"The CIA agent outside the door," he said. "He's been listening to my conversations."

"He's a sheriff, Walter," she said. "He's there because they think you're a thief."

She watched him take this in, glancing distractedly from her to the door. He seemed surprised by this information, which worried her. How could he not know what was going on?

"That's a nice necklace," he said. She touched the threaded shells resting on her chest. He never noticed anything she wore. Now she knew something was wrong.

*

After her mother died, Walter had written to Audrey, asking to "renew their relationship." The email had surprised her. It had been decades since he'd left her and her mother. His years of drinking and abuse had destroyed her parents' marriage. Audrey was a senior in high school then and it pained her to see her father leave, but she took her mother's side. Sometimes she yearned to see him, yet didn't want to appear disloyal to her mother. One night before high school graduation, he took her out for a celebratory dinner. Their conversation was awkward and as she watched him drink his dinner, she felt both sadness and pity for her father, then relief, when they'd finally finished their meal. She would start UCLA in the autumn and it was easier to ignore the pain, to push it away and leave it behind her.

She stayed in Los Angeles after college to teach, marry, raise a family. Over the years there were occasional phone calls, but she and Walter grew further apart, and neither one of them made much effort to change things. Sometimes she had wished it was different, especially after the twins were born, but this was how it was between them, and she'd accepted it.

Walter's email arrived shortly after her mother's funeral, thirty-five years after she'd kicked him out. By then Audrey and her husband had divorced, the twins were in college with their own lives, and she'd moved from Los Angeles into her mother's home in San Luis Obispo. She thought about Walter's letter for several days before replying. *Renewing?* Maybe *repairing* was needed—maybe even *overhauling*—and she told him so, in a return email. But after more consideration, she reasoned it might be time to have him in her life again, despite all the horrible history, and especially now, when she felt her mother's loss so acutely. So she agreed to see him in a second email, although for days later she questioned herself, feeling a betrayal to her mother.

Audrey and Walter got to know each other all over again—slowly at first, then more regularly, at coffee and donut shops, for movies and dinners. He'd been sober for many years and their relationship took on an ease she hadn't experienced before. It occurred to her this might be good for both of them. Sure enough, Walter's old self returned, but she seemed better able to manage it now, as a mature adult. Calling him "Dad" after all these years didn't feel right, so they agreed she'd call him Walter.

Now in the hospital room, after he'd recounted what happened at the pharmacy, he pulled the blanket over his chest.

"My morality is not going the way I thought it would," he said.

"You mean your *mortality*?" she asked. She adjusted the oxygen tubes in his nose and wrapped the straps around his ears a little tighter.

"I thought I would've had a heart attack by now," he said.

"You did have a heart attack," she said.

She fluffed a pillow and put it behind his head.

"Was it on the 15th hole, with a nine-iron in my hand?" he asked. "That's how I wanna go."

"No Walter, you had yours after stealing medication from your pharmacist, miles away from your favorite golf course," she said.

"I used to pay one dollar, now he wants five. What was I supposed to do?" he asked.

"Let's see, pay five dollars or get arrested for stealing your meds. That's a tough one, Walter."

*

After a week in the hospital, Walter was well enough to be discharged but not strong enough to go home. He transferred to a rehabilitation center. Right away he became more confused and irritable, unsure about the time of day, asking questions which didn't make sense. Audrey worried he was slipping into dementia. He hallucinated about his early Army days, although he'd only served for five years, decades ago. Walter's doctor suspected delirium, a state of confusion which sometimes occurs post-surgery or after a traumatic event.

"Is it temporary?" Audrey asked.

"Can't say," the doctor said. "But it's not unusual for an eighty year-old man recovering from a heart attack."

It became obvious to Audrey that Walter couldn't care for himself at home and returning there was out of the question.

She researched assisted living homes and found Ridgeview Retreat at the south end of town and convinced him it was only for a month or two. He argued he'd be better sooner than that, but she wasn't convinced.

Walter moved into Ridgeview with a suitcase and a few personal belongings. She helped him unpack and showed him how to find his beloved Dodgers on TV. Slowly he settled in, made friends, played daily card games, shared his California history books. Audrey was pleased to see him adjusting and getting along with other residents.

But it didn't take long before things turned sideways and the complaints began: the food was bland, the nurses unfriendly, the residents ignorant. Each time she saw him, he grumbled about Ridgeview.

As she was leaving one day, he told her he wanted to move to a hotel.

"A hotel? You can't stay in a hotel," she said. "They won't take care of you."

"What do you mean?" he asked. "They deliver food to your room, make your bed, clean your laundry, shine your shoes. What more do I need?"

"But it'll cost a fortune," she said.

"Like this place don't cost a few nickels?" he asked.

Audrey threw up her hands. She wasn't in the mood to reason with him.

"Let's talk about it tomorrow," she said, waving good-bye and closing the door.

Looking after Walter had become more work than she'd anticipated. Frankly, she never thought she'd be in this position, caring for her father after all their years of separation. What was her obligation to this man, someone who'd abandoned all responsibility to her and her mother? She imagined walking away from it all now, freeing herself. And yet, deep down she knew she couldn't do it. She wouldn't leave him. It had to do with being cast-off years ago and knowing full well how it felt on the receiving end. The bigger question was whether she could ever forgive him for it.

*

The first time Walter escaped from Ridgeview, Audrey was furious with the nursing staff. She couldn't believe they allowed her father to walk out the door, as if he were simply on a stroll to the park. Someone tried to stop him but Walter swung his fists, missing everyone in his path. In the end, they let him go and a supervisor phoned her.

"It's not as if he's institutionalized," the supervisor explained. "He can come and go on his own free will, if he's able."

"Yes, that's the point—he's not able!" Audrey yelled.

She'd been in Walter's house all morning, scraping charred bits of food stuck to the stovetop from his last fry up and disposing mysterious food from his packed refrigerator. And now she had a Houdini for a father. She picked up her car keys and was almost out the door when her cell phone rang again.

"Hey! A little close buddy!" Walter shouted into the phone. "Kiss my ass next time!"

"Walter? Where are you?"

"I'm on Highway 1," he said. She took in a deep breath, relieved to hear his voice, but suddenly realized he was standing on the two-lane coastal highway.

"What are you doing there?" she asked.

"Watching the elephant seals," he said. "I can't hear you too good Audrey, I'm on a payphone and cars are flying past me."

"Walter, you need to get off that highway," she said, controlling her tone to stay calm.

"Can you hear me?" he shouted.

A recorded message cut in, prompting more coins.

"Walter?" The line went dead.

Merging onto Highway 1, she passed a sagging grove of cypress trees, tilting toward the sea. She found her father several miles north just as he'd said, at the elephant seal rookery, where the massive creatures colonized a local beach. Audrey parked and watched him for a few minutes. He took photos of one lazy seal then another, because, she thought to herself, you can never have too many photos of lazy seals sunning themselves. She wrapped a sweater around her and walked toward him, leaning into the wind.

"No salt," Walter replied, when she asked him why he'd left.

She tilted her head and tried to make sense of this.

"The cooks don't salt the food?" she asked.

Walter shook his head.

"It's not good for the blood pressure," he said, rolling his eyes. "So they say."

"It can't be that bad," she said.

He counted off his fingers one at a time.

"No salt, no sugar, no fat," he said. "I already gave up booze. What the hell's left?"

His thin white hair blew in every direction in the breeze, exposing his pink scalp. Seeing him alone in these surroundings—the enormous seals, the wide expanse of the sea, cars whizzing by indifferently—made him appear small and vulnerable, unlike the insufferable man she'd known in childhood, the perpetual drunk who constantly yelled at her mother.

Walter turned to the seals again and they both watched them for several minutes.

"Your mother loved this part of California, coming up here from San Luis Obispo when you were young," Walter said.

Audrey inhaled the briny sea air.

"I remember," she said, quietly. She wasn't ready for this moment but it came anyway, the pure joy she'd felt on those trips as a young girl in the 1970's, when they'd driven almost an hour on the coastal highway to the nearby State beach, where they spent long afternoons lounging on the sand, searching tide pools, wading into waves. She'd forgotten about those trips until now, but felt as if she'd been longing for them her whole life.

Walter pointed his camera at a seal pup following its mama into the water. Click. Click. Heavy clouds rolled in and the wind suddenly turned cold. A foghorn bellowed from the lighthouse. Audrey wondered how many more photos he'd need of these seals.

"Look, over there," he said, pointing. "I call that one 'Grand Poobah.'" An enormous bull elephant seal stretched his thick neck and yawned awake, lifting his bulbous nose in the air.

*

"They're cute together," the receptionist said to Audrey, at Ridgeview's front desk.

Audrey was taking Walter out for lunch—a place where they salted the food, she had promised. Maybe a donut and coffee afterwards. She looked up from signing the visitor's book.

"Who's cute together?" she asked.

"Walter and Barbara," the receptionist said.

"Barbara?" she said, "He doesn't know anyone named Barbara."

"Oh yes he does," the receptionist said, smiling.

Audrey walked down the hallway to Walter's room. She opened the door a crack, just wide enough to see inside. A woman sat next to him, wearing a lavender sweater set, her auburn hair stacked in a bowl-shaped coif. The television blasted the Dodgers game, but neither of them were watching it. He was showing the woman one of his California history books, pointing to one photograph then another.

"There's Point Junipero Serra, the tallest mountain peak in the area," he said.

Seeing a woman so intimately close to Walter made Audrey draw back, away from the door. She stood still for a minute, puzzled. How did this happen? And when? She closed the door and told the receptionist she'd return tomorrow.

The next day, when Audrey parked at Ridgeview, she spotted Walter in the garden sitting on a bench with Barbara. They were holding hands. Every now and then, he chuckled. They appeared so besotted with each other, they didn't notice an elderly resident strolling past in a walker, clearing his throat and spitting two feet away from them.

"You wouldn't understand," Walter said later, in his apartment.

"Walter, it's not like I'm a child," Audrey said. "Try me."

"She pursued me," he said. "In the dining hall."

"Really?" she laughed. She pictured Barbara sidling up to her father, asking to borrow the salt from his table as she leaned into him. On second thought, she didn't want to imagine any of this.

"There aren't many men here with all their faculties. Upstairs and downstairs, if you know what I mean," he said, raising one eyebrow.

"Spare me the details," she said. "When did all this start?"

"A few days ago," he said. "But I first met her many years ago. I didn't realize she lived here until after I moved in."

"You guys didn't waste any time," she said. "I wish you'd told me."

Walter became quiet and peered out the window, then turned back to her.

"I didn't want you to think I was cheating on your mother," he said.

"That's an odd thing to say. How could you cheat on her?" she asked. "You've been divorced for decades and now she's passed."

Audrey recognized the tightening in her chest, which always meant she was about to learn something she didn't want to know. She felt it before her mother told her Walter was leaving them; when her own husband told her he was in love with someone else; when the doctor said her mother had passed away in the night.

"Your mother and I made amends before she died," he said.

Audrey looked at her father and blinked. Wait a minute. What did he say?

"Made amends?" she asked.

Walter nodded and tapped his finger on the arm rest. He took in a deep breath.

"What does that even mean?" she asked.

"We didn't say anything to you because we didn't know where it would lead," he said. "And it didn't lead anywhere after she was hospitalized."

"She never mentioned anything to me," she said.

Walter shrugged. "What can I tell you?"

"I don't believe you," she said. She crossed her arms over her chest. Frankly, she didn't think Walter had it in him to make amends with her mother.

Years ago, therapy had helped Audrey see the person Walter had been for most of her young life. He was never physically abusive, but she'd witnessed his drinking binges and explosive temper, and the verbal abuse was horrific enough. And how she hated the way he took it out on her mother. Audrey was the one who cleaned up the broken plates, after her mother disappeared to her bedroom and her father sat brooding in his chair. Once during dinner, he tipped a perfectly good steak onto the floor claiming it was overcooked, only to have the dog snatch it and race out the door, which made Walter go ballistic. A round of apologies and regrets always followed, but days later, his temper would flare again: the soup was scalding hot, the refrigerator was broken, the house wasn't clean enough. It was always her mother's fault. She never did anything right. These episodes continued as his drinking worsened—or worsened as his drinking continued, Audrey never knew which. What she does remember is how often she had wished for a new family.

When she attended sleep-overs at friends' houses, she saw how their fathers were home most nights, and their mothers weren't alone in the kitchen crying. No one came home tanked after work; no one lost their temper at dinner. By the time she was a teenager, Audrey was spending long hours in her friends' homes, away from her father and also from her mother.

It's what pains Audrey the most when she thinks about this time, just before her parents' separation. Something she'd realized later, when her twins were teenagers and her own marriage was crumbling: surely it must've saddened her mother to see her family falling apart. And at a time when she might've been comforted by Audrey's presence—with a chat over an after school snack, or a distracting trip to the town shops—Audrey was simply not around.

"I can't imagine it Walter, you making amends with my mother," Audrey said.

"She thought you'd be disappointed," he said. "She let me back into her life because I'd stopped drinking."

"But you'd stopped drinking years ago and didn't go back to her," Audrey said. "What was different this time?"

"I don't know. Our age, I guess," he said. "History, maybe. Loneliness, probably."

Audrey felt her stomach turn. How could her mother keep this secret? In her final days, there was no mention of it—no mention of meetings or dates, of his presence in the house, the very same house that was now Audrey's.

"We had some fun times, before she got sick," he said. "Went to the Sunset drive-in movies once, like the old days—you remember—we did that when you were a kid. Remember getting ice cream and popcorn at the snack bar? You were about ten or eleven."

"Yeah, I remember," she said, her face hot with anger. "But I remember it differently: you boozed your way through the entire double feature. You were so drunk, you tried putting the car keys into the radio. When mom took them away, you pounded the radio so hard, it broke."

Walter grew quiet. Audrey had felt powerless as a child, whenever her father went into a drunken rampage. She wouldn't allow him to make her feel that way again, now that she was an adult capable of remembering the truth.

"I need to sit with this for a while," Audrey said. She grabbed her purse and walked out.

As she drove out the parking lot, she considered again the inner struggle she'd been suffering for most of her adult life: how the person Walter had been to her and her mother—the drunk and cruel father and husband—stopped her from fully loving him.

*

Two days later, Audrey couldn't stop thinking about her parents' reconciliation. How was it possible, after all these years? Had Walter actually atoned for what he'd done to her mother? And had her mother forgiven him for it?

To distract herself, she cleaned Walter's garage, tossing old magazines and newspapers into the recycling, all of it smelling like mildew. This old house. He'd been here for years—a small two-bedroom bungalow just outside of town. She wondered if he'd want to live here anymore, now that he'd met Barbara at Ridgeview. Assisted-living romances changed with the weather, but this one seemed different. She saw the way Walter had nodded attentively at Barbara on the garden bench, as if hanging on to every spoken word. Had he listened to her mother in the same way, when they'd reunited? Her back pocket buzzed and she reached for her cell phone.

"He asked for a Maple Glaze, then fell over," said the woman at the donut shop.

"Walter? What's he doing there?" Audrey asked.

"Ma'am, it's a donut shop and he was buying one," the woman said.

"But he's supposed to be at Ridgeview. Did he escape again?" she asked.

"I don't know the answer to that, ma'am," the woman said.

"Where is he now?" Audrey asked.

"He's sitting at a table, eating his donut," the woman said. "He asked me to call you. Seems okay now, maybe a little dizzy."

Audrey drove to the donut shop. She was adjusting to the idea of her parents reconciling, but still felt furious they'd kept it from her. Knowing about it would've reassured years of uncertainty on her part, when she'd wondered if her father had ever loved her mother. She'd spent most of her youth wishing away her dysfunctional family. They might've had a chance to start anew, had they told her in the first place.

She turned off the engine and sat in the shop's parking lot for a few minutes. She wondered if she was too mired in the past, spending hours thinking about circumstances she couldn't change. Maybe the question she'd been asking was the wrong one. Maybe it wasn't a question of forgiving Walter.

Sitting across from him inside the donut shop her father seemed fine, albeit a little disoriented. She picked up a napkin and brushed the donut crumbs from his cheeks. He stared out the window towards the highway, absorbed in his thoughts.

"I lost myself," he said.

"What do you mean?" she asked, though she had a notion. He sometimes appeared adrift and misplaced, as if he'd left some part of himself on the side of the highway. This was the first time he attempted to articulate it.

"Your mother," he choked. "I screwed up."

Tears pricked Audrey's eyes and she felt her throat thicken, the way it had when she was a young girl, listening to her parents fight.

"Yes," she whispered. "Yes, you did."

He lowered his gaze and tried to continue but covered his face with both hands.

"I need to get out of here," he said. He struggled to stand but she put her hand on his forearm and he settled back into his chair.

"Why do you keep disappearing?" she asked.

He picked up a donut crumb and rubbed the sugar between his thumb and finger.

"Why do you keep finding me?" he asked.

Audrey didn't know how to answer. She took in the old man sitting in front of her: his sagging cheeks and drooping eyelids, the craggy wrinkles across his forehead. His thinly stooped shoulders. This was not the cruel man she knew long ago. And yet, how could she forget that man? If she stripped away all the old layers, at his core lay one simple truth: he'd failed her and her mother. Failed them in compassion and tolerance and empathy. And now it seemed, he might live his final years regretting it.

Maybe her mother predicted this might happen. Maybe after years of him treating her like she didn't matter, she knew he would remain unfulfilled and remorseful in her wake. Maybe she understood this all along and it was her final reckoning. But where did that leave Audrey?

She handed her father a napkin and he blew his nose, wiped his eyes.

He glanced around the crowded shop, but seemed oblivious to the comings and goings of customers. She stretched across the table for his hand. As a young girl, long before her parent's divorce, there were times when she had buried her small hand in his palm and his thick fingers curled around hers. Between them, she swung their hands together. How much she had wanted to prolong those moments then, to make them last.

"Tell me about Barbara," she said.

Walter's milky blue eyes met hers.

He shrugged. "What do you want to know?"

"Start from the beginning," she said.

For a little while more they sat together quietly talking, drinking coffee, amid the shop's busy chatter. And when it was time to go, they stepped outside into a morning so fine, even the cypress trees stood taller in the magnificent sun.

L. Mari Harris

In The House With The People

Our son told us he had a brother before he was born. I would take him clothes shopping and he'd point out a little t-shirt with green dinosaurs all over it that his brother would have liked. At dinner, he'd tell us his brother loved carrots but he didn't, so he'd pass if that was ok with us. We knew imaginary friends were common; we'd had them ourselves at his age. But we agreed this was different, this insistence on a brother that once was, yet wasn't.

He was a sensitive boy, prone to playing quietly in his room, cross-legged on the floor, orderly driving his toy trucks down street lanes he created with popsicle sticks. Tears would well up in his eyes when we found the occasional dead wasp on a windowsill. We thought how lucky we were, to have a son who cared so much about everything in the world. We worried he was so much more than we deserved.

We asked him if he'd like a little brother to play with. *I had one already*, he frowned.

We considered taking him to a therapist. We'd spent a year in counseling before having him, when we were figuring out if we could find ways to stop disappointing each other. We'd tried a temporary separation while in counseling, and I'd briefly dated an emotionless man who talked only in his sleep.

When our son was still an infant, we ran into the emotionless man on the street. You protectively wrapped your arm around me and our son snuggled against my chest. I didn't know you even knew what he looked like, and after the emotionless man had walked by without acknowledging us, you confessed you used to stand outside the apartment I'd rented for that short time and watch us sitting in opposite chairs next to the window. I remembered how fragmented I'd felt, sitting with a man who would only talk to me when I dreamed, how I'd longed on those evenings apart to call you up, tell you I had redefined *enough*.

On the first warm spring day, we went to the zoo. One of the polar bears had had twins, and the cubs were curled together, asleep near the edge of their pool. Our son stared and stared, his little hands gripping the bars of the fence. He wouldn't take his eyes off the polar bear cubs, wouldn't stop staring as he told us he'd used to curl up with his brother like that, and they'd hold each other tight and fall asleep with intertwined fingers. How he grew bigger while his brother who loved little green dinosaurs and carrots grew smaller, how they'd agreed a decision had to be made, how it made the most sense he would be the one to live in the house with the people who had once been so unhappy they split in half and toppled to the floor.

Seven Truths, One Memory, and Four Lies

Lie: Real dad says he'll be right back when you try to follow him out the kitchen door one day.

Truth: When she realizes real dad isn't coming back, real mom cries harder than you do, until you both have snot running down your noses.

Truth: Real mom starts hiring a babysitter on Saturday nights, and after real mom leaves, not looking like real mom at all, the babysitter lets you eat all the pizza you want while she giggles into the phone.

Lie: Fake dad never shows up, and never stays and stays and stays and stinks up the house like a rotting fish.

Truth: One morning, real mom has a purple and black bruise on her cheek, and you ask her if she's your real mom or an alien mom, because real mom is beautiful and perfect and never looks like damaged fruit.

Truth: Alien mom pokes her alien head out her bedroom door, tells you to keep it down, tells you *We're trying to sleep in here!* Shuts the door again until the afternoon sun burns.

Truth: Alien mom sells your dog. You come home from school to find the back yard empty, and you scream *But I loved him!* until you fall to the ground. Alien mom tells you to grow up, that love doesn't pay the bills.

Lie: You never tiptoe up to alien mom's bedroom door. Never lie on your stomach and sniff under the door. Never breathe *I hate you I hate you I hate you* until you fill the room.

Truth: Fake dad carves the roasted chicken with his hunting knife, says *Look what I can do with this bad boy.* Alien mom claps her hands and squeals like he's the best thing ever.

Truth: Fake dad tells alien mom to run out and get him another 12-pack. Alien mom winks at you like you're pals, says *Men. Whatcha gonna do?* You want to slash the tires of his stupid truck. *That's whatcha gonna do.*

Lie: One day, real dad walks into the kitchen and tells you

he forgot something. *You, silly, you! I forgot you!* And he swings you around in his big arms, and you laugh and laugh and laugh.

Memory: Real dad and real mom once took you to Yellowstone, where they pointed out a bear at the far end of a meadow covered in yellow and blue wildflowers. You couldn't really tell if it was a bear or not, but you had no reason not to believe them, because real dad and real mom never lied to you. Later, at the gift shop, they let you pick out a bag of smooth river rocks that cooled your skin as you rolled the little bag between your palms. Then you all stood around and waited for the geyser to blow.

Underpinning

We had lived in the house for several years before the first small crack appeared in the kitchen. Over the next several mornings when I came downstairs to start the coffee maker, I would trace my finger along the latest crack I found. They were all paper-thin, my finger barely feeling their ridges. I kept waiting for my husband to notice; wanted to point them out, tell him the sooner we stabilized the foundation, the better.

For weeks, the cracks only appeared in the kitchen, until one day I spotted them in the dining room, the hallway, and halfway up the stairs, as if the house was parched earth. I'd purposely stare over his head at the dinner table, hoping he'd grow curious and turn to see what had caught my attention, or at least ask me what I was up to. But he'd only say *pass the rolls* or *this needs more salt*, then he'd tell me he was going to go into the den to watch the game.

I found myself wandering from room to room every day, measuring the width of the cracks with my fingernails, an envelope, the blade of a hatchet I retrieved from the tool shed.

I hung pictures to hide the widest cracks, and when the flooring broke apart in a corner of the living room, I tossed the decorative Mr. and Mrs. pillows over the gap and turned the volume of the TV up louder.

When a hole the size of a basketball broke open in the ceiling as we were changing for bed one night, I held my breath, waited for him curse the day we moved into this house, that he *knew even back then this was a bad idea but I'd just had to have it*, that he'd *tried to tell me a million times*. But he didn't. He tied the drawstring of his pajama bottoms, said it had been another long day and would I mind shutting off the bedside light.

Soon, his breathing evened and slowed. I stared at the hole above us, inhaled a hint of staleness that drifted down and slowly filled the room. At one point, he turned over, pulled my side of the covers around his body in his sleep. I eased out of bed and made my way across the room, waited to turn on the bathroom light until I'd softly shut the door behind me. I turned the faucet on cold, dipped my head to drink.

I felt a tremor vibrate through the soles of my feet, a new crack appearing above the bathroom mirror, slowly crawling up the wall, then along the ceiling. I watched it spread to the opposite wall, down to the doorframe. And then the bathroom door splintered and fell.

And yet still he slept. I watched his chest rise and fall. He moaned once or twice, batted a hand at his mouth as if to brush away a spider or a fly. Another tremor shook the house as I caught his scent. I spread my arms, hovered over his sleeping body. Bared my teeth. Patiently waited for him to wake up, for him to see.

Maya Kanwal

A Shade for the Window

The woman materialized one bitter winter morning under the graffitied awning of the vacant taqueria. The shop had sat boarded up since its last tenant clattered away in a pickup truck ahead of a raging Houston storm. The woman, though slight in aspect, wielded a rugged rake as if it were nothing but a sisal broom. Haroon noticed her as he maneuvered his bicycle to his bus stop across six bustling lanes of Hillcroft Road.

Leaning his bicycle against the bus shelter, Haroon regarded the way the new woman's powder blue shawl draped on her head, flowed over her shoulder, was tucked just so behind one ear—she had to be Pakistani. She purged the sidewalk of a muddle of plastic bags and organic refuse as if the act marked the place as hers. Haroon had never seen an occupant of this stretch of road pay heed to the street front, all peevishly ensconced in their lodgings and bazaars as if what or who dwelled outside did not matter, as if they themselves could not matter outside their walls. Houston was a city of interiors. Haroon missed his grandparents' leafy verandah in Lahore, the childhood games he'd played there with cousins and neighbors. He often gave a disengaged new student in his class the benefit of the doubt because he remembered the wilds of American schooling he'd been released into as a gangly thirteen-year-old, ignorant about deodorant and mediocre at English. He'd picked up the English, some fashions as well, but the jokes, two decades later, still gave him trouble.

Perhaps the new woman struggled with English too. Even here, she wore her shawl as if a disapproving brother might appear around the corner any moment and chide her for lapsing in her modesty. She gathered the trash under the chipped tile counter beneath the awning. The late taqueria, converted from a shawarma stand, converted from a juice and tea shack, converted from an immigration, insurance, and tax office, stood in a two-story property that broke up a chain link of carnicerías on one side and halal meat stores on the other. No one expected the termite-gnawed structure to sustain life for long, let alone afford a living. No one knew who owned it, or why the developers of the adjacent strip lots clawed their way around it. Its sign board, painted and repainted, had faded and peeled so the names of its occupants merged indistinguishably. Over that counter Haroon had bought tacos—not halal—many a night after his mother had gone to bed, and before that, when the shop was a shawarma stand, he'd brought home shawarmas—halal—to his mother as a Friday evening treat.

He was on his way to the high school where he taught math. As on every morning, he had ducked under the gate of his apartment complex, careful not to brush flaking paint and rust with his gelled hair, and raised his hand in farewell to his widowed mother. She watched him from their window, a squat obelisk, her white dupatta still swathed around her head from her dawn prayers. She waited for him silently all day, the only non-Spanish speaker in the complex; then unleashed her pent-up Urdu on him when he returned.

The screech of a braking bus startled him. The woman, who'd glanced up at him several times, squinted and adjusted her shawl with an air of finality, as if to dismiss his gaze—a gesture he'd seen his cousins back home make in markets when strange men stared at them.

On the bus ride to school, he thought the woman, given her demeanor, might be in her forties. Over lunch in the teachers' break room, he recalled the shine on her cheek, striking even from a distance, and imagined her younger, closer to his own age. By the time he unlocked his bicycle in the afternoon, her face had resolved into a fine-featured blur of the starlets on the Hindi film posters in the desi grocer's windows, and he worried she might be barely twenty. That was the problem with women. Their attitude and their apparent age could not be counted upon to reflect each other.

#

On his return, as Haroon lifted his bike off the bus rack, he saw the abandoned building aglow with new life. Its tattered awning had been removed. Light from the setting sun danced off the shop's scrubbed aluminum shutters. The woman's shawl was aflutter in the window of the second story. Two shadows crossed the blue curtain back and forth. A teenaged girl emerged at the casement. Her eyes wandered down and connected with Haroon's. He waved, but she shrank back under the curtain. Self-conscious of his awkward interest, he pivoted toward home. But sensing another movement from the window, he glanced up again. The woman now peered out at him from behind the shawl. She held his eyes and didn't look away as he expected. The surprise put such steam into his legs, he cycled away, breaking up their wordless exchange.

As he tucked his bicycle under the stairs, the comforting smell of toasted flour from the rotis on his mother's griddle wafted down the stairwell. He stepped in to the sound of the slap of dough between her hands.

"Any news, Ammi?" His usual greeting, offered without pause as he passed the kitchen on his way to freshen up before dinner. He did not run the water as soon as he reached the bathroom, curious for once to hear if she had anything to share.

"All by the grace of Allah, son." Her usual response summarizing the monotony of her day. He turned the tap to full gush.

Returning to the living room, which doubled as his bedroom, he dropped to his bed to tear into the rotis laid out alongside a bowl of thick lentils. From his mother's bedroom he heard a shuffle different from the sound of her preparations for the sundown prayer.

She emerged shaking out a white cotton sheet. At one intersection of folds, the fabric had stiffened from age and crumbled. She clucked at it. "Never mind." She brushed away the detritus. "It will do."

"For what?" He tried to modulate his tone, maintain brevity

so as not to express too obvious an interest. His mother could neither abide being ignored nor being upstaged.

"After you've eaten—and don't hurry your meal—go give this to the new woman across the road."

"But why?" The sheet reminded him of those used to cover the floor at his father's funeral prayers.

"You men always need a reason." She groaned as she lowered herself into the only chair in the room. Its wicker frame creaked out a threat to snap another string from its woven seat. "Is nothing I need important?"

"Ammi, please." Exhaustion settled in the nape of his neck.

"She's hanging the shawl off her head for a curtain. Who knows where she came from? In what circumstances? A single mother, showing up like that—in a shop, not even a home." She sighed, her brow pained.

"The second story has living space—"

"Tch tch…" His mother dismissed his rationalizing. "She has a daughter with her. We should do what little we can to protect the honor of a young Pakistani woman."

She told him of how, when she had ventured out to the grocer's that morning, she had overheard the construction workers' mothers gossip about how no one had seen the new woman's man yet. They guessed the woman was a cleaner sent by the owner who was finally prepared to sell the building. They wondered about why she kept that shawl draped over her head. "If I could speak their tongue, I'd explain to them she's Muslim."

Even after two decades in these parts of Houston, she refused to converse with "Mexicans"—her designation for all non-desi brown people—in anything but broken English. Haroon wished she'd strike up a friendship with some of her neighbors, so she wouldn't be so dependent on his company.

He rose from his meal to rinse his hands. Catching himself in the mirror, he reached for his comb. Back in the living room, he picked up his mother's gift. "I'll be back."

#

At the shop, uncomfortable with the intimacy of the side door to the rooms above, Haroon knocked on the shutter at the counter. After a second knock, a stream of light flooded from the window above. The shawl had been pulled down.

The woman emerged from the side door, the shawl hastily flung over her head. "It's you."

She'd addressed him in the familiar form in Urdu. Her cadence mellifluous, even in such few words, did not have the quarrel of his mother, nor the wile of the grocer's wife or the Bollywood-inspired flirtatiousness of the grocer's daughters. Her's was the voice he imagined of the narrator of the Urdu fairytales he used to read as a child. Where had those books gone now? He couldn't remember having read anything but English in years.

She had guessed he spoke Urdu as well.

"Yes." He smiled to acknowledge her friendly tone, surprising himself. Flustered, unable to think what to say next, he gestured at the clean shutters. He wasn't sure if he meant to compliment her work or ask her about her plans.

"Thank you. My coffee stand would be open tomorrow if I had some beans and milk," the woman answered both his thoughts. She had understood.

"Ah, a coffee shop." That was all he could muster. He was speaking to a woman. But he spoke to women all day—his colleagues at the school, so many others he had business with. He remembered his business and handed the woman the white sheet with a brief explanation.

"Please, thank your mother for her kindness." She was as calm as he had been abrupt.

He had a question. How to ask it in Urdu without sounding too forward, now she'd chosen to use the familiar address between them? He fretted for the first time that he'd lost his finer sense for the language, speaking it for years only with his mother as a son, and, since his father's passing, as a provider.

"What name can I give my mother?" He'd managed not to say "you" or "your." He wished she'd volunteered it herself.

"Zeenat." She laughed. "And what name can I give my daughter when she asks who brought us this gift?"

A joke. He hadn't volunteered his either. He smiled, found himself shielding behind English. "Haroon. I teach. At Percy High. Math."

She nodded, then continued in Urdu. "We don't have much. Some clothes and dishes, a coffee machine for our shop, and… some sugar."

How strange, yet entirely fitting, that she would have nothing but sugar. He wanted to ask her more, hear her speak more. But he had no more messages from his mother.

"You should open your coffee shop in the morning anyway." He turned away before she could ask what he meant because he wasn't sure yet of anything except that his head rushed.

#

In the morning, hearing him clanging about the kitchen, his mother called out from her bedroom. "What are you doing? I just finished my prayers. I was going to make your breakfast." She stationed herself in the kitchen doorway. "Why the hurry today?"

"I'm leaving now." He brushed past her, a mug of milk and a sandwich bag of ground coffee in hand, ignoring her cries of *Allah, what has gotten into this boy today?*

His heart raced from having been so abrupt with his mother. His supplies balanced in one hand, he grasped his bicycle under his free arm. At the edge of Hillcroft he paused as delivery trucks and speeding commuters honked past each other. He looked over at the coffee shop, expecting the shutters to roll open any moment. There was no way he could cross his daily divide with this new burden.

His eyes roved his side of the road for options. The grocer, lazy pig of a man, never unlocked his doors before eleven. Haroon convinced himself that if he left his bicycle resting against the grocer's door, passersby might assume it belonged to the grocer.

Across, the street, the upstairs window was now shaded by his mother's white sheet, as if she had already blessed the dwelling in her own manner. It had been done out of kindness, out of concern. And yet, and yet. No gift was ever truly free. It was as if she had raced ahead of him, changed the course before he was even upon it.

In front of the shop, as he considered how to announce his presence, the shutter clattered open. Zeenat and her girl stood looking at him.

The girl smiled from behind her mother. She resembled her, but had the gaunt wiriness of youth who had begun to shed their adolescence. He hesitated to smile back because he'd seen the kids at school grin that way when they thought they knew more than the person they hid behind. The girl shrugged and receded to the back of the shop to pick up a book.

He set the milk and coffee down.

Zeenat picked them up. "Will you have some coffee?"

"Yes. Yes, thank you. I didn't have time for coffee at home this morning."

He glanced back to check on his bicycle. It had slipped to the sidewalk, forcing people to walk around it onto the street.

At a nod from her mother, the girl ran upstairs. She returned shortly with as many clean mugs as she could cradle.

Zeenat twisted open her jar of sugar, nestled inside which sat several crushed cardamom pods. As she started the coffee, Haroon told her about his school in the city. He complained about some tiresome students who did everything but the work he assigned them—all things he had planned to tell her as he tossed in bed the night before. In Urdu, he'd promised himself. If he did not talk about himself, he would have to ask her why she had come here, alone, barehanded. He did not want to know who she had been, because his mother was right, there was nothing good Zeenat could possibly say. If he kept telling her about himself, she'd keep asking more in that voice of hers.

When Zeenat turned to attend to the coffee, he checked on his bike. The girl caught him looking that way and came forward to peek as well.

Zeenat poured some of her brew into a tall mug, sprinkled on some sugar, swirled in milk and handed it to him.

He inhaled the subtle scent of cardamom that lingered in the steam. "Won't you join me?"

Zeenat splashed some coffee into a mug, handed it to the girl, and poured a bit for herself. The girl stole away with her coffee, as if afraid it might be taken back.

Zeenat set her own coffee down on the counter, untouched. "Hina's father died last year."

The girl didn't bother to look up from her book. She recrossed her legs nonchalantly as if that statement, the story to follow was stale to her. Haroon set his mug down too. How to keep sipping during such a revelation?

Zeenat glanced once at her daughter and then continued, "His family says I'm cursed since he turned sickly from the day I arrived as his bride in this country. They had expected my youth would guarantee them an heir." The girl kept her eyes averted. "Now they won't keep a cursed woman in their home."

How was it that she could bring herself to tell him all this? How did she know he would not shun her like others from the community might, others had? She was taking a chance. He nodded. "And your family?"

"They're still back in our village. My mother won't accept the shame of a daughter turned out of her marital home. They'd sent me here when I was as old as this one. How can they take me back now with a girl as old as the one they'd given away?"

Hina looked up. "And so, *you* have no home." She spoke in that way teenagers have, of telling ungracious cutting truths.

Zeenat closed her eyes as if drawing on her reserves of patience. "A home is where you make it." She did not turn around but raised her voice for the benefit of her daughter.

Haroon wondered about the girl's accusatory tone. He thought it unfair toward Zeenat. Perhaps Hina had imbibed her grandparents' rhetoric. Children were sponges. How alone

Zeenat must feel. "What will you do?"

"My parents' neighbor's uncle has owned this building for a long time." She described how Mr. Zakir had moved back in his old age because his family in Houston claimed they couldn't afford his healthcare. He was angry with them and refused to sell his only property or bequeath it to them. Somehow, her father convinced Mr. Zakir she could take care of it, though her mother was opposed to the shame of her living here by herself.

"But your husband's family won't have you, and your mother won't have you, so where does she imagine you could live?"

"Such questions are irrelevant for mothers, where moral matters are concerned."

He couldn't argue with the truth of that.

"So, here, I'll earn something and send my girl back to high school. She's missed so much already."

Haroon felt grateful for Zeenat's trust, a heady urge to convince her she could rely on him. Not in the way his mother did, as was her right and his duty. But in the way two people who owed each other nothing might.

"Hina," he ventured, "Would you like me to bring you some books to catch up?"

The girl looked up at him, and then behind him. She grinned once more. "Wasn't that your bike?"

He twisted to see what she meant by the past tense. A teen in sagging pants was wheeling away on his bike.

"Oy!" He raced to cross the road despite the traffic. The boy whipped his head back to look and lost his baseball cap. Haroon picked it up. He was about to throw it at the receding bike when he saw himself falling to the level of the thief. He tossed the cap into the scrub by the edge of the road and trudged back to the shop.

Hina had come up to the front to watch the proceedings. "Sucks," she said, expressionless.

He shrugged, accepting her commiseration.

Zeenat smacked her daughter's shoulder. "What language at

a time like this!"

Hina spun around, grabbed her book and left.

Haroon wished he could defend the girl on this technicality, even though he'd felt little sympathy from her earlier, perhaps even derision. But he didn't know how to explain "sucks" in its entirety in Urdu.

"It's alright," he managed.

"How will you get to work now?" Zeenat looked around the shop as if she might have something lying around that could be of use; as if she was used to hunting for possibilities even in a void.

Absurd. And he had been foolish. He raked his fingers through his hair for a while, then looked up across the road and considered his own street. "I have to go."

As he stepped away, he paused and turned back.

This woman was causing him go against his own survival instincts. First he'd abandoned his bike, and now he was returning to say the goodbye he should have a moment ago. Stopping to take leave never got him anything except instructions from his mother and requests for inconvenient favors from acquaintances. He had learned not to explain himself. "I'll ask the guys in the complex for a ride into town on one of their pickups. Probably get a new bike. But if I do, I'll have to get something for my mother too."

#

That evening, the unfamiliar sight of a cab pulling up to the apartments brought the small children out to ogle. As Haroon hauled a recliner up to the apartment, he ignored his mother's repeated refrains of *What was the need?*

Moments later, his mother, glowing in the bliss of her new chair, did not object to his also having spent a few dollars on books for the new girl. In fact, she sent one of the boys from downstairs to fetch Hina to come get them. Something in the air loosened her tongue; she attempted broken Spanish to instruct the boy.

Zeenat came with her daughter, so Haroon's mother

offered her tea and fed Hina a ghee-laden paratha. "The child needs some meat on her bones." Zeenat was subjected to a piqued glance.

When Zeenat wished Hina had a tutor, Haroon's mother asked what good her son was if he couldn't do this small favor for them. Haroon hesitated, worried about dealing with the girl's contrary attitude, but his mother glared at him. He relented, having learned by now the futility of challenging his mother's judgments of him founded on her own imagination of his intentions.

So, it came to be that he visited the coffee shop several times a week without his mother demanding any explanations from Allah. Instead, she sent along hot chicken curry for Hina, and once, at the Eid festival, even handed him a silk for the girl from her own storage chest. Zeenat made acquaintance with the grocer's wife and through the woman's community connections acquired some spare furniture, including a worktable for the coffee shop, at the end of which Haroon tutored Hina in math.

After her lessons, Hina preferred to take her assignments upstairs and Haroon and Zeenat waited in the coffee shop for her to return with her completed exercises. The two talked mostly of their childhood, both interrupted by a removal to this country.

The grandmother of the boy who had been dispatched to fetch Hina began to visit with Haroon's mother. They found that hand signals interjected with Spanglish and Urdu were adequate language for camaraderie between neighbors. Sometimes, Haroon came home to the sound of laughter that rang of conspiracy between his mother and her visitor. There was an anticipation in the air the women tamped down when they became aware of his presence, readjusting in their seats as he walked by.

One evening, after the visitor had scurried off just before he returned from the washroom, Haroon asked what had caused them to become such good friends all of a sudden.

"Hope." His mother flashed a smile of mutual understanding at him.

Never had a word from her sparked such a twinge of joy in his heart. "Ammi, we need to talk" He sat down to his meal, finding himself hungrier than usual.

"What is there to say, son?" She poured more milk into his glass. "Of course, I approve. I've been waiting for this day for years, and just when I had lost hope in this forsaken land, Allah delivered a daughter to me of his own accord. Now all I need to be at peace is some money for the wedding preparations."

"But shouldn't someone at least talk to her?" He was taken aback at his mother's assumption of acquiescence on Zeenat's part.

"Women understand, my son." She chuckled. "Never mind, never mind. I'll set your heart at ease and go over tomorrow to talk over what is already understood."

"But Ammi, there are things that should be discussed, things you cannot say for me." He pushed his plate aside. "I'll talk to her myself tomorrow."

"What could you possibly need to talk to her about that we women cannot resolve?" His mother sat upright, petulant again in a way she had not been since the new chair.

Where could he begin? If they ever had a lengthy discussion, it was rarely on any matter other than subsistence.

"Our home situation, for one." He got up. "We'd need room for four."

"My dear boy!" His mother eyed his unfinished meal. "What need would Zeenat have to move in with us when she has her shop to run? You and your wife can have my room."

He set down his glass of milk with care, afraid it might spill along with hasty words that would not serve his purpose. She should not be made to feel opposed. He was all she had. She knew that.

"You don't trust your mother, I see." She picked up the Quran that sat on her side table. Her eyebrows took on the pious aspect she reserved for special moments of supplication in prayer. "As God is my witness, I'll treat your wife well, and she will not need another mother."

He strode to the window and scanned the street. Cars rushed past, their headlights mocking him as if he were doomed to stand still forever. He could not bring himself to turn around, look at his mother's face. He could think of no other way to tell her. "I want to marry Zeenat, not the girl."

He heard his mother struggle out of her chair and limp off to her room.

His resolve broke. He followed her and halted in her doorway. She lay on her bed with her face to the wall, a scarf tight around her head—the way she lay whenever her head pounded with a pain caused by the only child born of her womb.

"Ammi, listen."

"You would bring a cursed woman into this house," she moaned at the wall.

He steeled himself for more lines from her favorite Urdu soap operas. "She's only a widow. Like you."

"Which is why she should know better and take pity on me. She did away with her first husband. And now she would enter my home and take away my only blessing. Woe be to the day I let her over the threshold of my house…"

He determined to cancel their satellite TV subscription on the pretext of expense. "She has never, Ammi, never intimated to me any desire of marriage."

His mother sat up. "Don't make it worse, son! Allah protect my ears from such abomination. Do you mean to tell me she consorts with you without considering marriage? Abuela warned me about her. I see now why they allow their own sons and husbands only one coffee a day at her shop, no matter how special they say it is."

"You don't understand." He was struggling. "I would never marry that poor child. Don't you see? She's too young."

"Too young for what?" His mother donned a confused expression. "Abuela says she might even have introduced to us her own granddaughter, who is the same age as Hina, if you didn't have the problem of not being Mexican."

"They're Nicaraguan! And why do you call her abuela? She's not your grandmother!"

"So? She calls me ammi. Am I her mother?"

"You've all lost your minds!" He turned away from her door, sickened, afraid of encountering "Abuela" if he stepped outside.

"I'm not saying anything needs to happen right away, son." She followed him out. "Can't I wait a bit more, when I've waited so long already?" Her voice turned conciliatory. "In any case, we may have to save for a year or two, to have enough for the wedding."

When he didn't respond, she snapped, "Don't underestimate me the way your father used to."

How could she equate him to the man who had smothered her to his last day? The man he swore he would never be to a woman, and especially not his mother. She must know this after all these years. He was tempted to pick her up by the shoulders and shake her. The shock of that impetus propelled him out of the apartment.

"Haroon!" His mother called after him. She sounded distraught, in true anxiety for herself. "What will Abuela say?"

He could think of only one person he'd ever felt the urgent desire to converse with. He traversed his street, found himself at the closed shutters of the shop, went around to the side door, banged on it with his fist.

#

When Zeenat found him at her doorstep, she saw his state and led him upstairs. She must know how inviting him into her living quarters appeared. But she didn't hesitate, so he didn't either.

The stairwell was uncomfortably dark and damp. Haroon was glad to emerge into a lamplit living room at the top. Shutting the door that led to the bedroom, Zeenat offered him a seat on a small plaid couch. Save for a round rug the chair rested on, the room was vast in its emptiness. He wondered if she knew the chair was called a loveseat. He could not take it because of the irony of it. And if he did, then where would she sit? It wouldn't be appropriate for them to sit so close together given all the proper distance the rest of the room afforded, despite its barrenness. Whatever his mother imagined about Zeenat, they had never gone past conversation. The more he wanted her, the more he wanted to wait for her. She was an enigma he hadn't wanted to resolve for two moments of present pleasure. She was to him the misplaced past he wanted for his future.

When he would not take the seat, she sat down first. With a wave toward the other side, she invited him to join her. He sat instead on the rug by her knees and could barely muster the strength not to take her hands uninvited.

Of all the things he wished to tell her in those moments, he found he had waited too long and dared only to begin with his mother's stated wish.

Zeenat listened, her face still, a flash in her eye. "And will you not tell me, what you wish?"

If only he could describe to her all that he dreamt, then pull a switch like a rail operator, split his track from his mother's, carry Zeenat away from the shadow of the accusations she had come here to transcend, to never look back. If only. "I told Ammi Hina is like a daughter to me."

Zeenat searched his face, waiting for more.

His ears burned. He had shifted the burden of their mutual admission, their next turn, to her. Of course, she gleaned this was not the entirety of his argument with his mother, the entirety of his confession to her. They remained silent for so long, Zeenat got up.

He had expected he'd leave if he could say no more, but he found himself unable to stand her leaving. He moved to the chair and reached for her hand to guide her back to the seat. To his relief, she let him. Her hand stayed in his.

Letting out a deep breath, he braced himself. "I told Ammi it is you I want to marry."

She gave him a wry smile. Slid her hand free.

"Have I said something wrong?"

"You once asked me my name so you could tell your mother."

#

When Haroon returned home, he followed the steps past his apartment door as if in a trance, broke out on to the bare flat roof of the building and fell asleep under the open sky. When the sun rose so high the cement beneath him was warm, he awoke. He tumbled downstairs past his apartment. On the ground floor, his bicycle waited for him as on every morning. If he stepped out, his mother might be looking out her window, her white prayer dupatta tucked around her head. She had never spent a night alone.

He tiptoed back up and cracked the door to the apartment. She wasn't at the window. Perhaps she'd taken to her chair to pray on her rosary for his safe return. Most likely, she'd taken to bed, her scarf knotted around her aching head.

He stepped in to the clicking of her gas lighter at the stove.

"I cooked your favorite sooji halwa after my fajr prayers." She did not turn to check on his state. "Go wash up. I even made poori dough—they'll be all fried up by the time you're back."

Halwa poori—each crispy bite a nutty-sweet creaminess enveloped in rich flaky pastry—the meal of communal celebrations. He slammed the apartment door behind him and ran past his bicycle, under the gate, down the street and to the edge of Hillcroft. It was so late, even the grocer had begun to rustle inside his shop.

The grocer poked his head out of his side door, a garbage bag in hand. Seeing Haroon, he snorted. "Why are you not at school today, teacher?" Without waiting for an answer, he flung the bag into a trashcan and slammed his door shut.

Haroon took in the closed shutters of the coffee shop. Upstairs, the dark window gaped. A ripped plastic bag fluttered over the counter of the shop and caught on the bar of the missing awning.

Cecilia Kennedy

Bottled

A cold Pilsner, which my mother carefully poured, arrived just in time for my tenth birthday. My mother served it to me, not to drink, but to examine. She wanted to see if I could sift out its secrets by tilting the glass and watching for signs. Sometimes, the bubbles made a thin line that rose to the top—and that meant change, for the better, though the winds might turn. Sometimes they gathered at the bottom, which meant a long wait or delay in a hopeful outcome. Shadows meant death, and caramel lines or swirls meant the birth of something—or someone. Mom poured all kinds of beers for customers who came to her Tarot card store and believed in crystals and fate, but the real attraction was the beer: lagers, stouts, ports—all of them whispering and bubbling their stories. Above the notes of citrus, cherry, or pine, I'd sift the layers to find that shift moment that made everything clear.

When Mom died, I saw the shadows in a pale ale, but then the bubbles trailed into a caramel swirl, which coincided with the opening of my own shop. And it has provided well, each pour successful—each story unique.

*

The wind shakes the chimes outside the store when I open the door on a Sunday afternoon. A woman comes in, a baby in her arms, and she looks at me the way a child would, eyeing a birthday cake.

"I've never been to a place like this before," she says, in one breath.

She probably thinks she's doing something forbidden, but not too wild—just adventurous enough to satisfy her curiosity.

"Is it true?" she says. "Do you tell fortunes in beer? Do I drink it? How does it work?"

"It's not really a fortune," I say. "It's just stories. The beer tells me something about you. Something you'd wish to know."

But I suspect the people who come to me already know. The reading is more for me. I'm listening for the whispers from the spirits rising from the dead to share their insights. They do more than just keep the lights on. They quench my soul. And I'm always thirsty for more.

This woman, I suspect, is a lager-type, so I choose one from the shelf that's already trembling. It doesn't take much effort to pull the cap off, and when I pour, slowly, tilting the glass so the foam won't spill out over the top, it still does, and I can't control it. I close my eyes and listen to what it's saying, the words becoming an echo in my ear, speaking of changes, imminent danger, uncontrollable outcomes, but they unite in one voice, meant for me: Leave at once!

I'm so rattled, I drop the bottle, and it shatters. I can barely mumble an analysis for the woman—a superficial reading—that leaves her looking deflated.

*

Today, a bridal party schedules a session, and I pull bottles off the shelf: spiced ales, pilsners, IPAs, stouts—and when I open them up, the messages are all intended for me, not the bridesmaids. The voices scream and shriek for me to leave and to stop what I'm doing. I'm at a loss because I love what I do. But word spreads that I'm a sham, and no one comes by the store. The shop fills with angry voices. Every beer I pour is cloudy, a storm in a bottle.

*

On the corner of Pine and Maple, an old brewery stands—abandoned. I go inside to see if I can smell the yeast or any semblance of beer. I miss it so much and the sweet stories it used to tell. I sit in the corner, near the vats and find a lone bottle. When I open it, it unleashes a scream, which I'm used to by now. As the bubbles pour out, I listen closely to the voice's own story of transformation, which I've ignored all these years in order to tell someone else's story. The bubbles rise to the top, which means change, for the better, I suppose.

So I take it as a sign and get to work in the factory, cleaning the vats, learning about hops and temperatures and sugars and yeast, bottling processes and disturbances that might throw everything off balance. When I'm done, and I've taken out my loan, I open my brewpub and use my instincts to choose the perfect beer for each customer, resisting the urge to tell them the future—just relying on a good pour and the soothing whispers that settle.

Paula Mirando

Mr Justin

You get detention for calling your social studies teacher by his first name in front of all the other kids. He says it's because he doesn't want the other students to feel left out because y'all have an existing relationship outside of the classroom—he's the coach for your CYO basketball team—but you're pretty sure it's really because Justin cares a little too much about his reputation at school. He gets flustered whenever someone undermines his authority as a teacher—or worse, mistakes him for a student. So when you slip up in the middle of class, he takes it the wrong way completely and responds with a lunch detention.

When you report to Justin's classroom at the beginning of fifth-period lunch, there's already hella people sitting with the desks pushed together and chopping it up over trays of cheesy potato wedges. Justin's on the far side of the room, wiping down the whiteboard. *Hey, Mr. Baluyot,* you call out, careful to call him by his last name so he knows you're sorry without saying it outright. *What's up, Jericho,* he answers, feigning exasperation. But then he smirks, covertly affirming that y'all are still cool.

You're surprised to see how poppin it is in Justin's classroom. You recognize Angelica, the new kid on the girls' CYO team who just transferred to Barnard-White from Saint Clement, sitting alone, a few of your cousin's friends in the corner reading love fortunes, and the guys you hoop with at lunch when you aren't kickin it with Elijah and the homies at the picnic tables.

You go up to the guys.

Aye, what y'all doing here?

It's Filipino Club.

What do y'all do? Sit around and eat lumpia?

From across the room, Justin reminds you that you aren't

there to socialize. He points to an empty desk in the corner and says to sit quietly and to finish the assignment from class.

The curriculum for eighth grade social studies centers U.S. history—or what Justin describes as "a version of history." It's a presidential election year, so even though your class is two cycles away from becoming eligible voters, Justin wants to "encourage civic engagement" by forcing y'all to fill out a worksheet on the candidates' stances on the hot-button issues. You folded it into a paper football and flicked it across the desk to Elijah until Justin snatched it out of the air.

Surrounded by all the lunchtime chatter, you unfold the worksheet and smooth out the creases. On the front side are short summaries of each candidates' platform and on the back is a chart labeled with different issues—gay marriage, the recession, the war in Iraq. Justin wants you to fill in the candidates' positions. You start to copy the exact wording from the front to the back, absorbing none of it.

Justin claps his hands to get folks' attention and welcomes everyone to the first meeting of Filipino Club. He has everyone go around the room to introduce themselves and share what brings them to the meeting. Most of the responses are reducible to

I'm Filipino and I want to learn about my culture, or

I want to eat Filipino food, or

All my friends are in it.

By the time the guy in front of you turns around to signal it's your turn, you realize you were so distracted listening to everyone else that you stopped writing mid-sentence.

I'm here for detention, you say, waving your half-completed worksheet in the air. Everyone laughs. You don't mind being the funny guy. *I'm Jericho, by the way.* You wink, then glance at Justin to gauge his reaction. He pretends to roll his eyes, but the twitch in the corner of his mouth betrays a smile he's trying to suppress.

Justin uncaps a dry-erase marker and asks folks to shout out what they know about Filipino culture and writes each response on the whiteboard:

Lumpia
Adobo
Pancit
AJ Rafael
Jeremy Passion
Tagalog
TFC
Do you have boypren/girlpren?
Tinikling
Candle dance (pandanggo sa ilaw)
No shoes in the house

Almost everyone adds to the list, except the quiet kids. You chime in to add the *Asian persuasion*, but Justin refuses to write that one down.

Anything else? Justin asks, looking over his shoulder and waiting a few seconds for last-minute responses. When no one speaks up, Justin faces the group, about twenty-five kids, smaller than the average class size. *Alright. Now, what do y'all know about Filipino history?*

We were colonized by Spain, someone says. *For, like, three hundred years.*

Anything else? Justin asks.

You wait for someone to add something, but no one does.

Isn't it strange that's all you know? he asks. *Why is it that, when talking about our culture, we can talk about the fun parts all day—but when it comes to our history, we begin and end with colonization?*

Justin erases everything on the board, all the references to fiesta foods and YouTube singer-songwriters and Lea Salonga as Princess Jasmine.

Filipinos first set foot on this land in 1587, before the United States was even a thought in Fuckboy Chris's head, but you won't find that in your history book. Most textbooks don't mention our cultures at all, which can make it seem like we don't have a history in this country, but we been here.

On the board, he writes: NO HISTORY, NO SELF.

Not knowing our own history creates a void inside us, he says, *a void that can't be filled by anything else.*

Justin returns to the board, the marker squeaking as he adds a *k* in front and a *w* after each *no*, the new phrase reading: KNOW HISTORY, KNOW SELF.

There's something about knowing your roots that does something for your identity—it fills a void that you didn't know was there. You gotta know where you came from to know where you're going.

You lean forward, feel the tectonic plates of your worldview shifting as you hang onto every drop of gospel that passes through Justin's lips.

He continues on about how October is Filipino American History Month because that's when the first Filipinos landed in Morro Bay. He says on the thirtieth, the school will hold an assembly to honor Filipino culture. Justin implores the club members to correct the exclusion—*erasure*, he says—of Filipino American history in the curriculum by sharing what y'all learn in Filipino Club with the rest of the student body.

The warning bell for lunch rings. Justin says that's all for this week, everyone is already in their own conversations, packing lunches into their backpacks as they head off to sixth period.

You go up to Justin to show him your half-filled worksheet. Instead of getting upset with you for goofing off again, he gives you the opportunity to finish it for homework. You thank him for the extra chance, but he brushes you off.

You stand there for an extra second, the paper still in your hand and your half-open backpack slung over one shoulder.

Hey—Mr. Baluyot? you ask, almost calling him Justin again, even though there's barely anyone left in the room to witness it.

Yeah?

Is it cool if I come by again next week? You hesitate to put yourself out on a limb, even though you know it isn't that serious and that Justin—Mr. Baluyot—probably doesn't give a shit.

You want another detention? he asks.

No, uh. You stumble—you never stumble. *For Filipino Club?*

Sure, he says, seemingly unfazed by your interest. He swipes the eraser over the whiteboard to clear away the catchphrase that's already begun to root itself in your subconscious. *Bring Elijah, too, if you want.* You wait for him to say more, maybe special encouragement to come through, but he doesn't say anything else. You take a tentative step back, give him another chance, but he has his back turned. You play it off like you didn't expect anything and leave without saying nothing either.

*

Next week at lunch, Justin lectures on the use of folk dances to mask the instruction of martial arts techniques. He asks whether anyone knows how to dance pandanggo sa ilaw, and this girl Jocelyn raises her hand. Justin invites her to join him at the front of the room and asks her to demonstrate the iconic flourish of the wrist. Because she's put on the spot, Jocelyn doesn't balance a candle or oil lamp in either palm, so the fact that she can twist her arm around without burning herself is less impressive than it should be. No one claps when she's done and her arms fall awkwardly to her sides. Justin thanks her, then tells her to pretend she's about to start again.

When she poses the second time, he cuffs his hand around her wrist, holding it in a lock. *Is this okay?* he asks. Jocelyn shrugs. *Say I'm a Spaniard trying to apprehend a villager,* he says. *I grab her wrist, but*—he turns to her—*do the candle move.* Jocelyn rotates her wrist in the same motion, freeing herself from his grip. This time, she receives scattered applause. Elijah whistles at her as she returns to her seat.

You dedicate every Friday afternoon in October to practicing for the assembly. Elijah complains that it's the weekend and y'all could be anywhere other than school, but he sticks with you anyway. The tinikling group practices on the basketball courts while the eskrima group wanders off to the mid-height chain-link fence which separates the school from the street, gear in tow. You, Elijah, and the other guys—except the baklas, who don't count—choose to be in the eskrima group. Y'all fuck around while Justin is too busy trying to make sure the dancers don't eat shit tripping over the bamboo to discipline you. You play-fight each other without art, whipping one another's arms with the arnis sticks Justin supplied, seeing who can strike hard enough to leave a mark.

Angelica and her weird friend Nina are also in the eskrima group, but they only talk to each other. They follow your gang of lost boys to the outer edge of the yard, arnis sticks still in their protective sleeves, but don't engage. They stand off to the side, not saying anything unless one of the guys tries to mess with them. Even then, Nina's the one who cusses them out. Angelica just watches.

You slap Elijah's ass when you catch Angelica staring at you, but then she snaps her head down to look at the sheath in her hands, thumbing the fabric. Whenever you try to talk to her, she clams up and looks to Nina for reassurance before responding. You don't know what you did to make her so awkward around you. She and Nina are always in Justin's classroom at lunch, so you mention it to him to see if he's heard them say anything about you. He's convinced Angelica's crushing.

Listen, it's not like I'm invested in my students' love lives, he says, *but it's obvious. Whenever you look in her direction, she looks the other way.*

I'm pretty sure she's just shy.

Nah, he says. *Trust me. She likes you.*

For a moment, you consider the implications if this is true. Angelica is what Tita Mai would call big-boned, but that's not necessarily a bad thing. Curvy girls, you think, can be cute. She's in CYO and Filipino Club, so you have those things in common, too.

But there's another half-second when you wonder why Justin's pushing you toward Angelica. You start to regret seeking his advice in the first place. Maybe you just liked the idea of him seeing you in another light—not just a student, but someone capable of being loved.

You take the queue from Justin and start talking to

Angelica. With enough exposure, you figure you could develop feelings for her, which is what you think is supposed to happen. You tease her to make her blush because bullying your way into a girl's heart is a trope in teleseryes, so there must be some merit to it. Still, you try to balance it out with some sweetness. You smile at her in the halls at school. You compliment her when she does well during practice. You even offer to be her eskrima partner when Nina stops showing up to Filipino Club, but she declines.

One day you catch Angelica wandering through the main courtyard, clutching her binder close to her chest, looking lost. You invite her to sit with you and Elijah and the rest of the homies. You appreciate that Elijah is polite to Angelica even though she's stiff and doesn't speak unless spoken to. He's been your best friend ever since first grade, when he shoved your soft face onto the blacktop for complimenting his long eyelashes. Whenever one of y'all invites someone into the fold, the other needs to approve. If they can't hang with Elijah, they can't hang with you either.

*

You got a busy schedule—CYO basketball practice on Tuesdays, CCD on Thursdays, Filipino Club on Fridays, and games almost every weekend during the fall season—which means you're spending a whole lot of your time in and out of school with Elijah and Justin.

Elijah's mom spends most of her time at home and is usually able to pick y'all up from practice, but tonight she can't—Auntie Emmie's cooking up a big batch of suman and needs to wrap each individual serving in a banana leaf before her client comes to pick up the order at 7:00. She's grateful when Justin offers to give y'all a ride home.

From all the extra time you've been spending with Justin, you start to realize that even if he's a hard-ass in the classroom, Justin's a cool dude. Wild 94.9 comes on when he starts the car, and it hits you that he isn't that much older than y'all, maybe ten years, Elijah's half-brother's age. You wonder if that's why he's so uptight about students calling him Mr. Baluyot.

Even though it's almost dinnertime, Justin swings by Tapioca Express on the way back to South Hayward from UC. Justin insists on paying for your drink. He hopes you'll pay it forward someday when you're in a similar position.

It's not as busy in the evening as it is right after school, so you're able to get a table easily. You sit and watch Elijah play with his Tech Deck while Justin waits by the counter for your order to come out.

So, Justin says, flipping his cup upside-down and swirling it to distribute the contents. He ordered something with actual tea, earl grey or oolong or Okinawa or something. In contrast, the artificial color of your green apple slush looks radioactive. *How are things going with Angelica?*

Angelica? Elijah asks. Sure, you've brought her around the lunch table, but this—the idea of you and Angelica—is news to him, and he's supposed to be your best friend. You stab a squid tube with your skewer to avoid the blend of confusion and betrayal on his face.

She sits with us at lunch sometimes, you say.

Don't make it too obvious you like her, Justin warns. *Guys got thick skulls, so they need the extra help, but for girls, it's overkill. Trust me.*

Even though Tita Mai will kick your ass for spoiling your appetite when there's food at home, you polish off the popcorn chicken and squid tubes before cutting out. In the car, Justin plays all the church slaps—Open My Eyes, Trading My Sorrows, Mighty to Save. You all know the words from mass and sing with your whole chests. You cherish these nights after practice. It's the only time you get to kick it with Elijah and Justin without adult supervision, even though Justin is technically an adult himself.

Justin drops you off first. He pulls up to the curb in front of Tito Paul's house. He reaches into the backseat and rummages around the trash on the floor for something. You notice that he has a tribal band tattooed to his right forearm, just below the elbow. You want to touch it, to trace the pattern with your fingertips. But as soon as the thought materializes in your mind, you swat it away.

What's that? Elijah asks. Justin hands you a paperback, the cover partially folded from having been kicked around the footwell by unknowing passengers.

Carlos Bulosan, Justin says. *May be too soon to call, but Jericho strikes me as a future historian. But you gotta know where you came from to know where you're going, so I figured he needs to read a classic from one of the forefathers of Fil Am literature.*

Justin's never mentioned his vision of you as a historian before, so you wondered where this prediction came from, and whether you're capable of living up to such a lofty expectation. A historian sounds so scholarly, so smart, but you're neither of those things. You're just some kid, not even a "gifted" student, not even good enough to make the A-team for CYO basketball.

They got books by Filipinos? Elijah asks.

You take the book into your hands. There's a portrait on the cover of a man in a suit with your same nose and monolids.

I can borrow this? you ask.

For sure, he says. *If you're into this kinda thing, I wanna encourage that interest. I could take you under my wing.*

You've always known you were Filipino, but it didn't mean anything to you other than the fact that the food you ate on Thanksgiving and Christmas was bomb and that it took forever to leave family parties. You remember that thing Justin said at the first Filipino Club meeting—something like, no history, no self. Before then, you wouldn't have thought someone who looks like they could be your uncle would've done anything worthy of being considered "history," but the book in your hand suggests otherwise, a tangible counterexample to what you previously thought you understood about your culture.

As expected, Tita Mai guilt trips you for skipping dinner. Never mind her. You head straight to your room, empty now that lola hasn't had the strength to leave the living room sofa since finishing her last round of radiation. You flip to the first page of Bulosan's book and read until you get a text from

Elijah.

>>*Wtf was that sht bout coach takin u under his wing?*

<<*wut u mean?*

>>*Hes creepin*

<<*how?*

>>*Wen he gave u d book*

The first thing that comes to mind is: maybe Elijah's right. Is it that weird for Justin to want to teach you these things? Half the guys on the CYO team already call him Kuya. They invite him to their club games and to be their Confirmation sponsor when they turn fifteen.

>>*N tips 4 pickin up Gel*

The second thing that crosses your mind is: maybe Elijah's jealous. Because he's supposed to be your best friend, but you told Justin about Angelica before him.

>>*Since wen u been feelin her neway?*

The thing is, you're not even sure if you're feeling Angelica like that. You hardly know her. She's real quiet and innocent, which you think is kinda sweet. It's cute that she's into rock music, despite her good-girl image. But do you *like* her? You don't know. Not yet.

You flip your phone shut and toss it to the foot of the bed. You pick up the book and flip through the pages until you're where you left off. You don't read except for school, and all the books Mr. Pacheco assigned this year are corny so you can't take them seriously. But this one is like a special assignment that Justin came up with, just for you.

At first, you imagine yourself as Allos, the protagonist, and Justin as both of your older brothers, providing books to prepare you for a future beyond your present circumstances. But as you read onward, the image in your mind's eye shifts, and you start to imagine Justin as the main character instead. Picture him in a field, wearing a wife beater and wiping the sweat from his brow, the tattoo on his forearm exposed. Justin unscrewing the cap off a plastic water bottle and lifting it to his full lips to take a long, hard sip.

*

You spend most of your weekday afternoons in Justin's classroom, even though the FAHM assembly's over and there's no more after-school practice. Usually there's at least one or two other guys in there, studying or playing Yu-Gi-Oh or chopping it up. You get a good amount of your homework done while Justin catches up on grading or whatever he does on school days. Sometimes you bug him with random questions, like what was he like when he was in high school and how did he start coaching and has he always wanted to be a teacher, and even though he rolls his eyes and asks whether you couldn't redirect this curiosity toward your studies, you feel he secretly enjoys the attention. Sometimes you don't leave school until 5:00 because you'd rather hang out with him than go home.

Your English teacher, Mr. Pacheco, assigns a report for every book you read in his class. He requires you to print it out and read it to the class, which is a waste of time cause no one listens and it takes hella days, but you have to do it because it's the only advanced class you're in and you don't want to blow it. You don't have a printer at home, so you ask Justin if you can use his computer to type up your essay and he agrees. Really, you could've gone to the media center, but you'd rather kick it with Justin than Mrs. Dennings-Leung.

You go straight to Justin's classroom after seventh period. When you get there, it's empty except for Justin, who's standing at his desk and biting into a green apple. He leans forward to type in his password with his free hand, then steps aside to let you behind the teacher desk. The computer chair is too low for you, so Justin pumps the lever under your seat to raise its height and corrects the position of your wrists so they don't rest on the table. Your skin tingles where your fingers touched you, like static without the shock.

You already wrote out the whole paper in your notebook, so all that's left is to type it up. You focus on the keyboard, typing with your pointer fingers and glancing up at the monitor after every few letters to check for mistakes. You shouldn't have messed around so much when you had keyboarding as your elective in sixth grade, the one class where the shit you learn is applicable in real life. Now you gotta hunt for every single letter.

By the time you tell Justin you're done, the soft light in the mottled glass window has dimmed to a dark gray color. The wall behind the desk is covered with wallet-size graduation photos from former students who loved Justin and hoped he would remember them. You understand the sentiment. Justin doesn't look away from the essay in his hand, eyes scanning the text. When he gets to the bottom of the page, he sets the paper down and presses his thumb and forefinger to his temples.

How are you getting home? Justin asks.

Bus.

Need a ride?

Justin's given you tons of rides home from practice, so you don't think anything of it. You follow him to the front of the school where Justin's Civic is parked on a patch of dirt and gravel. You toss your stuff in the back and hesitate before getting in. Whenever Justin's given you rides in the past, it's been you *and* Elijah, so y'all would sit together in the back. But today it's just you. You shut the door to the back seat and get in on the front passenger side. Justin gets in on the driver's side and waits for the car to warm up.

You get a chance to read Bulosan? he asks.

Even though you had to reread a few passages over and over again cause the prose was too dense, you finished the whole novel in a weekend.

Yeah.

What'd you think?

You don't want to disappoint him. You wish you could tell him that the book transformed you, that you *finally* understand what it means to be Filipino. There was so much in the book that was new to you, things you didn't know happened to Filipinos in this country, and things you wish you didn't know. A part of you wishes he'd given you guidance so you would know what to focus on and what it all *meant.* But at the same time, there's a voice in your head berating you for expecting him to hold your hand when he's already done so much to teach you about your history, and you couldn't even figure out this small piece on your own. You're afraid that if he finds out you don't get it, he'll realize you're dumb as rocks, not worthy of calling him your kuya. He'll realize you're not special, just some stupid kid.

It was alright.

Justin holds his palms up to the air vents, warming his hands. You do the same, rotating your wrists so you get both sides.

Hungry? he asks.

He backs out of the lot and drives down the road to 7-Eleven. He asks what you want. You'll eat anything. He leaves you in the car with the heater on while he runs into the store.

He's in there for a while. You look through the junk in the footwell of the passenger seat and find a McDonald's bag full of trash and a cloth CD case filled with a bunch of mixes labeled in Justin's handwriting: Disney classics, ballads, 90s R&B. You don't know why this is in the car, considering it only plays cassettes.

You get antsy waiting, afraid Justin will catch you snooping through his stuff. You take the keys and go inside. He's standing in the aisle, holding a bag of Bugles and two beef chimichangas in both hands. He hears the bell over the door ring when you walk in and beckons you over, asking if his selection is okay.

The bell rings again and when you turn around to see who it is, it's one of the preppy girls from your social studies class, Kayla. *Hey, Mr. B,* she says. Her eyes move from Justin to you. *Oh. Hey.* She's with her mom, who fake-smiles at Justin with closed lips before ignoring you both to request a pack of Marlboros from the clerk.

Justin breaks away to line up behind Kayla's mom, meanwhile Kayla walks up to you.

What're you doing here? she says.

Nothing, just getting some food with Mr. Baluyot, you say, trying to play it cool, like you and Justin kick it after school all the time, which is technically true. This girl is insignificant to you, but you're glad to be spotted outside of school with Justin. It cements your relationship as special, not confined to a single context. *He's gonna give me a ride home.*

Kayla's mom glances back to mean-mug Justin. *It's not like that,* he says, holding his hands up, palms out. You aren't sure what's got him so defensive, but his reaction makes you embarrassed for both of you.

Oh, okay, is all Kayla says, scanning the colorful row of plastic chip bags. *See you at school, I guess.*

Kayla's mom finishes paying and then so does Justin, and you all leave the store one after the other. Justin won't look at you as he gets into the car, or even after Kayla and her mom drive off. You run your mind back to figure out what you did wrong, but you don't know what it is.

Listen, he says, dropping his hands down from the wheel. A worry line creases his forehead. *I've been meaning to talk to you.*

You know I'm here for you, he says. *Whenever you need anything, I gotchu.*

The words are measured and deliberate, well-spoken but with enough vernacular mixed in to suggest that he's trying to level with you, to let you know he's just like you, which is something folks only do when they're talking down to you.

But I'm your teacher, he says. *I don't want folks to think I'm giving you special treatment. You understand?*

You don't, not when it was only a few weeks ago that he was treating you to boba and lending you books from his personal library. He said he thought you could be a historian. You don't even know what a historian does, but it made you feel like he saw something in you that no one else noticed or thought to nurture. He was supposed to take you under his wing.

I'm still your coach, though, he says, gazing out the windshield or into the rearview mirror, his gaze landing anywhere but on you. *I can still give you and Elijah rides after practice. You can still talk to me when something's bothering you.*

He drums his fingers against his kneecap. *Are we… cool?*

Justin bounces his leg, wiping the sweat from his palms on the dark denim of his jeans. You notice the faded brown oxfords on his feet and wonder if he's been wearing those to seem more teacher-y.

You reach across the center console to dap him up. Mr. Baluyot is a cool dude. You're the one who forgot your place.

Jill McCorkle

A Simple Question

There was something in the late winter light that tugged Anna's mind to that day and she wasn't sure why. Over twenty-five years had passed and yet there it was- a gray winter afternoon and a long-ago friend. They were in the parking lot across from the theatre—the Colonial—she remembers that part clearly, and she had to walk carefully to avoid lingering patches of ice. She wasn't wearing her boots, having opted to risk the good shoes, but then was sorry not to have the security of hard rubber traction. It was a Sunday in late February and the whole day had felt like dusk. The show crowd had thinned and the last of the cars were filing from the lot. They had gone to see *Death of a Salesman,* the matinee, and while walking around before the show, had actually seen Hal Holbrook sitting in a restaurant. Was it really him, they wondered. How could he eat? They stared too long because he smiled and raised his hand. She will never forget that, the image returning so clearly with the recent news of his death. But that day, in the city with Muriel, their words and laughter muffled by scarves and coat collars, it had made her recall seeing a striking man on Charles Street years before- an elegant camel hair coat and trimmed moustache. She told Muriel she knew it was either Walter Cronkite or Captain Kangaroo and after a stunned pause had let out a loud involuntary *Walter Cronkite*! He turned, smiled and waved and she was so relieved she hadn't screamed *Captain Kangaroo*! They laughed and then Muriel said she had something she wanted to ask- how had she said it*? I want to ask you something* or *I have a question*. Then she said that perhaps it would be better to wait until they were seated, or after the show, better without all the distractions. She said this when Anna stopped to study the menu of a restaurant, suggesting they eat there some time, perhaps the next time they met for a show.

At the time, Anna was thinking a lot about her apartment, a

small one bedroom, fourth floor walkup. She was thrilled not to have a roommate but also missed having someone to share her life, someone that is, other than Muriel who people might very well have thought was her mother. Muriel got divorced later that year so it could have been something about that, maybe she'd known it was coming and wanted to run her thoughts by someone else. And she often talked about her son who had left college in the middle of his freshman year and moved back home—so there was another possibility.

Anna had thought often what unlikely friends they were—Muriel was twice her age—and yet, they had a lot of common interests and taught at the same junior high school, both in language arts. They both loved walking around the city, going to the theatre and museums, and they both disliked their principal, a man who stood too close and explained everything in exaggerated enunciation as if talking to a toddler or dog. *Or imbecile*, Muriel once added. Anna was barely 25 when she took that job and had known no one so she had welcomed seeing Muriel each day, the wry glances at meetings and laughter at lunch.

It had been only natural that they began to get together outside of school. In those early years, Muriel was encouraging in all ways, telling Anna she would have a host of friends in no time, that she was a stellar teacher, that she imagined Anna would soon have all kinds of dates, and then who knew where life would take her. *Enjoy this window,* Muriel had said and laughed. *You won't believe how quickly things can change.* Muriel seemed old at the time, a husband and a child in the seventh grade, a house in the suburbs; she often brought baked goods—bread or cakes—for the break room at school. That was in the very beginning and Anna relied on her maternal goodness, the care and hopeful future projections of what Anna's life might bring. They laughed over Anna's domestic mishaps- the time she purchased MSG for a recipe, the fact that she didn't know a dryer filter had to be cleaned or that you shouldn't put grease down the sink. Back then, Muriel had said that she was the happiest she had ever been and felt closer to her husband than she ever dreamed possible. Their son had some challenges in school, but he was about to turn thirteen and doing so much better. They had hired a tutor; they were hopeful. Such a relief for him to have a friend, she had said.

Anna wasn't domestic at all then, but she loved everything about her first tiny apartment except the pigeons roosting on the windowsill and the squirrels living in the walls. At night she could hear them, acorns rolling, nails scratching, even though the landlord had assured her that he had it all under control. He said he really doubted they would find a way into the apartment. He said it had only happened once in the thirty years he'd been there; he could set a trap, and would if it got worse, but that really is a horrible sound, he said, not to mention that they'd all be smelling it. *It's a quandary*, he kept saying. *And remember—squirrels are not rats and it's almost spring.*

It was a breezy February day. Valentine hearts and cardboard cupids decorated the window of a stationery shop from the week before and she recalled Muriel commenting about the groundhog having seen his shadow—more cold coming. She doesn't remember telling Muriel about the squirrels in the wall and the way she could hear them scratching right near her bed, but she must have, especially with the mention of another rodent.

She recalled how she had envied those like Muriel with so much of life fixed and decided in their suburban backyards, garage doors that magically opened to a kitchen the size of her whole apartment, a life partner, a child, a pet. She was only at Muriel's home a few times, the son's bar mitzvah her first and she was only invited because she mentioned in the teacher's lounge that a friend had broken a date and she had nothing to do. Muriel even arranged a ride for her with another teacher in their school. Anna remembered how Muriel's husband had raised a glass and said *today you are a man and tomorrow you go back to seventh grade!* Muriel and her husband stood together that day, arms entwined, their son out on the dancefloor laughing with a new confidence to have this moment of popularity. Another time, Anna was shopping out that way and stopped by to return a book Muriel had loaned her and was invited in at what seemed a stressful time; there was an uncomfortable pause when she found the three of them in the kitchen, sitcom laughter in some distant room. The son was in high school then, applying to schools, smoking a lot of pot. Muriel said that every time she tried to talk to him, to understand what was going on in his life he said: *You want to know what's wrong with me? How about what the fuck is wrong with you?*

The question Anna recalls vividly was the one he asked at his party when he was thirteen and reading aloud from a book of riddles he'd received as a gift. The spotlight was on him and it was clear that his parents were enjoying his getting attention as much as he was. There were all the silly riddles of course—hands and legs/clocks and chairs—but the one Anna recalls was: *what is the question you can ask anywhere in the world, get different answers each time and yet always be correct.* She could see him there, hair cowlicked, crust of chocolate cake on the edge of his mouth. He was an awkward kid who came into the room and everything was instantly topsy turvy, lamp shades crooked and rugs flipped up; it seemed he was always on the verge of nervous laughter because he had a secret or knew something you didn't.

In high school, there were suspensions and drugs. He told his mother that he wished he was dead, and then later that he wished *she* was dead. Muriel had told Anna that while they were walking Beacon Hill on the third Thursday in May—a day devoted to the annual garden tour when they made their way along the uneven brick sidewalks to peer into tiny often sunless spaces transformed into paradise—brickwork in elaborate patterns, mirrors and fountains and statues. They read aloud the descriptions in the program, the various plant names like incantations that might open the wrought iron gates and heavy ancient doors that led to other lives: trumpet vine and bleeding hearts, astilbe, pulmonaria, laurel, lilac, euonymus. *What can a mother say to that?* She asked. *God.*

Another day, they made up their own tour based on Muriel's idea—apartments of long dead writers—three on Pinckney Street alone: Alcott and Thoreau and Hawthorne. Plath on Willow and Frost on Mt. Vernon. Muriel's idea was that they should read something at each stop, and she had books in her tote with pages carefully marked. They had stood at the foot of Pinckney Street, the river at their backs, before climbing up the hill and it was there Muriel had pointed to a third floor bay where she had once lived with two other young teachers, a view of the river and a preschool across the street where at recess, kids all bundled in snowsuits, held onto a long rope with a teacher on each end; if one started to slip on the icy bricks, they yanked the rope and popped them right back up.

"I wish you could have known my son when he was a toddler," she had said and smiled but it was hard to pull together the image of a windblown, bundled cherub with the awkward, riddle telling boy, and especially not the angry young man who wished her dead. "When I was your age and up in that window," she paused, then shook her head as if to dispel whatever words were coming next and reached for one of her many quotes selected for the day: Plath's *numb as a fossil. Tell me I'm here* to Alcott's *I hate ordinary people.* She never let the somber tone last too long, always looking for something that might bring a smile, and perhaps that was what was different on that February day. The lifts were getting harder and harder to find.

And for Anna, it was getting harder and harder to listen to the sadness and the denial in her voice, the blame of the boy's father, his teachers. It was hard to respond to the regret and grief, that episode his freshman year; everything seemed okay and then. *And then.* How many times had Muriel told that story? He drained his bank account and got out on the highway. They had no idea where he was, and it was days before he called from a motel in Tucson without any money. Her husband had called her an enabler, said he couldn't take it, and then got a divorce, a new wife, a new life but that was all later of course, and information Anna only heard second hand from another teacher in the school who lived in the same town. That day at the theatre, Muriel had checked her phone often, a weak smile if she saw Anna notice.

But what was the question? *There's something I want to ask you*, she had said. Did she wait for intermission, or did they never circle back? They had great seats, Hal Holbrook completely transformed into Willy Loman, and afterward, when they stood in the parking lot and talked about the play—how Linda Loman said: "he's only a little boat looking for a harbor;" they marveled at the power of those words and the effect of staring at the set—the house where they had lived and struggled—*lived*—while also seeing what was not on stage, the distant crash of Willy's car wrapped around a tree, the shocking end of it all and what about those haunting last words *we're free*. A mortgage all paid. Something completed, and yet. *And yet*. Anna will remember that for the rest of her life, that February day, the sharp smell of the river ready to thaw, exhaust from the Turnpike trapped in the low ceiling of gray. *We're free*.

At some point in one of the many conversations along the way, Anna had voiced horror that Muriel's husband kept a gun locked in his closet; she'd told Muriel she would *never* live with a gun in the house and that it was absolutely clear her son needed treatment, perhaps serious medication or tough love as she'd read about recently and seen on television, Oprah or Jane Pauley, someone talking in the background while she straightened her apartment for another day and looked forward to going out with friends her own age. Finally, friends her own age, too many friends it seemed and a relationship that would carry her into the future and her *real* life. "I bet once he gets straightened out, his dad will want to return and then you'll have a decision," she had told Muriel. "That will be a big decision, won't it? Whether or not you let him come back. And what about some day when your son gets married? You can tell all these stories to his fiancée and everyone will laugh." Now, she shudders with the thought.

Muriel smiled, or what at the time seemed a smile, as if to say, oh yes, how smart, you are so right. As if suddenly, the light blared through and she realized something she hadn't seen before and yet, now isn't it obvious that what she was really thinking was, *oh my dear ignorant friend, you know nothing. Wait until you have children; wait until the person you have vowed to share through thick and thin can't take it anymore. Just you wait.* But she also was above saying such a thing. The words *just you wait*, would not have occurred to someone like Muriel.

What time is it? That was the answer to that long ago riddle, the universal question that yields different answers but all correct. A thirteen-year-old boy stands in the spotlight, his five minutes of glory, proud parents with their arms entwined, kids from school gathered around him, new suit, shiny belt and shoes, a tie purchased just for the occasion. His party, his celebration, his step into manhood. On that day, he had friends and proud parents and the gift of not knowing all that lay ahead of him.

And here she is, years and miles from that day in a town not unlike Muriel's where children wait in front of the house for the school bus to arrive. A place where the local news reports are the kind that get laughed at by the rest of the world: someone dumped trash in the recycling bin at the grocery store- a squirrel was in a tree acting strange- heads of cabbage were tossed around and left on the school ground. *Why?*

Now, standing at the sink, making the bed, staring out the window, grading papers, the thought of all the words not spoken seizes her. *Dear Muriel,* she thinks. *Dear Muriel,* and she thinks how sometimes the Universe gives an answer before we understand the question. There in the dark theatre, there at the end, they sat in silence. The scene plays and even knowing what is coming, they are shocked by the crash, shocked by the humbling sense of loss and awareness of how vulnerable each life. Muriel has been dead for several years now, her son as well, and yet each time Anna remembers there is shock. By the time she heard about Muriel's illness, Anna was at a different school, and it was only by chance she ran into an old colleague who mentioned it—Muriel's years with her son and the sad choice he made, then her own health issues she kept to herself. This question comes to Anna: if she went to the city and walked those same steps, would she see something? Hal Holbrook in a restaurant? *Death of a Salesman* on the marquis? Willy Loman resurrected and once again filled with hopeful promises? Would she see her young single self step from her dark apartment and hurry along the city streets to see Muriel waiting there on the corner with a big smile, hands deep in the pockets of her down coat?

They sat that day, elbows touching, not a sound to be heard in the theatre as their minds fixed on the imagined accident in the distance, the same way her mind now can't think of Muriel's old house without seeing her son, hanging there in the mudroom where a Little Tykes tractor had grown invisible over the years. But that day, after the curtain call, after the lights came up, they walked outside where it was almost dark and lingered in the parking lot. It was their last outing. Anna is almost sure of that now, and what did she even do in her apartment that she rushed back to that day? She was eager to get home, hands in pockets and head bent to the cold, an urgency in her steps as she walked the many blocks. Did she stop in Blockbusters for a rental? DeLuca's for something she couldn't afford to eat? Did she call her still living parents or wait until the next day to avoid the slow blue Sundays that plagued her for much of her young life. Did she watch something mindless on television? Knit? Grade papers? Did she even wonder what it was Muriel had wanted to ask or was she distracted by the fact that there were squirrels in the walls and a pigeon roosting on her bedroom windowsill that overlooked an alley and dumpster, and she had boxes to pack, a move up ahead; she was moving into her life. It was a dark Sunday in February when she had no husband, no children, no mortgage. Her parents were alive and far away, healthy enough that she could complain about hearing from them and not worry for a minute. She hadn't known what it felt like for a parent to die or for a marriage to feel threatened, for a child to lash out in anger; she hadn't known how sometimes you just need someone to listen. That day she had walked quickly, protecting shoes she tossed out twenty years ago, then climbed the four flights of stairs to her dark tiny space where an old radiator whined and some creature with no sense of time clawed at the walls to get free.

John Saul

The Possibilities

The Possibilities (band)
from *Wikipedia*, the free encyclopedia

Name

The Possibilities was not intended to suggest the band members possessed any particular talent but that there were always possibilities for corrections, adjustments and improvements, especially given the extent of electronic sound engineering and recording techniques. In an interview (Rolling Stone RS 157) Joel FitzP, widely regarded as the band's leader, said literature had for hundreds if not thousands of years been doing exactly this—correcting, revising, aiming to achieve the best *possible* result. The band members saw themselves as exploring manifold possibilities. Ironically, the pervasive effect of auto-correction software may also be responsible for the band often—mistakenly—being referred to as *The Possibles.*

Personnel

Joel FitzP, leader, vocals and keyboards. Josh MacPherson, guitars. Graham Harrington (formerly of *Box of Swifts*), vocals, keyboard bass and cajón**[1]**. Julie Weston, vocalist, intermittent participant.

History

In its original constellation The Possibilities was formed in the Porthmadog area of North Wales in the 1990s. A 'riotous mixture' (Joel F) of backgrounds lay behind the band, with parents being a civil engineer (Graham H), decorator and chef (Julie), and egg merchant (Joel). Josh's mother Sally became a judge and his father a negotiator for a multinational oil company. Only Julie (see Wikipedia entry) had any directly musical background.

Development and legacy

The Possibilities prime dictum was to perform first and later to reflect (this could include study, reconfiguration, time out, and particularly lateral thinking) on what direction to take next. The music was mostly improvised, followed by or coupled with words, art and dramatic performance. When at the height of their joint career Graham H withdrew to the Orkney Islands, seeking both a change and the opportunity to write a much fuller improvised piece (which after constant transformation became the book *The Interest in Going North*), a spokesperson for the band let it be known one of their strongest impulses was to keep (some) 'things modern' at arm's length, in particular to avoid all [the kind of experiences] that television had hitherto been able to offer. (While the so-called yellow press was all too ready to describe this or themselves as the 'new Luddites', it was never technology itself that was brought into question.) Whereas in reality, the reality of everyday lives, people worked, ate, shopped, loved, or travelled (north, say), in the many dramas on television and other media there was a preponderance of dead, often mutilated bodies—there was a blatant disjunct between realities, between everyday experience and the scenes broadcast on screens. The audience for the latter is drawn in, to speculate who might have carried out the killings, and possibly why, while only rarely is any one of the bodies or their killers or pursuers in any way genuine. Graham H thus for instance reported himself 'entirely unsurprised' that he came across nothing of the sort when away on his sojourn north. Perceived as it was by The Impossibilities, this yawning chasm between media-created living and actual life led to the milestone creation now referred to as *The Pane*, not available in any purchasable or consumable form. At the height of critical success for *The Pane* band leader Joel FitzP also became embroiled in (a notorious murder case) what became known at the Allerton Affair, which was swiftly followed by the dissolution of the band.

Landslide (songs)

These songs, which exist only in very fragmented form, refer to the Landslide Indictments, so called for the legal decisions made in English-speaking countries within a short period of twelve months partly as a result of the activities of Julie Weston (see entry 'Julie Weston') and her associates. Unofficially at least, the entire texts/lyrics are attributed to her. Sound engineers for some time puzzled over why it had proven so difficult to acquire or improve the quality of recordings of public performances of Landslide (or indeed any works) by The Possibilities. A plausible explanation for this is that recording devices were controlled and if necessary confiscated at the concert doors, ostensibly to ensure that only one good-quality recording would be made (Steven Lay, Lay Music). At the doors it was also made clear that any obvious interference with the sound—calls or whistles overlapping with the beginnings, ends, or quiet passages of songs—would see the recording of that piece scrapped and destroyed. The rationale behind this is complex and based on a quasi-spiritual belief held by Graham H, who believed the act of recording would severely lessen the experience of a performance for both the recordist (and any of the audience aware of a recording) and musicians. This position, he explained before the camera on *SkyArts*, was a carry-through from the more widely known notion where the use of phones and selfies—he and others now claim, in the aftermath of decades of mobile phone usage—results in the transformation of experience, often to the point where the users in later life have absolutely no recollection of what they—according to any records or diary entries they may have—saw or heard. The audience seemed for the most part to be aware of this position and respect it. Among the band's devotees this position, or contention, became known simply as 'the Harrington'.**[2]** In a further twist to this ban on or disapproval of unauthorised or amateur recordings: unbeknown to all but an innermost circle, Steven Lay did not in fact make any recordings either—again, on account of 'the Harrington'.

Influences

Between them The Possibilities spanned an astonishing breadth of musical interests and influences. They included not only the well-trammelled repertoires of blues, folk and rock music, but also and more unusually, popular music of broader times. Jazz and classical influences were also apparent in their performances, as were moments, if not passages of rap and avant-garde. The more contentious the latter forms were, the more interested The Possibilities would be, most particularly Joel FitzP. In particular, attentive listeners have mentioned having heard MacPherson inserting melody from Tchaikovsky's violin concerto, albeit with the timing altered, just as Graham H could find the timbre of a George Michael, Cliff Richard or even Paloma Faith in his combination of voice and microphone. While 'Landslide' appears to have no strict musical connection to the song of the same name by the Dixie Chicks (now Dixies), the lyric 'and I took it down' was heard on occasion.

References

[1] A cajón (Spanish: [kaˈxon]; "box," "crate" or "drawer") is a box-shaped percussion instrument originally from Peru, played by slapping the front or rear faces (generally thin plywood) with the hands, fingers, or sometimes implements such as brushes, mallets, or sticks.

[2] "You mean we can't record this?"
"No, it's the Harrington."

Resources

Allerton (Joel FitzP, Sefton Press, People & Places series)
Call it Tender (Palm Court, 2007)
These Are Our Lives (Stinging Fly, Ireland 2006)
Landslide, a study in the dark (Schuldt, 2002)
New Musics 5 (Vintage, 1998)
Cold Comfort (Palm Court, 1996)
New Musics 2 (Vintage, 1995)

Border Lines (Palm Court, 1994)

This page needs **additional citations for verification.** Please help by adding reliable sources.

Allerton Affair

from *Wikipedia*, the free encyclopedia

The facts of what became known as the Allerton affair continue to be disputed despite all court judgements having been made and appeals exhausted. Allerton was a text created and made public by the musician Joel FitzP. 'We dipped into it from time to time,' he told the photographer Mark Albright. All charges against Joel FitzP were dropped when there surfaced DNA evidence which it was adjudged exonerated him. He did know the murdered woman**[1]** and had depicted her publicly and (so it was contended) in such a way as to have cast suspicion on his person**[2]**, but that was all. Suspicion unfortunately for him only increased when he decided to disown the text (and music, since lost or destroyed). The affair led to Joel FitzP withdrawing from public performances for almost three years, effectively ending his hitherto highly successful collaboration with members of the band The Possibilities.

This page is a **stub. You can help *Wikipedia* by expanding it.**

<u>References</u>

[1] details withheld at the behest of the family.

[2] The relevant text is in the public domain and is reproduced here:

[Allerton]

The Susan Duff syndrome: lying awake at night, the thought of someone appears. The one thought burgeons into several. Your head carries the thoughts with you, off the pillow, into the shower, down the stairs to breakfast, out of the door. Susan Duff being the first, the most persistent, the most frequent, the phenomenon is named after her.

It's years since I saw her last—on the tennis court in her almost-white kit, walking to the base line, about to receive serve. Her walk is unremarkable. The on-court air is a film of paprika, scuffed up from the red clay, which is essentially brick dust. This playing surface used to break up easily, particularly in summer, until dust covered tennis shorts and shoes, legs and forearms, hair, eyelashes, everything. I remember one club member in the shack by the courts declaring: This is no place to unwrap a sandwich. Said another: Blow your nose and it comes out pink. Pink is not accurate, but you can't stop people saying what they say.

Her age? Fifteen? She doesn't grow older. I must have seen her take the little path from the cabin to the road but don't remember her on it. She comes by herself, there's no sign of brothers or sisters, parents. She won't leave the court, she exists only there. Her walk to the base line is on a loop, which recently has been repeating for days, I should say nights.

Always when I went to the little club on the hill I hoped to see her. Because of her I selected my newest, brightest Slazenger balls before setting off; the thought of her had me checking my racket strings assiduously (as if I knew how to string them; I didn't). She was a girl, older than myself, who I innocently and passionately desired. Innocently, because I would do nothing. Desired? I desired only a few words or a little time together, not much by today's standards but for a fourteen-year-old in those days, a lot.

Her name I knew from the competition draw pinned up in the shack, although by then she'd been knocked out. Some people never get to hold a little silver cup and she was one. So was I. But she fitted the little club on the hill. Her sandy complexion perfectly complemented the court surface. In a warm-up with her partner and opponents, the surface would rough up enough to produce that red fizz amid which her legs and ankles blended so harmoniously. Even her freckles, careful freckles, were indistinguishable from particles of the dust. By 'careful' I mean they so matched the court it was as if someone had carefully arranged them. But so what? Why return to her in the dark, the dawn, take her with me down the street, onto the platform, the train, the office?

There were two courts. When I was fortunate enough—it activated the teenage thrill centre—to find Susan Duff also at the club (inexplicably, she was always there before me), I would as usual join three strangers, usually older, looking for a fourth to make up the numbers. Negotiating the gate that clanged so, they entered the courts as relaxed as if into their own garden. In contrast, I would be in the far more difficult position of yearning to look at Susan Duff while trying desperately to conceal the fact. Walking past her as casually as I could, I would drop the Slazengers (their brightness now embarrassing), or my racket would suddenly snag on the wire netting (a nigh physical impossibility, which I alone would manage), or I would tread on a lace that had grown too long (thus nudging me towards becoming a devotee of velcro); or the person in front would stop suddenly just as I was casually glancing aside (having resolved in all circumstances to look casual). Undone: the opportunity to take in Susan Duff's sandy hair and careful freckles would be lost. My embarrassment at whichever of these inevitable mishaps (then major, only now trivial, after years for them to settle and fade) would cause her to smile, but not at me, it would be with her head half turned towards the net. Not once can I remember her looking my way, and not once did we play a game together.

So, once again Susan Duff has arrived in the murky flotsam of sleep and hasn't left me all morning. She crossed the station barriers with me, rose twelve floors in the lift, and as I poke at this sushi lunch she's there still. I wrack my brain for more details. But I only see her, as always, walking back to the base line, her whites getting dusted in that colour, about to receive serve. In my head she never serves; a point with her is never completed, let alone a game, a match.

I remember there was also a church at the top of the hill. It had the same dark sandstone as the streets. Did Susan Duff go there, I think so. Her short hair suggested something conventional, even puritan. She could easily be imagined singing, praying. She may equally have given her soul to the Almighty, at least for the time being.

I doubt she'll flash before me at my dying moment. That I imagine differently: without a thought of dying, most likely I'll be in the middle of something. Someone is speaking; a van has pulled up outside; the doorbell has rung; I'm about to answer a question; but I don't. So no final flash-by, no last run-through—more likely is a steady stream, over years, of incidents and people. By day or night, little bits at a time flashing up, like flakes off the tennis court, Susan Duff, a church on a hill. That's where she fits in, as a glimpse, her getting dust on both legs. The surface had a fake-tan colour and may still have, a colour that managed to fit Susan Duff perfectly, and probably still would, and still does, there on the court on the hill in Allerton, as she walks back to the base line, waiting to receive serve.

Julie Weston (singer and activist)
from Wikipedia, the free encyclopedia
For other people named Julie Weston, see Julie Weston (disambiguation)

Julie Weston was a Canadian singer and activist whose work focused on the rights and aspirations of women.

Early life

Born in British Columbia, from where her doctor mother later took up an international post administering vaccination programmes, Julie Weston was brought up in Vancouver before later moving with her parents to Denver, Colorado. Both her mother and father, she said, were 'highly musical'. She would join them at the piano, sat between them on the piano stool, her feet well clear of the ground. As a young teenager she would go with brothers or sisters to concerts and to clubs, where—she remembered among several acts—she saw and heard Muddy Waters ('the thrill when he played, unrivalled') and ('with her small guitar, delightful') Mimi Farina. In Vancouver, despite their professional lives the family lived in 'the hippy quarter' of Kitsilano. 'You could do what you wanted, that was what mattered.' She ('we knew our microphones') and her two brothers and two sisters were regularly asked to sing to inaugurate local events.

Formative experiences

In her early twenties Julie accompanied a pregnant woman—'we happened to meet on the street, it was as simple as that'—to the courthouse in Denver, where a case involving the woman's fiancé and several acquaintances saw her vindicated. This led Julie to accompany other women ('when I saw them hurry up the courthouse steps, I knew there was trouble') and to informally organise women to accompany other women in numbers to similar cases and soon to more overtly political lawsuits. This informal organisation took place quietly and without show (stealthily, came the accusation from opponents). It never became a movement as such. Indictments against hangers-on of the ex-President and other figures on that periphery were quickly followed by numerous central persons landing in prison, even after appeals. Pornography, prostitution and sex trafficking were all causes she took up, 'speaking out regularly before stepping back into the shadows' (New York Times). Besides speaking out, she sang out, fearlessly ruffling feathers at will with her lyrics, most notably in the Landslide song series. Although Julie Weston did not herself take up law in the professional sense she studied law and wrote copious notes, which her sister Rusty described as being 'like essays, only very short, and not sweet'.**[1]**

References

[1] held by the estate of Julie Weston and not publicly available

Graham Harrington (musician)
from *Wikipedia*, the free encyclopedia

Graham Harrington is a musician, occasional producer and well-known recluse, also well-known for his Celtic roots.

Biography

Graham Harrington was born in Vienna (a fact his detractors like to point to, for its associations with psychotherapy and extreme ideas, Freud, Klimt, Oskar Kokoschka, etc.). The geography accompanying his birth was more or less accidental, he has been reported as saying. His parents were en route to Merseyside, first in Birkenhead, 'then it was Calderstones', from where his father was to work on the ventilation system in the Mersey Tunnel. Graham H, as he was known, was an only child. In the summer the family would visit North Wales, where his father's interest and knowledge became transferred into an obsession with the old slate mines and quarries. 'We were shafted', Graham liked to say. The Welsh connections however came to have increasing importance for the musically gifted teenager, given the easy contact in the area to artists, poets, amateur drama groups, even comics and performance artists. There was a 'rich vein', Graham also liked to say, unable to leave the mining imagery. The area had attracted philosophers (Bertrand Russell), naturalists (Caroline Mabey) and world-knowing travellers. Importantly, little Porthmadog had not its own bookshop but Cob Records, where in its trays and racks all music could be found.

Career and later life

In North Wales, possibly in response to the way in which the North American musicians of The Band had withdrawn from public attention to play and record privately in a remote area, Graham and fellow local musicians formed Box of Swifts and shortly afterwards retired to 'a very thick-walled farmhouse [in Snowdonia] where we got woken by the sheep thundering by'. The exact location is still a matter of contention among music journalists but it is thought this was high above

Porthmadog and close to the coast. Box of Swifts would descend unannounced into student gatherings in Bangor and Caernarfon—until they were expected, at which point they stopped appearing. The band had a life of some eighteen months before disbanding.**[1]** Taking up menial employment Graham Harrington soon afterwards joined Joel Fitzpatrick to found The Possibilities (see elsewhere). From there he 'widened out', as he put it, to become the radical alternative thinker he is best known as today.

<u>Breakdown and recovery</u>

Following a brief liaison with fellow musician Julie Weston (see recent entry) and occasional periods spent in the west of Canada, Graham Harrington developed an interest in the Tranquille Sanatorium. This institution in the Kamloops area of British Columbia had itself in fact closed, but it emerged that Graham was particularly interested in its physical building. This was just one in a series of obsessions, another being his adulation of the UK singer popular in the 1960s and the second half of the last century, Cliff Richard. The latter interest led to creation and the dissemination by Graham H of the text "D" (in part inspired by the song "D in love")**[2]**. In its text form—of this, arguably regarded as a work of art—D was also a riposte ('I can do this too') to the former band member, Joel FitzP, with whom the yellow press persistently maintained he was manically in competition. Together these concerns led him to voluntarily enter and submit himself to new lines of therapy at Burnaby Grove, a radical centre for experimental psychotherapy near Vancouver. It emerged that his main motive was simply to be able to live with his obsessions, such as those for Cliff Richard—music to which Joel FitzP, when questioned, also admitted an attraction**[3]**—for Bobby Vee, The Five Satins, June Carter, for as many years as he liked. His public outbursts led to the discrediting of the centre and, to a large extent, its eventual closure in 2008. Despite these difficulties he managed to move back to 'yet another life' in Scotland. At the time these events are recounted, Graham Harrington is thought to be residing at a remote cove in the Orkneys, while 'keeping careful watch' over Skara Brae and the Ring of Brodgar. He is reportedly alive and well, although missing the presence of trees.

References

[1] There exist low-quality recordings of some 30 songs, occasionally obtainable via eBay and similar providers.

[2] As this account will show, I have been graded. I am a D. Now convinced anything of significance will involve a D, I shall capitalise the Ds, to Draw attention to them. What follows Does Demand a certain amount of Devotion, to the task, of reading.

I.

Onwards. I arrived with Lucero at that pretty granite house, some say cottage, and whomp: in no time she and Jorge were taking the steep path oh it was a steep Atlantic coast path and Down we scrambled to the ruins where great waves crashed and sprayed, where she and he vanished to Do the Deed. It took Lucero only hours to Dump me and be charmed by him, my rival, at the house with its great pines in the corner of the field, a rural idyll, the remote stone cottage where he hung out, kept logs in a pile and chickens in a coop and bottles of brandy in shadowy cupboards, in other words lived—a schemer who came out from a darkness: Jorge de la Peña, lover of masks and masquerades, his mind full of skulls, smoky cemeteries and ghost riders in the night.

That's it, apart from the backstories, the Details, bags of them to be shovelled in, if you'd just be so kind as to hold open the tops of the bags, you shouldn't need gloves but that's up to you.

Young Lucero wanted Jorge; she Didn't me. She loathed the brogues, the neckscarf. Jorge wasn't everything to her, she said, but I was nothing, and could piss off. What can I say, what add? A Description of her appearance would be highly Distracting

but for the fact she was Drop Dead gorgeous, as they say in the tabloids, which is where I aim leaving it, that blonde hair, the blue eyes, the envy of many a cornflower, the perfect skin.
I've got gloves in the shed if you need them. Pigskin.

Her counterpoint in this Drama, the scheming Jorge, lover of pretences and foreign coins that could be passed off as local currency, seduced Lucero by the water. He was frequently by the water with her. The morning after our arrival—Day two out of the three-and-a-bit Days I'm reporting on—seeing an old tyre washed up among the seaweed, he rolled it into the sea, only a few yards from the grand hotel with its decorative balconies and those yuccas which had been looking rather sad. By the time Lucero showed up he was (still dressed) standing on the tyre as it floated, pretending to have trouble balancing, extracting the maximum in comedy until her head was turned, her gaze riveted, until the sandals of her imagination were kicked off into the bushes.

Only a handful of years later he would have splashed and fallen, for his alcoholic Decline was swift. She knew nothing of that, nothing of Jorge's Death, the trips to the hospital and the whores who loved him.
Meanwhile I was already well on my way to becoming a D—more through continuous assessment than a simple exam, a single error. D, fourth in line, alphabetically speaking. That's enough capitals, I'm Dropping them henceforth.

There are more bags under the sink. Here's a tip: rub both sides at the top and the plastic will separate better.

On day zero I had brought Lucero with me. On a cultural note, the era of hitchhiking, flower wearing and apples in barrels was all but over—but hitchhiking was still just about feasible. And so we stood on a roadside in the rain in Normandy. It rained without a break in Normandy. Everyone should spend an evening in the rain in Normandy. Day or night, it can rain a lot in Normandy. Eventually we came to Rennes. At a roundabout in the same rain on the outskirts we lay inside these giant concrete pipes and slept. On day zero on the outskirts of Rennes it rained and rained. We lay close. Come dawn I was anxious to move away from those giant concrete pipes. Lucero however wanted us to stay in longer. As I crawled out into the rain she was mad at me, as north Americans say. Or as Cliff Richard once sang. I wouldn't bet on it but Don't Be Mad At Me may be on the flipside of Please Don't Tease. Will his music ever be re-instated and does that matter, yes.

I heard Lucero later went to live on a farm, remote as this house, in Wales, mid Wales.

II.

Otherwise, I learned. Jorge was a living instruction manual on how to seduce: live quite remotely, keep logs in a pile and chickens in a coop and bottles of brandy in shadowy cupboards, but despite all the material details still make it feel as if he/you had arrived from nowhere, been parachuted in, with no baggage, no background. Make a stew, get out the brandy. Make a papier-mâché mask, paint it, it doesn't have to be great, hang it on the wall. Wait. Someone will show up. Hand the arrivals endless opportunities to be curious. Stand astride an old tyre in the sea. On dry land, take a curiosity out your pocket and fabricate a fine tale about its origins. A fossil, say, though a piece of fluff will do. Go home, get out another bottle, make a fire, stare into it, nod at the mask, laugh a little. Show off your chicken coop as soon as eggs are laid.

Day three. Time already to return with Lucero through Normandy and across the Channel, as had been the plan all along: that college of art and design awaits her. The return journey; in tears over leaving Jorge and she hates my guts. Missed the famous roundabout through looking the wrong way. Missed any swallows that might have swooped overhead, over the fields.

III.

I arrived with a pig, and what a chancho he turned out to be. No wonder I stormed off to the beach. Ah, Jorge. Jorge was dancing on a rubber tyre, the pig said I wonder why he's doing that, I said because it's fun, No said the pig, he wants something.

Chancho followed everywhere, down the slope on a summer evening, to the sunset over the water. Jorge sat a way off and then I sat with Jorge and then we sneaked round the back of the ruin and round a ledge to where, behind this wall and truth be told, I was happy to yield it was that simple. Afterwards we looked through a hole in the wall and the pig was right there, only looking in entirely the wrong direction as was typical, he shot out of those pipes the other morning when we could have relaxed but he didn't relax he always had to be doing, but what he did was irrelevant, like himself, irrelevant. When Jorge lit a fire in the hearth and it was lovely the chancho said He's doing it for a reason because it isn't cold we don't need to burn anything, typical chancho, no wonder he sleeps alone, only on our way back through Normandy we didn't quite. The cold in the barn we stopped at, god, we had to keep close to stay alive and then he got all interested, interested in himself really, my self was still back with Jorge and the cock and the chickens, there was something to crow about. What marks in love would you give me, he asked at daybreak, straw in his hair. Whatever's lowest, I said. D he said. He started singing D in Love which he said was an old Cliff Richard song. The B-side of something but not Please Don't Tease. Fine I said. Do not follow me, I said, from here on I'll be walking by myself. Chancho.

Notes

* Don't Be Mad At Me © Tepper-Bennett 1960, B-side of A Voice in the Wilderness

* D in Love © Tepper-Bennett 1960, B-side of I Love You

[3] This music—Graham H said in the 50th anniversary jubilee edition of the New Musical Express—was impelled as if into the great hush down a remote North Wales valley of his teenage years. 'Into that vast awesome space would go the spangled tones of a shiny-stringed red Fender guitar, while the bass sounded so softly as to be barely audible, then in came the voice, warm and true: Cliff. Behind the radical shifts of The Possibilities lay such figures, worthy of our respect for all time.'

Authority Control

General. VIAF. WorldCat

National libraries. United States, Canada, Ireland United Kingdom

Other Treve (France)

This page needs additional citations for verification. Please help by adding reliable sources. Contentious material about living persons that is unsourced or poorly sourced must be removed immediately, especially if potentially libellous or harmful.

Elixir

When a man finds a never-ending, eternally replenishing case of craft beer at the local grocery store, you can expect a corny allegory, the kind of groan-worthy and forgettable Twilight Zone episode sandwiched between two better ones. At best, this must be one of those SNL skits relegated to the last half hour, where the comedians stain the screen with their flop sweat while the guest host shrugs his way to the conclusion.

I, however, have read enough magical realism to not immediately check out. My last boyfriend, an aspiring drag queen, celebrated both the classic South American novels of his home country and the current flash fiction of his avant-garde contemporaries, small tales that are nevertheless bloated and spiky, like a rare fish you have to sign a waiver before eating. Either way, the stories traffic in impossible events, teasing the joy of fantasy right up to the end, when the helpless characters finally succumb to the absurdity of life.

This is all the more important because the man I have followed home, the one with the bottomless case of beer, is an English teacher at the same college where I teach Physics to three sections of glassy-eyed freshman. He represented his station perfectly at faculty happy hour, with his worn slacks and wrinkled shirt, the rumpled ends untucked, like late autumn leaves clinging to a tree. The first thing I heard him say was a proclamation about a recent indie movie, decrying its tangled themes and poor acting, and I thought, oh great, one of these guys. But he dropped the analysis after meeting me and seemed genuinely interested in writing in LaTeX, and the adjustments to moving to the mountains from the Bay Area. Eventually, the two of us peeled off from the other academics and began to chat about the deficiencies in the local bar scene, the one good movie theater downtown, the boyfriends we've each left behind in distant cities, and, when he was ready to reveal it, the secret beer stash, newly discovered. So new that I am the first to hear of it.

Two hours later, he's ushering me shyly into his kitchen. His whole house, a tiny place on the west side, exists to cover wall space. There's the bookshelves, of course, but also paintings and photographs and scraps of maps, and some kind of woven mat thing above the couch. In one corner, framed concert posters. In another, photographs of dogs. A defunct fireplace takes up most of one wall, the mantle displaying a white enamel clock with gold scrollwork, perfectly Liberace in its faux-French excess, the most fabulously gay item in the house. The wall art continues into the kitchen, where an identification guide for basic herbs hangs above the stove.

"Watch," he says, opening his dull white fridge. I peek around the door, and there, as promised, is the generic brown cardboard case of beer, the top open. He reaches in, easily halfway into the box, and pulls out a gleaming silver can, no label. He hands it to me.

"And now one for me." He takes another.

"Wow," I say, all deadpan sarcasm. After all, I didn't follow him home because I thought the story was true. I liked the way he told it. And that he's cute.

"You want to double fist?" he says. He takes out another, shoving it in my free hand. "Triple?" Another can. "Quadruple?"

He pulls out cans until I'm cradling eight in my arms. All silver, all without labels, too many to fit into that one twelve-pack box that is clearly half-empty.

"No way," I say, and tumble the cans into his sink. He steps aside while I inspect the box. Boring cardboard packaging. Exactly five cans inside: two in the middle cradled by three on the bottom. Tilting the box doesn't reveal a secret compartment below. I take one can, then another, looking away for a second to make sure both are secure in my left hand. When I look back in the box, five cans. I almost drop the two cans and look over my shoulder, sure he has sneaked up behind me to perform the trick, violating personal space I have not yet given him permission to violate. He stands at the opposite counter, too far to interfere, already drinking from his unmarked beer.

I put the two cans back in the case and shut the fridge before finding out if the seven cans turn back into five. "Okay, cool, you're a magician, too." Hair stands on the back of my neck, my cheeks are flushed. He got me. I believe the impossible, if only for a moment, which makes me a fool.

"I told you you wouldn't believe me," he says, opening one of the beers and handing it to me.

"I still don't believe you." I lean on the counter by him, but not too close, since this ridiculous scenario will require he deliver an actual apology before I touch him again.

The apology comes in the form of the beer. I'd forgotten this part of his promise, this extra layer of absurd storytelling. Earlier, at the bar, he told me the beer was not only bottomless, but the most amazing elixir on God's earth. Another fun lie meant to draw me in, tease me, show his playfulness.

I've had how many beers at this point in my life? Not just individual beers, but the categories they are shuffled into, rearranging as tastes change, alcohol content rising and rising before falling and rising again. Ales, pilsners, stouts, imperial stouts, IPAs, Brut IPAs, West Coast IPAs, hazy IPAs, session IPAs, mango IPAs. No new styles exist, just trendy fruits added to old beer, and new beer added to old whiskey barrels. The wonder of discovery is gone, replaced by appreciation for the familiar.

The smell of his miracle beer is bright, somewhere between the sweet malt of a lager and the sweet grape of a wine. The first taste reminds me of a Belgian beer, rich textures of fruit and spice, but it's far too light for that. The mouthfeel matches my initial impression of a lager, but without the salty carbonation that accompanies American pilsners, or the spicy German hops of craft lagers. After swallowing, I feel no crackling on my tongue, no bitter aftertaste, no lingering dryness that calls for another drink. I feel refreshed, like drinking a glass of water. No, it's more than that, both more substantial and more ethereal, like drinking the evening sun's reflection off a still mountain lake.

I look at him, and he's no longer smiling as he was before, no longer enjoying a rigged game at my expense. He watched it all, every emotion as I took my first sip, rolling the liquid across my tongue, assessing its quality with open wonder and disbelief. Yet he looks at me now with worry, as if I might not have experienced something magical, like this isn't the most unbelievable and unlikely thing that any human has ever come across. He seems to think I will say, "this shit is just Bud Light," or "the best beer is the one in your hand." Either way, his anxiety is palpable, tracing every tense line on his body, and his wide, blinking stare awaits my response.

I stare back in kind, afraid to admit that I tasted exactly what he claimed, that this is the best beer I've ever had, and yes, it comes in endless amounts, can after can from that stupid brown box. All I can do is admit I believe. It's all true. The fear, of course, is that he will laugh at me. He will drop the act, explain the trick, and reveal the magic as a technical series of hand gestures and misdirections. Fully excited by my naiveté, he will proceed to lay me out as yet another gullible sexual conquest lured in by the promise of the impossible.

But even worse, he might do none of that. In the most sublimely terrifying scenario, he will draw me close, kiss me, and admit that he doesn't know why the beer is so good, or why it keeps reappearing, no matter how many times we reach for it.

The clock has just struck midnight and the most fantastical possibility is that he is just as big a fool as I am.

Sara Streeter

The House Always Wins

As she pulls up to the house for the first time, Tess spots the white goat. It stands in the fenced-in side yard, chewing on tufts of weeds and watching as she steps out of the car. Grinding its mouth in a circular motion, the goat quickly loses interest in her. She debates whether to pet it, but veers toward the house.

The front door is bloated and warped from years of heat and cold, the forest green paint in shreds. The knob doesn't turn, but with force, the door opens with a groan and a thump. It's dark inside except for a teetering floor lamp in the corner. The main room oozes the dank, stale smell of beer. Flattened boxes from cases of Busch Light cover dingy floorboards. A brick fireplace's gaping mouth devours more empty beer boxes, along with cigarette butts and a few empty bottles. A well-oiled Remington shotgun hangs above the mantle.

Garrett emerges from the other room and wraps Tess in his arms.

"Hey, you."

She stands on her toes to kiss him, running her hands along his broad shoulders. They've been together for a year, but she still gets butterflies when he touches her. She likes Garrett because he's goofy, cute, and awkward—her favorite white-boy flavor. The same dumb puns, breakfast orders, and quiet moments together. It's comfortable.

Opening her eyes, Tess notices a yellowing Confederate flag tacked on the wall above a sectional with collapsed, stained cushions.

"What's up with that?" She points at the flag.

"It's Bobby's." He nuzzles her black hair. "Left over from when his parents lived here. He just never took it down." He tries to steer her away from the flag.

"And you're OK with it?" she prods him.

"Oh, come on, babe. It's just a flag. You know I don't believe in that stuff."

She bites her tongue. She doesn't want to start the weekend with an argument. As the son of conservatives, discussions about racism are simply not in Garrett's wheelhouse. She worried his parents wouldn't be able to wrap their heads around their son dating someone who wasn't white, but to her surprise, her race and their status as an interracial couple have, supposedly, been non-issues for his parents. It makes her feel like she is a non-issue too. She wonders if maybe they are just waiting out his Asian-girlfriend phase.

Garrett's bedroom is small but tidy. On the dresser, there are photos of the two of them from their anniversary at her favorite restaurant and his brother's wedding last year, both in Richmond, reminding her of how much fun they used to have when he lived there. Now Garrett's in Toano, worlds away from any nightlife. It's a dying small town rumored to be built on an Indian burial ground. Nothing feels alive there.

Garrett opens his top dresser drawer and points inside. She peers in and sees a clean toothbrush lying neatly on a paper towel next to a stack of folded boxers.

"You should keep your toothbrush in here too. Bobby never cleans the bathroom."

"I miss your old place," she says. "I mean, it was kind of gross too, but not like this."

"Bobby gave me a good deal on the room, and it's an easy commute to work. It'll just be until I figure out my next move."

Tess wonders what he thinks his next move will be. She wasn't thrilled when Garrett took the position updating computer software at the corrections facility. His first week there, a guy tried to stab him with a shiv made from two plastic sporks. "What can I say, some dudes want to spork me," Garrett chuckles whenever he tells the story. His new job, the crappy house, hurtled him backwards, away from the life together she imagined for the two of them in Northern Virginia. She would hang his artwork on the walls in their new apartment together, they would get a dog, and have happy hours with the nice couple next door. It would be perfect. She just has to get him out of Toano.

*

That night, she hears Bobby throw open the front door. His footsteps are full of booze, although he doesn't stumble. He slams his bedroom door shut. The house shudders, then sleeps.

*

The next morning, the living room is dim except for spastic light coming from a muted TV. Bobby sits at a folding table, cleaning the Remington next to an open Bud Light. It's a rare weekend off from his job at the 24-hour pancake restaurant. He greets the couple with jolly blue eyes and a wide smile.

"You must be Tess!" He sets the barrel down. He stands to give her a hug, and his embrace smells like gun oil, cigarettes, and a whiff of body odor. In an instant, Bobby's hands sneak below her shoulders, and she jerks out of reach. He gives her a boyish grin, the one she assumes he uses to get away with bad behavior. Not sure what to say, she shakes her head and rolls her eyes. Although he creeps her out, she remembers Bobby is Garrett's childhood friend and forces herself to gather her composure.

"I met your goat yesterday. What's its name?"

"That's Gloria." Bobby sits down and picks up the shotgun again, wiping it with a rag.

"Gloria? Cute. How long have you had her?"

He cocks his head. "My parents got her for me when I was 15 I think. She's awesome. If you want, you can feed her an apple later." He speaks with a tenderness, almost love, for the animal, then the moment passes. Bobby takes a sip of beer as he redirects his attention to the gun. "A few of us are heading out on the river later. Going to do some drinking on the river on my day off." Garrett smiles at the invitation and, without looking at Tess, throws his oldest friend a thumbs up.

*

Water licks her body and sprays her face as the three of them speed out on the river in Bobby's motorboat. Tess has already lost count of Bobby's drinks, but she tells herself he's the kind of guy who can hold his beer. They approach a secluded strip of beach with ten boats tied up in a row. Bobby slows the motor. Through strains of Lynyrd Skynyrd and 2Pac, Tess hears laughter and the satisfying crack of cans being opened. Cigarette smoke and weed waft through the air. Sunburnt guys with too many blurry tattoos stand waist-high in the river holding beer cans. In between sips, they ogle the girls on boats—a mess of bikinis, sunglasses, and loose flesh.

After they tie up, Tess climbs down to stand in the water next to Garrett. He slides his arm around her, and next to his tall frame, she feels protected from the gaggle of drunk white people. From under her sunglasses, she reflexively scours the group of partygoers until she finally spots another Asian girl, simultaneously relieved and annoyed to see her. The girl flirts with a group of white guys on the beach, who are clearly enthralled. Slender with black hair that kisses the top of her ass, the girl's string bikini clings to her bronze body like she was born wearing it. She catches Tess staring and abruptly looks away. Nearby, Bobby sees the direction of Tess's gaze. He crushes his can in a tight fist.

"I'd bet that one likes it rough," he mutters. "Chinese chicks will let you do just about anything." He roars with laughter at a joke that doesn't feel like one, his pale, wet belly jiggling in the hot sun. Garrett coughs loudly and tilts his chin towards the boat.

"Hey Bobby, that bottle of American Honey still in the cooler?"

*

Tess wakes up that night from an uneasy, alcohol-infused sleep. She hears a female voice in the living room along with Bobby and a few other guys. The girl's voice is soft and husky. Though she can't see her, Tess imagines her to be a box blonde from the river, complete with a "tasteful" Confederate flag tattoo on her ankle, tacky navel piercing from high school, lips prematurely wrinkled from a trusty pack of Camel Lights.

To quench her curiosity, she gets up to go to the kitchen. Gingerly stepping out of the bedroom, she sees the Asian girl from the beach sitting on Bobby's lap, a blank look on her face. Under a sheer mesh tank top, she's still in her bikini, long hair in a messy bun on top of her head, her once spotless eyeliner now smudged and drooping. The girl attempts to stand but crashes down on Bobby, who greedily pulls her back into his lap. Two shaggy white guys on the sectional hoot and cough puffs of smoke. Tess pauses mid step when she sees a row of orange pill bottles lined up on the coffee table. Garrett mentioned Bobby liked to party, but she figured it was just the usual alcohol and weed.

Hoping to avoid being noticed, she steps lightly into the kitchen and finds a water bottle in the fridge. She takes a sip and looks out the window to see Gloria asleep in her pen, so peaceful and innocent. How strange that Bobby loves the goat so much when he doesn't seem to care about much else—not himself, not his house, and not the unfortunate girl on his lap. Tess's mind wanders and she considers barging into the living room, pulling the girl off Bobby and shaking her soft, narrow shoulders. "Wake up!" Tess would scream and, with that, the spell over her would break. The front door would fling itself open, and the girl would be whisked out the door, away from the pills, away from Bobby's house.

Tess caps the water bottle and slinks back to the bedroom. On her way, she sees Bobby whisper in the girl's ear, his meaty fingers inching up under her tank top. The girl nods and reaches toward a pill bottle. Tess closes the door, relieved to be back in the bedroom, safe with Garrett. The situation she just witnessed makes her shudder, but she doesn't want to get in the middle. It's better not to be involved; confrontation has never been her strong suit. Back in bed, she reassures herself and falls asleep.

Tess dreams she hears a barely discernible knock on the

bedroom door. From the lumbering footsteps, she knows it's Bobby. Frantic, she looks at the door and sees it's unlocked. She hears Bobby go into the bathroom and slam the door. She hears him vomit, a guttural, ghastly sound, and she leaps up to lock the door. When she turns around, Bobby's standing beside her in the bedroom, blue eyes glowing in the dark, outstretched fingers inches from her skin. She wakes with a scream burning in her mouth.

*

Back in Arlington, Tess finds she's desperate to clean the musty smell of the house out of her clothes and hair. It fades after a few days, but at night alone in her apartment, she thinks she hears Bobby's slow, wasted footsteps. Even in the crisp white walls of her modern apartment almost 150 miles away from Toano, she can't shake the house from her mind. Two weeks pass and she begs Garrett to come visit her, insisting the trip to see him wore her down. The truth is she can't go back to that house; it's haunted by a man who's still alive.

A month later, when Garrett tells her Bobby got fired from the pancake restaurant for being drunk, she pictures Bobby strumming his guitar in the dark, the pile of empty beer cases steadily piling up, his beloved goat growing thin and desperate—the man and his house held together in their decay.

*

Monday 10:11 a.m.: Garrett calls while she's in her weekly team meeting.

"He's dead, Tess. Bobby's dead." His voice breaks. She clutches her phone and hurries out of the glass conference room.

"What? Oh my God. What happened?" It comes out a fervent whisper.

"Heroin."

Outside, she sits down on a bench and stares at the sky. Her suit jacket starts to strangle her.

"Shit."

They stay silent, listening to each other breathe. It's over.

The house wins.

*

When Tess pulls up to Bobby's house for the last time, the street is full of trucks with mud slicked on the sides, hatchbacks with Phish and FloydFest bumper stickers, old sedans needing coats of paint. They are Bobby's friends, the people who loved him, and she's come to join them for the country boy's last rites. It's beginning to get dark and as she gets out of her car, the smell of bonfire tickles her nose, and she hears the familiar twang of bluegrass. Garrett comes over and gives a tight hug, a sad smile on his face. Her hand in his, he guides her behind the house to the people circled around the fire. The rag tag group eyes the newcomer as he seats her in the blue camping chair next to his.

"Hi," she says with a little wave. "I'm Tess." The fire crackles in response. A dreaded blonde guy across from her nods as he continues playing the guitar. Everyone else, clutching red plastic cups and cigarettes, ignores her introduction. Tess sits back. She gets it. They don't know her, and she didn't like Bobby. There's no use in trying to make friends. She's just there to support her boyfriend. Garrett comes back and sets a cup full of a dark liquid next to her.

"Moonshine and Coke. Dan got it from a guy in the mountains last time we went tubing." She takes a sip and grimaces. "Go easy, it's strong," he cautions. It's worse than rubbing alcohol, but she knows to drink it if she's going to sleep tonight.

The evening goes on with music, drinking, and reminiscing. Tess pulls the hood of her sweatshirt up and takes big gulps, nodding along to the stories and jokes, even taking a hit or two from the bowl being passed around. As she reaches the bottom of her second, maybe third cup, she tears herself away from the fire to find the bathroom and makes her way to the living room. Emptier and cleaner than she could have ever imagined, it's almost unrecognizable. The flattened beer boxes are gone, and there is only an outline of where the Confederate flag hung on the wall for all those years. She wonders who cleaned, maybe some of Bobby's friends or his family. Tess shudders thinking about what they found—beer cans and bottle caps, stray pills, cigarette butts, mouse droppings. God knows what else.

The smell of stale beer lingering in the house begins to turn her stomach as she reaches the bathroom. She closes the door and presses her forehead against the grimy mirror. She knows if she pukes she'll feel better. Holding her hair away from her face as she hovers over the toilet, she recalls Garrett's warning about the bathroom and tries not to touch the seat. Hearing herself make horrible retching sounds, she thinks about all the times Bobby must have thrown up in the same bathroom. She wants to be sad about his passing, but she can't. His death, the heroin, it all felt inevitable.

When it feels like everything is evacuated from her stomach, she rinses her mouth and splashes her face in the sink. She walks out of the bathroom on wobbly legs towards Garrett's room, where he's staying until the end of the month. They've looked at a couple of apartments near her place in Arlington, but they have yet to agree on any of them. He always finds something wrong, the timing, the deposit, the smell of the lobby. Tess worries he's not going to grow up, and Garrett thinks she's pushing him too hard, but mostly they argue about the high cost of living and shitty Beltway traffic. She realizes the end of their relationship is probably inevitable, too.

Something behind her makes a sound. She freezes. She hears it again, unfamiliar footsteps, closer this time. She turns slowly. Standing a few paces away is the goat, silhouetted by the dim light behind her. Gloria looks at the human curiously. Tess exhales with relief.

"Gloria, old girl. What are you doing here?"

She extends a hand, but the animal backs away. A wave of laughter rolls in from the open window reminding her of Gloria's former owner.

"Bobby's gone, sweetie. I'm sorry." The words come out before she can catch herself. Oddly enough, she finds she means them. The goat takes another slow step back and then another. Tess is surprised by the thick, muddled emotion she has for the animal. Was this what Bobby felt for her? Through Tess's wasted state, a thin line of resolution appears; Bobby is free, and now it's Gloria's turn.

She carefully guides the goat to the empty living room and opens the front door. Bugs buzz and flock toward the light. Gloria walks to the threshold and hesitates, sniffing the cool, crisp air. Tess smooths the animal's coarse pale fur as together they take in the night.

"Go on," she says softly. "Get out of here."

Meghan Louise Wagner

Wild Sage

I spend my first year of art school wishing I was anyplace else. My first boyfriend is also a painting major and he teaches me to hate almost everything about my art. After we break up, I switch to illustration. I find new friends, wild ones, girls he always told me to avoid. Most nights, I follow them to bars that don't check IDs. We roam dance floors and pool rooms in search of men to buy us drinks. When we strike out, we head to house parties or DIY spots. We bob through crowds with plastic cups, waiting for someone to fill them. Sometimes we shove our way into living rooms where sweaty guys thrash to hardcore. Sometimes we hit warehouses packed with noise kids, nodding to feedback. Sometimes we wander through old sewing factories and find dreamy boys strumming guitars, singing like they're underwater.

No matter where we go, I drift away from the group. I sneak into hallways, creep down steps, duck into darkened kitchens where people pass cloudy bongs. This is something my friends yell at me about on Uber rides back to campus, on steps outside the dorm, beside coffee carafes in the student center. "Why do you always have to disappear?" they ask. And I never have a good answer. My mother says I was like this as a child, always getting lost in shopping malls and grocery stores.

One night, I stumble out of the sewing factory into an alley filled with puddles and weeds. Fuzzy patches of herbs grow along a pathway leading to a rusty gate. I walk through it and feel my high heels sink into the muddy grass.

The gate clangs shut behind me. By now, the music from the sewing factory sounds as if it's coming from a faraway party. A razor edge of light buzzes from the street. It's enough to see the shadow of a middle-aged man slumped in a lawn chair, and my first thought is that he might be the landlord.

I slip a pack of Camel Lights out of my purse and pretend

I'm there to smoke.

"I'm Angie," I say, lighting a cigarette. "My friend knows the band."

"You can go where you want," he says. "You don't need permission."

"I was just telling you."

"Got a cigarette?"

I pass him one. He takes a silver zippo from the pocket of his flannel shirt.

"It smells like Thanksgiving out here," I say.

"It's the wild sage," he says. "It grows all over this part of Cleveland."

"I've never noticed."

"You'll see it everywhere now," he says, as if this is a fact.

After our cigarettes, I walk back to the gate but it won't budge. I wiggle it a few times and my palms itch from the rust.

He stands and walks over. He's taller than me, even in my high heels. "Oh, no," he says, his voice low and facetious. "If we're trapped, it'll have to be like the Garden of Eden."

I am only scared for a second.

He jiggles the latch. The gate loosens and the door swings open. "There you go," he says, waving his hand, allowing me passage.

I stride back into the sewing factory and find my friends lounging on couches with guys from the band. I tell them all about the Garden of Eden.

"You mean Paul?" a floppy haired drummer asks. "The upstairs dude?"

"I don't know," I say. "He was like forty or something."

"If that guy tries anything on you, I'll kick his ass."

This makes my friends jealous, which makes me swoon, and after the next band starts their set, I go searching for Paul.

I find him in the back yard, sitting in the same spot.

"Do you want to hang out?" I ask.

"Sure," he says, crossing one leg over the other. "You got another smoke?"

*

He invites me up to his apartment which probably used to be a factory manager's office. It's all one room, separated by hanging sheets and curtains. No couches or chairs. He offers me a can of Schlitz from a mini-fridge. There's no kitchen, only a table with two boxes of generic wheat shreds, a percolator, and a waffle iron.

We sit atop a patchwork quilt on a twin size bed. The air tastes a little like sawdust. Orange light shines through the window from the post office across the street.

He lifts an acoustic guitar. "Wanna hear something?" He plucks a neon-orange pick from under the neck.

"Yeah, yeah, sure," I say, wondering if anyone will come looking for me.

He strums a few chords and sings a soft, melodic song that makes me think of golden embroidery. It's the most beautiful music I've ever heard another person make in real life. It almost doesn't sound real. His voice is deep and soft and clear like a famous folk singer you'd hear on a record, or in a movie, or in a giant concert hall—not upstairs from a shithole like the sewing factory.

I finish my beer and wait for him to try something on me, but he never does, so I'm the one who kisses him.

It startles him. He drops the guitar. He asks if I'm sure. And I say, "Yeah, yeah, sure," and he says, "No, I mean, are you really sure?" and I say, "Yeah, I'm really sure," and then he's the one who kisses me back.

*

In the morning, we eat eggs at the diner down the street and I see all the little lines around his eyes and face. His hair is dark and wavy, but gray at the sideburns, gray stubble on his jaw. We have no problem making conversation, but every time the waitress comes by to fill our coffees or clear our plates, she glares at us so hard we both forget what we were even talking about. We keep starting over.

After the check arrives, he thumbs through a mess of dollar

bills and asks if I can leave the tip. On our way out, he squeezes my waist as if we're an old married couple. "It's so refreshing being around someone like you," he says.

"Someone like me?" I ask, tapping my Uber app.

Before he answers, a homeless guy pushes a cart of scrap metal past us. He's got scraggly gray hair and is dressed in several layers of coats and flannels even though it's sixty degrees. Instinctually, I look down, no eye contact, but then Paul waves.

"Hey, Billy," he says, "what's good?"

"Hey, Paul, where's your sister?"

They laugh as if this is some inside joke. I don't get it. I order an Uber. It's six minutes away. I squint in the morning light, wishing I had my sunglasses, wishing I could teleport home, into my shower, under my covers. I can't believe this was my first one night stand.

The guy pushes his cart down the street and Paul steps closer to me, digging his hands into his pockets. "Sorry about that," he says. "I should have introduced you."

"It's fine," I say, waiting until the guy is around the corner. "How do you know that homeless dude?"

"Billy's not homeless," he says, chuckling. "He used to own the Ramble Room. He took me in when I got clean. I owe everything to that guy."

"To *that* guy?"

"Hey, you got another smoke?"

I fish out my pack, which only has two cigarettes left. We smoke them and when my driver arrives, we exchange a hug on the curb, as that seems like something we should do under the circumstances. His flannel smells like sage.

I pull away from him and say, "Please, don't tell anybody about this."

He laughs and bops my forehead with a quick kiss.

"We don't know the same people," he says.

*

I think about that the whole ride back to campus. The

whole day. The whole night. The next day, the next night, even when I'm back with my friends, roaming dive bars and dance floors. I think about it a few weeks later when I run into the drummer from the sewing factory at a house party. We make out on an itchy couch in the basement. His tongue feels like a helicopter propeller in my mouth and, the whole time, all I think about is Paul's soft quilt, his soft lips, his soft voice.

*

I drag through the rest of the semester. In high school, I was the girl that other kids crowded around to watch draw. They'd gush over my sketches of space pirates and alien princesses. Now my classmates say stuff like "it's fine, if you're going for a middle-of-the-road thing," "your techniques are decent but your subjects are so cliche." Eventually, I stop drawing aliens and princesses altogether.

One snowy afternoon over winter break, I'm sitting at the art museum with my sketchbook, trying to draw like Dirck van Baburen, when I hear this low, soft facetious voice talking about the end of the world.

It's Paul, and he's strolling through the 17th century Dutch gallery with a petite middle-age woman. They both look frumpy in big sweaters, flannels, loose jeans, scuffed shoes. I lift my charcoal and start to wave, but he walks straight past me as if I'm one of the statues.

The woman laughs. "If it's the end of the world," she says, "I'm holding out for a Picasso."

"I call dibs on this one," he says, nodding past me to a painting of two roosters in a cockfight.

They leave, still laughing. I pack up my sketchbook and follow them to the next gallery, eavesdropping. They're pretending the world has ended outside the museum and they get to pick which paintings to bring back to their apocalyptic hovel. Paul's friend has terrible stringy, blond hair and terrible taste. She chooses the most obvious pieces: Matisse, Cezanne, Warhol, Pollack.

Paul lingers longer, taking deep, meaningful gazes before

making any decisions.

In the last gallery on the modern art floor, he digs his hands into his pockets and whistles a golden melody. I stand on the other side of a glass sculpture, clutching my sketchbook, wondering if he even remembers me.

They circle the sculpture, studying its intricate prisms. "You know, babe," he says, clucking his tongue. "I don't think we need any of these."

I follow them down the steps, through the lobby, into the gift shop. They flip through racks of postcards, lift novelty coffee mugs, pinch novelty socks that say *Vincent Van Toe.* Paul doesn't buy anything but she brings a few decorative magnets to the register. I thumb through a coffee table book on Grecian urns.

After the gift shop, they walk to the coat check. She hands the tickets to the clerk. Paul helps her fit into a giant tweed blazer. He wears a faded bomber jacket with a cartoon character on the back, something so uncool it makes me embarrassed.

They walk out of the museum into the snowy, blue night. I sit at a table near the café and start a new sketch of cartoon ducks and mushroom clouds.

*

The next day, I'm studying pointillism and my phone rings with a number I don't know. I think it's probably the manager of the print shop calling to offer me the job I interviewed for last week. Instead, it's this low, soft, facetious voice asking if I know where to get good clogs.

"Loud ones," he says, "the kind that go click-clack."

I don't get the joke. I don't even know how he got my number. Yet, part of me wants to play along, ask if he'll wander around a museum with me some time.

But I don't.

I say, "Wrong number."

*

A few months later, my friends drag me to a strip mall bar that does live music and two dollar pitchers on Tuesday nights.

It's the kind of place with giant jars of pickled eggs on the counters and signs above the bathroom doors that say: "You Look Like I Need a Beer." Almost everyone is over forty and I don't know what we're doing here. My friends, who have to like everything ironically, grab a table by a small stage and order a pitcher and a round of eggs.

I'm prodding a pickled yolk with my tongue when Paul walks onto the stage with his guitar. Quickly, I swallow it, and scan the room. His girlfriend from the art museum sits at the end of the bar, drinking a draft beer that looks too big for her petite frame. I scrunch my shoulders, trying to make myself look as small as possible. One of my friends even says, "Isn't that the old guy from the sewing factory?"

However, once he starts singing, my friends shut up. They prop their elbows on the table and watch, entranced.

Later, on our ride back to campus, they chatter about how amazing that was. They make comparisons to Leonard Cohen, Eliot Smith, Sufjan Stevens. They don't get what he's doing in a place like Cleveland, playing strip mall bars. And I don't say anything. I don't add to the conversation at all.

*

Over the next few years, I see Paul sporadically. After the sewing factory gets shut down, we run into each other at new DIY spots: an old Mexican restaurant that's been converted into an art gallery; a former barber shop run by noise kids; drafty houses with creaky floorboards and nicknames like "The Open Wound."

At the start of senior year, I buy a used car and it breaks down two weeks later. I have it towed to a garage where a friend of a friend works. When I'm waiting for the bus, it starts to rain. Paul pedals past on a dirt bike that's too small for him. He skids to a stop, his hair soaked, and asks if I need a ride. I glare at him and say, "On that?" And he glares back and says, "I can grab Anthony's car,"—as if I should know who Anthony is—and so I say, "I'll take the bus," and he says, "Are you sure?" and I say, "Yeah, yeah, I'm sure."

A few months later, I'm buying bread and cheese in the express lane at Stop N'Save. Paul is two lanes over, trying to write a check for a gigantic fruit basket. The cashier says they'll only take cash or card. He asks for a manager. She says, "He'll tell you the same thing." I swerve into their lane and flash my debit card. I say, "I'll pay for it with my stuff." The cashier glances between us, waiting. Paul stuffs his checkbook into his shirt pocket and says, "Are you sure?" and I unload my groceries and say, "Paul."

We walk through the parking lot together and I ask what the basket is for.

"My girlfriend's aunt died," he says. "I got it for her uncle."

"You're giving him fruit?"

"Why?" he asks, stopping under a bright orange spotlight. "Wait. Do you think that's weird?"

*

After graduation, I get promoted at the print shop. My new job requires me to visit clients at their offices. I invest in a wardrobe of slacks and blazers and pencil skirts. I move into a duplex with a couple friends from college. They convert our living room into an art studio. In the mornings, when I brew coffee, the kitchen always smells like acrylics and burnt rice.

On weekends, we hit gallery shows. My high heels clack against the hardwood floors, my underarms sweat beneath my blazers. I feel like a giant when I enter crowded openings. I swerve around corners, barely glancing at the art, searching instead for secret doors and stairwells.

And sometimes I look for Paul, leaning against a wall, chewing on a toothpick, swirling a plastic cup of wine. In most crowds, he's a hazy spot of comfort. Someone I can talk to without putting on a face.

He glances at my navy blazer and pencil skirt. "Are you like a banker now?" he asks.

"No, I do graphic design," I say, reaching over him to grab cheese and grapes from the refreshment table. "I just came from a client's."

"Aw, too bad," he says, snapping his fingers, "I was gonna ask you for a mortgage."

*

I first meet Jason at a comic book themed gallery show. He's a painter, only a couple years older than me. We get to talking about how one of the pieces is definitely a rip-off of a Daniel Clowes panel. We spend the rest of the night hopping from bar to bar. He seems to know people at every stop. The bartenders give us free shots, slip us baskets of wings, let us stay after last call, invite us to their after-hours parties. As the pink sky rises, he asks if I want to go back to his place and see his paintings.

He lives in a warehouse in a mostly deserted part of downtown. On our way up the freight elevator, he mentions having anywhere between four and seven roommates, depending on the month.

"It's cheap rent," he says. "People come and go."

Inside, in the hazy morning light, it reminds me of a half-finished construction site. Exposed pipes, wide open ceilings, standing walls, buckets of paint. Jason has an entire room devoted to his studio. The main subject of his paintings is urban decay: mattresses leaning against telephone poles, cars on cinderblocks, skinny girls draped across chain-link fences. He tells me he never went to art school, he taught himself craft from watching You-Tube.

We don't wake until two pm. We spend the afternoon tangled in his sheets, half-drunk, still jubilant, talking about everything—neither of us taking a breath, lest the conversation ends. Around six pm, it starts to get dark again and he asks if I want coffee. I think about my usual Sunday evening routine of going to the gym, listening to true-crime podcasts, and prepping work lunches for the week. I know I'll be wrecked come Monday, but I don't care.

He dresses in a paint splattered t-shirt and a pair of red checkered boxers. I change into my sweater and mini-skirt from the night before, no nylons. He tosses me a pair of flip-flops and says, "There's always shit on the floor."

I sit on the kitchen counter as he boils water on the stove for a French press. While we wait, he pushes himself against me, sliding his hands along my thighs, lifting my skirt.

Heavy footsteps thump around the corner. I jerk upright and see Paul passing by with a foot long sub under his arm. He's dressed in army green coveralls and steel-toed boots.

"Hey, Jason," he says. "Hi, Angie." Then he hurries past the kitchen, disappearing down one of the haphazard hallways.

Jason buries his head into my chest, laughing. My cheeks burn. He hops away from me to turn off the stove and I lower my skirt, covering my thighs.

"How do you know Paul?" he asks, pouring water over the coffee grounds.

"From around," I say, hesitating. "I used to hang out at the sewing factory."

"No shit," he says. "I don't remember you."

And that's all we ever say about it.

*

Most weekends, I stay at Jason's. Unlike my place, there's almost always something happening at his. Three of his roommates are in bands, and when they practice, everyone hangs out afterwards. Some nights, they throw shows and the loft is packed tighter than most clubs.

But when there's nothing happening, Jason sulks. He'll drag around the loft, texting friends, scrolling Facebook, pestering me and his roommates. Entertaining him isn't so easy, since all my friends bore him, too. He works odd jobs, so his schedule is never set. Some days, he hauls lumber, other days he cleans foreclosed houses. Days he doesn't work, he starts drinking around two or three, and by seven he's looking to pick fights over nothing. There's no predicting what details will aggravate him. He'll complain about my high heels making me too tall, say I use too many cups of water to make coffee, groan about my ringtone, cough because my hair spray smells like lemon Pledge.

He does the same thing to his roommates and friends, but all of them seem to have their own ways of dealing with him. Paul is the best because nothing ever seems to bother him. He'll chuckle and shrug, crack a dry joke, and Jason will sulk off to find another target.

One night, when Jason's painting in his studio, I talk to Paul about this in the kitchen. He spreads peanut butter across bread and I sit on the counter, kicking my feet. Jason's got the music cranked so loud I know he can't hear us.

"If he's not constantly doing something," I say, "he just looks for fights."

"He's always been that way," Paul says, scraping the knife against the jar. "It's how he is."

"But why?" I ask. "Why is he like that?"

"Who cares?"

"He's my boyfriend."

He steps up to the sink to rinse his hands. He's so close I can smell that scent of sage and smoke that lingers on him. "Angie," he says, drying his hands on a rag, "understanding why he is the way he is won't make him any less annoying. You either like him for who he is or you don't."

I feel the warmth from the gas stove on my legs. A slick of sweat runs down my neck, my back, beneath my thighs. We've known each other for years, Paul and I, but I realize then that we don't know anything about each other.

Jason's music stops. Down the hall, his studio door swings open. He strolls through the loft, carrying an empty coffee mug, his forearms flecked with yellow paint. He pays no attention to Paul as he plucks a six-pack from the fridge.

"Hey, babe," he says, grinning. "Lou just texted. They're all at the Cathedral."

"Cool," I say, hopping off the counter, twisting straight past Paul. "Let's go."

*

Despite its name, the Cathedral is not a former church. From the outside, it looks like it might have once been a storefront, selling vacuum cleaners or hiking boots. Inside, a projector shows B-movies from the 1970's against the wall. Faded landscapes, primary colors, biker chicks in mini-skirts, demonic children, aliens in white robes, androids dressed as priests.

As the movie plays, Jason mingles with his friends and I wander. Whenever I go out with him, it feels like I'm crashing another person's high school reunion. Everybody looks familiar from far away, but when they come close, I realize they're just archetypes of old friends or classmates or crushes.

The movie erupts into a screaming frenzy. Loud, ominous music thumps. It's a killing scene. The biker chicks versus the aliens with the robot clergy caught in the middle. I can't keep track. It all blurs together. There's no real story to follow.

I slip into the room behind the projector and grab a cold beer from a dorm fridge. I step through another door that leads to a narrow hallway, lit only by a blurry, red EXIT sign. From there, I wind up in a fenced-in backyard where a dozen people stand around smoking and chattering. None of them notice me as I circle the yard, looking for something that isn't there.

*

About a week later, on my way up to meet Jason at the loft, I find Paul loading boxes into the freight elevator. I notice his guitar in the corner and ask where he's going.

"Moving in with Stacey," he says, as if I should know who Stacey is. "She bought a house in Parma."

"Oh," I say, disappointed. "You should have asked me for a mortgage."

"Aw," he says, wiping sweat from his brow, "maybe next time."

"So you're really leaving?" I say, more seriously, stepping over two army green duffle bags.

"We'll see each other around."

"But we don't know the same people."

"No," he says, smiling, "we don't."

*

Eventually, Jason and I break up over pizza crust. One night, I grab us a deep dish pie—not a thin n'crispy—and this prompts him to lecture me for twenty minutes about how I don't really know who he is or what he values. I grab the box and say I'll go back to the pizza shop and get another. I drive away and never return.

In the following months, I spend more time with friends. We actively avoid bars that don't check IDs. Instead, we go to local breweries and craft cocktail lounges. When we talk about our early college days, we swap stories about all the creeps who used to buy us drinks, who snuck us into their clubs, who cut lines for us in moldy basements. We swipe through Tinder and giggle over our mutual matches and their stupid mountain climbing pics. We have breakdowns over turning twenty-five, but by twenty-six we hardly fuss. I go on dates with utterly normal guys who work in finance and health care and law. When I bring them back to my apartment and show them my sketches, they gush, genuinely impressed, as if I'm some kind of artist.

*

One spring night, I'm walking with a date through downtown. The streets are busy and brightly lit. It's sixty-five degrees and every patio bar is packed. We're on our way to an upscale sushi lounge, the kind of place where celebrities eat when they're in town. My date is telling me how his marketing firm represents a local celebrity chef, which is how he was able to pull strings for the reservation. I don't catch the details because a golden melody curls around the corner, drawing me close.

Instead of turning right, I go left, and walk quickly toward the crowded patio of a craft brewery. Paul sits high on a stool, plucking his guitar. His face is lit by green and purple neon coming from inside the bar, electrifying his salt-and-pepper hair. It sounds like he's playing a cover song—something familiar, a song everybody ought to know—but I can't place. I never can with him.

I stand at the edge of the patio, behind a gate blooming with lavender and lemon verbena. Paul glances at me and flashes a surprised grin. It makes me smile more. As he continues singing, he nods at me, letting me in on an inside joke. A warm breeze rolls down the street, making the smoke and herbs and craft beer smell more alive. My date squeezes my shoulder, reminding me of our reservation. The crowd claps and Paul starts a new song, another one that sounds familiar. One I know I'll have in my head long after we walk off to dinner.

Amy Weldon

Malconformation

Ann Carter (1781?-1803)

Along the dark street Ann hurries toward a place to hide. Another cold night is coming on here in the hinge between winter and spring, the first week of March although she's lost track of the day. Beyond the wall of Parliament to her right, with cold bronze Cromwell on his horse, the Thames rushes past in its stinking bed. Frost rims the air like fur on a rich woman's coat. A glitter of late snowflakes catches and swirls in the wind.

Between her legs the bale of sodden rag is cold. She carries it always: her curse, her shame, slung about her hips like a stillborn child bound to her as penance. To leak and leak, to run and run, to make her howl with pain when it's touched. And, now, again, to lose her her place. "My God," said Mrs. Macready last week in her velvet parlor, lifting her nose when Ann entered with the ash-bucket and broom. "What's that horrid smell?" And Ann stood still, dumb as a mule, waiting for the eyes to land on her. They always did. And then Mrs. Pullen, the housekeeper, sat her down at the kitchen table, firm and dismally kind, the braids of onion and the chicken on its hook to be dinner that night for everyone in the house but her. "Oh, Ann, girl, the mistress says ye've got to go. Here's a reference for ye, a good character. Ye've earned it." There are so many things she can never say in this situation. *Good thing Mrs. Macready can't hear her guests calling her a jumped-up Scots merchant's wife, getting above her station. Good thing character's not of the body but of the soul. Because it's my body, again. Isn't it. The thing you can't stand to see.*

Ever since she left the village there's been house after lady's house, inn after inn after tavern with its pallet of straw in the back. And now, whatever hiding hole she can find. But there is always the body and the thing between its legs to haul from pillar to post, from doorway to bridge-arch to square of yellow light falling from window through which she can see the normal people drinking, eating, warming themselves, sitting still for as long as they like. Like a dumb child that's the cause of shame yet unknowing of wrong, her body begs her: *What'd I do to be so hungry, so wet and raw? So cold? Oh, why am I not fit to look upon?*

The weight of rags around her hips is familiar now. Even the chafe of the reddened skin is known. She'd bathed the thing between her legs when she was in work at Mrs. Macready's and could haul a kettle up to the garret she shared with the other maids. "Oh, Ann," jested Irish Bridget, "don't ye find it a trial to bath so often?" But then Bridget saw her legs, and the thing between them, and went white, even crossed herself. "Oh, Ann. I'll pray for ye."

"Yes, well," Ann said. That was the third house in a year or maybe fourth and she was tired of prayers. "It ain't exactly suited God to take this from me, has it?"

All those Christians. Comfort the afflicted. That's what they are taught.

Here it is now, the great arch of Westminster. On nights like this all the hiding holes are full. The crevices up under Blackfriars and London Bridge and Westminster Bridge as well, the broken-open cellar near the Swan and Hoop where the fire started and has never been repaired, the lean-tos behind the breweries, where you can find old wicked Sal and all the rest, sucking on the barrel-dregs. The word's got out among them that Lord Mayor's decreed the Abbey door be opened on such nights. "Tell us another," says Ann. "Every time I've tried it's locked. And anyway, who'd let us in?" With all that gold, and all the famous tombs. All that splendor and illustriousness. Against old wicked Sal, and Will, and Mary Jane, and her. But even if the door isn't open there will be the arch, the nooks in all the walls. Some place to get out of the wind at least. A hole for her against the river and the stars and all this city.

It's funny, what'll put men off. She's seen them at it with the poxiest girls anyone could name, their black mouths jarred open in mock delight as some butcher's boy pumps at them with his pimply arse, his buttocks red and shriveled like the menagerie baboon's. But when she's had to let some man lift her skirts – hurts even to touch that thing, but it's food – he stops at the sight of it and on his face is something like Mrs. Macready's horror. A shout, a curse, a blow she'll dodge near-automatically. But yesterday had come a pause, a halt, her skirts shoved down, a coin flipped to her, a shamefaced sidelong glance: "Ah, well, then. That's for ye anyway."

Under the great east arch of Westminster Abbey, she pauses. Carved in stone, the saints and honored dead in rows until they narrow down to the great wooden door itself. This massive iron latch – large as her head, large as the wad of swaddling cloth that catches her trickling – has never been open. But, here, right now, it is.

Into the vestibule and then into the nave she slips. It's dim in here, lit only by torches burning in brackets on the walls, pressed in by the dark and the weight of all this space. High overhead comes a rustling, a clicking coo: pigeons have found a hole, as every creature must. Great shapely arches rise up and up into the black. Windows are spotted with what in sunlight would be color but now are only patterns, flat and dim: something like a Savior with his hands outstretched, something like a face.

She looks down into shadows at her feet. The dead are here, all their names to be trod upon. *Sacred to the Memory of Mary Countess Shrewsbury, Beloved….* Why read of it. She had her letters before she left the village to come to this place, and she had some Bible too. Her mother had read to her the story of the woman with the issue of blood who'd crept to Christ and touched his robe, who'd made the Savior wheel and cry out *Who touched me there?* Surely on his face was the same quick unhideable disgust the woman saw on every face when they caught sight and smell of her, the thing she'd prayed not to see as she brought him her body to pray for healing, her body with its traitorous seep of hope from her heart down into her stomach, where it pooled and burned. Read the story. Learn your letters. Pray. *Why am I not fit to look upon?*

The village. The taunts: piss-a-bed Ann. The whispers: *Have you seen it?* When the great red spongy thing began to grow on her and then to push the piss out of her sideways to left and right, uncontrollable, her mother had helped her with the rags, had washed and washed. Her mother had soothed her when the village boys had pinned her down and yanked her skirts up and pointed and laughed. "What did they say to you?" Mam demanded, but Ann had let her tears choke away the words. She wouldn't stain Mam with big Ned Simons' voice: "Ah, just like a mushroom on her cunt. Who'll ever give a ride to that?" Mam took ill when the milk-cow kicked her on the temple by mistake and then the landlord took the cottage and so that had to be that.

Here in the Abbey's dark there's no defense against the words or, worse, the tears, so she lets them come. She flees deeper into the gloom, under an arch spangled with gold, past a row of pews, past the ranks of choirboy seats upright and bare. The altar looms before her – a great window admitting of the night – and she dodges left and hurries deeper still. There must be shelter somewhere to rest this body for the night, this leaking stinking shitting bleeding yearning thing. She longs to be shed of it, to abandon it to dust like all the rest of them around her now – the Kings of England and all the other men who nevertheless can't stop the leak of her water out of her, the stink that drives her door to door, the dark that fastens over the city like a breeches-clout, the dawn that streaks dark blue above the river on yet another day to be endured.

A door, a passageway up some steps and she is into a smaller room with another tomb in the center and a narrow aisle around. One torch is lit and burning at the far end, even here. Lord, what it must cost to fire and light this place. A stone queen lies face-up under a canopy, narrow pointed hands folded, high forehead a perfect blank, a body neat, tidy, odorless, composed. The glow discovers Ann the words on a plaque: *Near the tomb of Mary and Elizabeth remember before God all those who divided at the Reformation by different convictions laid down their lives for Christ and conscience sake.* The old ones in the village talked of burnings their own grandparents had seen, of stripping the altar of any cross or Popery. *Thou shalt not suffer a witch to live.* She left the village when Mam died. Before they could get around to burning her.

In the farthest corner Ann curls, tucking her feet under her skirt and pulling her shawl and her layerings tight. The stone seeps into her on all sides. So cold. The hip that's going gamey with the walking presses into the floor and pains her now so she turns over to ease it some. With her eyes shut and forehead against stone the headache eases too. She's thirsty but she dast not drink. For what she drinks will only leak right out again.

In her dream she's back in the village milking the cow, pulling those teats with the leaking jets of milk, warm from the creature's body, steaming in the chilly morning, her head against its flank: *ssst, ssst, ssst.* And then there's an old man with a lantern bending over her, shaking her shoulder. He's asking her name, trying to rouse her, saying something about a hospital. A hospital's where you go to die, but this is too much trouble to explain to this stranger now. Ann turns her face back to the wall. *Sleep*, she wants to tell him. *Please just let me* – But the words don't come. Against her forehead the abbey stone has begun to warm. This one place in all cold stinking London acknowledges her. And she'll stay here for as long as it will hold a knowledge of her body: of the circle of warmth, mute and innocent, it can yet cast.

The Edinburgh Medical and Surgical Journal, 1 April 1805. Case of Malconformation of the Urinary and Genital Organs in a Female. By Mr. Astley Cooper, Surgeon to Guy's Hospital, London. Vol. 1 No. II, p. 129.

Ann Carter, age 22, was admitted, on the 4th of March 1803, into St. Thomas's hospital under the care of Mr. Cline, on account of a fungous tumour on the lower part of the abdomen, through which the urine was involuntarily discharged. This misfortune she had laboured under from her birth; but when she arrived at the age of puberty, her situation, in that part of the country in which she was born, became insupportable to her feelings, on account of her infirmity being known. She therefore resolved to seek her subsistence in London, where she vainly imagined it might escape detection, and she soon procured the situation of a servant to a family in town. But being unable to retain her urine, her clothes were rendered offensive by it, and her bed was nightly wetted. Her infirmity was thus soon discovered by her employers, and she was dismissed from their service. By frequent disappointments of this kind, she was reduced to seek a miserable subsistence by begging, and spent days and nights in the streets of London, until, becoming ill from the effects of want, and exposure to the severity of the weather, she was carried by the police to an hospital; and, when admitted into St. Thomas's, she was so much reduced by poverty and sickness, that she died on the 8th of March, four days after her admission.

Tara Stillions Whitehead

None of This Is Real

On shooting day 42 of 59, we find Britney behind a white shower curtain in LA General's ER, her saline-tubed arm wrapped around a black pelican case of walkie talkies. The Prius her parents cosigned for is a mangled installation of metal and smoke and craft services at the bottom of the spitless LA river. The new Air Jordans she'd been flexing at crew call on shooting day 41 of 59 are missing their treads, have been shoved into a plastic bag with her name on it hanging at the end of her hospital bed.

"She growled at us!" the tattooed nurse with the fresh undershave says. He laughs and licks at his clear retainer. "She said *they* would fire her if she didn't bring them back to work tomorrow. Who are *they*? Is it *you*? Are *you* they?" He rounds Britney's bed to the wall of machines keeping her stabilized and hydrated. He writes down a few numbers and continues the story, "I was like, girl, you got a busted collarbone, fractured hip, and subdural hematoma the size of my ass. You're *not* going to work tomorrow. You're not going to work *next month.* The only place you're going is online and to PT. That's when she lost it. She started growling and crying. Like a fucking hyena. I said *girrrrl*—" an incomprehensible page crackles over the hospital intercom—"I said *girl*, you howlin' at a deaf moon. But...the others and I...we felt bad and were like okay, whatever, we'll let her keep them in the bed if it chills her out. Once we told her that—" he brings his hand down onto the clipboard like an anvil, "*boom!—good night.* She's been down for—" he checks his notes, "*twelve* hours now?"

We thank him for his assistance and compassion for Britney. We compliment him on his nightingale forearm tattoo. When he leaves, we take the walkie talkie case and speed back towards our shooting location Santa Monica. We make it to set ten minutes before crew call, open the walkie case. We are speechless. The radios are all charged and ready to go, which means they must have been plugged in at the hospital, which means Britney did exactly what we'd trained her to do.

*

The first time I stayed up all night to see the sunrise, I was ten.

I played *Pee Wee's Big Adventure* over and over on the 13" Magnavox in my room. My senses magnified as the night wore down, the TV taking on a fifth dimension. The whine of the VHS rewinding in the player became a song with hidden lyrics. I watched and rewatched the scene where Pee Wee and Simone huddle in the mouth of the T-Rex and wait for the new day to come. I wanted to see those impossible colors—the dawn's fiery entrance.

Just before daybreak, a fog moved in and blocked the sun. Everything looked flat, desaturated, compressed to death like old television show. I fell asleep at my desk before lunch and dreamed I was on a train to Hollywood, part of a massive search party looking for Pee Wee's stolen bike. Everything was technicolor. Everything was beautiful and worth investigating. I woke up to the lunch bell and decided a world of color is the only kind of world worth living in. I needed to figure out how to relocate to that world, to harness its light and orchestrate its soundscapes. I needed to discover how to bring that world to the colorless one, to make them one.

I needed to learn how to make movies.

*

On shooting day 45 of 59, I let the Best Boy Electric call the martini shot and spin the dials because he is pretty to watch and after twenty hours on set, words are cotton candy silliness in my mouth.

"That's a wrap," he says, eight times, once for each department channel on the radio.

The Actors are the first to leave and take their entourage of hair and make-up artists with them in the transpo van back to base camp where they will undress and hang their wardrobe and prop bags on the back of the trailer door. They will fall asleep in the passenger seat of the sleek black Suburban escort back to the hotel and will return before the union-mandated 12-hour turnaround is up. The producers have done the math. Forced calls cost less than adding days to shooting schedule.

I wait for the Best Boy—Juergen—at the lowered lift gate of the 18-wheel electric truck parked behind the talent trailers. He is hunched at a makeshift desk towards the front of the shipping container, purple LED lights spilling their psychedelic confetti over his black hair. He is filling out the electric department paperwork that he will give to me so I can enter it into the production report that I send to the office each night. The crew parking lot is empty except for us, a condor, and a long line of two-bangers, honeywagons and work trucks. The sun is about to rise over the Pacific Ocean.

Juergen takes his time with the pen and paper, fills each little rectangle on the matrix with a whole number and fraction to the closest twelfth. He knows I can't leave without his calculations—without him.

He means to keep me here, but he doesn't mean to keep me up. Fatigue isn't a weapon we use against each other, not on these marathon-style gigs.

We have sex in the passenger seat of his yellow X-Terra. He tells me he loves me for the first time. I tell him I have to finish the production report and give him a playful kiss on the neck.

I'm so tired I accidentally assign the camera department meal penalties in the grip department and forget to enter the mileage for our stuntman, who drove 160 miles roundtrip to set because he is terrified of flying. Two hours after Juergen called the last shot, I click send on the production report email.

I drive home full of Juergen and Red Bull and panic. It's 5:30am. The 405 is less parking lot, more drive-thru, and maybe that's why I almost miss the exit and cut too hard into the off-ramp. The retaining wall pinball-paddles me up over the embankment and back across five lanes of red and white lights. I come to a stop upside-down beneath a CBS billboard and a cement sky, suffocate into a colorless sleep.

*

In 1965, a 17-year-old boy stayed awake for 264 hours for his science fair project. On the eleventh day, he slept 14 hours and 40 minutes. The doctor supervising his high school science experiment reported no lasting physical side effects.

Within days, he could run a sub-7 5k and split half a cord of oak.

The conclusion? A body can endure. It can recover.

A person can survive without dreams.

*

After I fall asleep at the wheel, Juergen builds a living room set inside my bedroom closet. I wake up to him sitting in a director's chair beside my bed, the crackle of walkie talkie chatter everywhere.

"What's going on?" I look down at the filleted meat of my arms, the cadre of stuffed animals at the foot of my raised trundle bed, the center of which includes a fluffy orca spouting a satin banner with the words: "Life blows sometimes. Get whale soon!"

Our goateed Key Set PA, Edwin, emerges from the closet with a gift basket full of reusable hot and cold packs, trail mix, highlighters, and organic muscle balms. He parks the awkward boat of miscellany on top of my computer desk. "From the producers," he says and then disappears behind the palisade of blazers and college sweatshirts I've meticulously hung and organized by season.

I turn to Juergen, who is enthusiastically scraping the bottom out of a yogurt cup. "Orcas are dolphins."

Juergen draws the spoon across his tongue. "Huh?"

"Get 'whale'?" I say, pointing at the black and white toy. "Orcas. They're fucking dolphins."

Juergen swallows hard and sets the empty cup on the floor beside his director's chair. "Then why do they call them killer whales?"

My bedroom door opens. Our A Camera Operator and her

First and Second Assistant Camera crew members pass the foot of my bed with coffee in paper to-go cups. Marcy, the Second Assistant Camera, gives me a cheeky wave before disappearing into the closet.

"Juergen, what's going on? What's happening?"

"You can work from home now," he says. "No more commute."

"What about the company moves to the Malibu house? What about the exterior shoots on days 30 to 37?"

"Rewritten. The producers didn't want to lose you," he says. Then, "your dad doesn't mind. He even helped the construction set up the flats for a few of the club scene interiors. Your closet is much bigger than you think it is."

I'm twenty-seven, but I've been living with my parents in Venice Beach to save money for a down-payment on a bungalow in North Hollywood. I'm not sure how Juergen got here or managed to fit eighty-five crew members and their gear between the secret library of R.L Stine books and a Ponderosa my dad and I built when I was eight, but I'm actually more concerned about Juergen seeing the shameful artifacts of my later childhood—badminton trophies, unfinished crucifix lanyards, a paper shrine devoted to Leonardo DiCaprio and Baz Luhrmann's *Romeo & Juliet.*

He knows too much now.

I go to can't afford to lose this assistant directing gig. I need the union days. I can't afford to lose my health insurance. Especially since the arrhythmias started. Who can afford to pay out-of-pocket for an EKG every month? On no income?

A small part of me holds out hope that if I can make it through the next few weeks of this shoot, I might have enough reserve to take a month off and finish my feature script. I might have time to make it good, to get it agented, to land something that could get me out of these brutal, endless, grinding days of platforming someone else's dream.

"Oh my god," I say. I grab the clipboard Juergen has placed by my pillow and scan the call sheet I don't remember completing but must have because—there it is—my signature at the bottom. "My parents are going to kill me."

"I told you," Juergen says, "Your dad's cool with it." Then, "It was tricky to figure out crew parking and where to put the work trucks. Your neighbor with the surfing Jesus sculpture screamed at Lily in Wardrobe because her Jeep was blocking the view of oncoming traffic and almost got T-boned by the Sound van rolling up. But it's all good now. Locations and Production secured a basecamp three blocks away, in the old Blockbuster parking lot."

*

Shooting day 48 of 59. Juergen says the producers don't want me to have a walkie talkie. Really, it's doctor's orders. They say a surveillance in my ear will make the head trauma worse, which will slow recovery. Even though he isn't in my department, Juergen has been assigned to communicate between me and the crew. He creates a small working desk out of my pink six-drawer vanity in the corner of the room by clamping some black lights to the mirror and using my exercise ball as a chair.

"I can't work like this," I say.

"You don't need to work. It is all being done for you," Juergen says, bouncing and smiling at me in the mirror.

I'm in bed, but I don't sleep.

*

Shooting day 31 of 59. I see things. Shadow puppets in my peripheral vision. Crew members I don't know. I tell Edwin to bring me a sticky note with the day players' names on it, and he disappears into the closet for hours at a time, only to return with C-47s (clothespins) clipped together in varying configurations of a voodoo dolls and effigies.

My hands flicker like a television screen. Here they are. There they go.

Nine hours into our day, and two hours since I dismissed Edwin and his evil art creations, Juergen comes in from the hallway carrying a sandwich on one of my parents' stoneware plates.

"Your mom sends her best—and your favorite sandwich," Juergen approaches the bed and holds out the plate.

"So now you know," I say.

"Liverwurst and pickles. She asked if I wanted one," he says, "but I told her I only eat animals from the chest up."

"So by that logic you'll eat brains but you won't eat thighs?"

Juergen leans in close and whispers, "Do you know what a liver does?"

I swipe the plate from Juergen and set it by the glass and brass touch lamp on my side table. The room ripples like a pond in a breeze, a little bit of color escaping into the closet with each successive ebb.

"You okay?" Juergen asks.

"Where's Britney?"

"Britney who?"

"The set PA who crashed her—" I stop. Smoke is wafting in from the closet door.

Juergen catches my gaze, "They're prepping the dream sequence where Meredith kills Dolores so that she can have Herman all to herself. Jimmy's going a little wild on the fog machine, so I'm thinking of tripping a fuse on him."

"What am I even doing, Juergen? What is going on?"

"You're working. Recovering and working."

"I'm sitting in a twin bed. The twin bed where I lost my virginity to Brian Thum and fingered Kelsey Milhouse."

Juergen grins. "Liverwurst aside, the more I learn about you—"

"There's an eighty-person film crew making an entire season of episodic television inside of my closet, and I'm just sitting here with a clipboard I can't read and disappearing hands." I look at him, "Why am I here? *Am* I here? Am I asleep? Is this some kind of experiment to see how much *they* can fuck with me before I totally lose it and fold?"

Juergen looks at me with genuine confusion. "Just what you said. We're making a show. You crashed your car, and Randy decided to bring the show to you. To be safe. To get it done, too. But mostly to be safe. I don't know. Maybe they also want to avoid a lawsuit. Actually, now that I think about it—"

"This isn't real. None of this is real."

"Remember when we did the telenovela gig down in San Diego?" Juergen asks. "We used our housing stipends to buy all that speed and ended up in Vegas with only our phones and wallets? We laid on the floor of the Bellagio, under those huge glass flower sculptures they had on the ceiling, people walking around us in their Louis Vuittons, holding martinis and shit, until security came?" He laughs. "You kept telling them 'none of this is real.' You kept repeating it, over and over, all the way back up to our room where we sat in the shower for like two hours. Those security fuckers were laughing at you, but I knew you were talking about something else…"

"I repeat myself when I'm smashed," I say.

"Maybe," he says. "Or maybe the truth caught you with your guard down and was trying to make itself heard."

He unties his size fourteen Wolverine work boot and pulls out a small bottle of Becherovka, which I haven't seen since I broke my foot behind a frozen church in Hradčanská, Prague. He puts the green glass to his lips and smiles.

"I'm losing it," I say. "None of this makes sense," and then, "Where did you get that?"

Juergen inspects the bottle, as if seeing it for the first time. "You know…I don't know. Props department? To be honest, weird stuff like this has been happening to me a lot a lot now."

"Doesn't that bother you?"

He shrugs and takes a careful sip, "Not really."

Becherovka is a secret bitter. Vintage enough to seem exotic, but not ancient. As he continues to sip, the centuries-old breeze od cinnamon and clove stirs memory from my body and projects it on the back of my bedroom door: Me, standing on the Charles Bridge, peering into the scintillating brilliance of the Vltava. I don't have a camera or a phone or a motive. I don't need to capture the moment's simple beauty by suffocating it into artistic preservation. I am simply present. Ambitionless. Relishing the bitters burning through my empty stomach, the fiery colors of the world I thought had abandoned me that night when I was ten.

Juergen sees the projection, too. He climbs into bed next to me, and we watch the POV shot play out. He doesn't know it is my vision, but it doesn't matter. That's the subjective magic of film. The suspension of disbelief. The reason we are here.

He holds the bottle under my nose and rolls the wet glass across my lips. He strokes my hair while I sip myself into the past. The bedroom corners soften into merengue. Panic, the ever-ticking clock in my chest, lifts into the atmosphere. The gentle, flickering water montage on my door continues its interminable dance.

Juergen rises like a kite, tapes a blue gel over my bedroom window. Venice Beach becomes the Challenger Deep.

"The sun can pretend it's the moon now," Juergen says, sailing back to me, sweeping over the narrow shore of my body.

Everything is water now. We kiss the soft sand of each other's stomachs. We drown beneath blue sheets.

Hammers and power tools and periodic laughter indicate that the crew inside the closet is erecting a fourth wall.

Juergen slips his thumb into my mouth and drags his teeth across my chest. We listen for open radios, try to gauge how much time we have before they're ready to shoot the scene.

"You'll miss the safety meeting," I mumble into his neck.

I can't stop saying the things I am being paid of say. Thousands of hours on set will do that. It's not the art that replaces the person, it's the monotony. But there is still this humanness pulsing between my legs, feelings being felt without words to flatten them into comprehension. A library of feelings waiting for desperate researching. And Juergen does that. He crawls up inside of me with an eager mind. He opens the secret door to my inner home and peruses the bookshelves of my soul. He trips and falls through the threshold separating my living room and kitchen and pores over the secrets I keep hidden in the expired condiments in my refrigerator door. He lies naked in my bed, masturbates to the sound of me laughing, and then runs a bath until it overflows and I'm flooded from the inside out.

When he leaves, the emptiness feels different. Lived in.

When he leaves, I open my eyes and see that I am alone and the bedroom door is just a door. The memory has passed. Everything is quiet.

I can't remember the last time I had company over.

I can't remember the day I stopped living inside of my body.

*

A 37-year-old Boom Operator in Phoenix, Arizona, collapses in the middle of a take on the seventh day of shooting the remake of the fifth installment in the *Saw* series. The Unit Production Manager, trying to make a comeback after two failed Tom Arnold pilots, tells two Dolly Grips to carry the woman out to the empty field behind the sound stage so that the Set Medic can do compressions until paramedics arrive. The UPM hands the boom pole to the production assistant who was, unbeknownst to her, just out behind the generators doing whip-its with Craft Services and the Props Master.

As the actors reset to their starting positions, the UPM leans over to the Locations Manager. "Is there a way for us to contact the ambulance and ask them not to use their sirens?" she whispers, "Actually, if you don't mind standing down the street so you can flag them down, we catch the trucks before they get here, and that way they won't ruin the takes we need to get in before lunch."

*

Juergen puts his mouth over mine. Everything tastes like cinnamoned pine and blood. A voice crackles through the soft plastic surveillance piece dangling from his ear: "Five minutes until picture."

"You know that means ten minutes," he whispers. "Kevin will forget to jam the slate. Bonita's going to ask Roberto to give her a line read again. We have time."

There's only so much time for us to do what we need to do. The black gaff tape he uses to fix me to the headboard is paper thin, so I am very careful not to struggle or reach for him. We both know my bondage is one part illusion, two parts compliance, but I don't know if Juergen can feel my growing unease.

"Do you remember Charles Shaughnessy?" I ask. Juergen wraps my left wrist to the bed frame one more time and throws a glance at the closet to see if anyone from the crew is spying on us through the open sliding doors. "He was the dad on *The Nanny*. The British guy?"

"Yeah, I gaffed a life insurance commercial with him in Rancho Cucamonga."

"He saved me from electrocution once."

"Only once?" Juergen runs his lips from my wrists down to my chest.

"We were filming a pilot about a yacht club."

Juergen looks up, holds my face in his sturdy hands, "This is exactly why you can never go back to low-budget shows. If I'd been there, it wouldn't have been an issue."

"No, no. It wasn't an electrical department issue," I tell him. "If anything, it was a locations issue. We nearly capsized when a pod of blue whales breached nearby. I fell overboard into a school of electric stargazers. Charles jumped into the tender boat and came back to get me. He was a hero, but the script was terrible."

Juergen kisses my forehead and looks into my eyes, "This is what we do. It's crazy, but it's life. We live for this shit."

*

Before the famous actor shot and killed the up-and-coming cinematographer on a low-budget western outside of Santa Fe, New Mexico, the camera department protested the producers' decision to deny them housing, forcing them to gamble with their exhaustion and commute hours to and from set on a desolate stretch of road. The Producers, modern-day

Narcissuses powered on lithium batteries and viral Tik Toks, ordered black long-sleeve shirts with the phrase "You can sleep when you're dead" silkscreened across the front.

The morning of the murder, as the Camera Crew were collecting their lenses and monitors and preparing to disembark the runaway train of a production—for their dignity and humanity and livelihoods!—the Executive Producer paces the equipment staging area, bundle of burning sage raised high, and chants a mantra he purchased from @nativemedwogoddess, a supposed Dakota Nations medicine woman on Venmo, the night before. When he finishes the smudging ritual, he circles the dispersing Camera Crew, mumbling and scrolling his phone, "You feel that? You feel those low vibrations just *evaporating* right out of here?"

*

Day 50 of 59. My vision is crowded with floaters. Translucent cobwebs and tiny shadow puppets all using my corneas as a dance floor. I can't read the small text on the call sheet anymore, so Juergen sings it to me, line by line.

"Production notes: No open-toed shoes. Forced calls no longer prohibited. Meal penalties as needed. Must start-work-finish all principals today. No open radios on set. Safety meeting to be held thirty minutes after call. Must wrap out of location by 5am. Submit your NCAA brackets to Sammy by noon. Don't drink and drive."

The bedroom ceiling light flickers and goes dark. The plastic stars my parents bought me during our trip to Lick Observatory when I was eight form a harrowing constellation across the flat white sky. Two words:

BE FAMOUS.

*

The Segment Producer from *The Daily Show* is someone I know from film school in LA. I slept with her boyfriend before he was her boyfriend, took his virginity before I knew he was a virgin. I liked her a lot when we were in the same Punch-Up Techniques for TV Comedy Writing class. She had the dirtiest jokes and the stealthiest callbacks. She is Canadian and married to a cybersecurity expert who works from home and takes care of their 4-month-old daughter. I know this from browsing her Instagram posts, which she strategically adds to maybe once every three months.

I run into the Segment Producer from *The Daily Show* on a weekend trip to New York City to watch a one-man stand-up show I've been asked to help produce as a web series for a new streaming service. I've just left the staged reading and am headed towards my Air bnb in Chelsea, rewinding the tape in my head, feeling anxiously committed even though the topical jokes about abortion and gun violence and #metoo drew more ire than laughs, when I hear a woman call my name from across the intersection. It's a pleasant chance encounter. Organic and far enough removed from the film school days that I can set aside any shame or guilt I might still have over the regret I felt every time I saw her with the man whose virginity I took and didn't realize I'd been in love with, until it was too late.

"Congratulations on becoming a mom," I tell her.

"Oh my god, *shhhh*!" she says, ducking between me and a cement apartment staircase. "You're going to get me fired!"

"What are you talking about?" I look behind us, genuinely convinced that she had seen someone materialize out of the ether at the mention of motherhood.

My friend rises slowly, smooths her beige suit jacket down over an impossibly flat postpartum stomach. "Ever since our post-production supervisor was fired for having twins, we've decided not to talk about Skylar until she is in kindergarten."

"We?"

"Me and my husband."

"Kindergarten. That's like five years, Debbie."

"It goes so much faster than you think," she says with more joy than despair. "How about you? Do you have any…?"

"I don't even have a person, Debbie," I say.

The Daily Show producer's face relaxes into sudden disconnect. She checks her phone and starts drifting up 8th

Avenue. "I have a meeting with the censors in twenty minutes and need to go. It was so great running into you. Let's get together the next time you're in the city!"

"Hey, Debbie," I call. "Why did they fire her? Did she miss days at work? Stop showing up?"

"She was falling asleep in the sound mixes. And at the spotting sessions. And at the studio screenings. They said it was sleep deprivation and blamed the babies." She gives me a knowing look. "You know who they really blamed."

*

Shooting Day 59 of 59. I've forgotten the color of sky, the elevation of dreams.

"Striking!" The closet casts a rectangle of cold gray light across the bed. The sheets are soaking wet and smell like asphalt and gasoline.

The traffic noise escalates into a rainless thunder.

Juergen and I are separated by three lanes of traffic. He is a small figuring standing by the miniature closet door in my now infinite room. He cinches his work belt and waves at me. Even at this distance, his body is the exact shape of my longing.

I start to cry.

"What's wrong?" he shouts. Two U-Hauls and a funeral procession pass between us.

"I don't think I'm sleeping," I say.

"It's all sleeping and being awake. It's always been like that."

"No, this is different," I say.

The bedroom door opens, and two paramedics walk in and set two duffle bags on the floor by the open closet. They wait for a break in the traffic and jog over to me, immediately begin to tear me free from the headboard.

The Female Paramedic takes me under the arms, the Male Paramedic grabs me by the shins, and on the count of three, they hoist me off the bed and lie me on the glass-and-aluminum-littered asphalt of the freeway median. The Female Paramedic sprints to the exit shoulder and hands the defibrillator power cord to Juergen, who plugs into a black electrical box at the foot of the dresser right next to the closet door.

Juergen, looking into the closet, into the cool gray light, speaks confidently into the surveillance microphone, "Tell Rick we can power fucking Beijing if he needs us to. We'll get him a second sun, simulate a forest fire, whatever the fuck he wants."

"You dozed off," the Male Paramedic says. His eyes are shiny nickels that flash blue as someone turns the key light towards him. Desi from Hair and Makeup flies in, dabs a little paintbrush across my lips and blows a tear stick into my eyes to moisten them up.

"Looks are good," she says into the surveillance microphone clipped to her romper. She winks at me and jogs away, smacking her gum and zipping her fanny pack as she goes.

"What's happening?" I manage.

Someone dips a boom mic over my head. "Can we get a sound check real quick?"

"What?"

The Male Paramedic lifts his mouth to the shotgun microphone and sings the horn solo from "Tequila" by The Champs.

The Boom Operator, a day player I don't recognize, gives a thumbs up and the Male Paramedic turns back to me, smiling, "We're about to get going. Just waiting on the defibrillator to charge."

A colorless sun crests over the CBS billboard, casts its gray beams across my totaled car, the morning traffic.

I'm not struggling to breathe, but the Male Paramedic places an oxygen mask over my face anyway. I can hear the First Assistant Camera person call the shot to my left, but I can't see her—"Episode 59, Scene 7, Take One. A and B, common mark—soft sticks." A gentle clap indicates she's clapped the slate.

There's a brief pause. Someone calls out, "Set!" The Director says, "Action!"

I start to cry, "Am I dead?"

The Male Paramedic strokes my hair with genuine concern, his previously blue eyes now haunting daguerreotypes of silver and milk. "Don't worry, sweetheart. You just hang in there, okay? We're gonna get you back up and running in no time. I promise."

"But I'm not…"

The Female Paramedic enters screen left with the charged defibrillator, hits her mark so that she's a shadow perfectly backlit by the rising sun. "Charged to 900," she says.

"900 volts?" I panic as they continue to talk around me.

"Good God, we're losing her," the Male Paramedic cries, quickly taking up the paddles.

"Are we clear, Jack?" the Female Paramedic asks.

The Male Paramedic pauses, feigns intense reflection as he remembers his line. He looks deeply into my eyes until he finds it. "Damn it," he says finally, standing up, pulling a white shower curtain closed between us. "We've lost her."

Contributors

Sean Cho A. is the author of *American Home*, winner of the Autumn House Press chapbook contest. His work can be found or ignored in *Copper Nickel, Prairie Schooner, The Massachusetts Review, Nashville Review*, among others. Sean is a graduate of the MFA program at The University of California Irvine and a PhD Student at the University of Cincinnati. He is the Editor in Chief of *The Account.*

Anthony Aguero is the author of *Burnt Spoon Burnt Honey* with Flower Song Press. He has been twice nominated for a Pushcart Prize and was featured in *The Slowdown.* His poems have been published with *Carve Magazine, Rhino Poetry, Foglifter, Guernica* and elsewhere.

Darius Atefat-Peckham is the author of the chapbook *How Many Love Poems* (Seven Kitchens Press, 2021) and editor of Susan Atefat-Peckham's posthumous collection *Deep Are These Distances Between Us* (CavanKerry Press, 2023). His work has recently appeared in *Poetry Magazine, Poem-a-Day, Shenandoah, Rattle, The Journal, The Georgia Review*, and elsewhere. Atefat-Peckham grew up in Huntington, West Virginia, and currently studies English and Near Eastern Languages and Civilizations at Harvard.

Darnell Arnoult is the author of the novel *Sufficient Grace* and the poetry collections *What Travels With Us* and *Galaxie Wagon.* She has received the SIBA Poetry Book of the Year Award, Mary Frances Hobson Medal for Arts and Letters, the Thomas and Lillie D. Chafin Award for Appalachian Writing, and the Weatherford Award. She lives in Mebane, North Carolina, where she continues to write, coach other writers in virtual gatherings. and critiques manuscripts. Visit darnellarnoult.net for more information.

Chris Arthur is an Irish essayist currently based in Scotland. He's the author of several essay collections, most recently *Hidden Cargoes* (2022), and has published in a wide range of journals in the US and UK. *What Is It Like to Be Alive? Fourteen Attempts at an Answer*, his latest collection, is forthcoming from EastOver Press.

Amber Wheeler Bacon's work has appeared or is forthcoming in *Ecotone, Epiphany, Five Points, Post Road, New Ohio Review, Crazyhorse and Witness.* You can find her writing online at *Ploughshares, CRAFT, Fiction Writer's Review and New South.* She is the recipient of the 2018 Breakout Writers Prize sponsored by The Author's Guild and a 2021 scholarship from Bread Loaf Environmental. In 2020, her story collection, "We Were Vessels," was one of five finalists for Hub City Press's C. Michael Curtis Short Story Book Prize and a finalist for Moon City Press's Short Fiction Award. She received the 2022 Lit/South Award and teaches English at Coastal Carolina University.

Matt Barrett teaches creative writing at Gettysburg College and hold an MFA in Fiction from UNC-Greensboro. His stories and poems have appeared or are forthcoming in *The Sun, Best Microfiction 2022, SmokeLong Quarterly, River Teeth, The Minnesota Review, Pithead Chapel, The Forge, Contrary, Hobart, and Wigleaf*, among others. He tweets @MBarrettWriter.

Christine Barkley is an artist and writer based in the Pacific Northwest. Her writing explores themes of chronic illness, trauma, and nature. Her work has appeared or is forthcoming in *The Massachusetts Review*, *Salamander*, *Rust + Moth*, and *Autofocus*, among others.

Ace Boggess is author of six books of poetry, including *Escape Envy*, *I Have Lost the Art of Dreaming It So*, and *The Prisoners.* His writing has appeared in *Michigan Quarterly Review*, *Notre Dame Review*, *Harvard Review*, *Mid-American Review*, and other journals. An ex-con, he lives in Charleston, West Virginia, where he writes and tries to stay out of trouble. His seventh collection, *Tell Us How to Live*, is forthcoming in 2024 from Fernwood Press.

Greg Bottoms is the author of two short story collections, *Sentimental, Heartbroken Rednecks and Pitiful Criminals;* two works of literary journalism, *The Colorful Apocalypse: Journeys in Outsider Art* and *Spiritual American Trash: Portraits from the Margins of Art and Faith*; and three memoirs, *Angelhead, Fight Scenes,* and *Lowest White Boy*. His work has appeared in *The Believer, Harper's, The Oxford American*, and in numerous literary journals and anthologies.

Jacob Boyd is from Lansing, Michigan. He works in a bakery in Milwaukee. Poems of his have appeared in *American Journal of Poetry, Blackbird, Copper Nickel, Fiddlehead,* and elsewhere. His chapbook, *Stilt House*, was selected by Heather McHugh for the Emrys Press Award.

Wendy BooydeGraaff's fiction, poems, and essays have been included in *NOON*, *Flyover Country*, *X-R-A-Y*, *Slant: A Journal of Poetry*, and elsewhere. Born and raised in Ontario, Canada, she now lives in Michigan.

Hannah Bonner's poems have appeared, or are forthcoming, in *Asheville Poetry Review, Pigeon Pages, Rattle, Schlag, So to Speak, The Hopkins Review, The North Carolina Literary Review, The Pinch Journal, The Vassar Review, Tinderbox Poetry Journal, TriQuarterly*, and *Two Peach*. She is a creative nonfiction MFA candidate at the University of Iowa.

Evan Brooke's work has appeared in *The Threepenny Review, The Northwest Review, The Baltimore Review, The Chicago Quarterly Review*, and elsewhere. Her fiction has been shortlisted for The Moth Short Story Prize and the Writers' League of Texas Manuscript Contest. She is a writer and teacher in the Philadelphia area, and holds an MFA from the Bennington Writing Seminars.

Sarah Butkovic holds an MA in English from Loyola University Chicago. Her writing can be found in *The Decadent Review*, *Stella Veritatis*, and elsewhere.

N.J. Campbell is the author of *Found Audio.* He lives and writes in the Midwest.

Matt Cashion's story collection, *Last Words of the Holy Ghost,* won the 2015 Katherine Anne Porter Prize for short fiction, judged by Lee K. Abbott, and his novel *Our Thirteenth Divorce* won the 2017 Edna Ferber Book Prize, judged by Robert Olmstead. Other work has appeared in *The Sun, Willow Springs, Grist: A Journal for Writers, Carolina Quarterly, Moon City Review, Passages North, storySouth, The Writer's Chronicle*, and elsewhere. He lives in La Crosse, WI, where he works as Professor of Creative Writing at UW-La Crosse.

Kathryn Chiariello is an essayist and fiction writer from Washington, DC. Her work has been published in The Watershed Review and *Gargoyle.* Like all DC residents, she lacks voting representation in Congress.

Catherine Pritchard Childress lives in the shadow of Roan Mountain in East Tennessee. She teaches writing and literature at Lees-McRae College. Her poems have appeared in *North American Review, Louisiana Literature, Connecticut Review, The Cape Rock, Still: The Journal, Appalachian Review, Stoneboat,* and *drafthorse* among other journals. Her work has been anthologized in *The Southern Poetry Anthology*, Volumes VI and VII: Tennessee and North Carolina, and in *Women Speak*, Volumes VII and VIII. She is the author of the poetry collections *Other* and most recently *Outside the Frame*, published by EastOver Press.

Grant Clauser is the author of five books, most recently *Muddy Dragon on the Road to Heaven* (winner of the Codhill Press Poetry Award). Poems have appeared in *The American Poetry Review*, *Greensboro Review*, *Kenyon Review*, *Tar River Poetry* and others. He works as an editor in Pennsylvania and teaches at Rosemont College.

Nancy Cook runs "The Witness Project," a program of free community writing workshops in Minneapolis designed to enable creative work by underrepresented voices. Some of her recent work can be found in *Channel Magazine, decomp journal,* and the *Michigan Quarterly Review.* More about her work can be found at NancyLCook.com.

Eileen Cunniffe writes nonfiction that has appeared in *Global City Review, Still Point Arts Quarterly, Funny Pearls, Bluestem Magazine*, and *The RavensPerch.* Eileen's essays have been recognized with Travelers' Tales Solas Awards and the Emrys Journal 2013 Linda Julian Creative Nonfiction Award. Her first book, *Mischief & Metaphors: Essaying a Life*, was published in 2023 by Shanti Arts Publishing. Read more at www.eileencunniffe.com.

Bill Cushing lived in numerous states along with the Virgin Islands and Puerto Rico before moving to California where he lives in Glendale with his wife and their son. As an undergrad, he was called the "blue collar" writer because of his years working as an electrician on oil tankers, naval vessels, and fishing boats. Earning an MFA in writing from Goddard College, he recently retired from teaching at area colleges. A variety of his writing has appeared in print and online. He's published three books of poetry and is finishing up a memoir about his life working on ships.

Anthony D'Aries is the author of *The Language of Men: A Memoir* (Hudson Whitman Press, 2012), which received the PEN Discovery Prize and Foreword's Memoir-of-the-Year Award. His work has appeared in *McSweeney's, Boston Magazine, Solstice, The Literary Review, Memoir Magazine, Sport Literate, Flash Fiction Magazine*, and elsewhere. He was recently nominated for a Pushcart Prize and his essay, "No Man's Land," was listed as a Notable Essay in *Best American Essays* 2021. He currently directs the low-residency MFA in Creative and Professional Writing at Western Connecticut State University.

John F Duffy is a graduate of Columbia College Chicago. Currently a resident of southern Indiana, his debut novel "A Ballroom for Ghost Dancing" was published in summer 2022.

Since its inception, **Gary Fincke** has been co-editor (with Meg Pokrass) of the annual anthology *Best Microfiction.* His books have won the Flannery O'Connor Prize for Short Fiction, The Robert C. Jones Prize for Short Nonfiction Prose, and what is now the Wheeler Prize for Poetry. His latest nonfiction collection is *The Corridors of Longing* (Pelekinesis, 2022.) His latest collection of full-length stories is *Nothing Falls from Nowhere* (Stephen F. Austin, 2021). Besides having work chosen to appear *in Best American Essays 2020* and *Best Small Fictions 2020* , he has recently published flash fiction at such sites as *Craft, Wigleaf, Vestal Review, Atticus Review, Ghost Parachute, Pithead Chapel, New World Writing* , and *Flash Boulevard.*

Nick Rees Gardner has worked as a winemaker, chef, painter, show salesman, teacher, and addiction counselor. His criticism, fiction, and poetry have appeared in many literary journals, including *Epiphany, Atticus Review, Reckon Review, and Barrelhouse.* His book of poetry, *So Marvelously Far*, which tracks a life of substance abuse and recovery through a postindustrial Mansfield, Ohio, was published in 2019 through Crisis Chronicles Press; and his novella, *Hurricane Trinity*, is forthcoming in 2023 from Unsolicited Press. He currently lives in Washington, D.C., but still writes about Ohio.

Puloma Ghosh is a fiction writer living in Chicago, IL. Her work has appeared in *One Story* and *CRAFT* as a 2020 Flash Fiction Contest Winner, among other publications. She is a 2021 Tin House Summer Workshop Scholar and received her MFA from Bennington College, where she was the spring 2020 Residential Teaching Fellow.

Kathleen Gibbons received two Pushcart Prize nominations for her 2021 fiction publications in *Bellevue Literary Review and Air/Light Magazine.* Her short stories were finalists in contests for *American Short Fiction, The Sewanee Review, and Bellevue Literary Review.* She was a fellow at BookEnds, the novel development program of Southampton Arts at Stony Brook University and holds an MFA from the Bennington Writing Seminars. She is working on a novel set on California's central coast, and lives in Los Angeles with her family.

Lily Greenberg is a poet from Nashville, Tennessee, and the author of *In the Shape of a Woman*, published with Broadstone Books in 2022. Her work has appeared in *On* *the Seawall*, *Kissing Dynamite Poetry*, *About Place Journal*, *LEON Literary Review*, and *Relief Journal*, among others, and she is the 2021 recipient of the Dick Shea Memorial Prize for Poetry. Her work has been funded by Bread Loaf Writers, University of New Hampshire, and Maine Writers and Publishers Alliance. Lily holds an MFA from the University of New Hampshire and lives in the Hudson Valley where she serves as Grants Coordinator for Columbia University. Learn more at lily-greenberg.com.

Lauren Harkawik is a Vermont-based essayist, journalist, and fiction writer. Her nonfiction has appeared in *Autofocus, Salt Hill Journal*, and *Narratively*. You can read her more of her writing on www.laurenharkawik.com.

L. Mari Harris's stories have been chosen for the Wigleaf Top 50 and Best Microfiction. She lives in the Ozarks. Follow her @LMariHarris and read more of her work at www.lmariharris.wordpress.com.

Shayla Hawkins is from Detroit, Michigan. She is the author of *Carambola* and *Exquisite by September*. She is a winner of *The Caribbean Writer* Canute A. Brodhurst Prize for Short Fiction and The John Edgar Wideman Microstory Contest. *Exquisite by September* was a 2020 runner up for the Cave Canem/Northwestern University Press Poetry Prize and is now available from EastOver Press.

Craig Holt's short fiction and nonfiction have appeared in *Psychopomp Magazine, Jersey Devil Press, Exit 7*, and elsewhere. His first novel, *Hard Dog to Kill*, won the Independent Publishers Book Award gold medal. I received my MFA in creative writing from Bennington College. He is a fellow in the BookEnds novel incubation program.

Shilpa Kamat is a poet and educator currently residing in Northern California. She has an MFA in Creative Writing and has been published by a range of magazines from *Strange Horizons* to *Willowherb Review*. Her chapbook, *Saraswati Takes Back the Alphabet*, was a finalist for the Gloria Anzaldúa Poetry Prize and was published by *Newfound*. You can read more about her work at shilpakamat.com.

Maya Kanwal's work appears in *Witness, Meridian, Juxtaprose, Quarterly West* and other journals, has been anthologized by *The Doctor TJ Eckleburg Review* and nominated for the Pushcart Prize. She is an Inprint C. Glenn Cambor Fellow at the University of Houston Creative Writing MFA Program, and a Sewanee Writers' Conference and Bread Loaf Writers' Conference participant. Maya is a 2022 Inprint Donald Barthelme Prize in Fiction winner and *Witness Magazine* 2022 Literary Awards runner-up. She is Fiction Editor at *Gulf Coast Journal*. Follow her on Twitter @ mayakanwal

Christen Noel Kauffman is a 2022 National Poetry Series finalist and author of *Notes to a Mother God* which was a winner of the Paper Nautilus Debut Chapbook Series. Her work can be found in *A Harp in the Stars: An Anthology of Lyric Essays*, *Tupelo Quarterly*, *The Cincinnati Review*, *DIAGRAM*, *Smokelong Quarterly*, and *Hobart*, among others.

Armaan Kapur (he/him) is a writer and designer from New Delhi. His short prose has appeared in *The Reader Berlin, Apparition Lit*, and *Helter Skelter Magazine*. He is currently completing two full-length works: a debut novel about existentialism, and a collection of queer, speculative nonfiction.

Rimma Kranet is a Ukrainian-American writer with a bachelor's degree in English from University of California Los Angeles. Her work has appeared in *Brilliant Flash Fiction, Construction Lit, Coal Hill Review, EcoTheo Collective, The Common Breath, Drunk Monkey, Door Is A Jar Magazine* and in *The Short Vigorous Roots: A Contemporary Flash Fiction Collection of Migrant Voices*. She resides between Florence, Italy and Los Angeles, California.

Cecilia Kennedy (she/her) is a writer who taught English and Spanish in Ohio for 20 years before moving to Washington state with her family. Since 2017, she has published stories in international literary magazines and anthologies. Her work has appeared in *Maudlin House, Tiny Molecules, Rejection Letters, Kandisha Press, Ghost Orchid Press,* and others.

Cyn Kitchen is an associate professor of English at Knox College where she teaches creative writing and literature. She is the author of *Ten Tongues*, a collection of short stories. She also writes poems and nonfiction, some of which appear in *Fourth River, Poetry South*, *American Writers Review* and *Poetry Quarterly*. Cyn makes her home in Forgottonia, a downstate region on the Illinois prairie.

Matthew Landrum is a poet and translator. He is the author of *Berlin Poems* and translator of *Are there Copper Pipes in Heaven?* by Katrin Ottarsdóttir. He lives in Detroit.

Kris Lindsey is hopelessly curious and usually hungry. Following a thirty-year career in philanthropy, politics, and higher education, she switched gears to put her energy, time, and love into words. Her writing explores the intersections of identity, race, history, and place. She is at work on a book honoring 18 generations of Black resistance in America and assorted essays interrogating her personal ghosts. She is excited to share her first published essay in *Cutleaf*. She has forthcoming work in *The Audacity*. More info at www.kriswritenow.com

Jennifer LoveGrove is the author of the poetry chapbook *The Tinder Sonnets* and the 2017 collection *Beautiful Children with Pet Foxes*. Her novel *Watch How We Walk* was longlisted for the Scotiabank Giller Prize. She is currently at work on the full-length version of *The Tinder Sonnets*. She works at the University of Toronto and divides her time between downtown Toronto and Squirrel Creek Retreat in rural Ontario, Canada.

John C. Mannone has poems in *Windhover*, *North Dakota Quarterly*, *Poetry South*, *Baltimore Review*, and others. He won the Impressions of Appalachia Creative Arts Contest in poetry (2020), the Carol Oen Memorial Fiction Prize (2020), and the Joy Margrave Award (2015, 2017) for creative nonfiction. He was awarded a Jean Ritchie Fellowship (2017) in Appalachian literature and served as the celebrity judge for the

National Federation of State Poetry Societies (2018). His full-length collections are *Disabled Monsters* (Linnet's Wings Press, 2015), *Flux Lines: The Intersection of Science, Love, and Poetry* (Linnet's Wings Press, 2021), *Sacred Flute* (Iris Press, 2022), and *Song of the Mountains* (Middle Creek Publishing, 2023). He edits poetry for *Abyss & Apex* and other journals. A physics professor at Alice Lloyd College, John lives in southeast Kentucky.

Jude Marr (they, them) is a Pushcart-nominated nonbinary poet. Jude's first full-length collection, *We Know Each Other By Our Wounds*, came out from Animal Heart Press in 2020. Recent work appears in *Leavings*, Icefloe Press's *Work and the Anthropocene*, *Boats Against the Current*, and *Moria*. Jude is currently on the masthead at *SWWIM Miami* and *Poetry is Currency*.

Jill McCorkle has published seven novels and four collections of short stories, and her work has appeared in Best American Short Stories several times, as well as The Norton Anthology of Short Fiction. Five of her books have been New York Times Notable books, and her novel, *Life After Life*, was a New York Times bestseller. She has received the New England Booksellers Award, the John Dos Passos Prize for Excellence in Literature, and the North Carolina Award for Literature. She was a Briggs-Copeland Lecturer in Fiction at Harvard, where she also chaired the department of creative writing. She is currently a faculty member of the Bennington College Writing Seminars and is affiliated with the MFA program at North Carolina State University.

Ben Miller's work has appeared in *Best American Essays, Best American Experimental Writing, Kenyon Review, Raritan, AGNI, New England Review, Harvard Review, Antioch Review, Salmagundi, Yale Review, Southern Review, Fiction International*, and other venues. He is the author of *River Bend Chronicle: The Junkification of a Boyhood Idyll Amid the Curious Glory of Urban Iowa* (Lookout Books.) Awards include creative writing fellowships from the NEA and the Radcliffe Institute at Harvard University, and grants from the South Dakota Arts Council and the Schlesinger Library on the History of Women in America.

Jennifer Stewart Miller was born in Massachusetts and grew up in Vermont and California. She holds an MFA from Bennington College, a JD from Columbia University, and a BA from Michigan State University. Her book *Thief* won the 2020 Grayson Books Poetry Prize. Miller is also the author of *A Fox Appears: A Biography of a Boy in Haiku* (2015) and a chapbook, *The Strangers Burial Ground* (Seven Kitchens Press 2020). Her poems have appeared in *Hayden's Ferry Review, Poet Lore, RHINO, Sugar House Review, Tar River Poetry*, and elsewhere.

Douglas W. Milliken is a Maine composer, artist, and writer who, drawing from personal experience, examines intersecting themes of addiction, mental health, sexual ambiguity/fluidity, poverty, and childhood trauma. The author of two novels—*To Sleep as Animals* and *Our Shadows' Voice*—and the collection *Blue of the World*, he is also a founding member of the post-jazz chamber septet The Plaster Cramp, as well as the recipient of a Pushcart Prize and honors from the Maine Writers and Publishers Alliance, Glimmer Train, and RA & Pin Drop Studios, among others. www.douglaswmilliken.com

Paula Mirando is a queer Pinay writer from the Bay Area. Her writing has been supported by the Kearny Street Workshop Interdisciplinary Writers Lab, Voices of Our Nations Arts Foundation, and Philippine American Writers and Artists. Her fiction appears in *Waxwing* and she is currently working on a collection of linked short stories.

Rannvá Holm Mortensen is a leading Faroese visual artist. Her book-length poem, *Sólsmakkur*, explores themes of feminism, landscape, and the creative process. It is her first foray into poetry.

Karen Multer is a Chicago-based writer and composer, though she's never been able to shake her Wisconsin roots growing up on the back waters of the Mississippi River. There's something about ice fishing in a onesie that changes a person. Karen's a former Dramatists Guild Fellow and her work has twice been featured at the Kennedy Center Page-to-Stage Festival. She currently licenses her original music for TV and Film including ABC, CBS, HBO, Netflix, Disney Channel, and Amazon Originals.

Okwudili Nebeolisa is an MFA candidate at the Iowa Writers Workshop where he is a Provost Fellow and won the Prairie Lights John Leggett's Prize for Fiction. His poems have appeared in *The Sewanee Review* and *The Threepenny Review*, *Image Journal*, *Florida Review*, and have been nominated for a pushcart by *Beloit Poetry Journal*, *The Cincinnati Review*, and *Salamander Magazine*. His nonfiction has appeared in *Catapult* and *Commonwealth Writers*. He was first runner up for the inaugural Granum Foundation Fellowship Prize.

Naomi Shihab Nye's most recent books are *The Turtle of Michigan* and *Everything Comes Next, Collecte& New Poems<*, both from Greenwillow/HarperCollins. She is on faculty at Texas State University.

Carolyn Oliver is the author of three chapbooks and *Inside the Storm I Want to Touch the Tremble*, winner of the Agha Shahid Ali Prize in Poetry. Carolyn's poems appear in *The Massachusetts Review*, *Copper Nickel*, *Southern Indiana Review*, *Superstition Review*, *Shenandoah*, *32 Poems*, and elsewhere. She lives with her family in Massachusetts. Her website is carolynoliver.net.

Diane Payne's recent publications and forthcoming include: *Best of Microfiction 2022*, *Quarterly West*, *Invisible City*, *Miramachi Flash*, *Microlit Almanac*, *Spry Literary Magazine*, *Cutleaf*, *Another Chicago Magazine*, *Whale Road Review*, *Fourth River*, *Pine Hills Review*, *Tiny Spoon*, *Ellipsis*, *Bending Genres*, *New York Times*, *Unlikely Stories*,, *Hot Flash Fiction*, *The Blue Nib*, *anti-heroin chic*, *X-ray Literary Magazine*, *Oyster Review*, *Novus* ,*Notre Dame Review*, *Obra/Artiface*, *Reservoir*, *Southern Fugitives*, *Spry Literary Review*, *Watershed Review*, *Superstition Review*, *Windmill Review*, *Tishman Review*, *Whiskey Island*, *Quarterly*, *Lunch Ticket*, *Split Lip Review*, *The Offing*, *Elke: A little Journal*, *Punctuate*, *Outpost 19*, *Abandon Journal*, *McNeese Review*, *The Meadow*, *Burnt Pine*, *Story South*, and *Five to One*.

Annette Pearson is a former college writing instructor living in Austin, Texas, and on Galveston Island. She is currently working on a memoir about ambiguous loss, displacement, and finding one's way home, titled *This Is Where I'll Be.* Excerpts from that have been shortlisted for the 2022 Writers League of Texas Manuscript Contest and the Bellingham Review's Annie Dillard Award for Creative Nonfiction and will also appear this fall in *Kaleidoscoped* and *SmokeLong.*

David B. Prather is the author of *We Were Birds.* His work has appeared in many print and online journals, including *Potomac Review, Poet Lore, Northern Appalachia Review, Prairie Schooner, Sheila-Na-Gig,* etc. His work has been nominated for Best of the Net and the Pushcart Prize. He studied acting at the National Shakespeare Conservatory, and he studied writing at Warren Wilson College.

Joanne Proulx's critically acclaimed debut novel *Anthem of a Reluctant Prophet* was published internationally, won Canada's Sunburst Award for Fantastic Fiction and was named a best debut by The Globe and Mail and Kirkus Reviews. The novel was made into a feature film. Joanne's second novel, *We All Love The Beautiful Girls* was published in Summer 2017 by Penguin Canada and Grand Central in the USA. It was named as one of hundred best books by the Globe and Mail in 2017. A graduate of the Bennington Writing Seminars, Joanne lives, writes and teaches in Ottawa, Canada.

Rolli is a Canadian author, cartoonist, and songwriter. His fiction, poetry, essays, cartoons and drawings are familiar to millions of readers around the world and are staples of *The New York Times, The Saturday Evening Post, Playboy, The Wall Street Journal, Reader's Digest, The Walrus* and other top outlets. Rolli is the author of the acclaimed new book of poems and drawings, *Plumstuff.* Visit his website (rollistuff.com) and follow him on Twitter at @rolliwrites.

Bridget Muller Sampson lives on Martha's Vineyard with her husband and her rescue border collie, Pearl. Together, they run an inn and a restaurant in West Tisbury. Her short stories have been published in *Northern New England Review* and *Consequence.* Her stories have also been published and recognized by *Ruminate* magazine as the winner of the 2022 Waking Flash Prose Prize and by *Dappled Things* as the winner of the 2018 J.F. Powers Short Story Award. Bridget earned her M.F.A. in Fiction at the Bennington Writing Seminars and her B.A. in English Literature from the University of Virginia.

Jane Sasser grew up in a family of storytellers and began writing her own stories at the age of six. Her poetry has appeared in *JAMA, North American Review, The Sun,* and other publications. She has published three poetry chapbooks: *What's Underneath* (Iris Press, 2020), *Itinerant* (Finishing Line, 2009), and *Recollecting the Snow* (March Street Press, 2008). A retired high school English teacher, she lives in Fairview, North Carolina, with her husband and retired greyhounds.

John Saul is the author of the collections of short fiction *Call It Tender, The Most Serene Republic* and *As Rivers Flow* as well as the novels *Heron and Quin* and *Seventeen.* With stories appearing in publications throughout the UK and internationally, he has had work in Dalkey Archive's *Best European Fiction 2018* anthology and *Best British Short Stories 2016.* He lives in west London.

Ceri Savage is a British, Berlin-based writer with a BA in English Literature from the University of Exeter. Her writing is published in *The FU Review*, *The Honest Ulsterman*, and *ASP Literary Journal.* Ceri is the founder of Savage Edits, an editing business that provides self-publishing services to indie authors. Follow Ceri @ cerisavagewrites or www.cerisavage.com.

Alan Simmons was twice recipient of Illinois Arts Council Awards, Poet-in-Residence, City of Chicago, 1979-80, and Founder of the WPA, World Poetry Association, and The Main Event, World Heavyweight Championship Poetry Fights, Chicago, Illinois - Taos, New Mexico, 1979-2001. He has been quoted on the front page of the New York Times Living Arts Section. He was nominated for a 2021 Rhysling Award. His work has recently appeared in numerous magazines and anthologies including *Abyss & Apex, Kanstellation, Urban Arts, Illumen, The Novelette-Dark Fantasy*, and *The Reckoning.* He lives in Alameda, California.

After many years as a tour guide, landscaper, and failed law student, **C.L Schacht** now lives in Colorado, where he does none of those things. His work has appeared in *Analog, The Hopper, LandLocked, West Trade Review, The Bellevue Literary Review*, and others.

Claudia M. Stanek's work has been turned into a libretto, has been part of an art exhibition, and has been translated into Polish. Her poems have been published in her chapbook *Language You Refuse to Learn* as well as in *Book of Matches*, *Atticus Review*, *Rust + Moth*, *Aji*, and *Inscape*, among others. She holds an MFA from The Writing Seminars at Bennington College. A founding member of Just Poets (Rochester, NY), Claudia lives in Tennessee.

Sara Streeter (Hea Sook Han) is a transracially adopted Korean-American, recovering interior designer, and writer. Her work is published or forthcoming in *GASHER Journal, Fatal Flaw Literary Magazine, Hippocampus* and others. She is writing her first novel. Connect with her at https://sarajstreeter.com/.

George Singleton has published nine collections of stories, two novels, and a book of writing advice. His short stories have appeared in the *Atlantic Monthly*, Harper's, *One Story*, *Story*, *the Georgia Review*, *Oxford American*, and elsewhere. His non-fiction has appeared in *Oxford American, Garden and Gun, Bark, Gravy*, and is collected in *Asides–Occasional Essays on Dogs, Food, Restaurants, Bars, Hangovers, Jobs, Music, Family Trees, Robbery, Relationships, Being Brought Up Questionably, Et Cetera* (EastOver Press, 2023.) He lives in Spartanburg, South Carolina.

B.A. Van Sise is an author and photographic artist focused on the intersection between language and the visual image. He is the author of two monographs: the visual poetry anthology *Children of Grass: A Portrait of American Poetry* with Mary-Louise Parker and *Invited to Life: After the Holocaust* with Neil Gaiman, Mayim Bialik, and Sabrina Orah Mark. He has previously been featured in solo exhibitions at the Center for Creative Photography, the Center for Jewish History and the Museum of Jewish Heritage, as well as in group exhibitions at the Peabody Essex Museum, the Museum of Photographic Arts, the Los Angeles Center of Photography and the

Whitney Museum of American Art; a number of his portraits of American poets are in the permanent collection of the Smithsonian's National Portrait Gallery. His short nonfiction and poetry has been featured in *Poets & Writers, The North American Review, Nowhere, the Los Angeles Review, Tupelo Quarterly, The Southampton Review, Eclectica*, and *The Intrepid Times*, and he is a frequent reviewer of poetry and photography titles for *The New York Journal of Books*. He has been a finalist for the Rattle Poetry Prize, the Travel Media Awards, and the Meitar Award for Excellence in Photography. He is a 2022 New York State Council on the Arts Fellow in Photography, a Prix de la Photographie Paris award-winner, and an Independent Book Publishers Awards gold medalist.

William Vandegrift graduated from Bennington College and holdd an MFA in writing and literature. His work has appeared in journals including *Brevity, The Writing Disorder, Quarterly West, The Writer's Chronicle, Poetry Daily, Flash Fiction Magazine*, and in newspapers such as *US 1*.

Tommy Vollman is a writer, musician, and painter. For many years, he was a baseball player. He has written a number of things, published a bit, recorded a few records, and toured a lot. Tommy's work has been nominated for the Pushcart Prize and the Best of the Net anthology. His stories and nonfiction have appeared in *The Southwest Review, Two Cities Review, Hobart, The Southeast Review, Palaver*, and *Per Contra.* He has some black-ink tattoos on both of his arms. He's working on a short story collection and has a new record, Hope. He currently teaches English at Milwaukee Area Technical College and prefers to write with pens poached from hotel room cleaning carts. www.tommy-vollman.com

Amy Weldon is professor of English at Luther College and the author of *The Hands-On Life: How to Wake Yourself Up and Save the World* (2018), *The Writer's Eye: Observation and Inspiration for Creative Writers* (2018), *Eldorado, Iowa*: A Novel (2019), and the forthcoming *Advanced Fiction Writing: A Writer's Guide and Anthology* (2023).

Meghan Louise Wagner is a writer from Northeast Ohio. Her work has appeared in or is forthcoming from such places as *The Best American Short Stories 2022, AGNI, Okay Donkey, and Luna Station Quarterly*

Tara Stillions Whitehead is a writer and filmmaker from Southern California now working as Assistant Professor of Film, Video, and Digital Media at Messiah University in Pennsylvania. Her has appeared in several dozen journals and magazines, including Hobart, Fairy Tale Review, Cream City Review, and The Rupture. Her story, "Seven Bodied I Didn't Leave Behind" was included in Wigleaf's Top 50 in 2021, and she has received various Pushcart Prize, Best of the Net, and Best Small Fictions nominations. Her hybrid chapbook, Blood Histories, was released by South Carolina's Galileo Press/Free State Review, and her debut full-length collection, *The Year of the Monster*, which has been nominated for the Maya Angelou Book Award, is forthcoming with Unsolicited Press 9.27.22. A second collection of stories titled *They More than Burned* will be released by ELJ Editions in early 2023. This story comes from that collection.

Mary Winsor was raised in the Southwestern U.S., the setting for most of her stories and essays. Her writing appears or is forthcoming in *Locale: An Anthology of Time and Place, Threepenny Review, Northwest Review, Blue Mesa Review, Atticus Review, Ploughshares* and elsewhere. Mary is a graduate of the MFA program at George Mason University.

Luke Wortley is a writer living in Indianapolis, Indiana. His fiction and poetry have appeared or are forthcoming in *monkeybicycle*, *Hobart*, *Best Microfictions*, *Pithead Chapel*, *The Florida Review*, *Cincinnati Review*, and elsewhere. You can follow him on Twitter (@ LukeWortley) or visit https://www.lukewortley.com/.

Annie Woodford is the author of *Bootleg* (Groundhog Poetry Press, 2019), which was a runner-up for the Weatherford Award for Appalachian poetry. Her second book, *Where You Come from Is Gone* (2022) is the winner of Mercer University's 2020 Adrienne Bond Prize. Her poems have recently appeared or are forthcoming in *Beloit Poetry Journal*, *Michigan Quarterly Review*, *Mixtape*, and *Gulf Coast Online Exclusives.* Find more at her website, anniewoodfordpoet.com.

Corina Zappia's personal essays and reviews have appeared in *TriQuarterly, The Los Angeles Review of Books, Salon, The Rumpus, The Awl, Catapult, Serious Eats*, and *Gastronomica.* A former staff writer for the *Village Voice* and contributing food critic for *The Stranger*, she graduated with a nonfiction MFA from Bennington College. She lives in London.

Editors

Keith Pilapil Lesmeister is the author of the story collection *We Could've Been Happy Here* (MG Press, 2017). His fiction has appeared in *American Short Fiction, Gettysburg Review, North American Review, Redivider, Slice Magazine*, and many others. His nonfiction has appeared in *River Teeth, Sycamore Review, The Good Men Project, Tin House Open Bar, Water~Stone Review,* and elsewhere. He lives and works in rural northeast Iowa. Visit Keith's website: keithlesmeister.com.

Denton Loving lives on a farm near the historic Cumberland Gap, where Tennessee, Kentucky, and Virginia come together. He is the author of the poetry collection, *Crimes Against Birds* (Main Street Rag). He is also the editor of *Seeking Its Own Level: an anthology of writings about water* (MotesBooks). His fiction, poetry, essays, reviews and interviews have appeared in over 120 publications including *River Styx, CutBank, Iron Horse Literary Review,* and *The Chattahoochee Review.* You can follow Denton on Twitter @DentonLoving and visit his website at dentonlovingblog.wordpress.com.

Kelly March is a writer in North Carolina. A former newspaper reporter and editor, she is currently working on her first collection of essays.

Walter M. Robinson is a writer and physician in Massachusetts. His collection of essays, *What Cannot Be Undone,* won the 2022 River Teeth Prize for Nonfiction and was published by University of New Mexico Press in 2022. His recent essays appear in *wildness, Ruminate, Months To Years, The Sun, The Literary Review,* and *Harvard Review.* You can follow Walter on Twitter @WRobinsonWriter or visit his website at wmrobinson.com.

www.ingramcontent.com/pod-product-compliance
Lightning Source LLC
Chambersburg PA
CBHW030834190726
48285CB00004B/1218

* 9 7 8 1 9 5 8 0 9 4 4 9 5 *